textbook*plus*⁺

Equipping Instructors and Students with
FREE RESOURCES *for Core Zondervan Textbooks*

*Go to Textbook Plus to access **FREE** resources for Living God's Word* ·······························

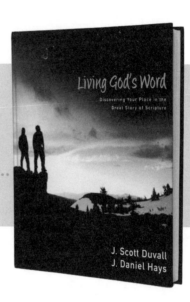

Living God's Word

Discovering Your Place in the Great Story of Scripture

J. Scott Duvall
J. Daniel Hays

*How To Access Resources

- Go to www.TextbookPlus.Zondervan.com
- Click "Register Now" button and complete registration process
- Find books using search field or "Browse Our Textbooks" feature
- Click "Instructor Resources" or "Student Resources" tab once you get to book page to access resource

➤ www.TextbookPlus.Zondervan.com

Living God's Word

Discovering Our Place in the Great Story of Scripture

J. Scott Duvall
J. Daniel Hays

ZONDERVAN®

ZONDERVAN.com/
AUTHORTRACKER
follow your favorite authors

ZONDERVAN

Living God's Word
Copyright © 2012 by J. Scott Duvall and J. Daniel Hays

This title is also available as a Zondervan ebook. Visit www.zondervan.com/ebooks.

Requests for information should be addressed to:

Zondervan, *Grand Rapids, Michigan 49530*

Library of Congress Cataloging-in-Publication Data

Duvall, J. Scott.
    Living God's word : discovering our place in the great story of Scripture / J. Scott Duvall,
J. Daniel Hays.
        p.   cm.
    Includes indexes.
    ISBN 978-0-310-29210-4 (hardcover)
    1. Bible — Textbooks. I. Hays, J. Daniel, 1953- II. Title.
BS605.3.D88   2011
220.6'1 — dc23   2011037200

Cover design: Rob Monacelli
Cover photography: Vernon Wiley, Getty Images
Interior design: Sherri L. Hoffman

Printed in the United States of America

12 13 14 15 16 17 /DCI/ 26 25 24 23 22 21 20 19 18 17 16 15 14 13 12 11 10 9 8 7 6 5 4 3 2 1

To our in-laws,
Bob and Joyce Bumgardner (parents of Scott's wife, Judy)
and
Charles and Elizabeth Reed (parents of Danny's wife, Donna),
with our deep gratitude that they lived their lives and raised their
families according to God's Great Story

CONTENTS

WHY THIS BOOK?

We are both college professors who also serve as teachers in the local church. For many years at our school (Ouachita Baptist University in Arkansas) we taught Old Testament Survey and New Testament Survey to all students. We realized somewhere along the way that we were failing our students in two primary ways. First, we were failing to teach our students how the whole Bible fits together. They were hearing about all the parts of the Bible but were never really seeing how it all comes together to form a single story. That couldn't be a good thing. Second, our students were not learning how to read the Story for themselves. Please don't misunderstand; Old and New Testament Survey have their place (upper-level college or seminary most likely), but we became convinced that they shouldn't take priority over learning the Story and learning how to read the Story well.

As a result, we changed from the two traditional courses to Survey of the Bible and Interpreting the Bible. We would make two passes through the Bible: once to explain the Great Story and a second time to explain how to interpret the Story responsibly. We also began creating resources for those courses. For the Interpreting the Bible class, we wrote *Grasping God's Word: A Hands-On Approach to Reading, Interpreting, and Applying the Bible* (Zondervan, 1998). The second edition came out in 2005 and the third edition in 2012. Because *Grasping God's Word* has been so well received, Zondervan approached us about writing a complementary book that would survey the Great Story of Scripture. And so *Living God's Word: Discovering Our Place in the Great Story of Scripture* was born.

How Is the Book Organized?

In terms of organization, *Living God's Word* follows the biblical story in a fairly straightforward manner, using "C" sounds as a pedagogical aid for students: Creation and Crisis, Covenant, Calling Out, Commandments, Conquest and Canaanization, Creation of the Kingdom, Communion and Common Sense, Crumbling of the Kingdom, Captivity and Coming Home, Christ, Church, and Consummation. The introduction provides a quick glance at the Great

Story, while the conclusion reviews the Story with a special emphasis on how it all fits together theologically. We also added a brief chapter to help students understand the period of time between the Old and New Testaments.

Each chapter includes the following:

- Enter Here → a story or illustration to introduce the topic of the chapter
- Be Prepared → reading or listening assignments (see comments in the following section)
- The Story Continues → an overview of the content of this part of the Story
- Making Connections → to show how this part of the Story relates to the whole Story
- Living the Story → to present ideas about how to live out this aspect of the Story
- Wrapping Up → a summary of the chapter
- Memory Verse → a Bible verse that gives the chapter in a nutshell
- Digging Deeper → recommended books and assignments

Students: The Importance of Reading or Listening to the Bible

Living God's Word is a guide to help you understand and live out the Great Story of the Bible. The subtle danger is that studying a book like this one might actually keep you from reading and studying the Bible itself, and that would be a tragedy. Above all, we want to encourage you to read or listen to the Bible.

The "Be Prepared" section presents key chapters of the Bible for you to take in. If you prefer a traditional book with pages you can flip and words you can underline and margins you can write in, great! If you prefer listening to the Bible, however, don't feel like you're a second-class Christian. In fact, people were listening to the Bible being read aloud long before they had a private copy to read silently to themselves. In the ancient world people read aloud or listened as others read aloud. By some estimates, only about 15 percent of the general populace in the first century was literate, although that percentage was probably higher among Jews and Jewish Christians since they treasured the Scriptures and taught their children to read (e.g., 2 Tim. 3:15).

Building on its Jewish heritage where the Scriptures were read every week in the synagogue, the early church placed a premium on knowing and memorizing the Scriptures. For instance, the apostle Paul refers to the common practice of having his letters read aloud (Col. 4:16; 1 Thess. 5:27) and encourages Timothy (and the church in Ephesus) to "devote yourself to the public reading of Scripture" (1 Tim. 4:13; cf. Luke 4:16; Acts 13:14–16). In Revelation 1:3, a blessing is pronounced on the person who reads the prophecy aloud and on those who listen: "Blessed is the one who reads aloud the words of this prophecy, and blessed are those who hear it and take to heart what is written in it, because the time is near." There is also an interesting but strong connection in the Bible between hearing God's Word and obeying God's Word (e.g., Matt. 7:24–27; John 14:23–24; Rev. 1:3; 3:3).

All this means that it's perfectly fine to listen to the Bible being read aloud. You could get an audio Bible of a dramatic reading of Scripture such as *The Bible Experience* and listen to this. Or you could download a Bible app like YouVersion for your phone or tablet or laptop and listen to the Bible that way. Whatever approach you take, we strongly encourage you to read or listen to God's Word as a way of preparing to understand and live out its message.

Acknowledgments

Anytime a book makes it to publication, there are many people to thank. We begin by thanking our wives (Judy Duvall and Donna Hays) for supporting us through yet another writing project. This volume is dedicated to their parents, our in-laws.

We are grateful to Zondervan, particularly Katya Covrett (Senior Acquisitions Editor) for entrusting this project to us. We are grateful for your confidence in us as authors, and we hope you will be pleased with the book.

We also thank our students for listening to our ideas and reading portions of the manuscript.

We are indebted to many scholars whose ideas have shaped our own in deep ways, including John Walton, Christopher Wright, Leslie Newbigin, Brian Walsh, Richard Middleton, Craig Bartholomew, Michael Goheen, N. T. Wright, Kevin Vanhoozer, Craig Blomberg, Darrell Bock, and Mark Strauss. While we do not know all these individuals personally, we have benefited from their contribution to God's kingdom through their writings.

Most of all, we are thankful to God for not giving up on the creation project and for graciously allowing us to participate in his Great Story and his ongoing mission.

Without intending to sound cliché, we genuinely pray that you will experience God's Story and discover your place in it. We give all glory to our Lord, the Author of the Great Story.

INTRODUCTION

Why is the story so often dismissed as not quite adult? . . . The story is the most adult form of language, the most serious form into which language can be put.[1]

— EUGENE PETERSON

Tell someone to do something and you change their life — for a day; tell someone a story and you change their life.[2]

— N. T. WRIGHT

The Value of Stories

Stories capture our attention better than almost anything, although video clips and music do a pretty good job. You'll be listening to a speaker, bored to death, when they start telling a story — "During my first year of college, I had a really good group of friends until we took a road trip to . . ." — and then you're hooked. It's almost impossible to stop listening to a story, especially if it's a good one told well.

Why do we love stories so much? They keep us interested for one. We can identify with the characters in the story, their personalities, choices, accomplishments, and struggles. We begin to see our reflection in some of the characters, and we want to find our own answers through what happens to them. We need to know at some deep level how the story ends, and we also have a built-in longing for it to turn out well. (That's why those "to be continued" episodes can drive us crazy.) Also, stories paint a holistic picture of life in all its complexity, emotion, and drama, and good stories do so honestly. Another reason we like stories is that they appeal to all people — young and old, well educated and uneducated, rich and poor. People of all cultures are drawn to stories. What about you — why do stories captivate you?

More and more people are realizing the importance of stories. As N. T. Wright puts it, "Stories are wrongly regarded as a poor person's substitute

---

1. Eugene H. Peterson, *Working the Angles: The Shape of Pastoral Ministry* (Grand Rapids: Eerdmans, 1987), 119.
2. N. T. Wright, *The New Testament and the People of God* (Minneapolis: Fortress, 1992), 40.

for the 'real thing,' which is to be found either in some abstract truth or in statements about 'bare facts.'"[3] Because stories capture reality more fully than other ways of speaking about life, Eugene Peterson is right to say that they are the most adult form of language. That's why the religious leaders of Jesus' day often got terribly upset when he told a simple story. We might say, "Come on, Jesus was just telling a story about a farmer (or whatever). Why does that bother you guys so much?" But in truth, Jesus' stories explained God and the world in ways that these religious leaders were opposed to. Big stories compete with other big stories for the right to explain how everything fits together and works. Stories are really, really important, and we are the ones who suffer when we dismiss them as nothing more than attention-getting illustrations.

Think about it this way: when we meet someone for the first time or when we are trying to get to know someone better, we don't just spill out random bits of information about our lives. No, we tell them a story, our story — "Every Christmas, my parents would ..." Somehow, we instinctively know that while they may appear simple, stories are actually very advanced, sophisticated, and complex. When we tell stories, we talk like adults.

Not all stories are created equal. Some stories are about ordinary things like going to the store to buy toothpaste or about watching a baseball game. Other stories, however, are basic or foundational because "they provide us with an understanding of our *whole* world and of our own place within it."[4] We use these great stories (or metanarratives) to make sense of life. These great stories are guiding and foundational because they seek to answer the most important questions of life:

- Where are we? What kind of world do we live in?
- Who are we? What does it mean to be a human being?
- What's wrong? What is the essential problem with us and the world?
- What's the solution? What can fix the problem?
- Where are we in the Story? Where do we belong and how does the Story affect our lives right now?

Everyone believes in or buys into a big story, whether they realize it or not. The only question is which great story we will accept as the one that tells us the truth about the way things really are. Which guiding story will we claim as our story?

The Bible, God's Great Story, claims to be the one, true Story that offers the best answers to the basic life questions.[5] It confronts and challenges other

---

3. Ibid., 38.

4. See also Craig G. Bartholomew and Michael W. Goheen, *The Drama of Scripture* (Grand Rapids: Baker, 2000), 18.

5. For more on how the Bible best answers the worldview questions, see especially Brian J. Walsh and J. Richard Middleton, *The Transforming Vision: Shaping a Christian World View* (Downers Grove, IL: InterVarsity Press, 1984); Leslie Newbigin,

stories, including the dominant stories of our culture and our own personal stories. For example, when the main story of our Western culture tells us that we can find meaning in life when we buy more and more stuff, the Bible flatly denies this. Finding meaning in life, according to God's Story, comes through important relationships, not through shopping, which ultimately leaves us empty and unfulfilled. Or when our society tells us that technological progress like social media is always a good thing, the Bible suggests that constant distractions and addictions can actually diminish rather than enhance life.

The longtime Christian missionary to India, Leslie Newbigin, was reminded of this fact by one of his Hindu friends who said:

> As I read the Bible, I find in it a quite unique interpretation of universal history and, therefore, a unique understanding of the human person as a responsible actor in history. You Christian missionaries have talked about the Bible as if it were simply another book of religion. We have plenty of these already in India and we do not need another book to add to our supply.[6]

The Bible is in fact a single Story that lays out a vision for the whole world.[7] We are familiar with story lines from everyday life—things like novels, movies, and TV shows. Your typical story opens with things going well. The author introduces the characters, gives us the necessary background information, and sets the scene. Generally, everything is good at the beginning. Then a problem or crisis arises that threatens one or more of the characters. Much of the story focuses on solving this problem (i.e., conflict resolution). Usually during the resolution phase there is a climax where everything rushes to a critical point and the overall story turns in one direction or the other. Finally, the resolution is worked out so that, in the end, things are even better than they were in the beginning. Not all stories work this way, but many do. If there is no happy ending, we label the story a tragedy. Here is how the Bible unfolds as a Great Story:

- Opening–Genesis 1–2
- Problem–Genesis 3–11
- Resolution–Genesis 12 through Revelation 18
- Climax to resolution–The life, ministry, death, and resurrection of Jesus Christ
- Closing–Revelation 19–22

The Gospel in a Pluralist Society (Grand Rapids: Eerdmans, 1989); Christopher J. H. Wright, *The Mission of God: Unlocking the Bible's Grand Narrative* (Downers Grove, IL: InterVarsity Press, 2006); Michael W. Goheen and Craig G. Bartholomew, *Living at the Crossroads: An Introduction to Christian Worldview* (Grand Rapids: Baker, 2008).

6. Newbigin, *Gospel in a Pluralist Society*, 89.

7. In Christopher J. H. Wright's recent book, *The Mission of God's People: A Biblical Theology of the Church's Mission* (Grand Rapids: Zondervan, 2010), he shows how the Great Story tells the church what it's supposed to do in this world.

To put the Great Story of the Bible into a memorable format, consider the outline below that uses "C" sounds as a memory tool.

The Great Story of the Bible

Creation and Crisis

At the beginning of the Story, God creates the world and places the first people in a wonderful garden where they enjoy a special and intimate relationship with him. Yet these first people and those who follow choose to act selfishly and rebel (or sin) against God. Their sinful behavior brings disastrous and deadly consequences: pain, suffering, death, and separation from God. The human race is not off to a good start.

Covenant

In response to the crisis of sin and rebellion, God starts to unfold his great plan of salvation. He establishes a covenant with Abraham, promising a land, numerous descendants, and a blessing. God promises to bless the rest of the world through Abraham. These covenant promises drive the Story throughout the rest of the Old Testament, and they find ultimate fulfillment in the coming of Jesus Christ.

Calling Out

As God moves to fulfill his promise to Abraham, he raises up Moses to deliver his people from slavery in Egypt. God's spectacular deliverance of his people from slavery through the exodus event becomes a pattern that foreshadows God's ultimate deliverance of his people through Jesus Christ.

Commandments

After God rescues his people from slavery, he gives them commandments to live by. These commandments are the terms by which his people can experience tremendous blessings as they dwell in the Promised Land with the holy God living in their midst.

Conquest and Canaanization

God uses Joshua to help his people conquer the "Promised Land" (Canaan). The good news is that they do successfully conquer the land and settle down. The bad news is that soon after the death of Joshua and during the time of the judges, God's people become just as sinful as the wicked Canaanites they were supposed to drive out of the land. Who will deliver them from this canaanization mess?

Creation of the Kingdom

The answer is David. Although the first king, Saul, is inept and fails to trust in God, David, the second king, is different. David trusts in God and delivers the people from the sinful influence of the Canaanites, restoring them to a true worship of God. He comes close to establishing a just and righteous kingdom filled with the blessings God intended for them. But just as this seems to be within reach, David commits adultery and murder, leaving us to look elsewhere for a "true righteous Messiah" or ultimate deliverer. After David dies, his son Solomon flippantly heads the nation toward idolatry. The dream slips away; the kingdom will soon crumble.

Communion and Common Sense

Throughout the Story, God has emphasized the covenant relationship with his people (e.g., "I will be your God; you will be my people; I will dwell in your midst"). The book of Psalms describes the intimate communion that God desires with his people. God also wants his people to live wisely in relationship to each other. These guidelines for wise living are presented in the Wisdom books.

Crumbling of the Kingdom

After Solomon dies, the nation has a civil war and splits into two: Israel (the northern kingdom) and Judah (the southern kingdom). The northern kingdom, Israel, is led continually by bad kings and falls into idolatry immediately. The southern kingdom, Judah, is led mostly by bad kings, and the few good ones they have are unable to stop the downward slide into idolatry. The prophets preach in this context, exhorting the people to turn from their sin and return to worshiping God and obeying his commandments. The prophets warn that if Israel and Judah do not turn back to God, terrible judgment will come and they will be driven out of the Promised Land. Yet the prophets also look beyond the coming judgment to proclaim a wonderful future time of restoration and blessing, led by the Messiah.

With few exceptions, no one really listens to the prophets, and thus the tragic judgment they proclaimed unfolds. The northern kingdom, Israel, is conquered by the Assyrians and its people are scattered. The southern kingdom is then destroyed by the Babylonians and the people taken to Babylon as captives. Israel/Judah has lost the Promised Land and the presence of God. All they have now is the promise and hope from the prophets of a future time of restoration and blessing ushered in by the coming Messiah.

Captivity and Coming Home

The defeated and shattered people of Judah are taken captive to Babylon, where individuals like Daniel illustrate that faithfulness to God during the captivity is still possible. Finally, after a time of living in exile away from the Promised Land, some of the remaining people return to Jerusalem and Judah under the leadership of men like Ezra and Nehemiah. The people are back in the land, but the situation for this small, struggling, rag-tag nation, still under foreign domination, is a long way from the wonderful time of restoration promised by the prophets. Obviously, the time of blessing and restoration still lies in the future, and the Old Testament closes with hope and expectation directed toward the coming, yet still future, Messiah.

Christ

About four hundred years later God sends the Messiah or Christ, who is Jesus of Nazareth, the Son of God. Jesus comes announcing the good news (or "gospel") of the kingdom of God in fulfillment of God's covenant promises. Jesus forms a new community of twelve disciples, teaches with authority, and works miracles. Jesus comes to save people (outcasts and sinners included) from their sins, not by leading a military revolution but by dying on the cross and being raised from the dead. This is God's plan to rescue his people and restore creation. With the coming of Jesus, the Story of how God will fix the world reaches its climax.

Church

Those who repent and put their faith in Jesus Christ and his gospel become part of the church. What Jesus began to do during his earthly ministry, he now continues to do through his people. But the church does not act on its own power. Rather, at Pentecost the Holy Spirit comes to live among the people of God, both corporately and individually, empowering them to witness to this good news and make disciples of all nations. Now we see how God is fulfilling his promise to bless all nations through Abraham. Through the Messiah's people, a multicultural community of Jesus followers composed of both Jews and Gentiles, God continues to rescue people from sin and restore creation.

Consummation

God's restoration plan is finalized when he destroys evil and fully and completely restores his creation. The enemies of God who have willfully rebelled against him—Satan, demons, and wicked human beings—will suffer judgment, while those who have followed God and Jesus the Messiah will live with him forever. The future hope trumpeted by the prophets now comes to pass. God's original plan of sharing the perfect community with his people becomes a reality.

God's longtime covenant promises are now completely fulfilled in a new heaven and new earth, where God will live among his people in intimate fellowship (see Rev. 21:1–4).

That is the grand narrative of the Bible, God's Great Story. When a person chooses to follow Jesus Christ, they are basically saying, "I want God's Story to become my story." That's what conversion is—embracing the Great Story of Scripture as our personal story. We could compare the Great Story of Scripture to a huge superhighway. Faithful people who lived ages ago traveled this

The Great Story of the Bible	
The Great Story	**Location in the Bible**
Creation and Crisis	Genesis 1–11
Covenant	Genesis 12–50
Calling Out	Exodus 1–15
Commandments	Exodus 16–40, Leviticus, Numbers, Deuteronomy
Conquest and Canaanization	Joshua, Judges
Creation of the Kingdom	Ruth, 1–2 Samuel, 1 Kings 1–11, 1 Chronicles; 2 Chronicles 1–9
Communion and Common Sense	Job, Psalms, Proverbs, Ecclesiastes, Song of Songs
Crumbling of the Kingdom	1 Kings 12–2 Kings 25, 2 Chronicles 10–36, Isaiah, Jeremiah, Lamentations, Ezekiel, Hosea, Joel, Amos, Jonah, Micah, Habakkuk, Zephaniah
Captivity and Coming Home	Daniel, Ezra, Nehemiah, Esther, Haggai, Zechariah, Malachi
Interlude: Time between the Testaments	
Christ	Matthew, Mark, Luke, John
Church	Acts, Paul's Letters, General Letters
Consummation	Revelation

same road long before it became so massive. Now, faithful people from many different cultures navigate the highway. When the Great Story becomes your guiding story, you merge onto that highway. Conversion involves merging. It's not just about "asking Jesus into your heart" but about becoming a part of and experiencing God's Story. Interestingly, the Christian movement was described as "the Way" in the book of Acts (9:2; 19:9, 23; 22:4; 24:14, 22).

Some of you might prefer another analogy, such as that of a thread being woven into a beautiful tapestry. Conversion would occur when the thread of your life begins to be woven into the larger creation. Whatever metaphor you choose to describe the Christian faith, please choose one where you become part of something much, much bigger than yourself rather than one where you try to cram God and all that he is doing into your individual life. Rather than remaining the center of the universe and just getting a bit of God added to your life, true conversion means that your whole life becomes reoriented around God, the one true Center. You join in what God has done, is doing, and will do to defeat evil, rescue his people, and restore his creation. It's also comforting to know that when you become part of God's Story, the Holy Spirit travels with you as your constant companion. And when you choose to follow Jesus Christ, you begin traveling with a whole new community of fellow believers who have merged into God's Story and are traveling the same story path. So you're never alone. Walking in the company of fellow travelers and the companionship of God's Spirit makes it easier to trust God during especially difficult parts of the journey.

Perhaps you can now see why all this talk about story is pretty important. It's not a stretch to say that the story you choose to live by becomes the most important choice you will ever make. And sadly, when you give no thought to your guiding story, then you are simply being swept along by the most powerful currents of your culture. We wrote *Living God's Word* to help you understand and make a wise choice about your guiding story.

Organization of This Book

The book is organized in a fairly simple way. Following this introduction you will find a chapter on every major part of the biblical story as outlined above. We also put a chapter in between the Old and New Testaments to help you understand that period of time. Then in the conclusion we summarize the Great Story and show how it answers the most important questions in life better than any other story.

ASSIGNMENTS

1. The biblical story and the story of Western civilization are often incompatible. Write out short answers to the five basic questions mentioned earlier in this chapter (p. 14), first from the point of view of the Western story and then from the point of view of the biblical Story. Your answers need to be thoughtful but not necessarily lengthy. Then write a concluding paragraph showing where the two stories overlap and where they are radically different. We will ask you to do this same assignment at the end of our study to see how much you have learned.

2. What metaphor of conversion have you grown up with, if any? Does your model lean more toward the "ask Jesus into your life" approach or the "merge onto a superhighway" model? Compare and contrast these two models of conversion.

CREATION AND CRISIS:
Who Am I and What Is Wrong?

Chapter 1

Enter Here

Who am I? Why am I here? What is wrong in the world? Who is God? What is he like? What does he want from me? What is the meaning of life? These are critical questions for us. The answers you come up with will shape your life. If you haven't asked these questions yet and thought seriously about the answers, it's time you did. The beginning of the Bible tackles these questions head-on.

Be Prepared

Read or listen to Genesis 1–9, 11.

The Story Begins

The Bible is basically a Story about God and people ... and the often troubled relationship between them. The Story is told through the lives of individual people (Adam, Eve, Abraham, David, Mary, Peter, etc.), but the central plot of the Story is universal in scope and much bigger than just the individual human characters in the Story. It is your Story and my Story as well ... and the Spirit of God invites us into the Story. In other words, this is also a Story about you and God and the relationship you have with him. Hang on to your hat! This is quite a ride! It is a fascinating and exciting Story, and the most important Story in all of human existence. We will call it the Great Story.

As we mentioned in the introduction, most stories have five basic parts or "movements":

1. The story starts out with a description of the setting, including an introduction of the major characters and a description of the initial situation; usually things are going well.

2. Then something happens that produces tension or some type of crisis; often one or more of the characters are threatened.

3. The characters struggle to resolve the crisis or tension (this part usually comprises the majority of the story).

4. The story reaches a climax or critical point where everything comes to a head.

5. The story comes to a conclusion or ending as the tension or crisis is resolved, often leaving the characters better off than in the beginning.

The Great Story follows this same basic pattern. Within the overarching plot of the Story, Genesis 1–11 plays a particularly important role for it covers the first two parts of the Story. Genesis 1–2 presents the description of the setting (God's creation), an introduction to the major characters (God and the people he creates), and the initial positive situation (close fellowship between the presence of God and his people in a wonderful garden).

Genesis 3–11 then describes the disruption of this situation. The people God has created rebel against him and repeatedly disobey him. Thus the close fellowship between people and God is broken and the wonderful life in the garden is lost, to be replaced by separation, disorientation, fear, and death. A crisis arises and there is tension. How will wayward and rebellious human beings ever be reconciled to God and be able to return to a situation of close fellowship and blessing?

Part 3 of the Great Story, the struggle for resolution of the crisis, begins in Genesis 12 as God takes the initiative and begins unfolding his great plan of salvation. The plot for most of the rest of the Story revolves around how God works to resolve the crisis and restore the close relationship between people and God that was enjoyed in the garden. The Story reaches its climax (part 4) in the life, death, and resurrection of Jesus Christ, through whom the resolution comes. The final, ultimate resolution (part 5), however, comes at the very end of the Story (Revelation 19–22) as God puts an end to all evil, death, and alienation and restores his creation. People once again will live a wonderful and blessed life in close fellowship with God in a gardenlike paradise.

What Is God Like?

"Apart from the Old Testament we will always have an impoverished view of God. God is not a philosophical construct but a Person who acts in history: the one who created Adam, who gave a promise to Noah, who called Abraham and introduced himself by name to Moses, who deigned to live in a wilderness tent in order to live close to his people. From Genesis 1 onward, God has wanted himself to be known, and the Old Testament is our most complete revelation of what God is like."[1]

— PHILIP YANCEY

God Creates a Wonderful World and Places the First People in a Fruitful Garden

The opening words of the Great Story are profound: "In the beginning God created the heavens and the earth" (Gen. 1:1). This is the most basic and

---

1. Philip Yancey, *The Bible Jesus Read* (Grand Rapids: Zondervan, 1999), 27.

foundational description of the setting for the Great Story and how we fit in. The implications of this opening statement are extensive and critical. We learn that God, the central character in the Story, is the Creator. We learn that people, the secondary characters in the Story, are part of the "creation." The most fundamental issues of life and the major questions about the meaning of life are tied up in this verse. If we accept this short opening statement, then a lot of things clear up. Our life will take on a certain ordered existence, much like the move from chaos to order depicted in Genesis 1. Our basic relationship to God will be defined: he is the Creator and we are the "created beings."

The implications are far-reaching. As Creator, God has the right and the authority to rule and to determine what is right and what is wrong, what is pure and what is corrupt, what constitutes obedience and what constitutes disobedience. Furthermore, if we accept this opening statement, we are acknowledging that God is sovereign and powerful, able to intervene in human history in miraculous ways. If we accept Genesis 1:1, we should not have any trouble believing that God parted the Red Sea, that Jesus fed more than five thousand people with two loaves of bread and a few small fish, or that God raised Jesus from the dead.

Genesis 1:1 also serves as a summary statement for the entire creation account of Genesis 1–2. The specific description of the creation actually starts in Genesis 1:2 with the mention of a chaotic watery world. That God creates the world out of "nothing" is certainly implied in Genesis 1, but the actual description in Genesis 1 focuses more on how God separates things, bringing order out of chaos and life out of nonlife. Genesis 1:2 also refers to the "Spirit of God" hovering over the waters. This is an early introduction into the Story of the close connection between God's Spirit and creative power, a theme that runs throughout the Story.

Notice that the creation episode in Genesis 1:2–31 is not told in a cold, boring, or mechanical manner. Rather, it is poetic and lyrical. There is rhythm, structure, and repetition ("evening and morning," "it was good," etc.). This chapter depicts God as totally unconstrained by the "laws" of nature, freely shaping his beautiful creation as an artist creates a painting or sculpture. Furthermore, the unfolding story of creation does not take place in a straight linear fashion but instead consists of two parallel cycles. During the first cycle (days 1–3) God establishes the critical domains of the creation, while during the second cycle (days 4–6) he goes back and establishes the occupants of those domains. This is illustrated by the following chart:

The Sovereign God

"From beginning to end the emphasis in the passage is on God's sovereign majesty. He is the subject; his actions, although expressed simply and briefly, are lofty and inspiring."[2]

– ALLEN ROSS

---

2. Allen Ross, *Creation and Blessing: A Guide to the Study and Exposition of Genesis* (Grand Rapids: Baker, 1988), 101.

The Domains	The Occupants
Day 1 (Gen. 1:3–5) God separates light from darkness.	**Day 4** (Gen. 1:14–19) God creates the sun, moon, and stars.
Day 2 (Gen. 1:6–8) God separates the sky from the sea.	**Day 5** (Gen. 1:20–23) God creates birds and fish.
Day 3 (Gen. 1:9–13) God separates dry ground from water.	**Day 6** (Gen. 1:24–31) God creates livestock, wild animals, and people.

Just as an ancient priestly king might build a temple and then assign positions to people and define their functions, so God creates the world, assigning positions to entities and closely defining their functions. At the end of the creation process and serving as the climactic event, God makes man and woman in his image. A summary of this task is presented in Genesis 1:26–31, and a more detailed account is provided in Genesis 2:4–25. Adam and Eve, the first two human beings, are not associated with any human tribe or race. That is, they are not called Hebrews, Israelites, or some other nationality. Instead they are described as being made "in the image of God." This implies that the "image of God" is "imprinted" on all people, regardless of culture, socioeconomic standing, or ethnicity. Everyone has this special status and value. Being in the image of God suggests that we all are similar to God in several aspects (spiritual, emotional, relational). Furthermore, it suggests that God appoints human beings as his representatives to administer his creation. That is part of their assigned function.

In Genesis 2 God places the first man, Adam, in a lush garden, made even more wonderful with the addition of Eve, the perfect match for him. Indeed, the creation account concludes with the institution of marriage. The man and the woman are together in a perfect match, living in a beautiful, bountiful paradise, and enjoying close personal fellowship in the very presence of God himself. Who could want anything more?

Sin, Rebellion, Separation from God, and Death

Of course, as you know, we spoiled it all. This is the part of the Story that dominates Genesis 3–11. God places his people in a wonderful world and desires for them to live happily in close fellowship with him and with each other. The human response? Genesis 3–11 chronicles four major sinful episodes that characterize the human response to God's great blessing. The result? Sin and rebellion by people against God have consequences. They produce separation from God and antagonism between people. They also result in death. So not only does Genesis 3–11 describe four major, representative sinful responses to God, but it also describes the tragic consequences. Throughout this section people move further and further away from God, scatter further

Literal Creation, Theistic Evolution, or Cosmic Temple Inauguration?

Even among evangelical scholars who believe in the inspiration and inerrancy of the Bible, there is little consensus on how to interpret Genesis 1. I have generally tried to understand Genesis 1 as literally as possible, recognizing at the same time that it has poetic elements and therefore is not a straightforward step-by-step mechanical account from a modern perspective of how God created the world. I see God working freely like an artist, unconstrained by the laws of nature, creating the world to look much like it does today, with mountains, valleys, rivers, beaches, and forests. From a scientific point of view, these elements take a long time to form. It seems probable that if God created the world to look like it does today—with sedimentary layers and fossils—then it had an "old" or "apparent age" look to it from the beginning. But obviously not everyone agrees with me. Many believe that the flood in Genesis 6–9 accounts for much of the geological and fossil data.

There are others within evangelicalism who affirm that God is indeed the Creator of the world, but maintain that he used evolutionary processes to do it. These scholars interpret Genesis 1 in a symbolic way, understanding the "days" as references to long periods of time and underscoring the places where the sequence in Genesis 1 aligns with the standard theory of evolution. To me, however, it is difficult to line up Genesis 1 (even symbolically) with standard evolutionary theory. Vegetation, after all, is created on Day 3, and the sun, critical for vegetation, is not created until Day 4.

Recently John Walton, an evangelical Old Testament and ancient Near Eastern scholar, has proposed an entirely different approach. He argues that if we read Genesis 1 against the background of other ancient literature from the Near East, we will realize that it is not addressing the creation of "material" or "matter" but rather describing poetically how God moves into the cosmos as his temple (place of residence) and assigns proper functions to all of the entities in his new temple (the universe). Walton summarizes:

> As in the rest of the ancient world, the Israelites were much more attuned to the functions of the cosmos than to the material of the cosmos. The functions of the world were more important to them and more interesting to them. They had little concern for the material structures; significance lay in who was in charge and made it work. As a result, Genesis 1 has been presented as an account of functional origins (specifically functioning for people) rather than an account of material origins (as we have been generally inclined to read it). As an account of functional origins, it offers no clear information about material origins....
>
> The account can then be seen to be a seven-day inauguration of the cosmic temple, setting up its functions for the benefit of humanity, with God dwelling in relationship with his creation.[3]

Walton maintains that there is no tension between science and faith in Genesis 1 because Genesis 1 is not addressing scientific concerns about the origin of the universe in any way. Has Walton convinced us and the rest of evangelical scholarship? It is too early to tell. He has certainly given us an entirely new way of thinking about Genesis 1.

---

3. John H. Walton, *The Lost World of Genesis One: Ancient Cosmology and the Origins Debate* (Downers Grove, IL: InterVarsity Press Academic, 2009), 162–63.

and further away from each other, and die. The paradise is indeed lost. These four sinful responses and their terrible consequences are as follows:

Sinful response #1: Adam and Eve rebel against God's boundaries for life in the garden (Gen. 3:1–24). We believe that Adam and Eve were real people, but their Story, while historical, is also representative for all people. Adam and Eve reflect the attitudes and behavior of all of us. God gives them a great life in the garden. They have each other, close fellowship with God, plenty of delicious food to eat … the good life! Yet they throw it all away. They fall for the lies and half-truths that the serpent, Satan, tells them, and they eat from the one tree that God had forbidden. When God confronts them with this, they each try to blame someone else.

The terrible consequences of sinful response #1: Sin disqualifies Adam and Eve from living in the paradise and they are banished from the garden. They no longer have the close fellowship with the presence of God that they once had. Driven from the garden, they no longer have food provided for them; now they must work hard in the hot fields to produce food just to stay alive. In fact, they will no longer live forever. Separated from God, death is now their destiny. Life will continue through childbirth, but even that will be difficult and painful.

The Lies of Satan

"The devil tempts us in the sin of spiritual pride, in that he deceives us about the seriousness of God's law and of God's wrath. He takes the word of God's grace in his hand and whispers to us, 'God is a God of grace, he will not take our sins seriously.'"[4]

— DIETRICH BONHOEFFER

Sinful response #2: Outside the garden, a man kills his brother (Gen. 4:1–26). Driven from the garden, Adam and Eve start reproducing more human beings. This is a miracle of life and a blessing from God. But how do the people in this new fledgling family society behave? One brother, Cain, kills the other brother, Abel. This is a terrible, yet unfortunately true, foreshadowing of human behavior. The pages of human history are filled with murder and war. Just watch the news. We continue to kill each other with some regularity.

The terrible consequences of sinful response #2: Cain is driven even further away from God, and he is now terrified that other people will try to kill him.

Sinful response #3: Human society embraces wickedness as the norm for behavior (Gen. 5:1–9:29). As the human population grows, the emerging societies accept immoral and unrighteous behavior as the norm. Genesis 6:5 sums up the grim situation: "The LORD saw how great the wickedness of the human race had become on the earth, and that every inclination of the thoughts of the human heart was only evil all the time."

The terrible consequences of sinful response #3: God destroys the world with a flood and starts over with Noah, the one righteous man he could find. Remember that back in Genesis 1 the phrase repeated over and over in reference to the

---

4. Dietrich Bonhoeffer, *Creation and Fall: A Theological Interpretation of Genesis 1–3* (New York: Macmillan, 1959), 143.

new creation was "God saw that it was good" (Gen. 1:4, 10, 12, 18, 21, 25, 31). Now, in ironic contrast, God sees "how great the wickedness of the human race had become." The world is not so "good" anymore. So God decides to destroy much of the creation and start over. Genesis 6–9 describes in detail the great flood that God sends. It is important to read this against Genesis 1, for the flood is described in terms that depict it as a reversal of the creation in Genesis 1. In Genesis 1 the waters above and waters below were separated (1:6–7), but now they collapse together into a great flood (7:11). In Genesis 1:9 God commanded the dry ground to appear, but now this is reversed and the dry ground is again covered with water (7:17–20). Most of the life created in Genesis 1 is destroyed and watery chaos returns. But in the midst of this, God preserves Noah and his family, along with representative animals, in the ark, and in essence the world is "re-created" as the waters recede (separate) and the animals and people once again inhabit the dry ground.

Sinful response #4: In defiance of God, people build a great tower to make a name for themselves (Gen. 11:1–9). Unfortunately, Noah's descendants do not remain faithful to God for very long. Soon they reject the reality that they were created in his image and thus are integrally connected to "his name" (1:26–27; 4:26). They desire to be great independently of God and to make their own "name" by which to be identified. They strive to accomplish this by uniting together to build a spectacular tower (probably a temple) that celebrates their own name instead of God's. They want to live separately and independently from God.

The terrible consequences of sinful response #4: God is offended by the tower and he confuses the language of the people (different languages emerge) and scatters this proud people into different groups. Genesis 10 is probably a description of the resultant scattering in Genesis 11:8–9, even though it is presented first. That is, Genesis 11:1–9 explains how the peoples of the world came to be so different and divided as described in Genesis 10.

Aspects of hope: Genesis 3–11 deals primarily with sin, rebellion, and the consequences—separation from the presence of God, enmity between people and God, scattering, death. But sprinkled faintly across this section are also glimpses of hope—short verses that imply something hopeful beyond the judgment and the dire consequences. For example, even as God announces the terrible consequences for Adam and Eve for eating the forbidden fruit (Gen. 3:14–19), he also decrees judgment on the serpent (i.e., Satan), indicating that through one of Eve's descendants the serpent will eventually and ultimately be crushed and defeated (Gen. 3:15).

Likewise, even as the consequences of Cain's murder of Abel are playing out, the Story quietly mentions the birth of another son, Seth, and then notes, "At that time people began to call on the name of the LORD" (Gen. 4:26). This indicates that even as most of the human race rebelled against God and rejected their relationship with him, there were some people—Seth and his son, Enosh, for example—who did indeed continue to worship God. Then in the great flood story (Gen. 6–9) it is important to keep in mind that not everyone was destroyed—Noah and his family were saved from the great flood.

These three references provide a brief aspect of hope in the midst of sin and judgment, and they foreshadow, if faintly, the ultimate deliverance that Jesus Christ will bring to resolve this great crisis. Finally, just as the Tower of Babel episode ends (Gen. 11:9), a genealogy is introduced that tracks the descendants of Noah from Shem, his son, down to Abram, later renamed Abraham. It is with Abraham that God will begin revealing and working out his master plan for providing deliverance and restoration for all who believe. So as this dismal unit (Gen. 3–11) concludes, it points forward with hope to Abraham, the father of faith.

Making Connections

Let's review where we are in the Great Story:

➤ **Creation and Crisis**
  Covenant
  Calling Out
  Commandments
  Conquest and Canaanization
  Creation of the Kingdom
  Communion and Common Sense
  Crumbling of the Kingdom
  Captivity and Coming Home
  Interlude: Time between the Testaments
  Christ
  Church
  Consummation

Living the Story

There is a lot in Genesis 1–11 for us to ponder and to apply. First of all, at the heart of our understanding of God and our relationship with him is Genesis 1:1 ("In the beginning God created the heavens and the earth"). Once we come to realize and accept that God is the Creator and Ruler of the universe (and not us!), then much of the confusion in life can be cleared up. Now we know who is worthy to be worshiped. Now we know who has the power and authority to set the standards for living. Now we can understand that God as Creator of the universe is involved in the world and in human history.

Likewise, it is instructive and encouraging for us to recognize that God's plan for the people he created was a wonderful life in the garden. God wanted them to have a good life in close fellowship with him. We can rest assured that

God wants the same for us and that his overall plan is moving in that direction (to bring about this great restoration for his people). Sin has tarnished the creation, often producing pain and sorrow for us. But the Great Story is moving forward to bring about a spectacular restoration and to bring us full circle back to the wonderful life with God in the garden.

Finally, as we come to grips with the terrible consequences of sin, we can begin to grasp the root causes of pain and suffering. God created a wonderful world. It is human sin that spoiled it and set all of the terrible consequences in motion—separation from God, alienation from other people, selfishness, murder, scattering, and death. This currently defines much of the world, if people are left to themselves. Fortunately, in Christ all of this will be overturned ... but that comes at the end of the Story. So keep reading.

Wrapping Up

God created the world and made human beings in his image. God's initial plan was for men and women to live together in harmony and peace in a garden-like paradise, walking in close fellowship with him, enjoying the blessings of his presence, and recognizing his role as Creator and Sustainer. The human race, however, which includes us, rejects this wonderful plan and rebels against God. Adam and Eve eat of the forbidden fruit, Cain kills his brother Abel, wickedness spreads throughout the entire race, and then even after starting over, people reject their identity with the name of God and attempt to become independent of God.

What will happen? What can be done? Can people on the earth ever be reconciled to God? Can the close fellowship between people and God seen in the garden ever be reestablished? Will there always be enmity and strife between human beings? Murder and war? And what about death? Is this the final and inevitable end for all of us?

Genesis 3–11 answers the question, "What is wrong?" It shows how human sin wrecks the peaceful setting of Genesis 1–2, creating a crisis and tension in the Great Story. God, however, is not content to sit back and watch his people continue to live in sin apart from his blessing and his fellowship. The rest of the Great Story deals with how God works to reestablish the fellowship he had with people in the garden. He also works to counteract death and to give his people eternal life. This is the Story of salvation, and it gets under way in earnest in Genesis 12 as God makes a promise to a man named Abraham.

Memory Verse

In the beginning God created the heavens and the earth. (Gen. 1:1)

Digging Deeper

Books

Longman, Tremper III. *How to Read Genesis*. Downers Grove, IL: Inter-Varsity Press, 2005.

Schnittjer, Gary Edward. *The Torah Story: An Apprenticeship on the Pentateuch*. Grand Rapids: Zondervan, 2006.

Walton, John H. *Genesis*. The NIV Application Commentary. Grand Rapids: Zondervan, 2001.

———. *The Lost World of Genesis One: Ancient Cosmology and the Origins Debate*. Downers Grove, IL: InterVarsity Press, 2009.

ASSIGNMENTS

1. List the seven days of creation and identify what was created on each day.

2. Some have alleged that Genesis 1 creates a tension between faith and science. Explore this relationship by answering the following: (a) Which elements of Genesis 1 do you find hard to accept "scientifically"? That is, which events in this chapter require faith to accept? (b) Which elements in evolutionary theory require "faith" to accept? That is, which events cannot be proven in a laboratory by observation but must be "assumed" or "accepted" on faith? (c) Briefly summarize your own personal view of creation and Genesis 1.

3. Discuss how the events in Acts 2:1 – 13 work as a reversal of Genesis 11:1 – 9.

4. Using a concordance, identify all the usages of the word "name" in Genesis 1 – 11. Discuss the role of "name" and "naming" in this unit.

5. Discuss the implications of Genesis 1 – 2 for your life.

COVENANT:
God Makes a Promise and Establishes a People

Chapter 2

Enter Here

"I, Danny, take you, Donna, to be my wedded wife. I accept the responsibility that God places upon me as your husband. I promise to love and to cherish you for as long as my life has breath...." Whew! Those were important words in my life. With those words I entered into a marriage relationship with a wonderful woman. I promised to love and to cherish her as long as I lived, no matter what. Incredibly, she agreed to the deal, also promising to love and to cherish me as long as she lived, no matter what. This was a crucial moment in our lives, as we entered into the most intimate and special of relationships. This relationship defines who we are ... and provides the foundational framework from which we make all the major decisions in our lives.

Marriage is one of the most basic *covenants* in our lives, and it provides us with a good model for understanding the covenants in the Bible. In the ancient world a covenant was a legal, binding agreement between two parties that brought them into a special relationship. It usually contained a number of promises. Just as my marriage covenant was one of the most important events in my life, so God's covenant with Abraham and his descendants is one of the most important events in the Bible. The promises God makes to Abraham in Genesis 12–17 will drive the Story throughout the rest of the Old Testament and, indeed, even into the New Testament.

Be Prepared

Read or listen to Genesis 11:29–17:27 and Genesis 50:1–26.

The Story Continues

As we concluded the previous chapter of the Great Story, we saw that the human race was not off to a good start. Adam and Eve ate of the forbidden fruit and were kicked out of the garden (Gen. 3). Cain then murdered his brother Abel (Gen. 4). After that, people became so sinful and rebellious that God had to destroy the world with a flood (Gen. 6–9). Then, as people began populating the world again, they once again became defiant and rebellious. They built the Tower of Babel, prompting God to scatter them across the earth (Gen. 11). Things didn't look too good for us.

Yet God in his grace had a plan to restore things … a plan of salvation for the people he created on earth. This plan began to unfold with the story of Abraham and the covenant that God made with him.

Abraham and the Abrahamic Covenant

At the beginning of this important episode of the Story, the central human character's name is Abram, a man from Ur in the region of Mesopotamia (Gen. 11:27–32). The name Abram means "exalted father." Later in the Story, after God makes his covenant with him, God will change his name to Abraham, which means "father of a multitude" (17:5). For consistency we will call him Abraham throughout our discussion.

Genesis 12:1–3 is one of the most amazing passages in the Bible. God tells Abraham to leave his home and his people and to travel to a land that God will show to him. Moreover, God promises Abraham that he will make him into a great nation, bless him, and make his name great (i.e., make him famous). Furthermore, God promises that Abraham himself will be a blessing to others; indeed, God declares that all of the peoples/nations of the earth will be blessed through him. God will also bless those who bless Abraham, but will curse those who curse Abraham.

This is the promise to Abraham. We can synthesize this promise into four primary components:

1. A promise of land
2. A promise of many descendants
3. A promise of blessing (on Abraham and through Abraham to the entire world)
4. A promise of blessings and curses on others, depending on how they relate to Abraham

When God makes this promise, Abraham does not possess any of these things. Any aspect that might humanly help him obtain these things, such as his existing home country and extended family, he is asked to leave behind as he travels to the new land, Canaan, which God has promised. When Abraham arrives in Canaan (later the land of Israel), God restates the land promise, "To your offspring I will give this land" (Gen. 12:7).

The stories that follow illustrate how God blesses Abraham and how the blessings on Abraham overflow to those around him. For example, even though Abraham makes some foolish decisions when he decides to go to Egypt and then lies about his wife, God continues to bless him and either blesses or curses

The Pentateuch and the Torah

The first five books of the Bible (Genesis, Exodus, Leviticus, Numbers, and Deuteronomy) are often called "the Pentateuch" by Christians. These same five books in the Hebrew Bible are referred to as "the Torah" by Jews.

others (like Pharaoh, whom Abraham encounters) in relation to how they treat Abraham and his wife (12:10–20). Likewise, in Genesis 14 God gives Abraham a great victory over the four kings who captured his nephew Lot.

In Genesis 15 God formalizes the promises of Genesis 12:1–3 into a covenant. That is, God makes several promises to Abraham that establish a relationship between them. In Genesis 15 God goes a step further and initiates a covenant-ratifying ceremony that formalizes the covenant between them. In the Story, Abraham has just finished defeating the four kings who captured Lot (Gen. 14), and he is probably apprehensive about possible reprisals. God tells Abraham not to fear, for he (God) is his "shield" and "very great reward" (15:1). At this point Abraham expresses some frustration to God, for although God had promised him a multitude of descendants, to date Abraham still has no children of his own. To answer this complaint, God takes Abraham outside, points to the sky full of stars, and says, "Look up at the sky and count the stars—if indeed you can count them.... So shall your offspring be" (15:5).

The next verse is one of the most significant verses in the Old Testament, declaring that "Abraham believed the LORD, and he credited it to him as righteousness" (15:6). Much later in the Bible, the New Testament apostle Paul will cite this verse to prove that even in the Old Testament, righteousness came through faith and not through works.

God next restates the "land" aspect from his original promise to Abraham (15:7). Abraham asks God how he will know for certain that this will be fulfilled. At this point God begins the formal covenant-ratifying ceremony (15:9–20). He has Abraham bring several animals and cut them in half, arranging the halves on the ground opposite each other. Later that night, as Abraham falls into a deep sleep, God reveals to him that his descendants will be oppressed for four hundred years in another country (we find out later this will be Egypt), but that God will then bring them up out of that land and give them the Promised Land (where Abraham currently was residing).

At this point a fascinating event takes place. A smoking pot with a blazing fire, representing God himself, passes between the halves of the cut animals. This is significant, for in the ancient Near East, apparently the formal practice for ratifying a serious covenant agreement between two people was to cut animals in half and then for both parties to pass between the halves. This probably was a symbolic way of saying something like, "May this happen to me if I am unfaithful to this covenant." Remarkably, in the covenant-ratifying ceremony between God and Abraham, only God passes through the cut animals. That is, God seems to be unilaterally binding himself to this covenant. Genesis 15:18 summarizes this event, stating, "On that day the LORD made a covenant with Abram and said, 'To your descendants I give this land.'" So in Genesis 12 God makes his initial promises to Abraham and in Genesis 15 he formalizes this promise into a covenant. Furthermore, all indications point to the fact that God alone binds himself to fulfilling this covenant.

In Genesis 17, when Abraham is an old man of ninety-nine years, God appears again and tells him that he will indeed establish this great covenant (17:2). God repeats the promise of numerous descendants, but he adds a few new wrinkles. He tells Abraham that he will be the father of many nations as well (17:5–6). God also informs Abraham that this covenant will be passed on to his descendants forever (17:7, 19). Then God tells Abraham that he and his descendants must undergo circumcision as a sign of this covenant (17:9–14).

With this demand for circumcision God is not changing the covenant into a two-sided covenant that has human obligations. Circumcision functions merely as a sign that Abraham and his descendants understood that they are under this covenant. It is a sign of identity with the covenant. The role of a wedding ring in a marriage is similar. The ring is worn as a sign and a reminder of the relationship. Wearing the ring in and of itself hardly fulfills

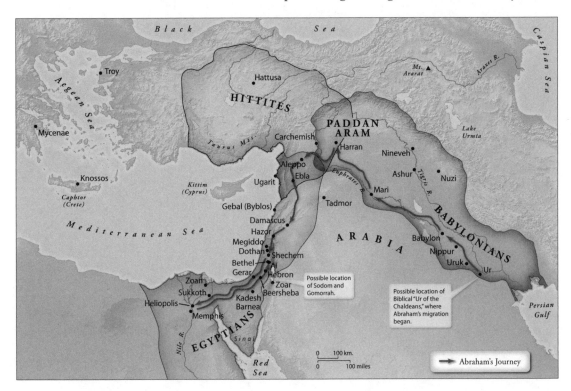

The Major Biblical Covenants

There are four major biblical covenants that play central roles in the Great Story: the Abrahamic covenant (Gen. 12–17), the Mosaic covenant (Exod., Lev., Num., and Deut.), the Davidic covenant (2 Sam. 7), and the new covenant (Jer. 31).

the obligations of the marriage (to love, to be faithful, to care for, etc.), but it does underscore one's identity as part of a marriage relationship. For Abraham and his descendants, circumcision functions in a similar fashion. The great, binding obligations of the Abrahamic covenant (land, numerous descendants, blessing) are still God's responsibility in the relationship. Circumcision simply marks out this new people, Abraham and his descendants, as part of this wonderful relationship. On God's part, he adds a new phrase that will become more and more prominently stated as the Story goes on throughout the Old Testament: "I will be their God" (Gen. 17:8).

Abraham is a real man and not a myth or a legend. His humanity is evident in that he stumbles (and doubts?) a few times. But overall he is a man of faith. He believes in God and in God's promises. He trusts in God, especially during times of crisis.

The Covenant Continues to Isaac, Jacob (Israel), and Jacob's Twelve Sons

As he had promised, God finally gives Abraham a son, Isaac. The birth of Isaac is miraculous, for both Abraham and his wife, Sarah, are very old and well beyond the age of having children. When Isaac grows up, in fulfillment of his promise to Abraham, God continues the covenant relationship with him, reaffirming it clearly and restating the core elements of the covenant: land, numerous descendants, and blessing (Gen. 26:3–5, 24).

As part of the covenant reaffirmation with Isaac, however, God also reveals a few new nuances of the relationship that will echo throughout the rest of the Bible. First of all, God chooses to identify himself from within the covenant context, declaring, "I am the God of your father Abraham" (Gen. 26:24). We will see this identifying characteristic of God repeated over and over throughout the Old Testament.

Second, God proclaims to Isaac, "I will be with you" (Gen. 26:3). This is a promise of God's powerful presence. Recall that Adam and Eve enjoyed God's presence in the garden back at the beginning of the Story, but they lost that wonderful privilege when they disobeyed God and were expelled from the garden. Now, as part of God's great restorative covenant with Abraham and his descendants, his powerful presence appears in the Story. God tells Isaac, "Do not be afraid, for I am with you" (Gen. 26:24). This is one of the most spectacular benefits of being in relationship with God. God's presence as a sign of holiness and empowerment within the covenant will continue as a theme throughout the Old Testament and into the New. Indeed, in the New Testament Gospels, Jesus will be identified as "Immanuel" (God is with us). Likewise, as the New Testament book of Revelation brings the Great Story to its consummating conclusion, the presence of God reemerges as a central theme (Rev. 21).

Isaac has two sons, Esau and Jacob. Even though Jacob is the younger of the two, he is chosen by God to be the one through whom the covenant continues. God reaffirms this to him twice (Gen. 28:13–15; 35:9–13). As part of God's reaffirmation of the covenant to Jacob, God changes his name to Israel (35:10; see also 32:28). In the book of Exodus Jacob's descendants will be formed into a nation, and they will take the term "Israel" as their national name.

Jacob will be blessed with twelve sons: Reuben, Simeon, Levi, Judah, Issachar, Zebulun, Joseph, Benjamin, Dan, Naphtali, Gad, and Asher, although the character of several of these sons is rather questionable. The Story in the final chapters of Genesis (Gen. 37–50) deals with Jacob and his twelve sons, with a particular focus on his son Joseph. Jacob favors Joseph, and the other sons resent it. In an attempt to get rid of him, the brothers sell Joseph as a slave to a caravan going to Egypt.

God, however, is with Joseph even as he languishes alone as a slave in Egypt (Gen. 39:2, 21). Remember that God's empowering presence is part of the covenant blessings. In addition, while in Egypt Joseph demonstrates that he is a man of character and faith. God blesses Joseph, and in an incredible "reversal of fate," Joseph rises from slave to a high-ranking government official, second only to Pharaoh himself. Remember that as part of the Abrahamic covenant, God had stated, "I will bless those who bless you, and whoever curses you I will curse" (Gen. 12:3). This plays out in Joseph's experience in Egypt. The Egyptians who treat him well are blessed. Because Pharaoh listens to him, Joseph is able to prepare Egypt for a coming drought. Thus Egypt escapes the terrible famine that strikes the region.

The family of Jacob, however, including Joseph's brothers who had sold him into slavery, does feel the devastating effect of the famine, and they end up traveling to Egypt to try to buy grain in order to survive. There they encounter

Theophanies

"Even more startling was the fact that the Lord himself appeared to these men in what has subsequently been called a theophany (Gen. 18:1). The reality of the living God's presence underscored the importance and authenticity of his words of promise, comfort, and direction. These appearances (also known as epiphanies) brought humanity, God, and his purposes for men and women into a very close nexus. All three patriarchs experienced the impact of God's presence on their lives (12:7; 17:1; 18:1; 26:2–5, 24; 35:1, 7, 9). Each appearance of God marked a major development in the progress of revelation as well as in the lives of these men. There he would again bless them, rename them, or send them on a mission that carried with it major consequences for the patriarchs, if not for the whole scheme of theology to follow."[1]

– WALTER C. KAISER JR.

---

1. Walter C. Kaiser Jr., *The Promise-Plan of God: A Biblical Theology of the Old and New Testaments* (Grand Rapids: Zondervan, 2008), 53.

The Patriarchs and Matriarchs of Israel

Abraham, Isaac, and Jacob are called the patriarchs of Israel. The word "patriarch" refers to the father or head of a tribe or people. The entire nation of Israel tracked their physical descent from Abraham through Isaac and Jacob; thus these three become the patriarchs of Israel. Likewise, the wives of the patriarchs—Sarah, Rebekah, Leah, and Rachel—are often referred to as the "matriarchs of Israel."

their brother Joseph, who is now a powerful person. Yet rather than look for revenge, Joseph forgives his brothers and the family is restored.

As Genesis ends, Jacob (Israel) and his family are in Egypt, enjoying the blessings that are available to them because of Joseph's status. Joseph's two sons, Manasseh and Ephraim, take their place alongside the other eleven sons of Jacob as family leaders from whom entire tribes will develop. At the end of the book, just before Joseph dies, he reminds the family to cling to the Abrahamic promises, stating, "God will surely come to your aid and take you up out of this land to the land he promised on oath to Abraham, Isaac and Jacob" (Gen. 50:24).

Making Connections

Let's review where we are in the Great Story:

Creation and Crisis
➤ **Covenant**
Calling Out
Commandments
Conquest and Canaanization
Creation of the Kingdom
Communion and Common Sense
Crumbling of the Kingdom
Captivity and Coming Home
Interlude: Time between the Testaments
Christ
Church
Consummation

In the opening chapter of the Bible we saw God's spectacular creation of the world. He placed Adam and Eve in a fruit-filled garden, abounding with numerous blessings. Perhaps the most important and most privileged blessing was the close presence of God. What a wonderful and blessed life God offered to Adam and Eve! Yet starting with Adam and Eve, and continuing through Genesis 3–11, several consecutive events occurred in which people demonstrated their propensity to defy and rebel against God. Adam and Eve ate the forbidden fruit. Then Cain murdered Abel. Next wickedness became so widespread that God sent the flood. Finally people defied God at the Tower of Babel and were scattered. Thus the Story moved from creation to crisis. What will this sin and rebellion lead to? Will the human race ever return to the garden and experience God's great presence? Will God destroy them or deliver them? How will he deliver such a stubborn and defiant people?

The answer is revealed through the covenant God makes with Abraham. God's great promise and covenant with Abraham (Genesis 12; 15; 17) is the solution to the problem of sin and rebellion seen so clearly in Genesis 3 – 11. It is with this covenant that God's wonderful plan of salvation begins to unfold. Indeed, the Abrahamic covenant will drive the Story throughout the Old Testament and into the New Testament, where it will find its ultimate fulfillment and consummation in Jesus Christ.

Living the Story

As we seek to see our place in this part of the Story, we first must remind ourselves of our role in the previous episode (crisis). The Story of sinful humanity in Genesis 3 – 11 as it rebels against God, crying out defiantly, "Not your way, but MINE!" is also our Story. Because of our sin we have been evicted from the garden and God's great presence and have been scattered into helpless groups across the face of the earth.

Yet God in his grace has approached us with a wonderful promise of salvation and blessing, in which he invites us to participate. We cannot work for this blessing or earn it. But like Abraham, we can receive the blessings of this great promise by faith. "Abram believed the LORD, and he credited it to him as righteousness" (Gen. 15:6). This is a critical juncture for us in the Story, for to continue on, we will need to believe and trust in God's promises—promises that find their ultimate fulfillment in Jesus Christ. Embracing God's great promises by faith will allow us to join the "people of God," that is, those to whom God has declared, "I am with you."

Memory Verse

Abram believed the LORD, and he credited it to him as righteousness. (Gen. 15:6)

Wrapping Up

The Abrahamic covenant (Genesis 12; 15; 17) is God's response to the sin and rebellion seen in Genesis 3 – 11. In the Abrahamic covenant God makes four basic promises: a promise of land; a promise of many descendants; a promise of blessing on Abraham and through Abraham to the entire world; and a promise of blessings and curses on others, depending on how they relate to Abraham. Much of the plot of the Great Story revolves around how God acts in human history to bring about the fulfillment of these promises.

Digging Deeper

Books

Hamilton, Victor P. *The Book of Genesis.* The New International Commentary on the Old Testament. 2 volumes. Grand Rapids: Eerdmans, 1990.

Ross, Allen P. *Creation and Blessing: A Guide to the Study and Exposition of Genesis.* Grand Rapids: Baker, 1988.

Schnittjer, Gary Edward. *The Torah Story: An Apprenticeship on the Pentateuch.* Grand Rapids: Zondervan, 2006.

Walton, John H. *Genesis.* The NIV Application Commentary. Grand Rapids: Zondervan, 2001.

ASSIGNMENTS

1. Discuss the similarities (and any differences) between the elements of the covenant that God promised to Abraham (Gen. 12:1–8; 15:1–21; 17:1–22) and the elements of this same covenant that God promised to Isaac (Gen. 26:1–25).

2. Read Genesis 21–22 carefully and answer the following questions: (a) Why was Isaac so unique and special to Abraham? (b) In 22:8 does Abraham really believe that God will provide a lamb or is he just hiding his intentions from Isaac? Give reasons for your answer. (c) This event in Genesis 22 occurs nearly two thousand years before the crucifixion of Christ, yet there are several similarities between the two events. List as many similarities as you can find. For a review of Jesus' crucifixion see Matthew 27:32–56 and John 19:17–27.

CALLING OUT:
"I am the LORD who brought you up out of Egypt"

Chapter 3

Enter Here

"Don't tug on Superman's cape!" This is a silly but true aphorism (short, pithy words of wisdom) that has often been combined with other short "duh" kind of warnings ("Don't sword-fight with Zorro," etc.) to convey a basic common-sense truth—don't mess with those who can easily give you a whipping. As this chapter of the Great Story unfolds, Pharaoh, king of Egypt, arguably the most powerful man in the world, ignores all such commonsense warnings and pits himself in a head-to-head power struggle against the God of Abraham, Isaac, and Jacob.

An Egyptian pharaoh enslaves God's people, works them mercilessly, and then massacres their baby boys. The next pharaoh continues this policy, ignoring God's demands to release the enslaved Israelites and stating defiantly, "Who is the LORD, that I should obey him and let Israel go? I do not know the LORD and I will not let Israel go" (Ex. 5:2). What will happen? How will God respond? He crashes down into history in a dramatic way to deliver his people and to crush the Egyptians completely. For the people who obey God, this is a time of spectacular deliverance; for those who oppose him, it is a time of terrible judgment.

In this chapter we will look at Exodus 1–15. We have called this part of the Story "Calling Out" because God "calls out" his people from Egypt and then forms them into the nation Israel. This is the great Old Testament version of salvation. The exodus deliverance event is to the Old Testament what the cross is to the New Testament. In fact, God frequently uses this event to define who he is. Throughout the rest of the Old Testament God often declares, "I am the LORD your God, who brought you out of Egypt" (e.g., 20:2). God is the one who saves his people. That is a critical part of his character that he wants us to grasp.

Be Prepared

Read or listen to Exodus 1:1–6:12; 11:1–10; 12:31–42; 13:20–14:31.

The Story Continues

The Tight Connection with Genesis

Exodus continues the Story of Genesis and it is tightly connected to the Story of Abraham, Isaac, Jacob, and Joseph. Remember that in Genesis 35:10 Jacob's name was changed to Israel. At the end of Genesis, his descendants are living in Egypt, where Joseph had risen to power and had helped to "save" Egypt from a terrible famine. Exodus 1:1 opens this new episode by connecting back to this family and letting us know that the Great Story is unfolding around this particular family. The book of Genesis mentioned the "sons of Israel" (i.e., Jacob's sons) twelve times. In Exodus, however, this term is used 125 times! This term, "sons of Israel," will be used to define the new nation that emerges in Exodus. In fact, many English Bibles translate the expression "sons of Israel" simply as "Israelites."

The covenant that God made with Abraham in Genesis (12; 15; 17) drives the Story of Exodus. Recall the critical components of the Abrahamic covenant. God promised Abraham (1) a land, (2) numerous descendants, (3) a great nation, and (4) blessings. God also promised, "I will bless those who bless you, and whoever curses you I will curse; and all peoples on earth will be blessed through you" (12:3). The fulfillment of these promises is everywhere evident in Exodus, driving the plot of the Story.

The Major Characters

There are three characters who dominate this part of the Story: God, Moses, and Pharaoh. Moses plays the role of God's ambassador/representative to Pharaoh. God also establishes Moses as the leader of the Israelites. But God himself also shows up frequently and plays a major role in this part of the Story. The book of Exodus as a whole gives us tremendous insight into the character of God.

There are actually two different pharaohs in the Story, one in Exodus 1–2 and another one in Exodus 3–15. The Story, however, tends to blur the two together, calling them both by the ambiguous name Pharaoh instead of providing their actual names. This is rather peculiar and probably carries some important significance. The Bible is not shy about giving us the names of foreign kings and pharaohs. In fact, this is the norm. In Exodus, however, the pharaoh is not named. Scholars are still arguing over who was the pharaoh of the exodus. This is probably one of the great ironies and lessons of the book. The name of that pharaoh, the most powerful man in the world, the one who challenges God himself, is lost. But everyone today knows the name of Moses. Note that even the names of the two midwives who protect the newborn Hebrews (1:15–21) are given—but not the name of either pharaoh. This is an ironic and poetic slam against the prideful pharaohs.

Pharaoh Oppresses the Sons of Israel (Exodus 1:1–2:10)

As the book of Exodus opens, part of the Abrahamic covenant is being fulfilled. The sons of Israel are still living in Egypt, but as promised to Abraham, this small family has grown into a significant-sized nation. Abraham, childless until late in life, now has thousands of descendants, a true sign of blessing. The Israelites, however, are still living within the borders of Egypt, and the blessing of proliferation now causes the Egyptians to oppose them. Joseph has been dead for a long time, and the new Egyptian pharaoh, perhaps from an entirely new dynasty, has no memory of him. Thus Pharaoh no longer views the Israelites as a source of blessing, as his predecessor during the time of Joseph did. Alarmed by the rapid growth rate of the Israelites, Pharaoh fears that Israel might turn and fight against him. Thus he tries three consecutive but unsuccessful plans to control the Israelites and their population.

Plan A (1:9–14). Work the Israelites to death. The irony here is that Pharaoh uses them to build store cities for him, a strategy that Joseph developed back in Genesis 41:46–49. This doesn't slow the population growth down at all. Pharaoh doesn't withdraw plan A; he just tries two additional efforts to control the Israelite birth rate.

Plan B (1:15–21). Order the midwives to kill all newborn Israelite boys at birth. This doesn't work either, because the midwives refuse to carry out this order, and then they cleverly deceive Pharaoh. God blesses the midwives for their defiance of Pharaoh and their care for God's people.

Plan C (1:22). Throw all newborn Israelite boys in the Nile River.

The Date of the Exodus

One of the ironies of the Exodus Story is that we are never told the name of either pharaoh involved. This is probably a not-too-subtle belittling insult against the pride and arrogance of the pharaoh. But since we do not know which pharaoh it was, scholars have trouble determining exactly when this Story happened. In fact, this is a contentious issue that scholars have argued about for some time (inconclusively).

Two major dates have been proposed. If we take the chronology suggested by 1 Kings 6:1 and work back from the reign of Solomon, we arrive at a date of 1446 BC for the exodus. If this is correct, then the pharaoh of the exodus would have been Thutmose III. This is a popular view of evangelical scholars who lean heavily on the Bible itself for chronological determinations. Using primarily archaeological data, numerous other scholars, including some evangelicals, argue for a later date of around 1280–1260 BC. If this is correct, then the pharaoh of the exodus would have been Rameses II.

Both sides have numerous arguments and counterarguments, and the issue can quickly become complicated. We think that the most important observation is the fact that the pharaoh's name is *not* given, in spite of the fact that providing the names of foreign kings and pharaohs is generally the pattern in the Bible. We feel that the Bible's silence on his name is part of the judgment against him.

Plan A, oppressive slavery, is bad enough, but plans B and C, the murder of newborn babies, are horrific. Remember that God told Abraham, "I will bless those who bless you, and whoever curses you I will curse." When Pharaoh enslaves the Israelites and then brutally murders their innocent newborn babies, we can only gasp and wonder with trembling how God will respond. After a series of serious warnings (the plagues), God responds with devastating force. In Exodus 11–12 God strikes down the firstborn of every Egyptian household, and in Exodus 14 he drowns the entire Egyptian chariot army in the Red Sea. It is divine poetic justice.

Moses, the eventual but unlikely hero and deliverer of Israel, is born in these terrifying times. His mother, desperate to protect her young infant son, coats a basket with pitch and constructs an "ark" of sorts (the same Hebrew word is used here as for Noah's ark in Genesis 6–9). She then hides her baby boy by placing him and this floating basket in the Nile River, in the reeds along the shore. Note again the irony. Pharaoh's decree was to throw all of the baby boys in the river; this mother complies (sort of) and indeed places her baby boy in the river.

At this point another huge irony occurs, for it is one of Pharaoh's daughters who finds baby Moses. She rescues the baby from the river (in defiance of her father, Pharaoh), and she determines to protect this baby and raise him as her own son. The future deliverer of Israel, the one who will bring Egypt to her knees in terrible destruction, is rescued and then trained by someone within Pharaoh's own household.

God Calls and Empowers Moses (Exodus 2:11–4:31)

Moses grows up, but to this point there has been no apparent word from God. We do not know what kind of religious training Moses receives. We can suspect that his real Hebrew mother teaches him about his heritage, but we do not know to what extent the Israelites in Egyptian slavery were maintaining the faith of Abraham.

As a young man, Moses sees an Egyptian taskmaster beating a Hebrew man. Moses intervenes and kills the Egyptian. He seeks to keep this homicide quiet, but soon everyone knows about it and Pharaoh himself orders Moses to be executed. Moses flees to the northeast into an arid region of the Sinai Peninsula where the Midianites lived. Here he marries a daughter of Reuel, a priest of the Midianites (most likely Baal worshipers), and settles down to live with them.

Whoa! All kinds of red flags ought to be going up. As readers we are wondering what in the world Moses is doing. Isn't he supposed to be the great deliverer of Israel? What is he doing marrying into a Midian priestly family? We know he is an Israelite, but the family of Reuel at first identifies him as an Egyptian. Then he marries into a Midianite family and settles down to become one of them.

The Promise of a Land

God had promised Abraham a land, and as the book of Exodus opens, that promise still lies unfulfilled. Movement toward the Promised Land will be a dominant theme throughout the rest of the Pentateuch and into the book of Joshua.

At last God steps directly into the Story, and things start to change. Exodus 2:23–25 are important transitional verses that change the Story dramatically. God hears the Israelites groaning and crying out in their slavery and "he remembered his covenant with Abraham, with Isaac and with Jacob" (2:24). Now things will start to happen.

It is important to note that this critical text (2:23–25) says nothing about Israel's faith. It does not say that they repented or offered sacrifices to God. It does not even say that they cried out *to God*. It just says that they cried out. God's response is based solely on his grace and his promise to Abraham (the Abrahamic covenant). God will proceed to call Moses and use him in a powerful way to deliver Israel and crush Egypt. But this action is a result of God's grace and his gracious promises, not a result of Israel's prayers or piety. The exodus, the great salvation event of the Old Testament, is not based on any kind of adherence to the Law (which will come later) or even on any kind of personal piety and prayer. God will provide the means and then offer the deliverance to anyone who wants to come.

In Exodus 3:1–4:17 God reveals himself to Moses and calls him to action. This passage brings together three major themes that are often closely associated throughout the Old Testament (and into the New Testament as well): God's presence, God's holiness, and God's power.

God appears to Moses from within a burning bush in the wilderness. God tells Moses to remove his shoes because the ground all around his presence is holy. He then gets right down to business. God declares that he has come down to rescue Israel from the Egyptians (3:8) and so is sending Moses to Pharaoh to demand their release. Moses, however, is not convinced that he is the right man for the job, and he raises several objections. God patiently answers each objection (3:11–4:17). In reassuring Moses, God promises him, "I will be with you" (3:12). Before too long Moses will learn that the presence of God brings incredible power.

God also tells Moses that after he has brought the Israelites out of Egypt, they will come and worship him on the very mountain where this burning bush encounter took place. God sees it as a done deal. Indeed, this promise is fulfilled in Exodus 19.

Moses, however, is still doubtful, and he next asks God rather pointedly what his name is. To this question God answers, "I AM WHO I AM" (Ex. 3:14).

"I AM WHO I AM"—The Names of God in the Old Testament

In the original Hebrew text of the Old Testament, two major names for God occur: *Elohim* and *Yahweh*. The word *Elohim* is used 2,570 times. It is a "generic" word that just means "god." It is similar to our English word "god" in that it can be used of the true God of the Bible (Gen. 1:1) or of pagan "gods." Most English Bibles will translate *Elohim* simply as "God" when the reference is to the true God of Israel and as "god" or "gods" when the reference is to pagan idols.

The name *Yahweh* is different. This word is used 6,800 times in the Old Testament. It functions as God's actual specific name. It is used especially in contexts of covenant relationship. The name *Yahweh* is probably related to the Hebrew verb that means "to be." God's self-identification of himself to Moses as "I AM WHO I AM" is a wordplay on this name (Ex. 3:14). Most English Bibles translate *Yahweh* as "the LORD," using small caps. The two names for God can be used together. A good example is Exodus 20:2, "I am *Yahweh* [the LORD] your *Elohim* [God], who brought you out of Egypt, out of the land of slavery." The nations surrounding Israel worshiped lots of gods (*elohim*). Israel's *Elohim* is *Yahweh*.

Then he identifies himself as the God of Abraham, Isaac, and Jacob (3:14–15). God also gives Moses three miraculous signs, apparently for him to use to convince the people back in Egypt that God really has appeared to him. Moses is also worried about his ability to speak well in public, so God tells Moses that his brother Aaron, who does speak well, can help him with that. Finally, with God's patience starting to run out, Moses agrees and returns to Egypt. He and Aaron gather the Israelite elders together, and Aaron tells them what God had said to Moses. The elders believe Moses and Aaron and they worship God. This positive reaction, however, will be short-lived.

Pharaoh versus God: The First Nine Plagues Fall upon Egypt (Exodus 5:1–10:29)

Now comes the real challenge. Moses and Aaron go to Pharaoh and tell him that the Lord God has demanded that he let the Israelites go into the desert to hold a festival to him. Pharaoh refuses, declaring, "Who is the LORD, that I should obey him and let Israel go? I do not know the LORD and I will not let Israel go" (Ex. 5:2). These are ominous words. Pharaoh is defying the word of God and challenging his authority over him. The consequences will be devastating for Pharaoh and for Egypt.

In the meantime, however, Pharaoh decides to flex his muscles. Not only does he refuse Moses' request, but now he decides to work the Israelites even harder, punishing them for Moses' audacity. The Israelites quickly turn against Moses, blaming him for the extra work and oppression Pharaoh has added. The truth is that the Israelites don't really "know" God very well either. Even Moses becomes discouraged.

God, however, reaffirms his plans to Moses, stressing that he will indeed bring the Israelites out of Egypt. God then makes a dramatic and important promise: "I will take you as my own people, and I will be your God." (Ex. 6:7). Both of these statements play important roles both in the book of Exodus and throughout the Old Testament. To define the most foundational core of his covenant relationship with Israel, God will frequently use the formulaic-type statement: "I will be your God; you will be my people." He will also frequently add a promise of presence to this formula: "I will dwell in your midst."

The second component of God's statement in Exodus 6:7 is: "Then you will know that I am the LORD your God." This phrase, along with several variations of the same idea, occurs repeatedly throughout Exodus. Through God's great acts in history as he miraculously delivers Israel from Egypt, everyone in the Story will "know that [he is] the LORD." The Israelites, and those who trust in God, will know him as the great savior and deliverer. The Egyptians, and those who defy God, will know him in judgment. Everyone will know him — either in deliverance or in judgment. This is a central message of Exodus.

At first Pharaoh hardens his heart and defies God, refusing to let the Israelites go. As things progress, however, God himself hardens Pharaoh's heart, for the time for repentance passes. As judgment begins, God is determined to see the entire scenario of judgment on Egypt play out (7:3–5) so that the Egyptians will know that he is the Lord.

The judgment unfolds through a series of plagues that God sends on Egypt. The plagues come in three cycles of three plagues in each cycle, with an introductory warning and a final climactic plague. The structure of the plague cycles can be illustrated by the chart below.[1]

	Plague	Passage	Forewarning by Moses?	Time of warning	Instruction formula given to Moses
Preliminary warning	Sign of the snake	7:8–13			
First series	Blood	7:14–24	Yes	In the morning	Meet/confront Pharaoh
	Frogs	8:1–15	Yes	None	Go to Pharaoh
	Gnats	8:16–19	No	None	None
Second series	Flies	8:20–32	Yes	In the morning	Meet/confront Pharaoh
	Livestock	9:1–7	Yes	None	Go to Pharaoh
	Boils	9:8–12	No	None	None

Continued on next page

---

1. This chart has been developed from one by Peter Enns, *Exodus*, The NIV Application Bible (Grand Rapids: Zondervan, 2000), 208; Enns credits much of the information on the chart to Nahum M. Sarna, *Exploring Exodus: The Heritage of Biblical Israel* (New York: Schocken, 1986), 76.

	Plague	Passage	Forewarning by Moses?	Time of warning	Instruction formula given to Moses
Third series	Hail	9:13–35	Yes	In the morning	Meet/confront Pharaoh
	Locusts	10:1–20	Yes	None	Go to Pharaoh
	Darkness	10:21–29	No	None	None
Climax	Death of firstborn	11:1–10; 12:29–30	Yes	None	None

Several of the plagues carry special significance. The first episode, the sign of the snake, not only functions as a preview of the coming plagues but pronounces judgment on Pharaoh. In ancient Egypt the cobra was used as a symbol to represent Lower Egypt, the primary region of Pharaoh's power. Most pharaohs had a gold or bronze cobra formed into the top of their crown, symbolizing the protective power of the pharaoh and representing his authority as well. When Aaron throws down his staff and it turns into a snake, Pharaoh's magicians think they can match this power by likewise turning their staffs into snakes. But the real sign and the significance of this event come when Aaron's snake swallows up the snakes of Pharaoh's magicians. This symbolizes that Moses and Aaron are much more powerful than Pharaoh and will indeed, if necessary, swallow (destroy) him.

The first two plagues (Nile water to blood, frogs) and the last plague (death of firstborn) connect back to Pharaoh's murder of the Israelite babies in Exodus 1. Pharaoh had been throwing the Israelite babies into the Nile to drown them, so God appropriately causes the entire Nile River to turn to blood. This not only reminds the Egyptians of what they have done to the babies of Israel, but it strikes at the heart of Egypt. The Nile River was the most central focus of Egyptian religious and agricultural life. As it turns to blood, it symbolically dies. The second plague (frogs) is even more directly connected to the death of the babies, for in Egyptian mythology, the frog is the symbol of a god named Heket. Heket is the patron god and protector of pregnant women. The plagues gradually grow worse, and in the climax plague, God strikes dead all of the firstborn in Egypt. This is a judgment that seems to be a direct result of Pharaoh's murder of the babies of God's children.

Besides connecting to the murder of the babies, some of the plagues carry other symbolism and significance. Several of them appear to be direct "put-downs" of Egyptian gods. For instance, one of the central gods in the Egyptian pantheon, and the god that is perhaps most closely connected to Pharaoh, is Re, the sun god. Thus the ninth plague (darkness) strikes directly at this god and its association with Pharaoh, symbolizing God's power over Pharaoh and his god Re and likewise foreshadowing the coming death of

Egypt's firstborn. Some scholars have suggested that all of the plagues are related to the gods of Egypt, but this seems to be overstated. However, some of the plagues definitely appear to be polemical (insulting put-downs) to the Egyptian gods.

Some scholars see in the plagues a reversal of the creation in Genesis 1. That is, God judges Egypt by taking that land symbolically in reverse back into the chaos that was before the creation. A few writers have suggested that the plagues were the result of a large volcano in the region. This view, however, seems unlikely and has little evidence to support it.

The overall point of the plagues is multifaceted; they demonstrate God's ultimate power over Egypt, Pharaoh, and his gods, and they serve as justice for the murder of the Israelite babies. Taken together, the ten plagues slowly and methodically bring Egypt and Pharaoh to their knees, crushing them economically, politically, and religiously. They finally do indeed know who "the LORD" is.

God Delivers Israel and Crushes Egypt (Exodus 11:1–15:27)

The tenth and final plague (the death angel) brings Pharaoh to his knees, and he finally capitulates and tells Moses to take the sons of Israel and go (12:31–32). As the Israelites hurriedly gather up their belongings and begin their departure, the Egyptians, glad to see these people finally leave and urged by God to look favorably on them, give them gifts of silver, gold, and clothing. So the Israelites do not sneak away like fleeing thieves, but rather they march away with plunder like a conquering army (12:35–36). In addition, numerous other people, probably from a range of nationalities, join the Israelites and leave Egypt with them (12:38). Thus we see another example of non-Israelites becoming part of the people of God and receiving the blessings of God. The "sons of Israel" who come out of Egypt are composed of numerous different nationalities, another fulfillment of the Abrahamic covenant.

This Story about the departure of Israel from Egypt is interrupted by a passage explaining the Passover. All of the Israelites who put blood on their doors, as Moses instructed, were "passed over" by the Lord as he went throughout Egypt striking down the firstborn. So the Passover celebration is established in Exodus 12 to commemorate this great event.

As the Israelites leave Egypt, the presence of God goes with them to lead them and protect them. The manifestation of this presence is seen in a pillar of cloud in the daytime and a pillar of fire at night that goes in front of the Israelites and guides them on their way.

God, however, leads them up to the shores of the Red Sea. Pharaoh hears of this, and he changes his mind about letting them go. He mobilizes his extensive chariot army and pursues the Israelites, thinking that he can trap them up against the Red Sea. The Israelites quake with fear, but God tells Moses to stretch out his hand, part the waters, and move the Israelites through the sea. Once again God states that now the Egyptians will know that Israel's God is "the LORD." God parts the waters of the Red Sea and the Israelites cross over safely to the other side. The Egyptian chariots, however, pursue after them into the bed of the sea. At that point God tells Moses to stretch out his hand again and cause the waters to return. Moses obeys and waters flow back into the bed of the sea, drowning every Egyptian soldier. Thus Israel now "knows" God as deliverer and Egypt now "knows" God as avenging judge. There is no middle ground.

This part of the Story ends with a song. Exodus 15 contains that song, which celebrates God's great actions in delivering Israel out of Egypt.

Making Connections

Let's review where we are in the Great Story:

> Creation and Crisis
> Covenant
> ➤ **Calling Out**
> Commandments
> Conquest and Canaanization
> Creation of the Kingdom
> Communion and Common Sense
> Crumbling of the Kingdom
> Captivity and Coming Home
> Interlude: Time between the Testaments
> Christ
> Church
> Consummation

In response to the disaster of human sinfulness in Genesis 3–11, God establishes the Abrahamic covenant with Abraham and his family (Gen. 12–50). At the end of Genesis this family (Abraham's descendants, Jacob and his twelve sons) is in Egypt. They have experienced some of the blessings promised in this covenant, but most of the promises are still to be realized in the future (Promised Land, numerous descendants, great nation, blessing on the other peoples of the world).

In Exodus 1–15 God steps directly down into human history to begin the fulfillment of the Abrahamic covenant. His people, the descendants of Abraham, are being brutally oppressed by the Egyptians, and God steps in to punish the Egyptians and to rescue his people. In essence, he "calls" them out of Egypt. But there is more. God calls them out from slavery in Egypt, but he calls them to be his people in the Promised Land. God delivers them from the horrible situation of slavery in Egypt with their babies being killed, to a fantastic situation of relationship with God in the Promised Land. Also, along the way he transforms Abraham's descendants from a small family to a nation, part of his promise to Abraham. We will see this develop more clearly in the next chapter.

Finally, it is important to note that while the focus of the Story is on the descendants of Abraham, the nation of Israel, other people are constantly hovering nearby. God delivers the descendants of Abraham out of Egypt, but as they depart, numerous "other peoples" join in, becoming part of "the people of God." This theme will continue quietly throughout the Old Testament and then move to center stage in the New Testament.

The exodus event is the paradigm or prototypical picture of salvation in the Old Testament, a dramatic foreshadowing of the salvation that Christ will bring in the New Testament. The prophet Isaiah will describe the coming of the Messiah as a "new exodus," but one that is even greater than this old one.

The exodus event is a Story of fantastic deliverance for God's people, but it is also a Story of terrible judgment on those who defy God and refuse to recognize him. The New Testament will present the gospel of Christ as the great new deliverance that replaces the exodus event, providing fantastic salvation for all who believe. But like the Egyptians in the exodus, those who defy God and refuse to recognize and follow Jesus as Lord will suffer judgment. This, too, is part of the gospel.

Living the Story

In this part of the Story we see how much God cares for his people and how he is faithful to his promises. In the early chapters of Exodus we notice that God is working quietly behind the scenes, even as his people are suffering through difficult times. Suddenly, however, he crashes into the Story and delivers his people in spectacular fashion. The New Testament likewise calls on us to trust in God during difficult times and to look forward expectantly to the time when Jesus Christ will come crashing back down into human history to deliver his people and to restore all things. God truly cares for us and he is always faithful to his promises.

In this part of the Great Story we also see the grace of God. He does not save Israel because of their "works" or their "worthiness." He saves them because of his grace and his promise to Abraham. As Christians we also celebrate the grace of God, for it is through his grace and his grace alone that we experience our great salvation in Jesus Christ.

Wrapping Up

Exodus 1 – 15 is about the exodus event. In fulfillment of the Abrahamic covenant, God delivers his people from oppressive slavery in Egypt. In this part

God said to Moses, "I AM WHO I AM. This is what you are to say to the Israelites: 'I AM has sent me to you.'" (Ex. 3:14)

of the Story, God's people, along with all those who join them, experience a spectacular and wonderful deliverance, while those who defy God and oppress his people experience terrible judgment. Through the exodus, God makes himself "known" to all—his people know him as deliverer and the Egyptians know him as judge and avenger.

Digging Deeper

Books

Enns, Peter. *Exodus*. The NIV Application Commentary. Grand Rapids: Zondervan, 2000.

Schnittjer, Gary Edward. *The Torah Story: An Apprenticeship on the Pentateuch*. Grand Rapids: Zondervan, 2006.

Stuart, Douglas. *Exodus*. The New American Commentary. Nashville: Broadman & Holman, 2006.

ASSIGNMENTS

1. Discuss each verse in Exodus that mentions Abraham (Ex. 2:24; 3:6; 3:15–16; 4:5; 6:3; and 6:8). Then summarize by describing the role Abraham plays in the first six chapters of Exodus.

2. Exodus 1–2 mentions numerous women. List them and briefly discuss how each one fits into the Story.

3. In Exodus 3–4 God calls Moses to lead the people of Israel out of Egypt. Discuss each of his objections and how God responds to his objections. How does this apply to us today?

COMMANDMENTS:
Terms for Living in the Promised Land with God in Their Midst

Chapter 4

Enter Here

When Danny's son was a toddler, Danny and his wife had a strict rule for the little tike that he did not like or agree with. The rule was this: *Do not put your fingers in the electrical outlets!* The toddler, of course, had no concept of electricity or of the danger it posed for him. Thus the commandment seemed unfairly restrictive to him. After all, those little holes in the wall were right at his level and his little fingers would just fit. With his limited experience, he simply could not fathom the danger.

Of course Mom and Dad could've concluded that total freedom for the young lad was what was best for him, and thus they could have placed him in the backyard to live. Here there were no electrical dangers and the toddler could freely poke his fingers into the knotholes in the fence and still be safe. However, because of rain, snow, broiling hot summers, freezing winters, and a toddler's general fear of the night, the parents opted to bring him into the house to live close to them. They wanted him to be blessed with a warm, modern home, and also to be in close relationship with them. But this meant being in close proximity to the deadly powers of electricity—thus the need for the rule.

In our Story, God wants to bless his young children (the Israelites) with a good life, and thus he plans to move them from the backyard (the wilderness) into the house (the Promised Land), where he will live in close relationship with them. But this requires a few basic rules.

Be Prepared

Read or listen to Exodus 19–20; Deuteronomy 6 and 28.

The Story Continues

The Continuing Picture of Salvation

In the previous chapter we saw how God dramatically delivered the Israelites from slavery and oppression in Egypt. We noted that this "exodus" event is a picture of what salvation is all about. Yet deliverance *from* something bad is only half the picture of salvation, because salvation also involves entering into relationship with God and then being delivered *to* something good.

In this chapter we will pick up the Story as the Israelites victoriously exit Egypt. We realize that this spectacular deliverance is but a prelude to something even bigger. God has wonderful plans for the Israelites. He delivers them from Egypt so that they can enter into a special, close relationship with him and then move triumphantly into the Promised Land with him living right in their midst, blessing them and protecting them. For all of this to work properly, the Israelites will need to keep certain terms; that is, they must obey certain principles that God delineates for them. These "terms" are called commandments. God gives these commandments to the Israelites on their way to the Promised Land to define the terms by which they can have a fantastic and wonderful life in the Promised Land with God living right there among them. This is the Story of Exodus 16–40, Leviticus, Numbers, and Deuteronomy.

Encountering God on Mount Sinai and Receiving the Commandments (Exodus 16–24)

In Exodus 19 God brings the Israelites to Mount Sinai. Moses has been here before, remember, for this is the location where God spoke to him from the burning bush, calling Moses to a special task (Ex. 3). The two events are related. In Exodus 3 God spoke to one man from a burning bush. In Exodus 19 God speaks to all of the Israelites and the entire mountain is ablaze. Both encounters stress the holiness and power of God. As God chose Moses for a special task in Exodus 3, now in Exodus 19 he chooses the entire nation to be a "kingdom of priests and a holy nation" (19:6). The entire mountain becomes

A Summary of the Ten Commandments

How to treat God:
The Lord alone must be worshiped; don't have any other gods.
Don't make or worship idols.
Don't misuse the name of the Lord.
Keep the Sabbath day holy by ceasing work on that day.

How to treat each other:
Honor your parents.
Don't commit murder.
Don't commit adultery.
Don't steal.
Don't give false testimony.
Don't covet other people's stuff.

Presence, Power, and Holiness

The theme of God's interconnected presence, power, and holiness runs throughout the Bible—from the garden of Eden to the tabernacle to the temple to the indwelling Holy Spirit to the new Jerusalem.

like a temple and the Israelites are able to encounter God, just like a priest would in a temple. This is a spectacular privilege for them, and it signals a special new relationship between God and the Israelites.

Next (Ex. 20) God presents to the Israelites the foundational terms for this new relationship. We know these terms as the Ten Commandments. They are cited twice, once here in Exodus 20 and again in Deuteronomy 5, representing the basis or the core elements of the new relationship between God and Israel. The Ten Commandments underscore for Israel God's strong emphasis on relationship and faithfulness—both between God and his people and also between each individual. The first four commandments focus on how the people should relate to God. The next six commandments provide the basics of how people should relate to each other. These Ten Commandments provide the most basic foundational terms for how Israel should live as the people of God—how they should treat God and how they should treat each other. The next several chapters in Exodus contain expansions, explanations, and applications of the Ten Commandments.

God has offered the Israelites a great deal. If they will but keep these basic rules, he will live with them in the Promised Land and bless them immensely. In Exodus 24 the Israelites accept the deal and ratify this "covenant" agreement. This covenant God makes with Israel at Mount Sinai on their way to the Promised Land is called the Mosaic covenant. Some scholars refer to it as the Sinaitic covenant. It complements the Abrahamic covenant, but it is not identical to it.

"I will dwell in your midst": The Promise and Implications of God's Powerful and Holy Presence (Exodus 25–40; Leviticus)

There is a three-part formula-like statement that God uses to describe the covenant relationship between him and his people: (1) I will be your God; (2) you will be my people; and (3) I will dwell in your midst. God's promise of giving his powerful presence to Israel—that is, coming down to actually live among them—is one of the most significant promises in the Scriptures, and it will echo throughout all of the rest of the Story. God relates to people directly through his presence. In addition, closely associated with God's presence is his power. Yet God is also a holy God, and his presence likewise brings a demand for holiness and cleanness for everything (and everyone) in the vicinity. God's presence among the Israelites will change everything in their lives.

First of all, if God is coming to actually live right there among the Israelites,

The Golden Calf Episode: An Unthinkable Interruption

In Exodus 25–40 God gives the details for how to build the tabernacle, the place where he will reside as he comes to dwell in their midst. His presence will be a wonderful blessing for them, almost beyond imagination. Shockingly, however, a horrible event interrupts the details of the plan for building the tabernacle. In Exodus 32 the Israelites grow impatient waiting for Moses to come down from a meeting with God on Mount Sinai, and they decide to build and worship a golden calf. So while God is giving Moses the Ten Commandments up on the mountain, the Israelites down below have already abandoned him and started to worship a golden calf.

God tells Moses that he will destroy Israel and make a new people out of Moses' descendants, but Moses talks him out of it, "reminding" God of his promise to Abraham. This is an ominous and incredibly ironic event. Even as God is instituting one of the greatest blessings ever (his presence), the Israelites are turning to worship an idol. This perhaps foreshadows the times ahead when Israel will turn away from God to worship idols, even after he has blessed them so richly.

he will need an appropriate place to live. Thus it is no surprise to see that the entire second half of Exodus (chs. 25–40) is largely filled with God's instructions regarding how to construct the tabernacle—a mobile, tentlike temple where God's presence will live. After a terrible interruption (Ex. 32) the Israelites do in fact build the tabernacle, and the climax of this section of the Story occurs in Exodus 40:34–38 as the glory of the Lord actually comes and fills the tabernacle. As promised, God's empowering and holy presence now dwells with his people.

Second, if the holy, awesome presence of God is actually going to come and reside within the midst of Israel, they will need to know how to deal with this new reality. How will they relate to him? How can they even approach him? How should they deal with the holiness of his presence and the demands that this holiness brings? The book of Leviticus answers these questions. Thus the flow of the Story from Exodus into Leviticus is logical and smooth. In the second half of Exodus the Israelites construct the tabernacle to function as the residence for the holy, awesome God of Israel. In the final chapter of Exodus God indeed comes and fills the tabernacle with his glorious presence. Leviticus, then, instructs the Israelites on how to live with the holy, awesome God in their midst. The holiness of God is a central theme, and four times in Leviticus the people are told, "Be holy, because I am holy" (11:44, 45; 19:2; 20:26).

Basically the book of Leviticus informs the Israelites that when the holy, awesome God comes to live in your midst, *everything in your life will change.* All of life must now be lived with the consciousness of God's great holiness. Thus Leviticus structures all of their daily life around categories of clean and unclean things, or holy and profane things. Because God is holy and mankind is sinful, Leviticus also provides details regarding sacrifices, which play an important role in dealing with people's sins and reestablishing relationship with God. Without the thorough explanation of the sacrificial system in Leviticus, our understanding of the great sacrifice of Jesus Christ in the New Testament would be seriously limited. Finally, Leviticus also explains to the Israelites how they can worship God and live with his blessings within the Mosaic covenant.

Disobedience and Wandering in the Wilderness (Numbers)

In the second half of Exodus, God makes the Mosaic covenant with Israel at Mount Sinai, leads them to construct the tabernacle, and then comes into the tabernacle to dwell in Israel's midst. Leviticus explains the implications and changes necessary for Israel to live and worship God since he now resides right there among them. The book of Numbers picks up the Story at this point as God leads Israel on to the Promised Land. Now that God has established a wonderful relationship with his people (the Mosaic covenant), he wants to move them into the Promised Land, where they can truly enjoy the blessings of their relationship with him.

In Numbers, however, an unbelievable thing happens. The Israelites refuse to enter the Promised Land. When they see that it will require faith and hard work to conquer the Promised Land, they rebel against God and refuse to follow him into the land. This is unthinkable! The whole point of the exodus event was to deliver Israel *from* Egypt and to deliver them *to* the Promised Land. This was the land that God had promised to Abraham back in Genesis. Now he is fulfilling the Abrahamic promise and actually giving Abraham's descendants the land. How can they refuse it? The entire Mosaic covenant that they have with God assumes and revolves around their living in the Promised Land.

But the Israelites do indeed reject the land, whining with exaggeration that it would have been better to have died on the way in the wilderness rather than to die while trying to conquer the Promised Land. God hears their ridiculous whiny excuse and turns it into a prophetic judgment against them. He sends them all back into the wilderness, where they will wander aimlessly for forty years until that entire generation dies off, just as they requested.

God still watches over Israel as they wander in the wilderness. Eventually the disobedient generation dies off and a new generation arises. God then leads this new generation of Israelites back toward the Promised Land. But God wants his people to understand clearly how they must live in relationship with him in the Promised Land, so right before they go into the land, he presents them with Deuteronomy.

The Terms for a Blessed Life in the Promised Land with God in their Midst (Deuteronomy)

The Israelites are now on the east side of the Jordan River, with the Promised Land lying just across the river. Unlike the earlier generation, this new generation seems eager to take possession of the land. God, however, wants to be sure that they understand the arrangement and the relationship they will have with him in the land. In a nutshell, Deuteronomy defines the terms by which Israel can live in the Promised Land with God in their midst and receive incredible blessings in life.

The title "Deuteronomy" means "the second law." It is not a "second law" in the sense that it is something totally new and unique, but rather that it is a second presentation to Israel of the basic laws first explained in Exodus 16 through Leviticus. Deuteronomy expands, explains, and clarifies some of the earlier laws as well as adding some new material. The Ten Commandments, first presented in Exodus 20, are repeated in Deuteronomy 5, likewise stressing that proper living for the Israelites involves a vertical component, how to relate to God, and a horizontal component, how to relate to each other.

The Israelites are exhorted to remain faithful to God and to worship and serve him alone as they move into the new land. They are cautioned against allowing the pagan inhabitants of the land to corrupt them with their idolatry and immoral practices. The Israelites are also challenged to live a life concerned with justice and to have compassion on those who are weak and vulnerable in their society: orphans, widows, foreigners, and the poor.

Deuteronomy is presented to the Israelites as a series of speeches that Moses delivers to them, just prior to entering the Promised Land. The basic literary structure and format of the book, however, resemble an ancient treaty form called a "Hittite suzerainty treaty." That is, God presents Deuteronomy to the Israelites in a format that would have been recognized fundamentally as a contract or treaty. Deuteronomy is basically a contract between God and Israel covering their life in the Promised Land. It has stipulations along with consequences. If Israel obeys the terms of the contract, their holy, awesome God will live among them in this wonderful land, blessing them with peace and agricultural prosperity. If, however, they choose to disobey or ignore the terms, opting to follow the ways of the pagan Canaanites instead, terrible repercussions will occur. Instead of experiencing the blessings of God, they will know the judgment of God. The curses predicted in Deuteronomy will unfold, and the good, peaceful, prosperous life will be filled with drought, famine, and foreign invasion. Eventually, God warns, they will lose his presence and the right to live in the Promised Land.

The book of Deuteronomy comes to a climax in chapters 28–30. There God summarizes the book and clearly explains things to Israel. Here is the deal, God tells them. If you follow the terms of Deuteronomy, you will live in the Promised Land as a blessed people and life will be wonderful. However, if you ignore me and disobey the terms of Deuteronomy, terrible things will happen to you, life will be a nightmare, and eventually you will lose the Promised Land. The choice, God declares, is yours.

Making Connections

Let's review where we are in the Great Story:

Creation and Crisis
Covenant
Calling Out
➤ **Commandments**
Conquest and Canaanization
Creation of the Kingdom
Communion and Common Sense
Crumbling of the Kingdom
Captivity and Coming Home
Interlude: Time between the Testaments
Christ
Church
Consummation

After God's great creation, people sin and alienate themselves from God (crisis). God, however, responds by making a wonderful covenant with Abraham, in which he promises numerous descendants, a land, and blessings, both to them and to the nations. The Abrahamic covenant will continue to drive the Story throughout the rest of the Old Testament and into the New Testament. In fulfillment of this covenant, God delivers Abraham's descendants, the Israelites, from bondage in Egypt (calling out). Now, in the commandments section of the Story, God takes the Israelites to Mount Sinai, gives them the Ten Commandments, and explains their relationship by a three-part formula: I will be your God; you will be my people; I will dwell in your midst. If he is to dwell in their midst, he will need a place to stay, so the second half of Exodus describes the construction of the tabernacle where God will dwell.

Leviticus defines how Israel is to live with the holy, awesome God in their midst. God leads the Israelites on to the Promised Land and tells them to subdue it, but the Israelites (have they lost their minds?) refuse to take it (Numbers). God lets that rebellious generation die off while wandering in the wilderness, and then he leads the children of Israel back to the perimeter of the Promised Land.

Here, then, he gives them the book of Deuteronomy, defining the terms by which they can live in the Promised Land with God in their midst and explaining how they can be blessed. These terms, along with the second half of Exodus, Leviticus, and Numbers, comprise the Mosaic covenant. Deuteronomy specifically defines the covenant or agreement between Israel and God. If they follow the terms in Deuteronomy, obeying God and staying faithful to him, he will bless them in the Promised Land. If they refuse to obey, turn to other gods, and act like their pagan neighbors, God will bring judgment on them and remove them from the land.

While the fulfillment of the Abrahamic covenant still hovers in the background, it is Deuteronomy that now takes center stage as the dominate background for the Story. Will Israel obey Deuteronomy and be blessed? Or will they disobey and be judged? This is the question that drives the Story through Joshua, Judges, Ruth, 1–2 Samuel, 1–2 Kings, and the Prophets.

Living the Story

It is good for us to remember that God is the one who defines our relationship with him. We are not free to set our own terms for how we choose to relate to God and worship him. He sets the terms and either we obey or we don't. Certainly we affirm that human beings are saved by faith through Jesus Christ and not through works. But the quality of life we live and the significance of our lives here on earth are related to our obedience.

God is also crystal clear in this portion of the Story that he is the one who sets the criteria for approaching him. He soundly and repeatedly rejects the notion that the Israelites can worship him through idols. Likewise, he demands that they worship him and him alone. Never in the Bible is there any suggestion that other religions provide alternate, but valid, approaches to God, and books like Exodus and Deuteronomy stress this over and over and over. God is not ambiguous about this. For us this message is clear. God has revealed to us that people can approach him and worship him only through his Son, Jesus Christ. The other religions, like that of the ancient Canaanites, are not just neutral; they are strictly forbidden.

Finally, this part of the Story places a significant emphasis on the presence and the holiness of God. This theme will continue throughout the rest of the Bible. For us today, we experience the presence and holiness of God through the indwelling of the Holy Spirit. As the ancient Israelites encountered the holy and powerful presence of God living right there in their midst (in the tabernacle), so we today live with the presence of God right within us. This is a frightening thought and should lead us to be extremely concerned with holiness in our lives. "Be holy, for I, the LORD, am holy" applies to us today.

Memory Verse

Hear, O Israel: The LORD our God, the LORD is one. Love the LORD your God with all your heart and with all your soul and with all your strength. (Deut. 6:4–5)

Wrapping Up

The commandments in Exodus, Leviticus, Numbers, and particularly Deuteronomy express the terms by which Israel can live in the Promised Land with the holy, powerful God right in their midst, and be blessed. Will they be faithful to Deuteronomy? This is the question that will drive the plot though the next part of the Story.

Digging Deeper

Books

Gundry, Stanley N., ed. *Five Views on Law and Gospel.* Counterpoints. Grand Rapids: Zondervan, 1996.

Schnittjer, Gary Edward. *The Torah Story: An Apprenticeship on the Pentateuch.* Grand Rapids: Zondervan, 2006.

ASSIGNMENTS

1. Compare and contrast Israel's encounter with God in Exodus 19 with Moses' encounter with God in Exodus 3:1–4:17.

2. Read the Ten Commandments in Deuteronomy 5:7–21. Choose any three of the commandments and discuss what each one means to us today.

3. In Deuteronomy 6, God is preparing Israel to cope with a major socioeconomic change. They will soon be changing from a nomadic, tent-dwelling society to a settled, more complex village/city society. Identify the dangers for the nation that the text cites. Discuss the role that the family was to play in keeping the nation faithful to God.

4. Compare the blessings for obedience with the curses for disobedience given in Deuteronomy 28. Discuss them in three categories: (a) economic; (b) political; and (c) personal/family.

CONQUEST AND CANAANIZATION:
Good News and Bad News

Chapter 5

Enter Here

We often encounter occasions in life when someone tells us, "Well, there is good news and bad news." In fact, this is a commonly enough shared experience that there are hundreds of "good news/bad news" jokes in circulation. Usually in these good news/bad news jokes the bad news is so bad that it completely negates the joy created by the good news. In a twisted sort of way, this irony somehow creates humor. Admittedly these are often corny, but consider the following example. The slave master on a Roman galley ship tells the slaves who are chained to their oars, "Men, I have good news and bad news. The good news is that you will get double rations for lunch today. The bad news is that after lunch the captain wants to go waterskiing." You can probably recall numerous other good news/bad news jokes.

While there is nothing humorous at all about the grim events in this part of the Story, nevertheless the good news/bad news contrast succinctly sums up this chapter of the Story perhaps better than any other analogy.

The good news? Under Joshua's leadership Israel successfully conquers the land of Canaan and settles down into the Promised Land.

The bad news? The following generations of Israelites abandon God and become just as bad as the wicked Canaanites they were supposed to drive out of the land.

Be Prepared

Read or listen to Joshua 1–7; Judges 1–2; 13–16; 19–21.

The Story Continues

As the Pentateuch (Genesis through Deuteronomy) ended, we were left with two major strands of plot that will push the Story along into the book of Joshua. First, although God had fulfilled several aspects of his promise to Abraham (numerous descendants, great nation, blessings on his people, blessings on those who bless them and curses on those who curse them), the promise of a land still had not been fulfilled. The whole point of delivering the Israelites from Egypt was to take them out of slavery and deliver them to a land of blessing. In the book of Joshua this promise will be fulfilled. The Israelites will cross the Jordan River and conquer the land of Canaan. They will then divide the land among the twelve tribes and settle down to enjoy the blessings of God in this wonderful Promised Land. In a sense the land then becomes similar to the garden back in Genesis 2. It is a place of blessing, empowered and sanctified by the presence of God.

The other plot strand comes from the commandments, and from Deuteronomy in particular. Deuteronomy, remember, presents the terms by which Israel could live in the Promised Land with God right there in their midst and find blessing. The question driving the Story is this: Will the Israelites obey Deuteronomy and be blessed? Following the death of Moses, as Joshua contemplates leading the Israelites into the conquest of the Promised Land, God reminds him, "Be strong and very courageous. Be careful to obey all the law my servant Moses gave you; do not turn from it to the right or to the left, that you may be successful wherever you go" (Josh. 1:7). Joshua will do a great job of obeying God and carrying out God's instructions. Thus he will be blessed with tremendous success in conquering the Promised Land.

Faith versus Disobedience and the Quick Siege of Jericho

Joshua 3–6 describes the spectacular victory that God gives Joshua and the Israelites over the strong fortress city of Jericho. First of all, God stops up the Jordan River so that the Israelites can cross over the river on dry ground, even in flood stage. This parallels the crossing of the Red Sea back in Exodus. Just as God parted the Red Sea to deliver the Israelites *from* slavery, so he now parts the Jordan River to lead them *to* a new life of blessing in the Promised Land. This parallels the New Testament picture of salvation for us — being delivered *from* sin and being led *to* a new life of blessing in the Lord.

God then destroys the walls of Jericho and delivers the city into the hands of Joshua and the Israelites. Normally a siege of a fortress city like this took over a year, and sometimes several years. God gives the victory to Joshua in seven days. The lesson is clear: obedience and faith in the Lord will lead to tremendous success in the task God has called them to, and they will result in great blessing.

While the main story line deals with the defeat of Jericho, there is a fascinating and important subplot that is closely interconnected. The stories of two individuals, Rahab (Josh. 2) and Achan (Josh. 7), open and close the Jericho episode like bookends. Rahab, a Canaanite prostitute living in Jericho, believes in the God of Israel and is delivered from the destruction of Jericho. She becomes part of the "people of God" and is even included in the lineage of David and Jesus. Achan, however, is a stark contrast to Rahab. He is an Israelite and thus should have been receiving great blessings in the Promised

Land. Yet he despises God and thinks he can greedily disobey God's basic commandments about hording loot from the conquered city. Thus, just as Rahab becomes like an Israelite and finds blessing, so Achan becomes like a Canaanite and finds judgment. In essence, the two trade places.

Located here at the beginning of the conquest, this subplot has a critical point. Gentiles (non-Israelites) who believe in and obey God can be included among the people of God and find great blessings, while Israelites who disbelieve and disobey God will be excluded, joining the unbelievers in judgment.

Conquering and Dividing the Land

After a short setback due to Achan's disobedience, Joshua gets the Israelites back on track to conquer the Promised Land. First he defeats the major cities in the southern part of the country (Josh. 9–10) and then breaks the back of the major resistance in the north (Josh. 11). Then Joshua divides up the land and gives each tribe its allocated area of territory (Josh. 12–21). Joshua 21:43–45 sums up the entire conquest:

> So the LORD gave Israel all the land he had sworn to give their ancestors, and they took possession of it and settled there. The LORD gave them rest on every side, just as he had sworn to their ancestors. Not one of their enemies

Understanding the Morality of the Conquest

For many people the gruesome details of the conquest are troubling. God orders Israel to completely annihilate the Canaanites. Sometimes, as in the case of Jericho, this involved the death of every man, woman, child, and animal. Is this fair? Does it conflict with our New Testament concept of God's compassion and love?

Reviewing a few points in the Story will help us better understand this event. First, note that the order to kill all of the inhabitants of a city applied only to cities that were inside the Promised Land. It was not a general rule of warfare for the Israelites.

Second, the Bible consistently stresses that the Canaanite culture was particularly immoral and corrupt. The perversion of the Canaanites in the Sodom and Gomorrah story (Gen. 19) functions as a prototypical picture of the society, a view reinforced by other texts that connect sexual sins and perversions to the Canaanites (Lev. 18).

Third, God acknowledged the offensive sin of the inhabitants of Canaan as early as the time of Abraham (Gen. 15:16), but in God's great mercy and compassion he opted to wait another four hundred years before judging them. The judgment carried out on the Canaanites by Joshua was not a new or novel idea, but something that had been permeating throughout the centuries prior to this.

Finally, it is rather ironic that in a story about annihilating the Canaanites, the first major episode deals with a dramatic exception to the rule (Rahab and her family). Her story, placed prominently at the beginning of the conquest, suggests to the readers that those inhabitants of the Promised Land who turned to the God of Israel in faith and obedience could be delivered and incorporated into the people of God.

withstood them; the LORD gave all their enemies into their hands. Not one of all the LORD's good promises to Israel failed; every one was fulfilled.

As the book of Joshua draws to a close, we see Joshua calling the Israelites to renew their covenant commitment and to pledge that they will continue to serve God and obey his commandments.

Thus the book of Joshua is basically a "good news" book. Joshua, the primary leader, is faithful to God and under his leadership the nation follows God. God blesses them and empowers them to complete the task he has called

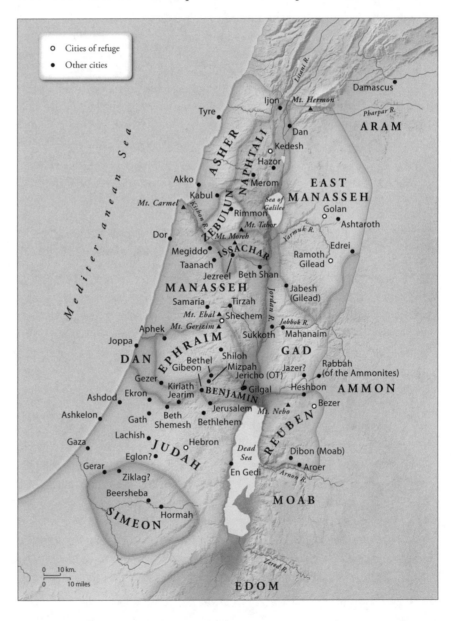

them to (the conquest). Now they are settled in the land and anticipating a time of blessing and "rest." However, even though the Story in Joshua is primarily a "good news" story, there has been a quiet undercurrent of brief hints to the contrary. Episodes like Achan's disobedience, along with brief references to territories and cities in the Promised Land that were not completely subdued, point to the fact that while the conquest is complete on the large scale, not everything is right. Once Joshua and the initial generation who led in the conquest pass away, the entire situation starts to unravel.

God at War?

"In Old Testament Israel's physical battles, God wanted to show forth his greatness, not a display of sheer human power. And though the true Israel—the church—doesn't wage war against 'flesh and blood' (Eph. 6:12) today, our warfare against Satan and his hosts has its roots in Yahweh [God's] wars in the Old Testament."[1]

– PAUL COPAN

Judges and the Downward Spiral of Disobedience

Judges 2:7 picks up on the success in the book of Joshua and declares, "The people served the LORD throughout the lifetime of Joshua and of the elders who outlived him and who had seen all the great things the LORD had done for Israel." After Joshua and the generation that conquered the Promised Land pass away, however, things in Israel deteriorate rapidly. The next generation, as well as those that follow, forsake the God of their fathers and worship other gods, particularly the Canaanite god Baal.

Judges 2:6 – 23 describes the terrible cycle that ensues for Israel. When the Israelites turn to other gods, God removes his protection and power from them, and foreign raiders or invaders overrun Israel and oppress them. Then God raises up a deliverer who rescues Israel from their oppressors. In the book of Judges these deliverers or tribal rulers are called "judges," but only rarely do they actually do any legal ruling or judging. However, soon after the rescue Israel will repeatedly plunge back into idolatry, even worse than before. So God once again removes his powerful protection, another enemy invades, and the cycle repeats.

Israel turns away from God to idols

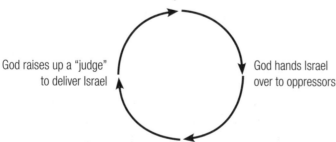

God raises up a "judge" to deliver Israel

God hands Israel over to oppressors

Israel suffers under foreign domination

1. Paul Copan, *Is God a Moral Monster? Making Sense of the Old Testament God* (Grand Rapids: Baker, 2011), 168.

This is the pattern that runs throughout the book. However, the pattern is not just cyclical. It is a spiral that moves downward morally and theologically as the book progresses. That is, as Israel spins around on this merry-go-round of disobedience, things get progressively worse until, as described below, they reach the bottom with a terrible crash.

Judges 1–2 presents the overview and the cycle. The particulars of the downward spiral are told through the stories of several specific judges (Judg. 3–16). Prominence is given to the stories of Othniel, Ehud, Deborah and Barak, Gideon, Jephthah, and Samson. Ironically, not only does Israel get worse as the Story unfolds, but so do the "judges." That is, with the exception of Othniel (the first judge) and Deborah (who serves more as a foil), the character of each judge is "tainted" in some way. Furthermore, these character flaws seem to grow more serious as the Story progresses, climaxing in the story of Samson, who cares nothing for God and has no inclination toward obedient living. Here is a summary of each of these major judges.

Othniel (Judg. 3:7–11), apparently a man of good character (see Judg. 1:9–15), starts the sequence off on a good foot, delivering the Israelites from their Mesopotamian oppressors. The text, however, doesn't mention anything about whether Othniel was able to return the people to a true worship of God.

Ehud (Judg. 3:12–30) delivers Israel by smuggling a sword into a private audience with the oppressing king and then slaying the fat, defenseless King Eglon. This act leads to Israel's deliverance, and in a sense this was a brave action. But it just doesn't seem like the valiant act of a heroic deliverer. For example, it is not the kind of thing that David (the upcoming Israelite hero of 1–2 Samuel) would have done. Furthermore, as in the case of Othniel, there is no mention of repentance or the return of the nation to God.

Deborah (Judg. 4–5) is one of the few "squeaky clean" judges and a brave heroine. Her faith and heroism, however, only underscore the timidity and cowardice of **Barak**, who was the one who was supposed to lead Israel into battle.

Gideon (Judg. 6–8) is more complex. On the surface he seems to be a brave deliverer who trusts in God. However, if we read carefully, we see that God has to give him sign after sign after sign (in total, four miraculous signs) in order to get Gideon to trust in him and to act. Then his story does not end well as he collects some of the captured gold (remember Achan!) and then forms a golden ephod (a vestlike garment that only priests wore) that is worshiped by his family (8:27).

Jephthah (Judg. 10:6–12:7) makes a rather stupid vow to God, swearing that if God gives him victory, he will sacrifice whatever comes out of his house first to greet him. After the victory, it is his daughter who runs out to greet him as he returns. Keeping his grim vow, Jephthah sacrifices his daughter. Ironically, the god of the Ammonites, whom Jephthah has just defeated, is the one most infamously known for requiring child sacrifice. The God of Israel abhors such things and would never have required that Jephthah keep such a vow.

The Nations in the Book of Judges

The specific enemies that oppress Israel in the Promised Land throughout Judges add to the irony of the Story. Othniel fights against Mesopotamians, Ehud against the Moabites, Deborah and Barak against the Canaanites, Gideon against the Midianites, Jephthah against the Ammonites, and Samson against the Philistines. The irony is that the Moabites, Ammonites, and Midianites were all subdued by Moses as Israel migrated to the Promised Land. To be fighting them again indicates that things are going backward. Likewise, Joshua had broken the back of the Canaanites, so to be struggling with them again is a bad sign.

Finally, the presence of the Philistines is ominous. The other groups are neighboring powers that were in the region at the time of Abraham. But the Philistines are a new group. Like Israel, they have recently migrated into the area. Thus they aspire to drive out the Israelites and dominate the Promised Land instead of Israel. What irony!

Finally, the sequence of judges climaxes with **Samson** (Judg. 13–16). Samson is set apart from birth to be a Nazarite, one who is designated to be committed to serving God (Num. 6:1–12). The requirements for a Nazarite are that he never touch a dead animal, never drink alcoholic beverages, and never cut his hair. God gives Samson great strength, empowering him to be a great warrior. Samson, however, chooses to live more like a selfish and spoiled bum than like a consecrated hero and deliverer. He sins frequently and even defiles his parents. He also fritters away the opportunity to crush the Philistines and drive them out of the land. When he does defeat them, it is always for self-serving purposes.

Eventually Samson tells the Philistine prostitute Delilah that if she cuts his hair, he will lose his strength (does he really believe this?). She does indeed cut his hair, he does indeed lose his strength, and the Philistines subdue him, blinding him and imprisoning him. Finally, at the end the Philistines bring him out to make fun of him at a party. His hair has now grown back and God gives him strength one more time. He pushes out the columns holding up the roof of the structure and kills all of the Philistines, along with himself.

Samson is a tragic figure. We can only wonder what would have happened if he had taken advantage of his great ability and actually rallied Israel and led them into battle. As the last of the judges in this sequence, he presents a good picture of Israel herself. That is, Samson appears to serve as a symbol of Israel. Incredibly gifted and full of tremendous potential, he chooses to ignore God and fritter it all away, chasing after foreign women (i.e., symbolic of foreign gods).

Unfortunately, the Story gets worse. The final chapters (Judg. 17–21) describe total anarchy and moral collapse, as the Israelites demonstrate that they have become just as morally corrupt and wicked as the Canaanites they displaced. The tribe of Dan decides to leave their allotted territory in the

Promised Land and migrate north to another area that looks easier to subdue. Along the way they pick up a Levite priest who has started serving household gods, including one he made himself.

Then, in similar fashion to the action of the Canaanites living in Sodom and Gomorrah (Gen. 19), the Israelite inhabitants of a city in Benjamin attack a visitor but end up raping his concubine instead. This visitor then cuts her up in pieces and sends a piece to each of the other Israelite tribes. They rally together and attack the tribe of Benjamin, nearly annihilating it. The book of Judges ends with the fitting words, "In those days Israel had no king; everyone did as they saw fit" (Judg. 21:25).

Throughout the book of Judges the Israelites have spiraled down and down morally and theologically. This can be seen especially through the fate of the women in the Story. Here at the end the Israelites hit the bottom with a spectacular and dramatic crash. Their priests, the Levites, are serving other gods, one of their tribes has left the Promised Land for a different region, and the morality in an Israelite city parallels that of Sodom and Gomorrah (the epitome of perversion). Finally, instead of fighting against the Canaanites or their other enemies, the Israelites are now fighting each other. What right do they have to the Promised Land anymore?

Making Connections

Let's review where we are in the Great Story:

> Creation and Crisis
> Covenant
> Calling Out
> Commandments
> ➤ **Conquest and Canaanization**
> Creation of the Kingdom
> Communion and Common Sense
> Crumbling of the Kingdom
> Captivity and Coming Home
> Interlude: Time between the Testaments
> Christ
> Church
> Consummation

Living the Story

From the life of Joshua we learn that if we trust in God and live courageously by his word, he will enable us to accomplish successfully the purpose he has for us. If we desire to find our purpose in life and if we hope to attain that purpose, it is critical that we seek the leading of God through his word to identify that purpose and to trust in his power and presence to accomplish that purpose.

From the time of the judges we learn that turning away from God and trusting in ourselves leads to total disaster in our lives. Then if we do not turn back to God in true repentance and commit to him faithfully, our lives will continue to spiral downward out of control into a deeper and deeper mess.

Wrapping Up

After God delivers the Israelites from Egypt, he gives them the commandments to enable them to live in the Promised Land with the presence of God in their midst and to enjoy the blessings provided by his presence. Then, after they accept the terms of the agreement, the commandments, God leads them into the Promised Land to drive out the sinful Canaanites and to occupy the land. Joshua and his generation remain faithful to God, and as long as they live, the Israelites are successful. This is the good news.

The bad news is that in the book of Judges the people turn away from God repeatedly. Thus morally and theologically, they spiral downward and things continue to get worse and worse for them. As we look to the next section of the Story, we can't help but wonder, "Who will save them from this mess?"

Memory Verse

"Keep this Book of the Law always on your lips; meditate on it day and night, so that you may be careful to do everything written in it. Then you will be prosperous and successful." (Josh. 1:8)

Digging Deeper

Books

Block, Daniel I. *Judges, Ruth.* The New American Commentary. Nashville: Broadman & Holman, 2003.

Copan, Paul. *Is God a Moral Monster?* Grand Rapids: Baker, 2011.

Hamilton, Victor P. *Handbook on the Historical Books.* Grand Rapids: Baker, 2001.

Hess, Richard S. *Joshua: An Introduction and Commentary.* Tyndale Old Testament Commentaries. Downers Grove, IL: InterVarsity Press, 1996.

Hubbard, Robert L. *Joshua.* The NIV Application Commentary. Grand Rapids: Zondervan, 2009.

ASSIGNMENTS

1. In these questions we take a deeper look at Samson. Compare Judges 13:1–5, 13–14 with Numbers 6:1–12 in regard to the requirements for a Nazarite. What restrictions were placed on Samson as a Nazarite? What restrictions were placed on his mother? What was the purpose of being a Nazarite? That is, what did it signify?

2. Read Judges 13–16. Discuss the various ways in which Samson violates the Nazarite requirements. How "set apart" or "holy" to Yahweh does Samson seem to be? How does the cutting of his hair and the consequent loss of strength relate to the Nazarite issue? Is Samson a Nazarite or isn't he?

3. Is Samson a hero or a bum? Give reasons for your answer.

4. Compare Samson to the nation of Israel of his day by discussing the ways in which Samson's life parallels the behavior of the nation since Joshua.

CREATION OF THE KINGDOM:
Nobodies and Somebodies

Chapter 6

Enter Here

Everyone loves a "rags to riches" story. This episode of the Great Story starts quietly with a young humble peasant "nobody" named Ruth, who struggles merely to find enough to eat each day. In dramatic contrast it ends with King Solomon living in wealth and splendor beyond imagination. You can't very well call Solomon a "nobody"! This episode has five main players—Ruth, Samuel, Saul, David, and Solomon—with David playing the central and most significant role in this part of the Story. He is the star. But read carefully and don't assume that this episode is straightforward and simple, for it contains lots of twists and unexpected turns in the plot. In fact, the "somebodies" don't do so well, and the "nobodies" turn out to be the real heroes and heroines.

"I'm Nobody! Who are you?
Are you—Nobody—too?"[1]

– EMILY DICKINSON

The other main character in this section is God himself. He starts out quietly, working behind the scenes to bless the foreigner Ruth and then calling softly to the small boy Samuel. As the Story progresses, God moves out of his quiet background role to become a major character in the Story. He is active in the lives of Saul and David, although he usually speaks to them indirectly through the prophets Samuel and Nathan. Then, dramatically and significantly, God appears directly to Solomon twice. Ironically—and this episode is full of irony—Solomon still turns away from God, and thus this episode of the Story ends with God's words of judgment to Solomon (1 Kings 11:9–11).

Be Prepared

Read or listen to Ruth 1–4; 1 Samuel 8–10; 17–19; 2 Samuel 7; 11–12; 1 Kings 11.

---

1. Emily Dickinson, "I'm Nobody! Who Are You?" *The Poems of Emily Dickinson*, ed. R. W. Franklin (Cambridge, MA: Belknap, 1998), 1:279.

The Story Continues

Remember what happened in chapter 5? In the book of Joshua, the "good news" book, Joshua leads the Israelites into the Promised Land (the conquest), defeating all of their major opponents in the land. In Joshua, by and large, things are going great. In the book of Judges, the "bad news" book, however, everything goes disastrously wrong, and by the end of Judges the Israelites have become just like the Canaanites they were supposed to drive out (the Canaanization of Israel). They sink about as low morally and theologically as a people can sink. Why doesn't God do something? Can they be saved from this disaster? Who will rescue them from this mess?

The answer is David. He is the hero whom God raises up to save Israel from their self-inflicted disaster. But God introduces David quietly by first working behind the scenes in the story of Ruth.

Ruth

After the horrific and gruesome events of Judges, the story of Ruth comes as a breath of fresh air. The contrast is startling. There are no kings and warriors here, nor are there any sieges, battles, or great military victories. There is only the quiet story of two simple but valiant women, Ruth and her mother-in-law, Naomi.

This part of the Story opens during the terrible time of the Judges, as a man named Elimelech takes his wife, Naomi, and two sons and *moves out of the Promised Land* to Moab. What is he thinking?! His two sons then marry Moabite women, one of whom is Ruth. When they live outside of the Promised Land and apart from God, bad things happen to this family, and all three men die (Ruth 1:1–5). Naomi, the man's widow, decides to return to Israel, and Ruth, her daughter-in-law, doggedly determines to go with her, declaring, "Where you go I will go, and where you stay I will stay. Your people will be my people and your God my God" (Ruth 1:16).

Once back in the Promised Land, this episode takes on a "boy meets girl" romantic twist as Ruth meets a strong "faithful-to-God" man named Boaz, who falls in love with her and marries her, likewise taking Naomi into his household to care for her. Soon a baby boy is born, a tremendous blessing that

Orphans, Widows, and Foreigners

The book of Deuteronomy frequently calls on the Israelites to care for orphans, widows, and foreigners. Occasionally it adds the poor to this list. In a certain sense Ruth falls into all of these categories—orphan, widow, foreigner, poor. As Boaz cares for Ruth, he is also fulfilling the commandments of Deuteronomy—and blessings result.

brings happiness, in contrast to the death of all the men at the beginning of this story. The point is this: once this family moves back to the Promised Land and trusts in God, blessing replaces tragedy.

But this sweet romantic story has an important twist at the end. The narrator of this story quietly tells us at the end that this baby boy born to Ruth and Boaz is named Obed. He becomes the father of Jesse, who will be the father of David (Ruth 4:13–17). Thus, in essence, the book of Ruth serves as an introduction to David. He is the hero who will crash onto the scene later in 1 Samuel 16. He is the one who will deliver Israel out of the disastrous mess seen at the end of the book of Judges.

1–2 Samuel

The main characters in 1–2 Samuel are Samuel, Saul, and David. However, 1–2 Samuel is first and foremost about David. The man Samuel plays a transitional and introductory role, and King Saul is but a foil to underscore the virtues of David, the real hero of this part of the Story.

Samuel (1 Samuel 1–7)

The book of Judges provides the background setting of the opening chapters of 1 Samuel. Things are bad. The tabernacle and the ark of the covenant are at a city named Shiloh, but an inept and incompetent old man named Eli serves as high priest, and his two disgraceful and self-serving sons are perverting the worship of God. In contrast, a humble, faithful woman named Hannah gives birth to a baby boy named Samuel, and as the Story unfolds a reversal of roles and position takes place. The high priest Eli and his two corrupt and immoral sons die and are replaced by Samuel, who, in contrast, is committed to serving God.

Samuel is a transitional figure. He functions as the last of the judges, but also serves as a priest. In addition, Samuel will anoint the first two kings and then serve as God's spokesman to the first king, Saul. In his role as spokesman for God, Samuel also functions as a prophet. So Samuel is the last of the judges, but also a prophet and priest. He will preside over the transition from "the judges" to "the monarchy."

One Book or Two?

First and Second Samuel were originally written in Hebrew as one long book on one scroll. All of the earliest Hebrew manuscripts of Samuel (part of the Dead Sea Scrolls discovery) place 1 and 2 Samuel together on one scroll as one book. When this book was translated into Greek (the Septuagint), however, the Greek letters required more space and thus this long book could no longer fit on one scroll. So the translators split it into two and placed it on two scrolls (1 and 2 Samuel). Our English translations follow this tradition. The same thing happened with 1–2 Kings and 1–2 Chronicles.

Strength through Weakness

A fairly consistent theme running throughout the Great Story is that God often works through what is humanly "weak" to create true "strength." In this portion of the Story, for example, we see God working through the simple peasant Moabite girl Ruth to bring about the savior of Israel, David. Likewise, the story of Hannah and Samuel underscores the reversal of roles and fortunes as the weak ones, Hannah and her son Samuel, replace the strong ones, the powerful high priest Eli and his terrible sons. Hannah sings of strength through weakness and the reversal of the roles and fortunes of the low and the powerful in her song of 1 Samuel 2:1–10.

Finally, this theme is illustrated dramatically as the small shepherd boy David defeats the huge warrior Goliath and then later becomes king. This theme culminates in Jesus Christ, for his life and the cross are the ultimate demonstration of strength through weakness.

King Saul (1 Samuel 8–15)

Israel's general experience with judges has not gone well, and in 1 Samuel 8 the Israelites demand that Samuel give them a king so that they can be like everybody else. They especially want a king who can "go out before us and fight our battles" (1 Sam. 8:20). Although this request reflects a lack of trust in God, nonetheless God tells Samuel to go ahead and appoint a king for them. Apparently even though God is not impressed with the people's motives behind their request for a king, he is intent on using the Israelite monarchy to bring about his purposes and to point prophetically to the kingdom of God. Remember, too, that eventually the Messiah, Jesus Christ, will come and reign as the ultimate king, bringing God's plan to its consummation.

Since the people want a king who can lead them in battle, God selects Saul as the first king, a man who fits their criteria. He is one of the tallest young men in Israel—a head taller than anyone else (1 Sam. 9:2). God helps Saul to get off to a good start, strengthening him through three significant things:

- God gives Saul the Spirit to empower him (1 Sam. 10:6, 10).
- God gives Saul a great initial military victory, which leads to his confirmation as king by all of Israel (1 Sam. 11:1–15).
- God gives Saul the wisdom, advice, and public support of Samuel (1 Sam. 10:24–25; 11:14; 12:12–15).

King Saul, however, matches these three gracious, empowering gifts of God with three momentous boneheaded mistakes, reflecting his lack of trust in God:

- In 1 Samuel 13 Saul grows impatient and does not wait for Samuel to come and offer a sacrifice prior to the battle. In disobedience to Samuel, Saul offers the sacrifice himself.
- In 1 Samuel 14 in the midst of a battle Saul makes a foolish vow like Jephthah did in Judges 11. Fulfilling this silly vow would have led to the

death of Saul's brave son Jonathan. Fortunately, the army stops Saul from fulfilling his vow and executing Jonathan.

- In 1 Samuel 15 Saul directly disobeys a clear command from God to destroy the Amalekites. Then he tries to blame his actions on the men in the army. For God this is the last straw. Samuel informs Saul, "You have rejected the word of the LORD, and the LORD has rejected you as king over Israel" (1 Sam. 15:26).

David (1 Samuel 16 – 2 Samuel 24)

Since Saul has proven dramatically that he is unworthy to be king, in 1 Samuel 16 God leads Samuel to anoint a new king. This time, instead of the people, it is God who selects the primary criteria, declaring, "Do not consider his appearance or his height. . . . The LORD does not look at the things people look at. People look at the outward appearance, but the LORD looks at the heart" (1 Sam. 16:7). God then leads Samuel to anoint David.

From the beginning we see how different David is from Saul. When Saul is introduced into the Story, he is looking aimlessly for his father's lost donkeys (1 Sam. 9). In contrast, when David is introduced into the Story, he is watching over his father's sheep (16:11; 17:34 – 37). In fact, one of the main themes driving this portion of the Story is the stark contrast between Saul and David. Saul, a gifted individual by human standards, is a failure as king, while David, a man after God's heart, has incredible success as king, at least for a while.

Most of the Story in 1 Samuel 17 – 31 revolves around the contrast between David and Saul. In fact, as mentioned above, Saul's role in the Story is more of a foil to underscore how smart, brave, and dedicated David is. Yet keep in mind that even though Samuel anoints David as the next king, Saul is still on the throne with no intention of peacefully handing it over to David.

In 1 Samuel 17 David explodes onto the national scene by bravely attacking and killing the huge warrior Goliath in one-on-one combat, a fight that should have been conducted by Saul since he was the largest and best armored of the Israelites. After David's victory Saul becomes jealous of him and attempts to kill David several times. David, however, when given the chance to kill Saul, instead spares Saul's life, which once again underscores the contrast between them. Throughout this section of the Story (1 Sam. 18 – 28), Saul slowly loses his sanity. Finally, in 1 Samuel 31 Saul is killed in a battle with the Philistines.

After Saul dies, there is a period of civil war between David and the house of Saul (2 Sam. 1 – 4). In 2 Samuel 5 David is confirmed as king by the entire nation of Israel. He then conquers the city of Jerusalem from the Jebusites and establishes his capital there. Next he defeats those pesky Philistines, finally driving them out of the country. In 2 Samuel 6 David brings the ark of the covenant to Jerusalem and returns it to the center of Israel's national worship.

One of the most significant events in David's life occurs in 2 Samuel 7. David wants to build God a "house" (meaning a temple). Instead, God declares that he will build David a "house" (meaning a dynasty). Indeed, 2 Samuel 7 is one of the most important chapters for biblical history and theology, for here God establishes the Davidic covenant. As part of this covenant, God promises that a descendant of David will be established on the throne of a kingdom that will last forever. Later in the Old Testament the prophets will clearly merge this covenant promise with the hope for a future Messiah, identifying the coming messianic king as a descendant of David. Likewise, the New Testament proclaims that Jesus Christ is the fulfillment of this promise to David and is the promised messianic Davidic king.

David, meanwhile, is fantastically successful as the new king. He unifies Israel and establishes his capital at Jerusalem. He brings the ark of the covenant to Jerusalem and reinstitutes a true and proper worship of God. As 2 Samuel 5–10 illustrates, *David is the one who finally completes the conquest*, the task originally assigned to Joshua and the people in the book of Joshua. He expands the borders of Israel nearly to the boundaries promised to Moses. Thus David is the one who truly delivers Israel from the disastrous disobedience we saw at the end of Judges. He is the hero, the savior, the messiah (anointed one).

But ... the Story does not end here. True, David is a great man, and so far he has been soaring. He is the hero of the Story. But he is not the Messiah; he is merely a man, and in 2 Samuel 11 he crashes.

Second Samuel 11 contains one of the most tragic episodes in the entire Story. David, our hero, sends his army off to war, but he stays behind in Jerusalem (is he bored?). Gazing down from his rooftop one evening, he sees a beautiful woman, Bathsheba, bathing in her courtyard, unaware that David could observe her. Although God has already provided David with seven wives, he decides that he wants Bathsheba right then, even though he finds out that she is married to Uriah, one of his leading soldiers who is away fighting with Israel's army at a major siege. With his eyes closed to everything he knows about God, David takes Bathsheba and sleeps with her. We are not told what her feelings are in this matter. Before long she becomes pregnant, and David has a serious problem on his hands.

As David tries to "fix" the mess, yet still keep his terrible sin concealed, the situation deteriorates for him. He tries to get Uriah to return to Bathsheba and sleep with her so that he and everyone else will think the baby is Uriah's. The loyal soldier Uriah, however, refuses to go home, even after David orders him

David on the Wave of History

"We are invited to watch while history works its relentless way toward God's intention. History is not a blind force or an act of sheer power. There is a purpose at work that regularly astonishes us. It is a power that disrupts and heals. David is now carried on the wave of this purpose. The ones who trust the story ride atop this flow of history with David. They ride there with David every time they tell or hear the story. The others, like Saul, either die or go mad."[2]

– WALTER BRUEGGEMANN

---

2. Walter Brueggemann, *First and Second Samuel* (Interpretation; Louisville: John Knox, 1990), 140.

to. Caught up in trying to scheme his way out of the consequences of his sin, David sends orders to his commander Joab to place Uriah in the front of the battle lines and then withdraw, so that Uriah will be killed. Joab complies and Uriah dies. David then marries Bathsheba and she gives birth to a son. At the end of the chapter, however, the narrator quietly notes that "the thing David had done displeased the LORD" (2 Sam. 11:27).

In 2 Samuel 12, God sends the prophet Nathan to confront David about this great sin. David does not try to defend himself, but acknowledges and confesses his sin. God forgives David of his sin (2 Sam. 12:13), but the terrible consequences of the sin cannot be removed. The baby dies and David's kingdom starts to unravel.

It is important to note that David's affair with Bathsheba functions as a great pivot point in the Story of 1–2 Samuel. Up to this point David has been incredibly successful, growing in power and establishing a great kingdom. He consistently defeats his enemies; indeed, he completes the conquest of the Promised Land. He is the hero and everyone loves him. After the Bathsheba event, however, everything starts to go bad, and the rest of 2 Samuel simply chronicles David's struggles and problems. David's son Amnon rapes Tamar, Amnon's half-sister and David's daughter. Tamar's brother Absalom then kills Amnon, his half-brother, in revenge (2 Sam. 13). Eventually Absalom leads a rebellion against David, and David flees Jerusalem in disgrace. As David, the former champion and hero, trudges out of Jerusalem in retreat, a man from the clan of Saul pelts him with rocks. What a contrast to the time when the young David valiantly slew the Philistine champion Goliath!

Eventually Absalom is defeated, but in the process he is killed by David's commander Joab. Thus David's victory is bittersweet, and he mourns the loss of his son. Yet even now, Humpty-Dumpty (David) cannot quite be put back together again.

> ## Easy Historical Date for David
>
> For an easy-to-remember ballpark number, place David around the year 1000 BC.

The glorious kingdom of David is gone with the wind. Other rebellions break out (2 Sam. 20) and even the Philistines reappear as opponents (21:15–22). The last four chapters (chs. 21–24) serve to summarize David's reign, including the good and the bad, but the book ends with a positive forward look as David dedicates an altar on the site of the future temple (24:18–25).

Solomon (1 Kings 1–11)

The books of 1–2 Kings follow right on the heels of 2 Samuel. As 1 Kings begins, David has grown old and is about to die. Although he has several wives and numerous sons, he follows the prodding of Bathsheba (quite ironic!) and appoints her son Solomon as the next king. From the beginning things seem a bit odd, for in the case of both Saul and David, the selection had been done by God. Here, as the successor to David is chosen, God is silent.

As David passes the throne to his son Solomon, the old king gives a serious charge and critical advice to his son. "Observe what the LORD your God requires," David warns. "Walk in obedience to him, and keep his decrees and commands, his laws and regulations, as written in the Law of Moses. Do this so that you may prosper in all you do and wherever you go" (1 Kings 2:3). David is referring primarily to the book of Deuteronomy, reminding Solomon that obedience to Deuteronomy is of critical importance. God himself will speak directly to Solomon twice, reiterating what David declared: if you obey the Law of Moses (Deuteronomy) you will be blessed, but if you disobey, bad things will happen (1 Kings 3:14; 9:4–9).

On the surface Solomon's reign seems to go well. He forms important alliances by marrying the daughters of foreign kings. He consolidates and expands the kingdom he inherited from David. Because of God's love and his promise to David, God blesses Solomon with wisdom and great wealth, which Solomon uses to build magnificent, awe-inspiring buildings in Jerusalem. He builds a grand palace and residence, along with residences for his many wives. More importantly, he constructs a spectacular, breathtaking temple for God and places the ark inside the temple in the "the Most Holy Place." Then a cloud fills the temple and the presence of God comes to dwell right there in the temple (1 Kings 7:13–8:13). Solomon also builds a huge standing army with large numbers of chariots (the latest in military technology). He builds a fleet of ships to sail on the Red Sea. Wealth pours into the empire. Everything about Solomon's empire is spectacular ... at least on the surface.

Nevertheless, the warnings given to Solomon by David and by God himself in regard to keeping the Law of Moses (the book of Deuteronomy) keep echoing throughout the book, which causes us to read the text a little more carefully and a little more critically. First, central to Deuteronomy and at the core of the Ten Commandments is the call to worship God and him alone. Yet early in the Solomon story (1 Kings 3:3), we see that things are not quite right in this regard: "Solomon showed his love for the LORD by walking

Kings and Chronicles

First and Second Chronicles cover much of the same historical time period as 1 and 2 Kings do, but with a different emphasis. First and Second Kings conclude the Deuteronomy-based history and stress the failure of Israel and Judah to obey Deuteronomy. They look back at the largely tragic time period of the kings, explaining why the terrible exile (judgment) came. First and Second Chronicles, on the other hand, reflect more of a forward-looking account of the kings, pointing beyond the exile and stressing worship and the continuity of the Davidic covenant.

according to the instructions given him by his father David, *except* that he offered sacrifices and burned incense on the high places." That little word "except" is extremely important, subtly suggesting an early indictment on Solomon.

Second, Deuteronomy 17:14–20 provides a specific set of criteria for the king to live by. God gives three specific rules for the Israelite kings:

1. The king must not acquire a great number of horses (probably chariot horses), especially horses from Egypt.
2. The king must not accumulate large amounts of silver and gold.
3. The king must not "take many wives."

A fourth aspect that is implied, though not stated, is a warning against any serious relationships with Egypt, the land from which God delivered them.

If we read the story of Solomon against the backdrop of Deuteronomy 17, a different assessment of Solomon emerges. On the surface, the narrator of the Story appears to praise Solomon for his spectacular kingdom, but beneath the surface, we observe that those very things the narrator seems to praise are, in fact, violations of Deuteronomy 17. Indeed, the same list appears:

1. Twice the narrator states the large number (12,000) of chariot horses Solomon accumulates (1 Kings 4:26; 10:26). The narrator is also careful to point out that Solomon obtains many of these horses from Egypt (10:28).
2. The abundance of silver and gold in Jerusalem is likewise emphasized (1 Kings 10:27).
3. The issue of "many wives" is almost ridiculous, for the narrator tells us that Solomon had seven hundred wives of royal birth (many of them foreign) and three hundred concubines.
4. The narrator telling the Story stresses Solomon's marriage to Pharaoh's daughter, highlighting the connection to Egypt, which was prohibited (1 Kings 3:1; 7:8; 11:1).

So while the Story appears on the surface to be praising Solomon, in actuality the text is subtly criticizing him for his failure to be faithful to the terms God gave Israel in the book of Deuteronomy. Finally, in 1 Kings 11:1–13 the sobering truth is stated plainly. Solomon has turned away from the God of Abraham to worship many other gods, even building worship sites for these detestable pagan gods. Some of these gods, like Molech and Chemosh (11:7), were known for requiring child sacrifice. Angrily God states that he will tear the kingdom out of Solomon's hands and give it to a subordinate; only because of God's great love for David does he delay this judgment. Nonetheless, at this point the nation of Israel begins a long, tragic downward slide into idolatry, which eventually leads to the end of the kingdom and to exile.

Making Connections

Let's review where we are in the Great Story:

Creation and Crisis
Covenant
Calling Out
Commandments
Conquest and Canaanization
➤ **Creation of the Kingdom**
Communion and Common Sense
Crumbling of the Kingdom
Captivity and Coming Home
Interlude: Time between the Testaments
Christ
Church
Consummation

The book of Deuteronomy, part of the "commandments" chapter, continues to provide the theological background for this part of the Story. God delivers the people of Israel from Egypt, enters into the Mosaic covenant with them, and then gives them the wonderful Promised Land. Deuteronomy, part of the Mosaic covenant, provides the terms by which Israel can live in the Promised Land and be blessed. After God gives them Deuteronomy, the question that drives the Story throughout the rest of the Old Testament is this: Will Israel obey Deuteronomy and be blessed in the Promised Land? The sad answer is, "No."

In the previous chapter we saw that Joshua led the people into the Promised Land and got them off to a good start. Judges, however, was a disaster as the people turned away from God and spiraled downward theologically and morally, ultimately becoming just like the Canaanites. Who will rescue them from this mess? The answer is David, at least in the short term. He is the "Messiah-like" king and hero who delivers Israel from the disaster of Judges. David completes the conquest and establishes Jerusalem as the capital. He restores the true worship of God to Israel. But as we read, we realize that David is not the Messiah, for he is but a human being, and as a mere man he stumbles, leaving us looking forward to the real Messiah who will not have the weaknesses of David.

Solomon then builds a spectacular kingdom, but Solomon is a big step down from David. Beneath the glitzy veneer of Solomon's kingdom we see that things are not right and Solomon is not obeying Deuteronomy. In fact, he helps the kingdom of Israel begin her long, disastrous affair with idolatry.

Another important connection is to remember that David composes a large number of the Psalms. These songs emerge out of David's virtues and his heart after God. Simply believing and obeying, while important to God, fall short of what he really wants from us. Psalms reflects communion with God and worship of God, in all stages of life—both the good times and the bad times.

As Israel stumbles in her inability to obey the Law (Deuteronomy), God continues to graciously forgive the people and restore them according to his promise to Abraham. In addition, in 2 Samuel 7 God makes a covenant with David. This Davidic covenant plays an important part throughout the rest of the Story. As Israel fails to keep the Mosaic covenant (the Law, especially Deuteronomy), she experiences the promised consequence of judgment. Yet also operating are the gracious promises God made in the Abrahamic and Davidic covenants; thus there is hope for the future through the coming Messiah.

Living the Story

The humble yet faithful life of Ruth provides us with a model we can learn from. In difficult times she clings faithfully to Naomi and to the God of Israel. She behaves virtuously and with dignity, and eventually she is blessed tremendously. She probably never realizes that God is working quietly through her and using her to raise up the deliverer of Israel. In reality she is not a "nobody" but a "somebody." We never know what God's future plans are or how we fit into those plans. We do know that we are important to him and that he does indeed want us to play a role in his plan. In God's eyes, there aren't any "nobodies" in his kingdom, only "somebodies." In the Great Story, Ruth emerges as greater than Solomon. What about you?

Likewise, there are numerous great applications we can draw from David, especially from his earlier years. He is a humble man with a heart that yearns for God. His trust in God produces incredible bravery in his life. Thus he provides us with a great model of how we should seek to have a heart for God and how we should strive to combine humility with bravery. Both of these derive from and are strengthened by our faith in God.

There are also lessons for us to learn from David's great tragedy, his affair with Bathsheba. David's total collapse in the Bathsheba event demonstrates that none of us is so mature in our Christian life or so strong in faith that we cannot fall to temptation. When David looks over the wall and sees the beautiful Bathsheba bathing below, we find ourselves shouting at our hero, "Walk away! Don't linger and let sin take hold of your imagination! And get back out to the battlefield where you are supposed to be!" But he doesn't and his life ends up in shambles. The same is true for us. When you find yourself being tempted toward an adulterous affair, you need to look into those beautiful or handsome eyes that are tempting you and *see your life in ruins*. Realize how many other lives will be negatively impacted (or wrecked) by your action as well! Walk away immediately! Distance yourself from anyone who might present themselves as a possible temptation to you. Don't think arrogantly that *you* cannot fall into such temptation.

Ultimately, David at his best as the righteous king points us to Christ. Likewise, the Davidic covenant points us to Christ, the one who will come as the perfect, righteous King and rule eternally over God's great kingdom. In David's failure, we are still pointed to Christ, realizing that no man or woman can fulfill the role of Messiah and Savior. While great leaders like David can help us, ultimately we must trust only in Christ. He will never let us down. He will never fail as David did.

Wrapping Up

Setting: Who will save the poeple of Israel from the mess at the end of Judges?

Ruth: a humble peasant girl. God works quietly through her to raise up David, the deliverer.

Samuel: prophet, priest, and the last judge. He provides the transition from the era of the judges to the monarchy. He anoints the first king, Saul, and the second king, David.

Saul: the first king of Israel. He is the kind of king the people want, one who is big and powerful. God gives him three gifts to empower him to be successful. However, he responds by making three rather stupid mistakes/disobediences, and thus God takes the kingdom away from him.

David: the hero of this part of the Story. In contrast to Saul, David is God's kind of king. He is humble and trusting. He delivers Israel from the mess of Judges. He completes the conquest and reestablishes true worship of God. But as a man, he falls into temptation and crumbles through his affair with Bathsheba. The Davidic covenant, however, continues, for it is based on God's gracious promise. The date for David: 1000 BC.

Solomon: Given great power and potential, he squanders it all by disobeying the book of Deuteronomy and embracing idolatry. Yes, he builds the spectacular temple, but so what? God is not impressed with glitz, but with faithful obedience. The nation begins its tragic downward slide.

Memory Verse

"The LORD does not look at the things people look at. People look at the outward appearance, but the LORD looks at the heart."
(1 Sam. 16:7b)

Digging Deeper

Books

Arnold, Bill T. *1 and 2 Samuel*. The NIV Application Commentary. Grand Rapids: Zondervan, 2003.

Bergen, Robert D. *1, 2 Samuel*. The New American Commentary. Nashville: Broadman & Holman, 1996.

Block, Daniel I. *Judges, Ruth*. The New American Commentary. Nashville: Broadman & Holman, 2002.

DeRouchie, Jason S., ed. *What the Old Testament Authors Really Cared About*. Grand Rapids: Kregel, 2011. See the articles on Ruth, 1–2 Samuel, 1–2 Kings.

ASSIGNMENTS

1. Compare and contrast the two "bookends" of this section, Ruth and Solomon.

2. Compare and contrast Hannah and her son Samuel with Eli and his two sons.

3. In what way does Jesus fulfill the Davidic covenant (2 Sam. 7)?

4. Compare and contrast David's encounter with and marriage to Abigail (1 Sam. 25) with his encounter with and marriage to Bathsheba (2 Sam. 11).

COMMUNION AND COMMON SENSE:
Worship and Other Ways to Live Wisely

Chapter 7

Enter Here

Communion means to have a close, intimate exchange of thoughts or feelings. Worship is a big part of communion with God, but communion is really broader than worship, and it stresses the two-way nature of the relationship. Communion with God involves sharing intimate thoughts and feelings with him—and then listening and meditating on his response.

Communion is at the heart of the book of Psalms. Israel's pagan neighbors "worshiped" their gods; that is, they offered sacrifices, burned incense, celebrated festivals, and so on. But there was little relationship or communion between the people and the gods. The God of Abraham was dramatically different. When he entered into covenant relationship with Israel, he stated, "I will be your God; you will be my people; I will dwell in your midst." This implied a real relationship, complete with communication and communion.

Yes, worship is an appropriate response to God, and it is part of communion. But communion goes beyond worship. The book of Psalms leads us into communion with God. Certainly the Psalms teach us how to worship, providing us with great models of how to praise God. But the Psalms also teach us how to cry out in confusion and pain and how to listen to the voice of God in the midst of crisis and hurting. This communion with God is part of the Great Story. It is what God desired from Israel, and it is what he desires with us today.

The second part of this chapter deals with the Wisdom Books (Proverbs, Job, Ecclesiastes, and Song of Solomon). Not only did God want his people to have a close, meaningful relationship with him, but he wanted them to have a close, meaningful relationship with each other. Likewise, he desired that his people live meaningful and blessed lives in the Promised Land. That meant that they needed to live wisely and not foolishly. The Wisdom Books give practical guidance to those under the covenant on how to live wisely in the nitty-gritty, day-to-day course of life.

Thus the dramatic historical events we have been following in the Great

Story will pause for a moment to allow for teaching and reflection on communion with God and living wisely with each other before God. This, too, is part of the Story.

Be Prepared

Read or listen to Psalms 1; 8; 9; 19; 22; 23; 74; Proverbs 1; 10–11.

The Story Continues

Psalms

As we saw in Chapter 6, David is the hero who rescues the Israelites from the mess in Judges and gets them back on track in regard to worshiping God properly. David is a "man after God's own heart," and he has a close, intimate relationship with God. David is also a musician, who learns that music is a wonderful and appropriate way to have communion with God. A "psalm" is simply a religious song. David composes 73 of the 150 psalms in the Bible and firmly solidifies the tradition of using psalms for public worship and private meditation, a tradition that has continued down to us today.

The book of Psalms is a collection of 150 individual psalms, grouped into five "books." The individual psalms were probably written, collected, and organized into these five books over a relatively long period of time, starting primarily with David and continuing into the postexilic period. One exception, however, is Psalm 90, written earlier by Moses. We cover this span of the Great Story in Chapter 6—The Creation of the Kingdom, Chapter 8—The Crumbling of the Kingdom, and Chapter 9—Captivity and Coming Home. The order of the five books is probably due to the chronology of the collection process. This grouping into five probably is intended to parallel the five books of the Pentateuch (Torah). Each of these five books ends with a statement of praise to the Lord. The five books are as follows:

Book	Contents	Ending
Book 1	Psalms 1–41	"Praise be to the Lord ... Amen and Amen" (41:13)
Book 2	Psalms 42–72	"Praise be to his glorious name forever ... Amen and Amen" (72:19)
Book 3	Psalms 73–89	"Praise be to the Lord forever! Amen and Amen" (89:52)
Book 4	Psalms 90–106	"Praise be to the Lord ... let all the people say, 'Amen!' Praise the Lord." (106:48)
Book 5	Psalms 107–150	"Let everything that has breath praise the Lord. Praise the Lord." (150:6)

The entire text of Psalm 150 is a call to praise the Lord, so this psalm as a whole is the praise that concludes the overall collection of Psalms.

I n the Hebrew Bible, the title of the book of Psalms is *Tehillim*, which means "praises."

The various psalms can be grouped into two major and very different categories, reflecting the contrasting contexts of the authors within the Great Story. First, there are "praise psalms," in which the psalmist seeks to thank and praise God for all of the blessings he has received. Sometimes the psalmist simply praises God because God is so wonderful and praiseworthy. In other cases a praise psalm might function something like a modern "testimony," in which the psalmist shares with the community how God delivered him from some great crisis. Generally these praise psalms come out of life contexts when things are going well (at least now) and the psalmist is enjoying the rich blessings of God.

The second category of Psalms is "lament psalms." A lament is a poetic woeful cry of pain and anguish, an ancient style of theological singing that resembles "the blues." Throughout the Great Story God's people often experience pain and suffering. Even the strongest and most faithful of people (like David) can sometimes feel totally overwhelmed and confused. "Where is God?" they cry out honestly. "Why doesn't he deliver me?" they ask. Later, during the exile, they will pour out their hearts to God, asking, "How long will you be angry at us?" The psalmists are brutally honest in these laments. Part of being in communion with God is honestly expressing one's hurt, sorrow, and confusion to him. There is no fake, superficial religiosity in these lament psalms. Yet usually, as the psalmist cries out in pain and sorrow, he slowly comes to grips with the fact that God is really with him, and he ends the sorrowful psalm with a statement of trust in God.

The Great Story provides the background context for the book of Psalms and can be seen throughout the psalms. The psalmists praise God for creation and for establishing the covenants. The great deliverance from Egypt (calling out) is

C. S. Lewis on "Praising God"

"I think we delight to praise what we enjoy because the praise not merely expresses but completes the enjoyment; it is its appointed consummation. It is not out of compliment that lovers keep on telling one another how beautiful they are; the delight is incomplete till it is expressed. It is frustrating to have discovered a new author and not to be able to tell anyone how good he is; to come suddenly, at the turn of the road, upon some mountain valley of unexpected grandeur and then to have to keep silent because the people with you care for it no more than for a tin can in the ditch; to hear a good joke and find no one to share it with.... The Scotch catechism says that man's chief end is 'to glorify God and enjoy Him forever.' But we shall then know that these are the same thing. Fully to enjoy is to glorify. In commanding us to glorify Him, God is inviting us to enjoy Him."[1]

– C. S. LEWIS

---

1. C. S. Lewis, *Reflections on the Psalms* (San Diego and New York: Harcourt, 1958), 95–97.

extolled as the paradigm of salvation, and some psalms praise God for that as well. The blessings that could be found in obeying the Law are enumerated, and obedience to the commandments (especially Deuteronomy) is stressed in several psalms. Likewise, the gift of the Promised Land (conquest) and the establishment of the kingdom are listed as other reasons for praising God.

Yet other psalms discuss the somber issues of disobedience and judgment. David cries out in sorrowful confession and repentance after the Bathsheba affair (Psalm 51). Later the shattered and disoriented Israelites in the exile also realize the consequences of sin, and they pray for forgiveness and restoration. Finally, several psalms contain messianic components. Psalms that extol the earthly Davidic king quickly merge into extolling the Lord as the ultimate king and thus often imply messianic fulfillment as they look forward to the establishment of the Lord's dominion over all.

The Wisdom Books: An Overview

As we have seen in the Great Story, if Israel stays faithful to God and obeys the terms in Deuteronomy, they will live in the Promised Land and be blessed. Throughout the Story the Israelites are exhorted to trust God and obey his commandments. This will lead to national blessing. On an individual basis, however, if someone opts to live recklessly and foolishly, directing their day-to-day life with stupid decisions, they will suffer the natural consequences of their foolish behavior. Thus in the Wisdom Books God gives guidance to help his people to live wisely.

Living the "good life" in the Promised Land involved trusting in God and obeying his commandments, but it also involved making wise, discerning decisions. Throughout most of the Great Story, the imperatives for the characters in the Story, as well as for us, are "trust!" "believe!" "be faithful!" and "obey!" The imperatives for this part of the Story (the Wisdom Books) are "think!" "reflect!" "discern!" and "understand!"

We see that a mature follower of God should have not only great faith, but

Messianic Psalms

There are numerous psalms containing nuances of messianic promises, but Psalms 2 and 110 clearly refer to the coming Messiah. This connection is stated numerous times in the New Testament (Matt. 22:41–45; Mark 12:35–37; Luke 20:41–44; Heb. 1:5). Likewise, Jesus quotes Psalm 22:1 ("My God, my God, why have you forsaken me?") while hanging from the cross (Matt. 27:46), indicating that the suffering described in Psalm 22 may refer to both David's suffering and that of the Messiah, Jesus. Psalm 22:15–18 describes the crucifixion of Christ with incredible specificity.

also wisdom for day-to-day living. Faith and practical wisdom are not separate or antithetical; rather, they are interconnected, even complementary. Proverbs 1:7 declares, "The fear of the LORD is the beginning of knowledge." The Wisdom Books help God's people within the covenant to make wise decisions in life, not only by providing some practical guidance in making specific choices, but also, and more importantly, by developing strong character.

The four Wisdom Books are Proverbs, Job, Ecclesiastes, and Song of Songs. These books do not present independent universal promises, but rather

> **Words of Wisdom from Hollywood?**
>
> "Life is hard; it's harder when you're stupid."
>
> **– JOHN WAYNE**

valuable, and contextual, insights into wise and godly living. Proverbs is the foundational, "baseline" book of wisdom. It presents the norms of life, things that are normally true. Proverbs teaches that if you work hard, you will prosper, but that if you are lazy, you will not prosper. This is normally true, though not universally true. It is not a promise but rather an insight into what happens normally in life.

The other three books (Job, Ecclesiastes, and Song of Songs) present exceptions to the norms of Proverbs. Job deals with a situation in which the norms of Proverbs are turned on their head—bad things are happening to a good and righteous person. Ecclesiastes teaches that the norms of Proverbs are good for day-to-day living (being wise is certainly better than being stupid), but that strictly rational, wise approaches to life ultimately come up short; moreover, without faith, wisdom will not provide any meaning in life. The Song of Songs addresses the wild and crazy love between a man and a woman—truly an experience that is outside the ordered, rational life depicted in Proverbs.

Thus Job, Ecclesiastes, and Song of Songs balance Proverbs. The four of them must be taken together for a complete picture of wise, godly living. Truly wise people will embrace the norms of Proverbs and use these to build their character. However, as part of their character, truly wise people will also develop the discernment to recognize and deal with the exceptions to the norms of life.

Proverbs

Wisdom in the book of Proverbs involves combining faith in God with an understanding of how day-to-day life works and showing how to make good decisions. As mentioned above, Proverbs explains the norms of life—how things normally work. Thus this book is extremely practical. It addresses such topics as work, friends, child-rearing, husbands and wives, sexual immorality, honesty, gossip, anger, patience, poverty, wealth, and the need for understanding.

The teachings in Proverbs repeatedly use four typical types of people to illustrate and characterize the point being taught. The main characters of Proverbs are listed in the following table:

Term used	Description
The *Simple* (or *Naïve*)	This person is not very smart and doesn't want to be. They have faith but no discernment, so they are likely to believe anything with their misplaced faith.
The *Fool*	This person is not smart either, but they think they are. They are too clever in their own eyes to need faith or to seek wisdom, for they know it all already.
The *Scoffer* (or *Mocker*)	This person is smart, humanly speaking, but they do not have faith in God; thus, their intellect does not translate into true wisdom and they become merely clever, bitter, and arrogant skeptics.
The *Wise*	This person is smart and discerning, always eager to listen and learn more. Yet they also have faith in God and always integrate their learning with their faith.

The book of Proverbs exhorts its readers to strive to be the *Wise* person and not the *Simple*, *Fool*, or *Scoffer*.

Proverbs 1:1–7 introduces the book and connects wisdom with faith in God. The first major unit (1:8–9:18) contains a father's wisdom to his young and gullible son. The middle section of the book (10:1–29:27) contains a large collection of one-verse (but two lines of text) pithy statements that are typically called "proverbs." Proverbs 30 contains proverbs by an unknown wise man named Agur. The final chapter (ch. 31) is attributed to the mother of "King Lemuel," another character unknown to us. So just as Proverbs opens with a father giving instruction to his son, so it closes with a mother giving advice to her son (31:1–9), followed by a description of a wise and noble wife.

Job

In the book of Proverbs everything in life makes sense. Good, righteous, hardworking people prosper and do well, while mean, lazy cheaters don't. Most of the time this is true (i.e., it is the norm). But it certainly isn't always true. Sometimes terrible things happen to good people. Car wrecks and cancer seem to strike randomly. Companies go under and thousands of hardworking employees are left without work, through no fault of their own. Impoverished countries experience devastating famines, and even strong Christian communities suffer greatly. How should God's people, especially those who are wise, cope with these great incongruities in life? The book of Job tackles this problem.

This book is very different from Proverbs. Job is a story, complete with beginning, middle, and end. Most of this story is told through a series of poetic dialogues spoken by Job, his friends, and finally God himself. The message is likewise different from that in Proverbs, for Job struggles with the difficult question of how wise, godly people are to handle terrible tragedies in their lives that seem completely unfair or without any logical explanation.

As the book opens, Job, a righteous and faithful man, is blessed with health, wealth, and a large family. Because of a challenge from Satan, however, tragedy strikes him and he loses everything. Using the theology of Proverbs, his friends assume that Job must have committed some great sin. Job knows he has not committed any great sin and he struggles to understand why this has happened to him. He begins to question God's justice and how God runs the world. He wants a hearing before God to clear this up.

At this point God himself shows up and speaks directly to Job. God, however, has not come to hear Job's objections and questions, but rather to clarify his right to run the world. In essence, God asks Job just how much he (Job) knows about running the universe. God seems to be asking Job just to trust him. God then rebukes Job's friends and restores Job's health, wealth, and family. God never tells him why all of this happened. The following four points synthesize the message that Job presents to balance Proverbs:

1. God is sovereign and his people are not.
2. God knows all about the world, while his people actually know and understand little.
3. God is always just, but he does not always explain his justice to his people.
4. God expects his people to trust in his character and his sovereignty when unexplained tragedy strikes.

Ecclesiastes

Ecclesiastes is a search for meaning in life. In Proverbs life makes sense and can be understood. The writer of Ecclesiastes, called the "Teacher" or the "Preacher," however, uses the rational approach of wisdom to take a good hard philosophical look at the world, where he finds all manner of inconsistencies and injustices. The book of Ecclesiastes is a story about a search for meaning

Popular Everyday Proverbs in the World Today

Practically every culture and language of the world have some kind of proverbial teaching or pithy one-line statements of wisdom. North American and British culture have dozens of them. "You can lead a horse to water, but you can't make him drink." "If you can't stand the heat, then get out of the kitchen." "Don't count your chickens before they're hatched." In regard to chickens, our favorite proverb comes from Ethiopia. One of their most frequently cited proverbs goes like this: "Slowly, slowly, the egg grows legs, and then suddenly one day walks away." This is a proverb about patience, recognizing that to a casual observer, not much seems to be happening to an egg. In reality, the chick is developing and the results will appear suddenly. So don't get impatient. What are the favorite proverbs from your culture?

All Is *Hebel*

One of the central words in Ecclesiastes is the Hebrew word *hebel*. Ecclesiastes 1:2 (in Hebrew) contains eight words, and five of them are *hebel*. Our English Bibles translate this word as "meaningless" (NIV), "vanity" (KJV and ESV), and "absolute futility" (HCSB). *Hebel* is normally used in Hebrew to describe breath and vapor, especially cloud vapor — that is, things that look as if they have solid substance but in reality do not. Clouds usually disappear as one draws close. The Teacher in Ecclesiastes discovers that the search for meaning from strictly a rational or "wisdom" approach is *hebel*. From a distance it looks like something solid of substance ought to be there, but in reality there isn't. The prophets will use this same word to describe the idols.

that the Teacher makes as he seeks to understand the world through wisdom and the logic of Proverbs. He discovers that while the rational, ordered approach to life (i.e., wisdom) is helpful and certainly to be preferred over foolishness and stupidity, nonetheless this "wisdom" approach does not give him a framework to grasp the meaning of life.

At the end of the search the Teacher comes back to faith, which was, after all, the real starting point for Proverbs. His conclusion, stated at the end of Ecclesiastes, is that one should "fear God and keep his commandments, for this is the duty of all mankind" (12:13). He realizes that wisdom is a good approach to life, and certainly much better for day-to-day decisions than folly is, but he finally acknowledges that wisdom does not answer everything and does not provide ultimate meaning in life. Only as one acknowledges God as Lord and Creator of the world does one find meaning in life.

Song of Songs

Marriage and the relationship between a man and woman form a significant, even foundational, part of human living. Thus it is no surprise to see that as the Great Story teaches practical wisdom, it also addresses marriage and sexuality. Proverbs presents the rational and reasonable side of love and marriage. It warns against lazy, drunken men and noisy, nagging women. Faithfulness in the marriage is stressed, and the devastating effects of adultery and unfaithfulness are presented. Proverbs 31 presents the ideal wife — a smart, dignified, hardworking woman. The wise man (an ideal husband) is presented throughout Proverbs while fools and scoffers are exposed for what they are. So Proverbs has great advice regarding whom one should marry. Yet Proverbs is limited to the public view. In Proverbs husband and wife are quiet, reserved, hardworking, discerning — in essence, dignified and respected.

Song of Songs, on the other hand, is quite different. This book is "X-rated," for it deals with the private, intimate side of marriage. The major topic in Song of Songs is human sexuality. This book celebrates the wonderful gift of human sexuality as enjoyed within marriage. Song of Songs has three major movements: (1) The Courtship (1:1–3:5); (2) The Wedding (3:6–5:1); and (3) The Honeymoon (5:2–8:14). This book is comprised of short songs that a man and a young woman sing to each other. Sometimes their friends sing too. The songs are mushy, corny, and somewhat sexually explicit.

This story is probably an idealized account of newly married lovers, written or collected by Solomon, but not necessarily autobiographical of King Solomon, who had a thousand wives! The book is not describing Solomon, but rather illustrating for God's covenant people how wonderful love between a man and a woman can be. It is also telling God's people that the dignified demeanor of the couple in Proverbs is proper in public, but once the lights go out at home and in private, then the sweet, mushy compliments whispered in the ear are what's best. This builds strong marriages and happy lives. This, too, is wisdom and part of the "good life."

Making Connections

Let's review where we are in the Great Story:

Creation and Crisis
Covenant
Calling Out
Commandments
Conquest and Canaanization
Creation of the Kingdom
➤ **Communion and Common Sense**
Crumbling of the Kingdom
Captivity and Coming Home
Interlude: Time between the Testaments
Christ
Church
Consummation

Based on his promise to Abraham (covenant), God delivered the Israelites from slavery in Egypt (calling out). He then gave them the terms for living successfully in the Promised Land with him in their midst blessing them (commandments). The conquest was completed and the kingdom was created.

At this point God expands on the terms for living successfully in the land. That is, starting with David, he teaches Israel the importance of praising God and crying out to him when in pain and trouble (communion). He also teaches them common sense (wisdom). Part of being godly and walking with God is being wise and discerning, able to navigate wisely and in a godly manner through the complicated decisions necessary in day-to-day living. The praise and communion of Psalms also balance and are, in turn, balanced by the wisdom of Proverbs, Job, Ecclesiastes, and Song of Songs. Faith is an integral part of true wisdom and vice versa.

This critical connection is illustrated graphically but negatively in the life of Solomon. Given great wisdom by God, Solomon nonetheless fails to integrate this wisdom with faith and faithfulness. Thus he has great organizational skill and builds a fantastic kingdom complete with an awe-inspiring temple and palace. But in the end, for all his wisdom he misses or simply ignores the point expressed in the opening chapter of Proverbs, the closing chapter of Ecclesiastes, and the entire book of Psalms.

The New Testament will continue to stress the theme of communion with God, modifying it and expanding it within the context of knowing Jesus as Lord (being "in Christ") and enjoying the indwelling of the Spirit. Discernment and wise living (common sense) likewise continue into the New Testament, for they are critical for godly living and the building of unity in the church. Both Jesus and Paul give practical advice on many of the same topics discussed in Proverbs. Also, the New Testament book of James draws heavily from the Wisdom Books of the Old Testament.

Living the Story

God desires to have close communion with us, both individually and as a community. The book of Psalms continues to be a fantastic avenue for us to use in approaching God from all contexts of life. The psalms provide great models for worshiping and praising God; indeed, Christians love Psalms because the psalmists can often help us express our praise and adoration to God much better than we can on our own. Reading and singing praises to God from Psalms lifts our spirits and helps us refocus on the important issues of life.

Likewise, the psalms teach us how to cry out to God in times of pain and suffering. They teach us that it is okay to hurt and to question God, to be confused and frustrated. Expressing our deepest pain, sorrow, and confusion to God is part of communion—and it is the first step on the road to recovery. God desires to hear how we feel. He will help us to endure the pain and suffering. Ultimately, he will deliver us from pain, suffering, and injustice.

The Wisdom Books likewise are brimming over with practical applications. Proverbs teaches us to seek wisdom and to strive for discernment and understanding. It challenges us to be patient and understanding, slow to speak, encouraging to others, faithful in our relationships, hardworking, honest, kind, humble, and compassionate toward the poor. Job exhorts us to trust in God's character even if we can't understand why tragedy has fallen on us. Ecclesiastes points to the futility of searching for meaning apart from a relationship with God. Finally, Song of Songs advises us to be madly in love and wildly passionate in our marriages.

Wrapping Up

The individual psalms fall into two primary categories: praise and lament. Both are part of walking in close communion with God. The Wisdom Books provide guidance for wise, godly, day-to-day living. Proverbs describes the norms of life while the other three books describe the exceptions: Job (why bad things happen to good people), Ecclesiastes (the limitations of rational thinking alone to give ultimate meaning to life), and Song of Songs (the irrationality of wild and crazy love in marriage).

> ### Memory Verse
>
> *Blessed is the one*
>   *who does not walk in step with the wicked*
> *or stand in the way that sinners take*
>   *or sit in the company of mockers,*
> *but whose delight is in the law of the LORD,*
>   *and who meditates on his law day and night.*
>
> *(Psalm 1:1–2)*

Digging Deeper

Books

Goldingay, John. *Psalms.* 3 vols. Baker Commentary on the Old Testament: Wisdom and Psalms (Tremper Longman, ed.). Grand Rapids: Baker, 2006–2008.

Kidner, Derek. *The Wisdom of Proverbs, Job and Ecclesiastes: An Introduction to Wisdom Literature.* Downers Grove, IL: InterVarsity Press, 1985.

Longman, Tremper III, and Peter Enns, eds. *Dictionary of the Old Testament: Wisdom, Poetry and Writings.* Downers Grove, IL: InterVarsity Press, 2008.

Waltke, Bruce K. *The Book of Proverbs.* 2 vols. The New International Commentary on the Old Testament. Grand Rapids: Eerdmans, 2004–2005.

Wilson, Gerald. *Psalms,* vol. 1. The NIV Application Commentary. Grand Rapids: Zondervan, 2002.

ASSIGNMENTS

1. Select two of your favorite psalms that are "praise psalms." Explain why you like the psalms and what they mean. Then select two psalms that are "Lament Psalms" (choose from Psalms 3–5, 7, 9–10, 13, 14, 17, 22, 25–28, 31, 35, 39–43, 52–57, 59, 61, 64, 69–71, 77, 86, 88–89, 109, 120, and 139–142). Explain what you think these two psalms mean and what it is about these psalms that you like.

2. From Proverbs 10–29 select three proverbs that you really like and explain what each of these three proverbs means.

3. Using a concordance, identify at least ten proverbs that describe the *fool.* Combine these proverbs and describe the characteristics of a fool.

4. Discuss the Teacher's search for meaning in Ecclesiastes 2.

CRUMBLING OF THE KINGDOM:
The Prophets and the End of Israel and Judah

Chapter 8

Enter Here

The Great Story is not a myth or fairy tale. It is a true Story about real life and real people. Some of them do not live happily ever after. Many times in life we stand at critical crossroads and make important choices that affect our lives forever. God offered the Israelites a wonderful deal. They could live in the Promised Land with God himself living in their midst, protecting them and blessing them bountifully. They could live the good life and have a close, meaningful relationship with him. This is the offer in Deuteronomy. Should they accept and live this good life? Duh. This looks like a no-brainer.

Yet unbelievably, Israel spits in the face of God and rejects his offer. Like an unfaithful spouse spurning a happy marriage and running recklessly into adulterous affairs, Israel rejects God and chases after the pagan gods of her neighbors. Not surprisingly, the "good life" and the blessings from God soon disappear. God repeatedly begs them to repent and come back, but they continually refuse. Eventually the end comes and a horrific nightmare descends on Israel.

The end of this chapter in the Story is tragic beyond comprehension. The Promised Land lies in ruins, ravaged by the brutal Babylonian army. The presence of God is gone, and the temple lies in ashes; indeed, all of Jerusalem has been destroyed. Thousands have been killed and the defeated, shattered remnants of the once-powerful kingdom of Israel trudge off sorrowfully into exile in a foreign land. The simple but stark historical account of the kingdom's demise is told in 1 Kings 12 through 2 Kings 25. A more detailed and complex account is provided by the Prophets, who show us the pain and agony that God goes through as Israel ignores him and experiences the consequential judgment.

Fortunately, however, there is a bright side to this chapter in the Story. The Prophets look beyond the destruction of Jerusalem and the exile and describe a wonderful time of future restoration when the Messiah will come to establish a righteous kingdom filled with true eternal blessings, in contrast to the current corrupt and crumbling kingdoms of Israel and Judah.

Be Prepared

Read or listen to 2 Kings 25; Isaiah 1–2; Jeremiah 3–4; Ezekiel 8–10; Isaiah 52:13–53:12; Jeremiah 31; Ezekiel 34.

The Story Continues

The haunting question is this: Will Israel follow God and obey Deuteronomy and thus live in the Promised Land with God's great presence and his blessing? This question continues to drive the Story. In 1–2 Samuel God established the monarchy in Israel, and he revealed that he could use the kingdom as a means for blessing Israel. Indeed, in the hands of King David, Israel flourished and experienced great blessings. David, however, stumbled (the Bathsheba affair), and the status of the kingdom blessings seemed to go "on hold."

When David's son Solomon became king, God offered him the incredible kingdom blessings, once again contingent on obedience to Deuteronomy. First Kings 1–11 recounts the wealth and blessings God bestowed on Solomon, demonstrating how wonderful things could be if the king and the people walked with God in obedience. Tragically, Solomon frittered it away, blatantly disobeying Deuteronomy, marrying foreign princesses, and worshiping their gods, even constructing worship sites for these gods in and around Jerusalem. Israel was sliding into idolatry and the blessings of Deuteronomy were slipping away. The situation is grim. Will Israel follow God and obey Deuteronomy? The answer is no.

1 Kings 12 through 2 Kings 25

Solomon had constructed numerous spectacular buildings and city fortifications. Yet to do this he had conscripted many Israelites into forced labor (like the Egyptians did!), in violation of Deuteronomy. When Solomon dies, his son Rehoboam, the new king, announces that he will continue, even increase, the forced labor of Israelites. So the people say, "Enough is enough," and a civil war breaks out. The kingdom now splits into two. The southern kingdom, comprised of two tribes, Judah and Benjamin, with its capital at Jerusalem, is called Judah. The northern kingdom, comprised of ten tribes with its capital at Samaria, is called Israel.

Jeroboam, the rebel leader who becomes the new king of the northern kingdom, decides that he does not want his people traveling to Jerusalem, the capital of their new enemy Judah, in order to worship. So he constructs two new worship sites for his people, one at Dan and one at Bethel. He then places a golden calf idol at each site and declares blasphemously, "Here are your gods, Israel, who brought you up out of Egypt" (1 Kings 12:28). Remember the golden calf episode back in Exodus 32? It is hard to imagine how this new king and his new kingdom could do anything more offensive and blasphemous to God than this!

Most of 1 Kings 12 through 2 Kings 25 describes the reigns of the many kings who rule over Judah and Israel, often giving assessments of their reigns. These kings can be summed up simply by the following:

- All of the kings of Israel are bad.
- Some of the kings of Judah are good, but most of them are bad.

The people of Israel, now split into two competing kingdoms, once again spiral downward theologically and morally. Deuteronomy is ignored and many of the kings and other leaders embrace idolatry. The splendor of Solomon's Empire is dismantled and his wealth is carried off bit by bit throughout 1–2 Kings. A few good kings in Judah (Asa, Hezekiah, Josiah) try to stop the slide, but the momentum is too great and their reforms are short-lived and swept away as soon as they die. Through his prophets, God begs his people to repent and return to him, but both Israel and Judah continually refuse to acknowledge God and to repent.

> **Bare-Bones Dates to Know**
>
> The northern kingdom (Israel) is destroyed by the Assyrians in 722 BC.
>
> The southern kingdom (Judah) is destroyed by the Babylonians in 587/586 BC.

Because of his great grace, God gives his people additional time, waiting on them to turn back to him. In this regard, 2 Kings 13:23 inserts an important theological comment into the Story, stating, "But the LORD was gracious to them and had compassion and showed concern for them because of his covenant with Abraham, Isaac and Jacob. To this day he has been unwilling to destroy them or banish them from his presence." So although Israel and Judah continually fail to obey the Law (the Mosaic covenant, particularly as defined in Deuteronomy), rather than judge them immediately as the Law warns, God graciously relies on his promise to Abraham and patiently endures their disobedience and waits for their repentance.

Unfortunately, that repentance never comes, and things continue to get worse. Eventually God's patience runs out, and the judgment described back in Deuteronomy 28 starts to pour out on Israel and Judah. The northern kingdom, Israel, with all bad kings and the two golden calves, falls first. In 722 BC the terrifying Assyrians invade and destroy Israel, scattering the inhabitants of the land into numerous other countries. The few good kings in the southern kingdom buy Judah some more time, but eventually the idolatry and injustices of the other leaders and the people overwhelm the feeble attempts by the few good kings to reform the nation. The last few kings of Judah are some of the worst, and Judah falls to the Babylonians in 587/586 BC. Jerusalem is destroyed and the people are carried off into exile in Babylon.

In the middle of 1–2 Kings, however, the normal sequence of describing the kings and their reigns is interrupted. The stories of Elijah and Elisha, two powerful and faithful prophets of God, are inserted into the midst of the royal accounts, providing special insight and comment on the unfolding events. While the overall story of 1–2 Kings focuses on the fate of the two nations Israel and Judah, the Elijah/Elisha stories focus on individuals. That is, even though the nations are plunging headlong toward destruction as a result of nationwide sin, individuals are being saved through faith. The Elijah/Elisha stories also demonstrate that neither the king nor the pagan gods like Baal, the primary Canaanite deity, have any power. Only the true God of Israel has power. Finally, these stories teach that even though the monarchy and the vast majority of the nation have abandoned God and embraced idolatry, there will always be a small remnant of faithful people.

The Prophets

The Prophets are God's spokespersons who deliver God's message to the Israelites. Although Moses is also referred to as a prophet, the group that we normally refer to as the Prophets (i.e., Isaiah, Jeremiah, Ezekiel, etc.) come to prominence during the monarchy (i.e., the time of the kings). Remember that God and Israel have entered into a covenant agreement (the Mosaic covenant), defined by the book of Deuteronomy. If Israel keeps the terms of Deuteronomy, they will live in the Promised Land with God in their midst and be richly blessed. If they refuse to follow Deuteronomy faithfully, instead turning to other gods, curses will fall on them and they will be expelled from the Promised Land. First and Second Kings tell the grim story of how Israel and Judah, usually led by corrupt, sinful, and self-serving kings, severely disobey God and abandon any attempt to obey Deuteronomy.

The Prophets come in this theological context. In essence it is helpful to view them as God's "prosecuting attorneys." With Deuteronomy (the Mosaic covenant) in their hand, they proclaim the outrageously sinful violations of the covenant committed by the king, the corrupt priesthood and false prophets he controls, the other leaders of the nation, and the common people. They likewise proclaim the earth-shattering consequences that will come if the king and the people do not repent and turn back to God.

The other important context for understanding the Prophets is the historical context. The historical setting for most of the Prophets, as mentioned above, is during the time of the monarchy. Dominating the history of this era, and extremely important for understanding the Prophets, are the two "superpower" empires that rise to prominence during this era, conquering much of the region. First, the Assyrians expand their empire across the ancient Near East, easily conquering the northern kingdom Israel and destroying its capital at Samaria in 722 BC. The Assyrians attack Jerusalem in 701 BC, but in response to the ministry of Isaiah and the faithfulness of the Judahite King Hezekiah, God delivers Jerusalem at this time and defeats the Assyrians (Isaiah 36–37; 2 Kings 18), although before long Judah submits to the nominal control of the Assyrians anyway.

The Assyrians are then defeated and displaced by the Babylonians, who conquer Judah and completely destroy Jerusalem in 587/586 BC, forcing the majority of the population into exile in Babylon. Thus the people of God lose

Organizing the Prophetic Books by Size

Traditionally the Prophetic Books are categorized by size. There are the four Major Prophets: Isaiah, Jeremiah, Ezekiel, and Daniel; and the twelve Minor Prophets: Hosea, Joel, Amos, Obadiah, Jonah, Micah, Nahum, Habakkuk, Zephaniah, Haggai, Zechariah, and Malachi. Keep in mind that the terms "major" and "minor" refer to size and not significance. Also, originally, the twelve Minor Prophets were placed on one long scroll and called "The Book of the Twelve."

Organizing the Prophetic Books by Content (Theology)

The destruction of Jerusalem by the Babylonians and the consequential exile was a watershed event, profoundly influencing the prophetic message. Thus in regard to content, it is helpful to group the Prophets according to where they stand in time in regard to the exile. The Prophets who lived and wrote before the exile and during the exile are called preexilic/exilic Prophets. A group of them have similar content, which we will call the standard prophetic message. Those preexilic/exilic Prophets reflecting the standard prophetic message are Isaiah, Jeremiah, Ezekiel, Hosea, Joel, Amos, Micah, Habakkuk, and Zephaniah. Nonstandard or unique preexilic/exilic Prophets include Daniel, Obadiah, Jonah, and Nahum. Then there are three Prophets who live and write after the exile is over: Haggai, Zechariah, and Malachi.

the Promised Land. Both Daniel and Ezekiel are part of the exiled population taken to Babylon. Most of the standard Prophets preach their message just prior to one of these two invasions. Thus when the Prophets warn the Israelites and Judahites to repent and to turn from their idolatry *or else judgment will come*, the judgment they are usually referring to is the coming invasion of either the Assyrians or the Babylonians.

The Standard Prophetic Message

While there is much diversity within the Prophets, their standard, basic message can be synthesized down to three basic points:

1. You (Israel and/or Judah) have broken the covenant (i.e., Deuteronomy). You must repent!
2. No repentance? Then judgment is coming!
3. Yet there is a glorious future time of restoration coming after the judgment through a righteous King, the Messiah.

You can open your Bible to almost any place in Isaiah, Jeremiah, Ezekiel, Hosea, Joel, Amos, Micah, Habakkuk, and Zephaniah and most probably the message will fall into one of these three major themes. This three-part message of the Prophets is critical to the Story and thus each point merits a discussion.

Point 1: You (Israel and/or Judah) have broken the covenant (i.e., Deuteronomy). You must repent!

The Prophets spend a great amount of time detailing the specific and consistent ways in which the king and the people have broken the covenant agreement, usually as defined in Deuteronomy. The Prophets will call these actions "sin," "rebellion," "hardness of heart," "iniquity," and "turning away from God," among other things, and they list these out as "indictments" or "charges." These indictments (i.e., charges of the sinful and rebellious actions against God) can be synthesized down into three basic categories, which the Prophets repeat over and over.

First and foremost is *idolatry*. All of the standard Prophets stress this. The northern kingdom, Israel, abandons God as soon as she splits away from Judah, establishing calf idols in Dan and Bethel. Other gods are soon added to their worship practices. In the southern kingdom, Judah, the king and the people think that they can lower the God of Abraham and make him to be just another god in their pantheon of numerous pagan gods. Thus they begin worshiping the pagan gods of their neighbors, such as the Canaanite gods Baal and Asherah, the Moabite god Chemosh, and the Ammonite god Molech, among others.

The second major covenant violation that the Prophets charge Israel and Judah with repeatedly is that of *social injustice*. The book of Deuteronomy called Israel and Judah to have a right relationship with God (i.e., the vertical dimension). But Deuteronomy also called on God's people to have a right relationship with each other (i.e., the horizontal dimension). God is concerned with justice among his people. Repeatedly in Deuteronomy there is a call for fairness and justice in the courts, in addition to special efforts to be made to care for people who do not have the socioeconomic status or resources to defend and/or care for themselves.

In the Old Testament context, as decreed in Deuteronomy and proclaimed over and over in the Prophets, the special people who need to be protected and cared for fall into the categories of the poor, widows, orphans, and foreigners. As the nations of Israel and Judah turn away from God, they become concerned only with themselves, and thus those in power begin oppressing those who are not, manipulating the already corrupt legal system so that the rich can become richer and the poor become poorer. The Prophets are scathing in their critique of this. They emphasize that social injustice is as equally sinful and rebellious as is the sin of idolatry!

The third major indictment the Prophets make against Israel and Judah is that of trusting *religious ritualism*. Drawing from the religious practice of the peoples around them, the Israelites and Judahites embrace the idea that God is not concerned with their actual behavior so long as they carry out the proper religious rituals (sacrifice, incense burning, fasting, celebrating festival days, etc.). Thus they believe that they can behave immorally toward each other, oppress the poor, worship Baal, and still be all right in the eyes of God so long as they still make some sacrifices and burn incense to him.

God, speaking emotionally and powerfully through the Prophets, rejects this idea. What God wants from his people is a close relationship. Religious rituals, if practiced properly (as described in Leviticus, Exodus, and Deuteronomy), served as the means to solidify and deepen the relationship. The Israelites, however, are attempting to replace the relationship with only the rituals. Furthermore, they think that the rituals will cover over all of their other blatant sinful violations of the covenant (like social injustice). The Prophets proclaim without any ambiguity that religious ritual without faithfulness to the covenant (worshiping God alone and practicing social justice) is worthless. In fact, God declares that he detests such practices.

So the three major indictments or sins that the Prophets underscore are idolatry, social injustice, and religious ritualism. The Prophets use poetic language and numerous analogies and figures of speech to communicate the seriousness of these sins. One of God's most favorite analogies in the prophetic books that he uses to illustrate his view of sin is that of an unfaithful spouse in a marriage. Repeatedly in the standard Prophets God will speak of himself as a faithful, loving husband and Israel/Judah as an unfaithful, adulterous wife. Sin, the Prophets declare, strikes at the heart of the relationship with God. It is a rejection of God and a refusal to be faithful. Such rejection hurts God just as an unfaithful spouse creates pain for her mate.

A critical aspect of point 1 is repentance. The Prophets will repeatedly call on the people to repent and turn back to God. They beg and plead and warn and threaten — all in an attempt to elicit some repentance. Even as the judgment hurtles down on Israel and Judah, the Prophets will cry out that it is not too late to be delivered, if only they would repent.

Point 2. No repentance? Then judgment is coming!

The tragedy of this chapter in the Great Story is that neither Israel nor Judah does repent. Even as the Prophets beg and plead for repentance, God informs them that the Israelites and Judahites will not repent. Thus the Prophets also proclaim and describe the terrible judgment that is coming. As noted above, most of the Prophets preach just prior to or during the Assyrian invasion or the Babylonian invasion. If you don't repent or since you haven't repented, the

The Christian and Justice

"Now we are in a position to see even more clearly what the Bible means when it speaks of *justice*. In general, to 'do justice' means to live in a way that generates a strong community where human beings can flourish. Specifically, however, to 'do justice' means to go to places where the fabric of shalom has broken down, where the weaker members of societies are falling through the fabric, and to repair it. This happens when we concentrate on and meet the needs of the poor. How can we do that? The only way to reweave and strengthen the fabric is by weaving your*self* into it."[1]

– TIMOTHY KELLER

---

1. Timothy Keller, *Generous Justice: How God's Grace Makes Us Just* (New York: Dutton, 2010), 177.

Prophets declare ominously, a terrible and horrendous invasion is coming. The Prophets are not squeamish about describing this judgment. Their images of judgment are graphic and disturbing. That is the point.

Several of the Prophets (Jeremiah and Ezekiel, for example) actually live through the destruction of Jerusalem. Thus within those books we find both predictions of the coming judgment and then descriptions of how their prophecies of judgment are fulfilled. Ezekiel 8–10 is particularly important. In this passage God takes Ezekiel to the temple in Jerusalem to see the extent of the idolatry the king and people of Judah are participating in—right in God's temple! This sin has become so great and abominable to God that he now *leaves the temple*. This is a huge event, for the presence of God dwelling in the midst of his people was at the heart of the relationship between God and Israel. The presence of God will not return to the temple until Jesus Christ walks in through the gates.

Point 3: Yet there is a glorious future time of restoration coming after the judgment through a righteous King, the Messiah.

The kingdom of Israel crumbles, underscoring the failure of the many human kings, priests, and other leaders, as well as the people in general, to

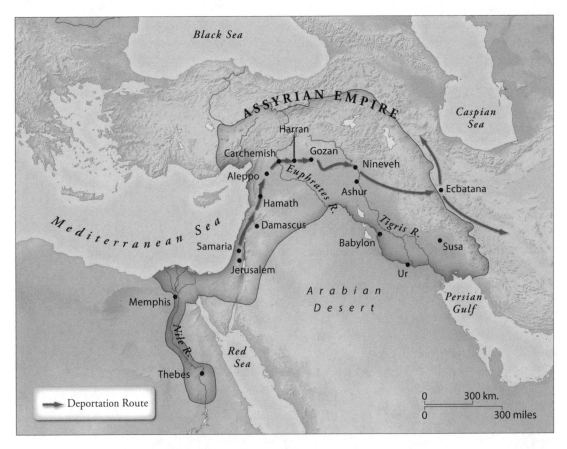

The Day of the Lord

The Prophets use the phrase "the day of the LORD" to describe the time when God will crash into human history, bringing judgment on those wicked ones who have defied him and bringing salvation and blessing to those who have trusted in him. Other related terms such as "that day" or just "the day" are also used. Blurred into this concept of the day of the Lord are the invasions by the Assyrians and Babylonians, as well as the events related to the first and second comings of Christ. The New Testament likewise uses numerous similar phrases and words such as "that day," "the day," and others to describe the future return of Christ, a time of terrible judgment on those who have rejected him and a time of great rejoicing, blessing, and ultimate justice for those who trust in him.

obey even the most basic components of Deuteronomy (the commandments). The Prophets describe the coming destruction in great detail; their texts on this subject are terrifying.

Yet sprinkled throughout the Prophets are passages of hope. In the midst of the doom and gloom of the coming judgment, the Prophets look beyond the failure of the present "human-led" kingdom and describe a glorious future kingdom ruled by a wonderful and righteous Messiah. This glorious King will restore Israel, but he will also gather the Gentiles (non-Israelites) to himself as well. Thus this glorious Messiah will not only answer the problem of Israel's failure to keep the Law (Joshua–2 Kings), but he will answer the worldwide problem of sin as described in Genesis 3–11.

The Nonstandard Prophets

The message of the nonstandard Prophets (Daniel, Obadiah, Jonah, Nahum, Haggai, Zechariah, Malachi) is not unrelated to the basic standard prophetic message, but the focuses and the contexts of these Prophets are different. Daniel illustrates how the Israelites can live faithfully before God even during the exile. Likewise, while the other Prophets focus on the kingdom within the context of Israel and Judah, Daniel broadens this view to present God's involvement in world empires, both present and future.

Obadiah and Nahum preach judgment against Edom and Nineveh, two of Israel's enemies, respectively. The prophet Jonah preaches directly to the Assyrians in Nineveh rather than to the Israelites and Judahites, as the other prophets do. The *message* of Jonah, however, is probably directed to Israel and Judah, for the Ninevites do precisely what the Israelites and Judahites don't do — repent and be saved. The repentant response of the Ninevites in Jonah underscores how ridiculous it is that God's own people turn a cold heart to him and refuse to listen to the Prophets and repent.

Special Contributions of Individual Prophets to the Theme of Hope and Restoration

Isaiah describes the future time of messianic blessing as a *new exodus*, with a greater and more spectacular intervention of God than even that seen in the old exodus from the time of Moses. Isaiah also describes the coming Messiah as a *suffering servant*, one of the great ironies fulfilled by Jesus.

Jeremiah proclaims that in the future God will establish a *new covenant* to replace the shattered, old Mosaic covenant. Jesus inaugurates this new covenant at the Last Supper. Jeremiah also tells the exiles that they will be in Babylon for *seventy years*.

Joel and *Ezekiel* add a radical and new dimension to the promises of the coming messianic kingdom. They proclaim that in the future God will indeed *place his Spirit within each person* who trusts in him. Thus, as God's presence in the temple is lost, an even greater presence of God is gained, a presence provided by the pouring out of his Spirit on his people.

Haggai, Zechariah, and Malachi are all postexilic Prophets, living and preaching in a much different context (after the judgment and during the return to the land). We will discuss them in Chapter 9—Captivity and Coming Home.

Making Connections

Let's review where we are in the Great Story:

Creation and Crisis
Covenant
Calling Out
Commandments
Conquest and Canaanization
Creation of the Kingdom
Communion and Common Sense
➤ **Crumbling of the Kingdom**
Captivity and Coming Home
Interlude: Time between the Testaments
Christ
Church
Consummation

The covenants play an important role in the Great Story, and they are particularly important to this stage of the Story. Israel and Judah refuse to obey the conditions stated in the Mosaic covenant, especially as defined by Deuteronomy. Thus they lose the great blessings of this covenant, such as the presence of God in their midst and the wonderful life in the Promised Land.

Yet even as the Prophets proclaim judgment based on violations of the Mosaic covenant, they also reach back to the unconditional promises that God made to David and Abraham, and thus they can proclaim hope for a future restoration. In the Prophets, judgment comes based on the terms of the Mosaic covenant (a two-sided covenant), but the wonderful messianic restoration will come based on the Davidic and Abrahamic covenants (one-sided covenants).

The New Testament is tightly connected to the Old Testament Prophets. The New Testament writers, especially the apostle Paul, will pick up this theme and explain it more clearly using the terms "law" and "grace." We are unable, Paul will explain, to keep the Law (i.e., the commandments) because of our sinful nature. The consequence of this failure is death. But praise be to God, Paul quickly adds, because we can be saved by grace, through faith. Like the Old Testament Prophets, Paul connects the Law to the Mosaic covenant and grace to the Abrahamic covenant (Rom. 2–4; Gal. 3).

Likewise, the Prophets proclaim that a righteous and just King from the line of David is coming to restore Israel, gather the Gentiles to himself, and make all things right. The New Testament clearly identifies this Savior and King as Jesus Christ.

Living the Story

In the name of "tolerance" many in the Western world today argue that there are many ways to God. They propose that all religions lead to the same God, and thus no one can say that only their religion is correct. The Bible, of course, categorically rejects this line of thinking, and the Prophets address it clearly. Can the true God be reached through other religions (i.e., through the worship of other gods like Chemosh and Baal)? The Prophets are not ambiguous on this issue. Their answer is, "No, no, no, no, no!" Likewise, then, can people today reach the true God through avenues other than through the Messiah, Jesus Christ? The Bible is clear and unambiguous, answering, "No, no, no, no, no!"

Another important application to grasp from the Prophets is in regard to our sin and the character of God. The Prophets teach us that God loves us dearly and wants a close, loving relationship with us. Indeed, the primary analogy God uses to explain this relationship to us is that of a marriage. Sin must be understood in this context. Sin is not like a speeding ticket. A speeding ticket is a violation of the law, and if one is caught, one pays a penalty. But no one is hurt, assuming you don't have an accident. Uncle Sam or the State Highway Department isn't offended or hurt by your speeding violation. Rather, God tells us that sin is more like adultery. It is a betrayal of a relationship. It brings pain. The ones you love the most dearly are the very ones who can hurt you the most deeply. The same is true for our relationship with God. Willful sin in our lives is a rejection of our relationship with him, and it brings pain to God.

Finally, the Prophets teach us about law and grace. We will never be able to be good enough and to keep the law well enough to find salvation through this route. Fortunately, and according to the great messianic promises of the Prophets, God has chosen to save people by his grace through their faith in his Messiah, Jesus Christ.

Wrapping Up

First and Second Kings tell the tragic Story of Israel's and Judah's rejection of God and their covenant with him (Deuteronomy). The kingdom splits into two: Israel in the north and Judah in the south. The northern kingdom of Israel has all bad kings. The southern kingdom of Judah has some good, but mostly bad kings. Israel falls to the Assyrians in 722 BC. Judah falls to the Babylonians in 587/586 BC.

Memory Verse

We all, like sheep, have gone astray,
each of us has turned to our own way;
and the LORD has laid on him
the iniquity of us all. (Isa. 53:6)

During this time, the Prophets proclaim three basic interrelated themes:

1. You (Israel and/or Judah) have broken the covenant (i.e., Deuteronomy). You must repent!
2. No repentance? Then judgment is coming!
3. Yet there is a glorious future time of restoration coming after the judgment through a righteous King, the Messiah.

Digging Deeper

Books

Bullock, C. Hassell. *An Introduction to the Old Testament Prophetic Books.* 2nd ed. Chicago: Moody Press, 2007.

Chisholm, Robert B. *Handbook on the Prophets.* Grand Rapids: Baker, 2002.

Hamilton, Victor P. *Handbook on the Historical Books.* Grand Rapids: Baker, 2001.

Hays, J. Daniel. *The Message of the Prophets: A Survey of the Prophetic and Apocalyptic Books of the Old Testament.* Grand Rapids: Zondervan, 2010.

McConville, J. Gordon. *Exploring the Old Testament: A Guide to the Prophets.* Downers Grove, IL: InterVarsity Press, 2002.

ASSIGNMENTS

1. Read Isaiah 52:13–53:12 and Mathew 26–28. Discuss the ways in which Isaiah's prophecy was fulfilled by Christ.

2. Compare and contrast the calls of Isaiah (Isa. 6), Jeremiah (Jer. 1), and Jonah (Jonah 1).

3. Explain the ways in which Jesus in John 10:1–21 is connecting back to Ezekiel 34.

4. Be able to stand up and recite the three points of the standard prophetic message, as well as the three indictments.

CAPTIVITY AND COMING HOME:
Surviving the Exile and Returning to the Land

Chapter 9

Enter Here

The survivors. We all like survivor stories. This chapter is about those who survived. Some of their descendants even made it back home.

The judgment came. The Babylonians burned Jerusalem and the temple to the ground and forced most of the dazed survivors to move to Babylon. The presence of God was lost. The Promised Land was lost. What would happen next? This part of the Story tells about life in the exile and the slow but steady return back to the land. This Story is told through the books of Daniel, Esther, Ezra, Nehemiah, Haggai, Zechariah, and Malachi.

Daniel provides a model for how one can live in the exile and yet serve God faithfully. Furthermore, right in the shadow of the gigantic Babylonian and Persian Empires, Daniel will put the concept of world empires into proper perspective, demonstrating that God has not lost control of history. Indeed, God's kingdom will not be destroyed and his dominion will never end. His kingdom is supreme.

The subtle story of Esther shows that God looks after his people in the exile, even if they aren't always following him faithfully.

Ezra and Nehemiah describe the return back to the Promised Land—the challenges, victories, and failures of reconstituting the people of God back in the land.

Finally, we will get the prophetic perspective with the postexilic prophets Haggai, Zechariah, and Malachi, who address the people back in the land. Some of the same old problems emerge.

Be Prepared

Read or listen to Daniel 1–3; Nehemiah 1:1–6:3; Haggai 1–2; Malachi 3–4.

The Story Continues

The Great Story, of course, is one that moves through time, so the historical context is constantly changing. In Chapter 8 we noted that the northern kingdom, Israel, was destroyed by the Assyrians, who dominated the region during the eighth century BC and into the seventh. Toward the end of the seventh century the Assyrians in turn were conquered and displaced by the Babylonians, who conquered and destroyed Jerusalem and the southern kingdom, Judah. At the beginning of the book of Daniel, the Babylonians are still in power, but during Daniel's life and ministry the Persians come to power. Throughout all of the other books we will be discussing in this chapter (Ezra, Nehemiah, Esther, Haggai, Zechariah, and Malachi), the Persians are the dominating and ruling empire of the region. This geopolitical fact will play a role in how we understand this portion of the Great Story, as you will see.

Daniel

In our Christian Bibles the book of Daniel is included with the Prophets, but although he does do a lot of prophesying, he and his message are different from the rest of the Prophets. Daniel was one of the first Judahites carried off into exile by the Babylonians. The first six chapters of this book tell the story of Daniel and his three friends, first in Babylon and then in Persia. Their valiant faithfulness to God even during severe persecution (thrown into a roaring fiery furnace; thrown into the lions' den) provides a powerful model for how the displaced Israelites are to continue to trust in God even during the difficult times of the exile.

As we saw in the stories of Elijah and Elisha (Chapter 8), even in a time of national apostasy and national judgment, individuals like Daniel could still serve God faithfully. The major theme of Daniel 1–6, however, stresses that even though the king of Babylon has destroyed Jerusalem, he is powerless before the God of Daniel. Likewise, even as the Persians take over, expanding their rule over a vast empire that includes the Jews from Judah, the stories in Daniel underscore that the God of Israel is actually the one in charge.

The second half of Daniel (chs. 7–12) is much different than the first half; it focuses on God's great plan for the future, especially in regard to the contrast between the powerful human empires of the world and God's great future empire. The book of Daniel teaches that even in difficult times when forces hostile to God appear to be dominating, God wants his people to live faithfully, trusting in him and in his promise that he alone controls world history and that he will certainly bring about his glorious future kingdom, all in due time.

As the Story moves into Ezra, Nehemiah, Haggai, Zechariah, and Malachi, we see portions of the exiled Israelite community moving back to Judah and struggling to reestablish their society and culture. What Daniel 7–12 clarifies for us is that this rag-tag bunch of Jews struggling to rebuild Jerusalem under Persian rule hardly fits Daniel's picture of God's great future empire, which will replace all of these flimsy human empires, such as the Babylonian and Persian Empires. Daniel—and the other Prophets, too, if we read them carefully—keeps us looking forward beyond the time of Ezra and Nehemiah for the coming kingdom of God.

Ezra-Nehemiah

Because of Judah's continued disobedience and refusal to repent, eventually the judgment stipulated in Deuteronomy 28 fell on her. In 587/586 BC the Babylonians invaded Judah, destroyed Jerusalem, and exiled most of the population to Babylonia. In 539 BC, however, the Persians overrun the Babylonians and inherit these exiles and the land of Judah. In 538 BC the Persian king Cyrus decrees that the Judahite exiles can return to their homeland if they want to. At last! A chance to return to the Promised Land and rebuild! The captivity is over and the time of coming home has arrived. The books of Ezra and Nehemiah describe how the exiles return to the Promised Land and struggle to rebuild Jerusalem, the temple, and their society.

The exiles return in three major waves. The first wave starts in 538 BC, immediately after the decree of Cyrus. Led by a man named Zerubbabel, this group returns to Jerusalem and begins a feeble attempt to rebuild the destroyed temple (see Ezra 1–6). Ezra, a priest, leads the second wave in 458 BC (Ezra 7–10), and Nehemiah, a governor, leads the third wave back to Jerusalem in 445 BC. Ezra focuses on rebuilding the temple and reconstituting the people of God (i.e., getting the system for properly worshiping God up and running). Nehemiah will focus first of all on rebuilding the walls and gates of Jerusalem. God empowers Nehemiah to rebuild them in a miraculously short period of time in spite of hostile opposition by several formidable regional powers.

In the later chapters of Nehemiah, he joins Ezra in trying to get the reconstituted society properly running, particularly in regard to obeying God (e.g., keeping the Sabbath day). While Nehemiah has spectacular success in rebuilding the walls and gates, he and Ezra have limited success in returning Israel to a proper worship of God. The destruction of Jerusalem and the exile have eliminated idolatry as a serious problem for the Jews. They will never fall into pagan idolatry again. The other problems such as social injustice and religious ritualism, however, continue to plague the returned exiles, and Ezra and Nehemiah struggle to get them to deal with these problems adequately. The book of Nehemiah does not end well, for the people are returning to their old ways of social injustice and religious formalism, and a frustrated Nehemiah seems unable to influence them to change. Rebuilding the proper religious and social character of the nation is much more difficult than rebuilding the city walls or the temple.

As the standard Prophets had predicted, the exile is over and Israel is

Ezra-Nehemiah as One Book

The books of Ezra and Nehemiah were probably originally written as one book. Later, probably because scribes were having difficulty fitting all of this material on one scroll, the book was split into two and placed (comfortably) on two scrolls. As mentioned in Chapter 7, the same thing happened with 1–2 Samuel, 1–2 Kings, and 1–2 Chronicles.

gathered back in the Promised Land. Jerusalem and the temple have been rebuilt, albeit on a modest scale. However, the Story in Ezra-Nehemiah demonstrates clearly that this is not the great spectacular restoration that the Prophets promised! A Davidic king does not sit on the throne; in fact, the Persians are still in control. Justice has not been established, and while idolatry has been eliminated, the other sins of social injustice and religious ritualism have crept back in. Finally, and importantly, there is no mention anywhere of God's presence returning to the temple.

In other words, things are hardly back to "the way we were." The old Deuteronomy-based status quo blessing of living in the Promised Land with God in their midst, blessing them richly and making them strong politically, is gone with the wind. We along with the ancient Israelites in the Story are left with the great prophetic promise that one day God will send a wonderful Deliverer who will change things forever.

Esther

The story of Esther is an entertaining "rags-to-riches" drama of a young Jewish girl who, through her stunning beauty and character, is selected to marry the powerful king of Persia. In her new role as queen she courageously intervenes in a plot to exterminate all of the Jews in the Persian Empire.

Reading this enchanting story is fairly easy, but interpreting it and fitting it into the Great Story are more complicated. There are several unusual features in Esther. First, no one in the book ever prays to God, asks him for direction, or gives thanks to him; in fact, God is not mentioned in the book anywhere. This is in strong contrast to Ezra and Nehemiah, and especially Daniel, who pray to God regularly and are quick to praise God for all he does. Second, the central players in the Great Story are those Jewish exiles who return to the Promised Land. The hope and the future lie with them. Esther does not return to the land; instead, she marries a pagan king. Esther represents those who stay in captivity.

So, what is the point of this book? Not everyone agrees, but we maintain that Esther is a story of God's great grace toward those Jews who do not obediently return to the land. While no one in Esther prays to God or worships him, he is still working behind the scenes and using people like Esther to protect his unsuspecting scattered people, so that eventually the great promise can be fulfilled in them.

Haggai, Zechariah, Malachi

Haggai, Zechariah, and Malachi are called postexilic Prophets because they live and preach after the exile. Haggai and Zechariah minister in Jerusalem around 520 BC, approximately eighteen years after the first wave of exiles return from Babylon to Jerusalem. Haggai focuses on rebuilding the temple. As the years pass and pressure mounts, the first wave of returned exiles has abandoned any idea of rebuilding the temple. They have, in essence, relegated the worship of God to the outer fringes of their concern. Haggai challenges them to move the worship of God to the center of their lives and to rebuild the temple. In contrast to the preexilic situation, the people in Jerusalem at this time listen to Haggai and obey him.

Zechariah is also concerned with rebuilding the temple and exhorting the people to live and to serve God properly while they wait for the coming kingdom. The major emphasis in Zechariah is, in fact, on the coming day of the

Elijah and John the Baptist

Elijah was a powerful prophet who lived during the time of the Israelite and Judahite kings. His story can be found in 1 Kings 17–19 and in 2 Kings 2. John the Baptist is a New Testament character who precedes Jesus and introduces the ministry of Jesus. What is the connection between these two? In Malachi 3:1 God declares that he will send a messenger to prepare the way before him. Then in Malachi 4:5 the messenger seems to be identified as Elijah. God states that he will send Elijah just prior to the great day of the Lord. At this point Malachi's prophecy is puzzling.

But as we turn the page from Malachi to Matthew and even into Mark and Luke, we discover that these gospel writers identify John the Baptist as the one who fulfills this prophecy (Matt. 11:10; Mark 1:2; Luke 7:27). That is, they declare that he is the one who comes to prepare the way before the coming of the Lord (Jesus). John the Baptist also appears in the opening chapter of the gospel of John (these are two different men named John). The crowd listening to John the Baptist sees the obvious connection between him and the prophecy in Malachi 4:5, so they ask him point-blank if he is Elijah (John 1:21). Surprisingly, he says no, choosing to identify himself instead with the prophecy of "the voice of one calling in the wilderness" (John 1:23; cf. Isa. 40:1). Jesus, however, seems to clearly identify John the Baptist as the fulfillment of the Malachi 4:5 prophecy. Well, is he or isn't he?

The solution lies in Luke 1:17. An angel of the Lord informs John's father, Zechariah, that his son will indeed "go on before the Lord, in the spirit and power of Elijah ... to make ready a people prepared for the Lord." John thus fulfills Malachi 4:5 in that he embodies the "spirit and power" of Elijah. So Christ can identify John as the essence of Elijah, fulfilling the Malachi prophecy, while John himself can say that he is not literally Elijah.

Lord and the establishment of God's spectacular kingdom. It is no surprise, then, that Zechariah has numerous messianic prophecies. Both Haggai and Zechariah mention the Persian rulers, a stark reminder that the glorious Davidic kingdom prophesied by the Prophets is still in the future. The return of the exiles to Jerusalem signals the beginning of that restoration, but the real fulfillment of that promise still awaits the coming King, the Messiah.

The book of Malachi does not contain any precise dates, unlike Haggai and Zechariah, but Malachi is probably a contemporary with Nehemiah (around 430 BC) and thus later than Haggai and Zechariah. The captivity is over and the Jews have returned home to Jerusalem. But the glorious kingdom is still in the future. Malachi focuses on how Israel will live and worship God in the meantime, while they await the coming day of the Lord and the establishment of his kingdom. Malachi addresses several problems relating to worship and living—unacceptable sacrifices, corrupt priests, refusal to support the temple, and social injustice. Several of these problems we saw emerging in Ezra-Nehemiah, and they will continue past the time of Malachi and will characterize much of Israel's worship system at the time of Jesus, 460 years later.

The book of Malachi is the last book in the Old Testament (in our Christian Bibles). It is significant to note that it ends with an exhortation to the people to obey God's commandments while they wait expectantly for the coming of the prophet "Elijah," who will signal the dawning of the great day of the Lord and the coming of the Messiah.

Making Connections

Let's review where we are in the Great Story:

Creation and Crisis
Covenant
Calling Out
Commandments
Conquest and Canaanization
Creation of the Kingdom
Communion and Common Sense
Crumbling of the Kingdom
➤ **Captivity and Coming Home**
Interlude: Time between the Testaments
Christ
Church
Consummation

Because Israel failed to keep the terms of Deuteronomy and failed to listen to the Prophets' call for repentance, the kingdom of Israel crumbled. The Babylonians destroyed Jerusalem and carried off most of the population into captivity. The Prophets, however, had preached more than just sin, repentance, and judgment. They promised that beyond the judgment and time of captivity, a great, glorious kingdom of God would be established. This wonderful kingdom would fulfill the Abrahamic and Davidic covenants, complete with a descendant of David on the throne. Israel would be regathered in the Promised Land and be joined by the nations of the world in worshiping God.

Daniel and Esther give us a contrasting picture of life in the captivity. Ezra, Nehemiah, Haggai, Zechariah, and Malachi tell the Story of the return of the exiles back to Jerusalem (coming home). But they are all crystal clear that this is not the great restoration that the Prophets foretold. Perhaps this is the beginning of that restoration, for Israel *is* back in the Promised Land. But things are different from the picture of restoration painted by the Prophets. Ezra, Nehemiah, Haggai, and Zechariah all stress the reality of Persian rule and dominance. There is no Davidic king on the throne in Israel. There is no Israelite king at all. Furthermore, the presence of God, which departed from the temple just prior to the Babylonian invasion (Ezek. 8–10), has not returned to the temple. This is important. The exiles have rebuilt Jerusalem and the temple, but, in stark contrast to earlier days, there is no mention of God coming to take up residence in that restored temple. To experience the wonderful blessing of God's presence living among his people, the Jews will have to wait for Jesus.

The Old Testament ends with the hopeful expectation of the coming Messiah, who will bring in the kingdom of God and restore all things. Thus there is but a slight break between the end of Malachi and the beginning of Matthew and the introduction of that Messiah. Indeed, more specifically Malachi 3:1 declares, "I will send my messenger, who will prepare the way before me." The New Testament identifies this messenger as John the Baptist, whose preparatory ministry introduces Jesus Christ (Matt. 11:10; Mark 1:2; Luke 7:27). After the captivity and the coming home, the next episode in the Great Story is the big event—the coming of Christ.

Living the Story

The stories of Daniel and his friends standing strong in their faithfulness to the Lord during trying times provide us with great encouragement likewise to stand strong in our faith, even if all of the world seems opposed to us. Moreover, just as God told the exiles through the prophet Daniel, so he tells us not to be too overawed by the powers that be in the world. They are temporary at best, and God still rules the earth. He will bring about the consummation of his kingdom in his own good time. In the meantime, we should live in trust and faithfulness to him, as Daniel and his friends did.

Nehemiah gives us numerous great lessons in leadership. He was a man of prayer and faith, but he was also a man who put his faith into action.

Sometimes we back away from serious challenges, claiming that the "door is closed." We then look around for something easier, with an "open door." Nehemiah teaches us that sometimes the true Christian leader is one who responds to the "closed door" by kicking it in—or looking for an open window. If God is with us, as he was with Nehemiah, and if we are in his will, we should not shirk away from difficult ministries or projects.

The people in this part of the Story were living between the beginning of the restoration and the fulfillment of the restoration. In a sense we are also in this situation. Jesus has begun the "already" part of the kingdom. It has started, and we are part of it. But we are still in the "not yet" period in the sense that the kingdom is not yet at the consummation stage. Thus we can learn from Daniel, Ezra, Nehemiah, Haggai, Zechariah, and Malachi to live by faith in the interim time, trusting in God, working to strengthen and build up his people, and looking forward with longing for the actual consummation of the kingdom when Christ will return and rule.

Wrapping Up

After a short time of exile in Babylon (the captivity), the Israelites are allowed to return back to Judah and Jerusalem (coming home). Daniel demonstrates how one can live in a tough environment in exile and still be faithful to God. His prophecies proclaim that God is still in control and one day will sweep away all of these feeble human empires and establish his great kingdom. In Esther we see that not all Jews returned back to the land (as they should have). Yet God still watches out for them, even though they are not always faithfully following him. Ezra and Nehemiah tell of the return to Judah and the rebuilding of Jerusalem. Ezra and Haggai focus on rebuilding the temple. Nehemiah focuses on rebuilding the walls and gates of Jerusalem. Zechariah and Malachi exhort the people to live faithfully for God even as they wait expectantly for the coming of the Messiah.

Memory Verse

"Multitudes who sleep in the dust of the earth will awake: some to everlasting life, others to shame and everlasting contempt." (Dan. 12:2)

The Israelites are back in the Promised Land. However, this is but the beginning of the great restoration and the great coming kingdom that the Prophets spoke so glowingly about.

A rebuilt temple is constructed, but it is nothing without God's presence. The Old Testament ends with hope and anticipation. Soon the King will come and bring the presence of God into the temple and dwell among God's people.

Digging Deeper

Books

Boda, Mark J. *Haggai, Zechariah.* The NIV Application Commentary. Grand Rapids: Zondervan, 2004.

Hays, J. Daniel, J. Scott Duvall, and C. Marvin Pate. *Dictionary of Biblical Prophecy and End Times.* Grand Rapids: Zondervan, 2007.

Kidner, Derek. *Ezra and Nehemiah.* Tyndale Old Testament Commentaries. Leicester, England, and Downers Grove, IL: InterVarsity Press, 1979.

Longman, Tremper III. *Daniel.* The NIV Application Commentary. Grand Rapids: Zondervan, 1999.

ASSIGNMENTS

1. Read Nehemiah 1–7. Discuss how Nehemiah balances faith with good planning and grim determination.

2. Read the book of Esther and our discussion of that book. Do you agree or disagree with us in our assessment of Esther? Explain why you agree or disagree.

3. Re-create a story similar to Daniel 3 (in the fiery furnace), but in a modern setting.

INTERLUDE:
Time between the Testaments

Chapter 10

Enter Here

No one in my family is very good at waiting. We are not known for our patience. I am particularly guilty of this, especially in regard to meals. If an elaborate meal is being prepared at our house, it is extremely difficult for me to wait until everything is completely cooked and prepared before I start sampling the cuisine. I can hear the noise of food preparation in the kitchen, especially if it is full of relatives all helping with the meal; I can see the various pots and pans of food on the stove; and I can smell the wonderful aroma that fills the entire house. My anticipation grows and waiting gets harder and harder.

But the meal is not quite ready yet, and I often receive reminders of that. "Don't lift that lid! You'll let the steam out of the rice." Or, "Put those rolls back in the oven! They are still doughy." Or perhaps, "Don't lick that spoon! That is for stirring, not tasting!" Finally, at just the right moment, everything comes together and a fantastic meal is spread out on the dining room table. Everyone sits down together, prays, and, at last, eats this wonderful meal.

The interlude in the Great Story, the four hundred-plus years between the last Old Testament prophetic word and the birth of Christ, is a time of waiting. God is at work in the world, and all of the Old Testament promises will come together in spectacular fulfillment ... at just the right time.

Be Prepared

Take a break. There is no additional reading assignment for this chapter.

The Story Continues

Israel survived the exile and a remnant returned to the Promised Land. As we saw in the previous chapter, as the Old Testament comes to an end, the Israelites are back in Judah (to be called Judea under the coming Roman rule in the New Testament) with Ezra, Nehemiah, and Malachi trying to rebuild the

Brief and Limited Independence

The Judeans (our modern English term is "Jews") are able to drive out their Seleucid rulers (dynastic successors to Alexander the Great in Syria) in 164 BC, and they enjoy a brief time of relative independence. However, crippled by weak leadership and embroiled in a squabble over which brother would be the next high priest and king, they are easily subdued by the Romans and brought into the Roman Empire.

shattered community. The year is about 430 BC. A small, modestly decorated temple has been rebuilt, but the presence of God has not yet returned. The city of Jerusalem has been reestablished and the worship of God has been reinstituted, but the stories in Ezra, Nehemiah, and Malachi let us know that things are not quite right. Idolatry has been eliminated in Israel, but several other problems can be seen bubbling up to the surface: hypocrisy in worship, corrupt priests, second-rate sacrifices, and social injustice. There is no Davidic king on the throne and the Persians rule over Judah. The kingdom promised by the Prophets has not yet come, but as Malachi closes out the Old Testament, he and the rest of the Prophets keep the Story pointed forward in anticipation and expectation of the coming Messiah. God's people are to trust in him, cling to his word and promises, watch, and wait. He is coming.

The time lapse between the final prophecy of Malachi and the birth of Jesus is about 430 years. Thus we have over four hundred years of silence in regard to biblical revelation. During this time, however, a lot of significant historical events take place that will shape the world into which Jesus Christ is born. The world in the time of Malachi is very different from the world that the apostle Paul later turns upside down with the gospel. God seems to be waiting for just the right time to send Jesus Christ into the world to bring the Great Story to its climax.

The Empires

The strong, imperialistic empires in the biblical world play a large role in the setting of the Great Story. Thus we have seen the Assyrians' rise to power in Mesopotamia be used by God in 722 BC to destroy disobedient and idolatrous Israel, the northern kingdom. Then the Babylonians defeated and displaced the Assyrians as the dominant Mesopotamian power. They are likewise used by God to destroy the southern kingdom, Judah, and her capital city, Jerusalem, because of her covenant disobedience and idolatrous rebellion (587/586 BC). The Persians are the next major power, displacing the Babylonians in 539 BC. The Persians are ruling over Judah as the Old Testament ends.

A huge change takes place in the late fourth century BC (starting around

334 BC). Alexander the Great unites Macedonia and Greece and then conquers the Persian Empire, including Asia Minor, Syria, Palestine, and Egypt. Alexander and his successors attempt to install Greek culture (often called Hellenism, from *hellenikos*, "Greek") in all of the cities throughout this entire region. This includes establishing the Greek language as the primary "trade language," as well as the "intellectual or literary language" of the entire region.

The Romans rise to power next and displace the Hellenistic successors of Alexander the Great as rulers of the region. In 63 BC the Romans conquer Jerusalem and in 37 BC they install a local supporter named Herod as king over Judea and some of the surrounding regions. Known as Herod the Great, he is king over Judea when Jesus is born. The Romans will be in power throughout the biblical world for the entire New Testament time era (i.e., first century AD).

Scattered Jews and Synagogues

Other important developments and transformations take place during this 430-year interlude. While some of the Israelites in exile do return to Judah, many of them remain scattered across the remains of the Babylonian and Persian Empires. Throughout this period they will continue to spread out across Asia Minor and much of the Mediterranean world.

Many, however, did return to Jerusalem and the surrounding areas. In the Roman era this region is called Judea, and the people are called Judeans (or Jews). The religion of these people, although based initially on the Old Testament, also undergoes some changes. The synagogue, an institution absent from the Old Testament, now emerges as one of the central features of their

Tabernacle, Temple, Synagogue, Church

As you read through and engage with the Story, it is important not to blur tabernacle, temple, synagogue, and church together into one. The tabernacle, remember, was a mobile tent that God dwelt in as he traveled with Israel from Egypt to the Promised Land. The tabernacle ceased to exist when Solomon replaced it with the temple, a permanent structure in Jerusalem. The temple of Solomon was destroyed by the Babylonians and rebuilt modestly by the exiles who returned. Herod the Great expanded the temple, building the spectacular structure that we see mentioned in the New Testament.

Synagogues are quite different. They are smaller local buildings, scattered all over Judea and other areas of the world wherever Jews live. Priests serve in the temple while rabbis serve in the synagogue.

The church, of course, is strictly a New Testament–era innovation. There are no churches (or synagogues, for that matter) in the Old Testament. But New Testament churches are clearly patterned on the Jewish synagogue, modified by Christian doctrine and practice. In the first century AD Christians probably met primarily in homes and less frequently in other existing buildings (including Jewish synagogues occasionally), but by the third century AD many Christian congregations were constructing their own buildings.

worship and plays a prominent role in their observance of the Sabbath, a situation different from that described in the Old Testament.

Likewise, the emergence of local rabbis teaching at these synagogues is a new phenomenon. Led by these rabbis, the worship began to focus on the Torah (i.e., the Old Testament Pentateuch) and Sabbath observance. The name given to this new system of religious practice and belief emerging out of the Old Testament is Judaism. The temple continues to play an important role in their religious life. However, during the Roman era, the high priesthood in Jerusalem becomes primarily a political position and the priesthood in general becomes corrupt.

Making Connections

Let's review where we are in the Great Story:

> Creation and Crisis
> Covenant
> Calling Out
> Commandments
> Conquest and Canaanization
> Creation of the Kingdom
> Communion and Common Sense
> Crumbling of the Kingdom
> Captivity and Coming Home
> ➤ **Interlude: Time between the Testaments**
> Christ
> Church
> Consummation

In the Great Story we are in the interlude portion. The exiled people of God are back in the Promised Land, but the great and wonderful messianic restoration that the Prophets promised has not come yet. The people are called to trust in God and wait for the Messiah.

Living the Story

This short part of the story doesn't have any specific biblical text for us to apply. However, it is easy for us to see God at work behind the scenes during this portion of the Story. The Bible is silent during this period, but God is not inactive. He is preparing the world for Jesus and waiting for just the right moment. We can learn much from this. Sometimes God calls on us to wait faithfully. This can be difficult, whether we are waiting for a meal to be prepared or waiting for God to move our Story forward. We always want things to go more quickly. But God is not in a rush, and in his great wisdom he waits for the perfect time to act.

Wrapping Up

When Jesus is crucified, Pontius Pilate, the Roman governor of Judea, places a sign on the cross that reads, "Jesus of Nazareth, King of the Jews" (John 19:19–20). This sign is written in three languages: Aramaic, the current spoken language of the Jews; Greek, the language that Alexander the Great and his successors imbedded across the entire region, and Latin, the official language of the Romans, who currently rule the region. Thus in this ironic sign we see the three major aspects of the interlude period brought together.

As the New Testament era dawns, we see that God's timing is perfect and that the time is now right. Paul, a Jew born in Asia Minor, can speak fluently in both Greek, the language of most of the cities in the Mediterranean world, and Aramaic, the spoken language of the Jews. Paul is also born as a Roman citizen. The Romans had established a relative political stability in the world and had constructed an extensive system of outstanding roads. Roman citizenship gave one certain rights and privileges, along with a certain amount of legal protection.

At this unique time Christianity sweeps into the world. Paul and the other early missionaries are able to travel throughout much of the Roman Empire. Speaking Greek, Paul can be understood by most people in all of the cities he visits. Speaking Aramaic and trained as a Jewish scholar, Paul is also able to enter local synagogues and proclaim Jesus Christ there, which often provides him with a starting point and a foothold in each new city. Carrying Roman citizenship, Paul receives a certain amount of imperial protection, and small provincial city rulers do not have the authority to obstruct him or imprison him without just cause.

So in the fullness of time, Jesus is born.

Digging Deeper

Books

Ferguson, Everett. *Backgrounds of Early Christianity.* 3rd ed. Grand Rapids: Eerdmans, 2003.

Jeffers, James S. *The Greco-Roman World of the New Testament: Exploring the Background of Early Christianity.* Downers Grove, IL: InterVarsity Press, 1999.

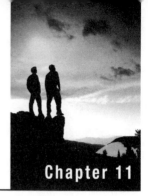
CHRIST:
Jesus Enters Our World

The Word became flesh and made his dwelling among us.
— JOHN 1:14

Enter Here

You've probably heard of John the Baptist, the prophetic figure who prepares the way for Jesus. But have you heard of his dad, Zechariah? John's dad was a priest (Luke 1:5 – 25). On a special occasion, he was chosen to enter the Holy Place in the temple and burn incense — quite an honor. In the Holy Place, an angel appears to Zechariah with the good news that he and his wife, Elizabeth, will have a son, who will prepare the way for the Messiah. But Zechariah doubts the angel and, as a result, is not allowed to speak for months until the baby is born.

When the baby finally arrives and the time comes to name the child, everyone expects him to be named Zechariah after his father. But Zechariah writes on a tablet, "His name is John" (Luke 1:63). Zechariah's doubts have been transformed into trust, and immediately he is allowed to speak again. His first words are words of praise to God for speaking to his people through his son, John, and through the Messiah, who, as we know, is Jesus (Luke 1:64 – 79).

It has been about four hundred years in the Great Story since we've heard God speak. He has been relatively silent since the time he spoke through the prophet Malachi. But that is about to change. God is getting ready to speak, perhaps even "shout" to his people. The writer of the New Testament letter to the Hebrews sums it up well:

> In the past God spoke to our ancestors through the prophets at many times and in various ways, but in these last days he has spoken to us by his Son, whom he appointed heir of all things, and through whom also he made the universe. (Heb. 1:1 – 2)

We come now to the "Jesus chapter" of the Great Story. It's not the final chapter, but it's the most important one in the sense that Jesus stands as the climactic center of God's plan to rescue humanity and restore his creation.

Be Prepared

Read or listen to Matthew 1–4; 11; Mark 1–3; Luke 1–2; 8; John 1–4.

The Story Continues

The Christmas Story

When you think of Christmas, you might think of movies such as *White Christmas* or *Miracle on 34th Street* or *It's a Wonderful Life* or *Home Alone* or *Elf* or *A Christmas Story* with its famous line: "Be careful or you'll shoot your eye out." You may envision time with your family opening presents or eating a big meal or decorating the tree. There is probably a nativity scene somewhere in the house portraying the first Christmas with unrealistic serenity. You can be sure that amid all the commercialism, Christmas carols, family traditions, and football, most of us have drifted a long way from understanding what the first Christmas was really like.[1]

The real Christmas story begins when God breaks centuries of silence and speaks through his angel Gabriel to two families, giving them the good news that they would each soon have a son. First, Zechariah and his wife, Elizabeth, are promised John, more famously known as John the Baptist (Luke 1:5–25, 57–80). John is often compared to the prophet Elijah because he had the arduous task of preparing the hearts of the people to receive their Savior. Persuading people to repent or change directions spiritually is perhaps the most difficult kind of ministry.

Second, Mary and Joseph are promised Jesus (Luke 1:26–56). When you

---

1. For a realistic look at what the Bible actually says about Christmas, we strongly encourage you to read Verlyn Verbrugge's little book, *A Not-So-Silent Night: The Unheard Story of Christmas and Why It Matters* (Grand Rapids: Kregel, 2009). Verlyn uncovers the dark side of Christmas — the pain, humiliation, fear, and danger — and gives us a realistic view of how God the Son actually entered this world and how it affected all the people involved.

Genealogies

Both Matthew and Luke include genealogies of Jesus (Matt. 1:1–17; Luke 3:23–38). Genealogies (or ancestries) were important in the ancient world to show a person's social standing and status and to establish a ruler's legitimacy. Matthew shows that Jesus was the legal descendant of Joseph and therefore a descendant of King David (Israel's greatest king) and Abraham (the father of the Jewish nation). This genealogy confirms that Jesus was the Jewish Messiah. But Matthew's inclusion of five women, all of whom were Gentiles except Mary, shows that Jesus is also the Savior for all people.

Taking a different angle, Luke traces Jesus' genealogy all the way back to Adam, emphasizing that Jesus is the Savior for all humanity.

Virginal Conception

The Bible makes it clear that Mary conceived by the supernatural influence of the Holy Spirit without any form of human sexual intercourse (see Matt. 1:18, 20, 25; Luke 1:35; 3:23; Mark 6:3; John 8:41). This miracle is best described as the "virginal conception" rather than the "virgin birth," since there was nothing unusual about the physical birth of Jesus.

The virginal conception reminds us that salvation is not a human achievement but a gift from God. Human beings can't even produce a Savior without God's help. It also reminds us that God shows his power and grace through human weakness. Most importantly, the virginal conception tells us that Jesus is both human and divine. Jesus is 100 percent God and 100 percent man. His being is the same as God's being, but he is distinct from the Father. Being God, Jesus is able to save us from our sins. Being man, Jesus is able to understand and relate to us.

read about Gabriel appearing to Mary, you must remember that she is a young teenager living in a small town far removed from the center of religious life in Jerusalem. She's also an unmarried virgin. Then one day out of the blue she gets a visit from an angel who tells her that she's going to have a baby. No wonder Mary is "greatly troubled" by the angel's message (1:29).

Mary learns that her son will be no ordinary child. She is instructed to name him Jesus, a Greek translation of the Hebrew name Joshua, meaning "Yahweh saves." His name reflects his mission to rescue people from Satan and sin. Jesus, she is told, will be "great" and will be called "the Son of the Most High God," indicating that he is God's chosen Messiah. Mary also discovers that Jesus will receive the throne of King David and will rule over a never-ending kingdom. Mary tries to absorb the shock that her baby will be Savior, Son, and King.

Joy and Pain

"Often a work of God comes with two edges, great joy and great pain, and in that matter-of-fact response Mary embraced both. She was the first person to accept Jesus on his own terms, regardless of personal cost."[2]

– PHILIP YANCEY

This is no ordinary day in Nazareth, and Mary has a lot to think about. God delights in using the weak and lowly to carry out his mighty, powerful will. He exalts the humble and takes down the proud and haughty. Mary's response to this startling news was nothing short of amazing: "I am the Lord's servant," she tells the angel. "May your word to me be fulfilled" (Luke 1:38). What humility and faith and courage!

The situation is this: Mary and Joseph are betrothed, meaning that they have entered a legally binding arrangement that normally lasts about a year and can be broken only by divorce or death. The time of betrothal would be

2. Philip Yancey, *The Jesus I Never Knew* (Grand Rapids: Zondervan, 2002), 32.

Honor and Shame

In the first-century world of Palestine, honor and shame were extremely important community values. Honor was all about respect and peer approval and was based on family, education, wealth, social relationships, achievements, and the like. Shame, by contrast, was the removal of such respect and the disapproval of peers due to some action looked down upon in the society. People were motivated to attain (or retain) honor and to avoid shame. Western culture today seems more motivated by individual and economic concerns than by community values, but in the ancient world honor and shame were primary concerns. Now you can see why Joseph and Mary faced a huge social dilemma, since pregnancy prior to marriage was indeed a shameful situation.

followed by the formal wedding ceremony. Can you imagine how Joseph feels when Mary tells him (prior to the formal wedding and any sexual relations) that she is pregnant and that God is responsible? Now he faces a dilemma made even more urgent by the honor and shame culture in which he lives—how to balance his love for Mary with the necessity of upholding his honor and reputation as a righteous man.[3] Out of compassion, Joseph decides on a quiet (rather than a public) divorce. But God intervenes through a dream, something he does repeatedly with Joseph, and tells him to accept Mary as his wife after all (see Matt. 1:18–25; 2:12–13, 19, 22). Like Mary, Joseph is also told to name his son Jesus.

Because Joseph belongs to the house and royal line of King David, he must travel to Bethlehem, the town of David, to register for the census. (The Old Testament prophet Micah had predicted that Jesus would be born in Bethlehem—see Micah 5:2.) Incidentally, it wasn't necessary for Mary to go along with Joseph to register, but it's likely that she had been kicked out of her house for bringing shame to her family. Can you imagine making a hundred-mile trip during the final stages of pregnancy? But Mary simply had no place else to go.

They arrive in Bethlehem but find no room in the "inn"—not a hotel but a guest room in a regular house (see Luke 22:11; Luke uses a different word for "hotel" in 10:34). It's possible that some of Joseph's relatives occupied the guest room and would not allow the disreputable couple to stay with them. As a result, Mary gives birth to Jesus in the only place left: down below where the animals stayed. She lays her newborn son in a "manger" or animal feeding trough. Could God the Son have entered this world in a humbler way?

Although he is rejected by some, two unlikely groups do recognize and worship the newborn King. The Lord appears first to ordinary shepherds with the announcement, "Do not be afraid. I bring you good news that will cause

---

3. For more on the honor and shame culture, see John Dickson, *Humilitas: A Lost Key to Life, Love, and Leadership* (Grand Rapids: Zondervan, 2011), especially ch. 5, "*Philotimia*: Why the Ancient World Didn't Like Humility."

great joy for all the people. Today in the town of David a Savior has been born to you; he is the Messiah, the Lord" (Luke 2:10–11). Since God could have chosen any group of people to which to announce the birth of his Son (such as the Jewish high priest or the Roman emperor), why did he choose lowly and despised shepherds? It appears that God himself is humble. This goes along with the "sign" the shepherds are given when searching for Jesus—you will find him lying in a feeding trough, a sure sign of humility (Luke 2:12).

The second group enters the story later. Although our traditional nativity scenes include the three kings, Scripture makes it clear that they arrive months later when the family is actually living in a house (Matt. 2:11). And the Bible doesn't actually mention three men (only three gifts) and doesn't say they were kings (only magi). The real irony, however, is that even pagan astrologers come to worship King Jesus. In addition to the shepherds and the magi, all of heaven erupts in celebration at the birth of Christ (Luke 2:13–14). God is stepping into history to seek and save the lost, and heaven simply can't keep quiet!

Jesus' Childhood

Jesus will grow up in a law-abiding Jewish family. They have him circumcised when he is eight days old and later take him to the temple in Jerusalem (just a short distance from Bethlehem) to "present him to the Lord" (Luke 2:22; see Lev. 12:1–8). The fact that the family offers two birds as a sacrifice rather than a lamb probably indicates that Jesus will grow up in a relatively poor family.

During their visit to the temple, they encounter two older saints, Simeon and Anna, who speak about Jesus' identity and mission. Simeon praises God: "My eyes have seen your salvation, which you have prepared in the sight of all nations: a light for revelation to the Gentiles, and the glory of your people Israel" (Luke 2:30–32). Anna speaks of Jesus as the "redemption of Jerusalem" (2:38). Both clarify that Jesus has come to offer salvation to all people, Jews as well as Gentiles.

Jesus is worshiped by angels, shepherds, older saints in Jerusalem, and magi, but he is not worshiped by everyone. Soon after the magi leave, God warns Joseph in a dream to take Mary and Jesus to Egypt to escape the evil intentions of King Herod. This journey fulfills Scripture as Jesus' experience matches the experience of the people of Israel, whom God also called out of Egypt (Matt. 2:13–15; cf. Hos. 11:1). The magi outsmart Herod, driving him mad

No Room in the Inn

"There was pain in Bethlehem on Christmas night. There was rejection in Bethlehem. We today stand by the manger and marvel and rejoice at the Child born to Mary in a barn. 'Joy to the world, the Lord is come,' we sing. But on that first Christmas night there were no doubt tears in the eyes of Joseph and Mary. Nobody in their family circle would help them. Nobody cared. The only ones who did come to the manger to witness the child were the lowly night-watch shepherds, directed there by God himself, while the prim and proper—yes, and self-righteous—relatives were right upstairs, missing the most awesome birth in the history of the human race. How incredibly sad!"[4]

– VERLYN VERBRUGGE

---

4. Verbrugge, *A Not-So-Silent Night*, 57.

with rage and resulting in the murder of all the little boys two years old or younger in the vicinity of Bethlehem. After Herod's death in 4 BC, God instructs Joseph through a series of dreams to return to Judea, more specifically, to Galilee (Matt. 2:19–23). As a result, Jesus grows up in Nazareth, a tiny, remote village where we are told he "grew and became strong," being filled with God's wisdom and grace (Luke 2:40).

Jesus' parents raised him as a pious Jewish boy. He had been circumcised and dedicated to the Lord as the firstborn. He would have been educated in the local synagogue where he surely learned the Scriptures in Hebrew. (Jesus was probably trilingual: speaking Aramaic at home, Hebrew in religious situations, and Greek in business and political settings.) Jesus probably grew up in a working poor family. Both Joseph and Jesus were carpenters — craftsmen who worked with wood, stone, or metal — so they were used to hard physical labor. Jesus had half brothers and sisters born to Mary and Joseph after Jesus was born (see Matt. 1:24–25; 12:46–47; 13:55–56; Mark 3:31–35; 6:3; John 2:12; 7:3–5, 10; Acts 1:14; 1 Cor. 9:5).

The only picture we have of Jesus between his infancy and adult life is recorded in Luke 2:40–52. At age twelve Jesus goes up to Jerusalem with his family for the Passover Feast. When the family leaves to return home, Jesus stays behind in Jerusalem talking with (and impressing) the Jewish religious experts. When his frustrated parents come back and finally find him, Jesus responds, "Didn't you know I had to be in my Father's house?" (Luke 2:49). Here we get a glimpse of his unique relationship to the Father and his God-given mission.

The "silence" of the Bible about Jesus' childhood probably speaks volumes about the essentially normal life Jesus had as a boy and young man. We can be confident that Jesus — being fully human — experienced many of the same things we experience: dangers, sorrows, joys, trials, disappointments, rejection; and as the writer to the Hebrews says, he is "able to sympathize with our weaknesses" (Heb. 4:14–16). We are told in Luke 2:52 that Jesus returned to his small hometown, Nazareth, where he lived obediently, growing in wisdom and stature and in favor with God and people (Luke 2:52).

John the Baptizer

God gave John the Baptist the task of preparing the people for Jesus. But John was not a Baptist ... or a Methodist or Presbyterian or the founder (or even member) of any denomination. He was John the "Baptizer" (i.e., one who immerses people in water). He was a strange man with an extremely difficult ministry.

Why does the Bible make such a big deal about John and his message? As we said earlier, it's been hundreds of years since God sent a prophet to speak to his people. When John appears, looking a lot like the Old Testament prophet Elijah, the people get excited about hearing a fresh word from God (2 Kings

1:8; cf. Matt. 17:10–13; Mark 9:11–13). Is God about to keep his promises and send the Messiah? The prophets had predicted that someone would come to prepare the way for the Lord (Isa. 40:1–11; Mal. 3:1–2; 4:5–6). John is the man!

John seeks to prepare people for the Messiah by preaching a sermon with two points (see Matt. 3:1–12; Mark 1:1–8). First, they need to repent or turn away from their sins. John is not just challenging individual Israelites; he's calling for a change of heart among all of God's people. John warns them to be genuine in turning back to God, a genuineness marked by how they live, not just how they talk (see Luke 3:7–14). As people come to John and confess their sins, he baptizes them in the Jordan River, a river carrying deep symbolic significance for Israel. God's people had once crossed that same river to enter the Promised Land. Now John baptizes in the Jordan to signal that God is doing a new, mighty work. (John's baptism was a baptism of repentance to prepare people for the Messiah and does not carry the added significance of Christian baptism today.)

> ### An Old-School Prophet
>
> "Holding no job and having no official position, John dressed in caveman clothing and lived off the land [eating bugs and honey]. He chose to preach not in the cities, where he could have found a ready audience, but in the wilderness. Such a person preaching along a rural highway today would cause people to speed up and lock the car doors, not rush out to hear him. We design homeless shelters for people like John."[5]
>
> **– TIM STAFFORD**

The second thing John proclaims is that a more powerful person is coming. John denies that he himself is the Messiah but instead portrays himself as the best man at a wedding. His role is to honor Jesus as the bridegroom. John says with reference to Jesus: "He must become greater; I must become less" (John 3:30). Whereas John baptizes with water, Jesus, the more powerful one, will baptize people with the Holy Spirit and fire, a symbol of judgment (Matt. 3:11–12).

John has what we might call a "fading ministry." His job is to prepare the people for Christ and then fade into the background as Jesus takes center stage. John does his job well. His wholehearted devotion to God lands him in prison, where he stays for a long time before being beheaded by Herod Antipas (see Mark 6:14–29). John is like a bridge between the Law and the Prophets on the one hand and the good news of the kingdom of God proclaimed by Jesus on the other hand (Luke 16:16).

Jesus' Baptism

As people confess their sins and experience John's baptism of repentance, they prepare themselves for the coming Messiah. How would the Greater One arrive? What would the Mighty Deliverer do first? There is a dramatic pause in the Story as we anticipate Jesus' grand entrance. Then one day as John sees Jesus approaching, he says to those around him, "Look, the Lamb

---

5. Tim Stafford, *Surprised by Jesus: His Agenda for Changing Everything in A.D. 30 and Today* (Downers Grove, IL: InterVarsity Press, 2006), 18.

of God, who takes away the sin of the world" (John 1:29, 36). What happens next shocks everyone.

Jesus comes up to John and insists on being baptized. John objects at first but reluctantly agrees. Although Jesus is sinless and doesn't need to repent, Jesus is baptized in order "to fulfill all righteousness" (Matt. 3:15). What a weird statement. This phrase could mean many things, but most agree that it shows Jesus identifying with sinful humanity, especially with the nation of Israel, which does need to repent. Tim Stafford explains the importance of Jesus' repenting of Israel's sins:

> Jesus very deliberately started a movement. He did not start it from scratch, however. Jesus adopted and embraced a very ancient movement— that of historic Judaism. He would shape and reshape it for the purposes of God, just as Moses and Samuel and David had done before him. That's what great leaders do. He began, however, with a full embrace of his people just as they were, sins and all. Jesus did not cause Israel's problems, but he took on her tragedy. He entered into Israel's experience, carrying her load. He would end his life in the same way: bearing the sins of Israel.[6]

As Jesus comes up out of the water, two important things happen: the heavens are ripped open, and the Holy Spirit comes on Jesus to anoint and empower him for public ministry. Although Jesus will baptize people with God's Spirit, he himself needs to walk in the power of the Spirit during his time on earth.

Next, the Father speaks from heaven, proclaiming, "This is my Son, whom I love; with him I am well pleased" (Matt. 3:16–17). The Father combines three Old Testament texts to announce the kind of Messiah Jesus came to be. He will be a King in the line of King David ("this is my Son," from Ps. 2:7), a willing sacrifice ("whom I love," from Gen. 22:2), and a servant ("with him I am well pleased," from Isa. 42:1). In other words, Jesus will be a Suffering-Servant King. His crown will be tied to a cross, where he will serve people by offering the ultimate sacrifice of his life for their sins. Interestingly, Jesus' baptism also symbolizes the coming death, burial, and resurrection—his ultimate baptism (Luke 12:49–50).

Jesus' Temptations

As the newly crowned King, we might expect Jesus to head straight for the temple to begin his reign. Most Jews in the first century longed for God to step into history and establish an earthly kingdom. They desperately wanted the Messiah (or "Deliverer") to defeat their enemies, the Romans. But rather than going straight to Jerusalem to set up his kingdom, Jesus is "led by the Spirit into the wilderness to be tempted by the devil" (Matt. 4:1). Jesus will

---

6. Ibid., 29.

go to Jerusalem at the appropriate time, but first he must pass through the fire of testing in the wilderness, a testing that Israel had previously failed (see, e.g., Ex. 15–19). As Messiah, Jesus came to deliver people from enemies far more dangerous and powerful than the Romans. In the wilderness, Jesus faces temptations as old as the garden of Eden (cf. Gen. 3:1–7 with Matt. 4:1–11). He follows the lead of the Spirit and enters the desert for an epic battle with the devil to determine the fate of the world.

Temptation is not sin but rather an invitation to sin. Jesus is tempted, but we know that he never sinned (Heb. 4:15). After fasting for forty days — parallel to Israel's forty years in the wilderness — the tempter attacks Jesus spiritually. He begins by saying, "If [better: 'since'] you are the Son of God," indicating that Satan is tempting Jesus to use his divine power in selfish ways. Specifically, Jesus is tempted in three ways:

- Matt. 4:3–4: to do the right thing at the wrong time
- Matt. 4:5–7: to test God rather than trust God
- Matt. 4:8–10: to make his work for God more important than his relationship with God

In every instance, Jesus is tempted to take a shortcut to accomplishing his life mission. But every shortcut contains a deadly compromise that would eventually destroy his devotion to the Father. The Father already told him at his baptism that he would be a Suffering-Servant King. Now Jesus must resist the temptation to become King in an easier way, a way that avoids the cross. Satan's strategies haven't changed, so don't be surprised when you are tempted to pursue a God-given mission at the wrong time or in the wrong way.

Jesus answers every temptation with truth from Scripture, introduced by the phrase "it is written" (Matt. 4:4, 7, 10). He quotes from Deuteronomy 6–8, in which Moses challenged the people of Israel to obey God as they prepared to cross the Jordan River and enter the Promised Land. After his baptism in that same river and prior to entering his public ministry, Jesus too faces a test in the wilderness. Will he prove faithful and obedient where Israel has failed? When put to the test, Jesus quotes God's Word in context and wins the battle over evil. After an intense spiritual battle, the devil leaves him and angels come to minister to him (Matt. 4:11). Jesus wins the opening battle in the cosmic war with evil. The next move for Jesus is to announce the arrival of God's kingdom.

Are We Trying to Use God?

"Once you have made the world an end and faith a means, you have almost won your man, and it makes very little difference what kind of worldly end he is pursuing.... We do want, and want very much, to make men treat Christianity as a means; preferably, of course, as a means to their own advancement, but, failing that, as a means to anything."[7]

– SCREWTAPE, IN C. S. LEWIS'S
SCREWTAPE LETTERS

---

7. C. S. Lewis, *The Screwtape Letters* (New York: HarperCollins, 2001; orig. 1942), 34, 126.

Making Connections

Let's review where we are in the Great Story:

> Creation and Crisis
> Covenant
> Calling Out
> Commandments
> Conquest and Canaanization
> Creation of the Kingdom
> Communion and Common Sense
> Crumbling of the Kingdom
> Captivity and Coming Home
> Interlude: Time between the Testaments

➤ **Christ:**

> **Jesus Enters Our World**
> Jesus' Message
> Jesus' Journey to Jerusalem
> Jesus Dies on the Cross
> Jesus Is Raised from the Dead

> Church
> Consummation

We see strong connections to other parts of the Story by looking first at how the coming of Jesus fulfills God's covenant promises. There are four major covenants mentioned in the Old Testament: the Abrahamic covenant (Gen. 12–17), the Mosaic covenant (Exodus–Deuteronomy), the Davidic covenant (2 Sam. 7), and the new covenant (Jer. 31).

We are probably most familiar with the Mosaic covenant. After God delivered his people from slavery in Egypt, he sustained them during their time in the wilderness, entered into a covenant with them, and gave them the Promised Land. Part of the Mosaic covenant spelled out how God wanted his people to live in the land in order to receive his abundant blessings. Would Israel live in obedience to God? Sadly, the answer is no. They repeatedly chose to rebel against God. The Prophets are like God's prosecuting attorneys, who charge the people with breaking the Mosaic covenant through idolatry, social injustice, and religious ritualism. As a result, Israel experienced God's terrible judgment. The glory left the temple, Jerusalem was destroyed, and Israel was taken captive by her enemies. But the Prophets' message includes a measure of hope. They also spoke about a time of restoration that would follow the time of judgment.

While judgment is a reality because the people have broken the Mosaic covenant, a future restoration is coming because of God's covenants with Abraham and David. The Abrahamic covenant was actually established hundreds of years *before* the Mosaic covenant. God made promises to Abraham and entered into a covenant relationship with him (Gen. 12; 15). We read in

Genesis 15:6 that "Abram believed the LORD, and he credited it to him as righteousness" (cf. Rom. 4:3, 20–24; Gal. 3:6; Jas. 2:23). In Genesis 17, God alone bound himself to fulfill this covenant. Although the Mosaic covenant has been shattered, God continues to fulfill his covenant with Abraham. He will bless Abraham with many descendants and through Abraham bless all the nations, depending on how they relate to Abraham. But where does God's covenant with David come into play?

God's covenant with David plays a key role in *how* God keeps his promises to Abraham. God promised King David that he would have a descendant on his throne who would establish an everlasting kingdom (2 Sam. 7). The Prophets made it clear that this future Davidic King would be the Messiah and in him lay the future hope for God's people. Now we can understand why Matthew and Luke begin their gospels by identifying Jesus as the Davidic Messiah. Matthew shows the covenant connection in the first verse of his gospel: "This is the genealogy of Jesus the Messiah the son of David, the son of Abraham" (Matt. 1:1). Luke records Zechariah's words:

> He has raised up a horn of salvation for us
>   in the house of his servant David
> (as he said through his holy prophets of long ago),
>   salvation from our enemies
>   and from the hand of all who hate us—
> to show mercy to our ancestors
>   and to remember his holy covenant,
>   the oath he swore to our father Abraham. (Luke 1:69–73; cf. 1:54–55)

Jesus is the Messiah who fulfills the everlasting covenants made with Abraham and David. He is the righteous King who will restore Israel, gather the Gentiles to himself, and renew all of creation. His kingdom will never end!

Another major connection we see with this part of the Story relates to God's desire to live in harmony with his people. He didn't need to create us, but he did so in order to love us and live with us in perfect community. He created Adam and Eve and walked with them in the garden of Eden prior to sin's entering the picture and spoiling paradise. He then made special appearances to people like Abraham, Isaac, Jacob, and Moses. God eventually instructed Moses to build a tent or tabernacle, a portable sanctuary where his personal presence would dwell (Ex. 25:8; 29:44–46). Later, King Solomon built a temple in Jerusalem, declaring, "I have indeed built a magnificent temple for you, a place for you to dwell forever" (1 Kings 8:13). Tragically, as time went by, God's glorious presence left the temple because his people turned away from him.

Finally, God came to us in Jesus, who is "Immanuel," meaning "God with us" (Matt. 1:23). Jesus' entry into the world demonstrates God's stubborn desire to restore paradise and live forever among his people. In Romans 5:12–21, the apostle Paul explains that while the actions of the first Adam destroyed our

Incarnation and Aquariums

"I learned about incarnation when I kept a salt-water aquarium. Management of a marine aquarium, I discovered, is no easy task. I had to run a portable chemical laboratory to monitor the nitrate levels and the ammonia content. I pumped in vitamins and antibodies and sulfa drugs and enough enzymes to make a rock grow. I filtered the water through glass fibers and charcoal, and exposed it to ultraviolet light. You would think, in view of all the energy expended on their behalf, that my fish would at least be grateful. Not so. Every time my shadow loomed above the tank they dove for cover into the nearest shell. They showed me one "emotion" only: fear. Although I opened the lid and dropped in food on a regular schedule, three times a day, they responded to each visit as a sure sign of my designs to torture them. I could not convince them of my true concern.

"To my fish I was deity. I was too large for them, my actions too incomprehensible. My acts of mercy they saw as cruelty; my attempts at healing they viewed as destruction. To change their perceptions, I began to see, would require a form of incarnation. I would have to become a fish and 'speak' to them in a language they could understand. A human being becoming a fish is nothing compared to God becoming a baby. And yet according to the Gospels that is what happened at Bethlehem. The God who created matter took shape within it, as an artist might become a spot on a painting or a playwright a character within his own play. God wrote a story, only using real characters, on the pages of real history. The Word became flesh."[8]

– PHILIP YANCEY

relationship with God, the actions of Jesus, a kind of "second Adam," provided a way for that relationship to be restored. Jesus came to reverse the curse on humanity.

We get a complementary perspective on Jesus' entry into our world through the gospel of John. Rather than including a traditional birth story, John shows us how God himself came to us with the mission of restoring the broken relationship with humanity.

John 1:1–3: "In the beginning was the Word, and the Word was with God, and the Word was God. He was with God in the beginning. Through him all things were made; without him nothing was made that has been made."

Notice how much John 1:1 sounds like Genesis 1:1: "In the beginning God created the heavens and the earth." In Genesis 1, God creates through his word or speech ("and God said ..."). That is how God expresses himself. Notice the many parallel themes in Genesis 1 and John 1 (e.g., creation, darkness, light, life). Throughout the Old Testament, we notice that God's word has a personal quality to it (e.g., Ps. 19:1–4; Isa. 55:10–11). Now, John says, this personal "word" of God has appeared in an actual person, Jesus of Nazareth (John 1:1; Rev. 19:13). Jesus is the perfect expression of God.

John 1:14: "The Word became flesh and made his dwelling among us. We have seen his glory, the glory of the one and only Son, who came from the Father, full of grace and truth."

---

8. Yancey, *The Jesus I Never Knew*, 38–39.

The Word became "flesh." John could have put it more respectably by saying that Jesus became a "human being" (*anthrôpos*) or Jesus took on a "body" (*sôma*); instead, he uses a tangible, almost crude term—"flesh" (*sarx*). Jesus was made or born "flesh." He completely and fully entered into our human situation in all its weakness and frailty. The technical term for God becoming man is *incarnation*, a word that means "being in flesh." In order to rescue us from our sins, God met us where we were. God the Son became a flesh-and-blood human being.

We are also told that God "made his dwelling among us." Notice how God's presence is connected to his glory later in the verse. During the wilderness wanderings of Israel, God filled the tabernacle with his presence and his glory (Ex. 40:34–35). John 1:14 says the Word (Jesus) "pitched his tent" or "tabernacled" among us. God came to live among us in the person of Jesus Christ, and God's glorious presence can now be seen in Jesus (cf. Rev. 21:3).

John 1:18: "No one has ever seen God, but the one and only Son, who is himself God and is in closest relationship with the Father, has made him known."

If you want to know what God is like, look at Jesus. No one has seen God the Father, but God the Son has clearly revealed or explained him. The word that is translated "made known" means to "exegete" or lead out. Jesus Christ leads out or makes known or reveals the true character and nature of the invisible God (Col. 1:15–20). Only Jesus Christ, who has the very nature of God, can really show us what the Father is like.

Living the Story

We can live this aspect of the Great Story in at least four important ways. The first and most obvious way is that we can accept God's gift of a Savior. Jesus' birth divided (and continues to divide) humanity into two camps—those who worship the newborn King (e.g., shepherds, magi, angels) and those who despise him (Herod). Jesus is God's gift to humanity. It would be an eternal tragedy to reject the most precious Christmas gift of all.

Second, Jesus' birth gives us a window into the heart of God, a humble God. If you were God and had to enter a world you had created in order to fix a problem, how would you enter that world? Whatever scenario you might imagine, one thing is for sure: most of us are simply too selfish to do things anywhere close to the way God actually did things when he entered our world. Paul's challenge to the church in Philippi now makes sense:

> Do nothing out of selfish ambition or vain conceit. Rather, in humility value others above yourselves, not looking to your own interests but each of you to the interests of the others.

> In your relationships with one another, have the same mindset as Christ Jesus:

> Who, being in very nature God,

> did not consider equality with God something to be used to his
>   own advantage;
> rather, he made himself nothing
>   by taking the very nature of a servant,
>   being made in human likeness. (Phil. 2:3–7)

When we humble ourselves, we are most like God.

Third, we also learn that God is not afraid of scandal. Some of us are too cautious about life when it comes to protecting our reputation. Living wisely is important, but there are times when we need to do the right thing and love people regardless of what the self-righteous think. Consider the scandal that accompanied the birth of Jesus Christ:

- Mary, a young teenager, gets pregnant without being married. A betrothed woman who became pregnant was considered an adulteress, an act punishable by death according to Jewish law.
- To the neighbors, Jesus is considered an illegitimate child.
- Joseph has to choose between divorce and a ruined reputation even though he is innocent.
- Joseph has to live with Mary's claim of innocence.
- Mary has to live with the Spirit's miraculous work in her body, knowing that very few people in her lifetime will ever believe her story.
- The entire family lives in a small town … enough said.

In what ways is God calling you to live more courageously?

Fourth, we have much to learn when it comes to Jesus' temptation experience. Satan always gift wraps evil and presents it as something good without any mention of the disastrous consequences. We need to take the long view rather than falling for the shortcut. As George McDonald once put it, God "resisted every impulse to work more rapidly for a lower good."[9] John Ortberg describes a mature person as "someone who can do the right thing at the right time in the right way with the right spirit."[10] If it's not God's timing, it's not God's will.

Wrapping Up

After a long period of silence, God speaks through his new covenant prophet, John the Baptizer. John comes to prepare the people for their Messiah, who will fulfill God's covenant promises to Abraham and David. Jesus courageously enters our world in humility. He lives an essentially normal life as a devout Jewish boy and identifies with sinful humanity through his baptism.

---

9. George McDonald, *Life Essential: The Hope of the Gospel* (Wheaton, IL: Harold Shaw, 1974), 25.

10. John Ortberg, *The Life You've Always Wanted: Spiritual Disciplines for Ordinary People* (Grand Rapids: Zondervan, 2002), 54.

He passes the initial test in the wilderness battle with the devil. Where the nation of Israel had failed, Jesus succeeds. Since Jesus withstands the wilderness test, he is now prepared to launch his heavenly mission. As one famous Bible verse says it, "For God so loved the world that he gave his one and only Son, that whoever believes in him shall not perish but have eternal life" (John 3:16).

Memory Verse

The Word became flesh and made his dwelling among us. We have seen his glory, the glory of the one and only Son, who came from the Father, full of grace and truth. (John 1:14)

Digging Deeper

Books

Blomberg, Craig L. *Jesus and the Gospels: An Introduction and Survey.* 2nd ed. Nashville: Broadman & Holman, 2009.

Stein, Robert H. *Jesus the Messiah: A Survey of the Life of Christ.* Downers Grove, IL: InterVarsity Press, 1996.

Strauss, Mark L. *Four Portraits, One Jesus: An Introduction to Jesus and the Gospels.* Grand Rapids: Zondervan, 2007.

Verbrugge, Verlyn. *A Not-So-Silent Night: The Unheard Story of Christmas and Why It Matters.* Grand Rapids: Kregel, 2009.

ASSIGNMENTS

1. Read Matthew 1–2 and Luke 1–2 and make a list of the names or titles given to Jesus. Then write a paragraph summarizing what these names and titles tell us about who Jesus is and what he came to do.

2. Read Luke 1:39–56, especially focusing on Mary's "song" (the *Magnificat*) in 1:46–55. (a) Summarize what Mary thanks God for in her song. (b) Read Hannah's song that follows the birth of Samuel (1 Sam. 2:1–10) and compare it to Mary's song. (c) Write a paragraph or two explaining how Mary's song is unique to her and how it is typical of the experience of all Christ-followers.

3. Matthew focuses on how the birth and childhood of Jesus fulfilled Scripture. Read Matthew 1–2 and identify the five times that he cites the Old Testament. Write a paragraph explaining why you think Matthew presents Jesus as the fulfillment of Israel's long-awaited Messiah.

4. Sometimes we have a hard time imagining that Jesus was really a human being. The Bible clearly teaches that Jesus was fully God and fully man. Use your imagination to recover a sense of Jesus' humanity by describing the ordinary things that Jesus must have experienced as an authentic human

being growing up in a small town (e.g., pimples, getting a splinter, learning about girls, getting thirsty).

5. Satan's temptation strategies in the garden of Eden with Adam and Eve (Gen. 3:1–7) and in the wilderness with Jesus (Matt. 4:1–11) are similar. Read both accounts and make a list of the tempter's strategies that are common to both situations (e.g., raises doubts about God's Word, appeals to their physical desires, etc.).

CHRIST:
Jesus' Message

Chapter 12

Enter Here

The Social Network is a 2010 film about the launching of Facebook, the social media website that started in 2004 on the campus of Harvard University. Would anyone have expected Facebook to grow to over 750 million users by 2011? The total population of the United States as of the 2010 census is just below 310 million. It's no exaggeration to say that Mark Zuckerburg (and others?) started a social revolution.

Jesus also started a revolution. Christianity is the largest world religion, numbering in the billions. To begin his revolution, Jesus teaches a simple but profound message with authority, gathers a community of followers who endorse the message, and performs miracles to verify the message. In this section of the Story, you will learn about Jesus' public ministry, a ministry that focuses on the kingdom of God.

Be Prepared

Read or listen to Matthew 4–7; 13; Mark 1–7; Luke 3–7; 15.

The Story Continues

When Jesus is "about thirty years old" (Luke 3:23), he begins his public ministry in Galilee, a region in the northern part of Palestine. His public ministry may be divided roughly into three periods:

1. Year of *obscurity*: baptism, temptations, teaching, and first miracles
2. Year of *popularity*: calling of disciples, more teaching and miracles, large crowds
3. Year of *rejection*: opposition from religious leaders, confession and transfiguration, raising of Lazarus, and final week in Jerusalem

As Jesus begins his public ministry, he preaches one of his first sermons in the synagogue at Nazareth, his hometown. On that occasion, Jesus is well received at first. But the longer he talks, the more angry the audience becomes, so that by the end of his message, they are ready to throw him off a cliff ... literally (you can read about that interesting episode in Luke 4:14–30). Jesus gets this kind of reaction throughout his ministry. What is he doing and saying that attracts devoted followers and, at the same time, invites fierce opposition? Let's take a look.

The Kingdom of God

We are told that after John the Baptizer is put in prison, Jesus begins proclaiming the good news of God. "The time has come," he says. "The kingdom of God has come near. Repent and believe the good news!" (Mark 1:14–15). The good news is tied to the kingdom of God, and Jesus is announcing the arrival of that kingdom. According to that same Luke 4 sermon, the arrival of the kingdom is directly connected to Jesus himself in a personal way. Few would debate that the "kingdom of God" is Jesus' favorite topic in his teaching, yet we hear little about it today.[1] What does Jesus mean by "kingdom of God," and what does this have to do with the Great Story?

Basically, the phrase "kingdom of God" refers to God's personal rule or reign over his creation, including his people. Jesus' view of the kingdom of God draws on two important ideas that run throughout the Old Testament. First, the Jews believed that God reigns now as sovereign King over all creation—"The Lord has established his throne in heaven and his kingdom rules over all" (Ps. 103:19; see also Isa. 43:15; Pss. 99:1; 145:13). God is King over all now! Second, a time will come when God will establish his kingdom on earth—"For the Lord Almighty will reign on Mount Zion and in Jerusalem, and before its elders—with great glory" (Isa. 24:23b). The Jews divided history into "this age" and the "age to come" (also known as the messianic age), and they very much looked forward to the age to come.

This new age would be a time of righteousness (e.g., Isa. 11:4–5), and people would live in peace (e.g., Isa. 2:2–4). It would be a time of the fullness of the Spirit (Joel 2:28–30) when the new covenant spoken of by Jeremiah would be realized (Jer. 31:31–34; 32:38–40). Sin and sickness would be done away with (e.g., Zech. 13:1; Isa. 53:5). Even the material creation would feel the joyful effects of this new age (e.g., Isa 11:6–9).[2]

---

1. The phrase "kingdom of God" (or "kingdom of heaven" in Matthew's gospel, due to his sensitivity to his predominantly Jewish audience) occurs eighty-seven times in the Gospels and is found in the central teachings of Jesus such as the Sermon on the Mount, the Farewell Discourse, and many of his parables. See Robert H. Stein, *Jesus the Messiah* (Downers Grove, IL: InterVarsity Press, 1996), 126.

2. Gordon D. Fee and Douglas K. Stuart, *How to Read the Bible for All Its Worth* (Grand Rapids: Zondervan, 2003), 146.

A Jewish Understanding of the Kingdom

God Sets Up Earthly Kingdom

This Age	Age to Come
Sin and rebellion	Comfort and safety
Suffering	No evil or suffering
Satan and the demonic	Wholeness
Diseases and death	Righteousness
Darkness	No death, only life
War with evil	Presence of God

The Jews held strongly to these two important ideas — God's present, universal reign over all now and God's future reign on the earth. They longed for the day when God would enter this world, defeat his enemies, and establish his kingdom on the earth.

Knowing this, you can imagine why Jesus' message is considered outrageous. He has the courage and boldness to say that now, with his coming, the kingdom of God has actually arrived! While the Jews believed that God would intervene at the end of the age to defeat evil and set up his kingdom, Jesus is declaring that he is establishing God's kingdom on earth now! This is radical stuff. Jesus proclaims the kingdom, heals the sick, drives out demons, feeds the hungry, and forgives sinners — all signs that the kingdom of God has arrived. In Jesus' words and actions, the kingdom of God has become a present reality (Matt. 11:11–12; 12:28; 18:1–5; Luke 17:20–21).

Jesus urges people to come under the personal reign of God or, in other

What Does It Take to Enter the Kingdom of God?

Matt. 5:20: To enter, our righteousness must go beyond that of the Pharisees and become a sincere, heart righteousness.

Matt. 7:21: To enter, we must do more than call Jesus "Lord"; we must do his will.

Matt. 18:3; Mark 10:15; Luke 18:17: We must become like little children to enter.

Matt. 19:23–24; Mark 10:23–25; Luke 18:24–25: Entering the kingdom is almost impossible for rich people.

Matt. 21:28–32: Entering the kingdom requires repentance and belief/trust.

Mark 9:47: We must deal with our sin in a radical manner in order to enter.

Luke 9:59–62: Entrance requires making Jesus and the kingdom our greatest priority.

John 3:5: We must be born again/from above in order to enter the kingdom.

words, to enter the kingdom of God. To do so, people must "repent and believe the good news." Repentance is the "no" that leads to the "yes" of trusting God. Repentance involves a change of life direction, not just a superficial or temporary emotional experience. It's much more than mere regret.

Coming under the reign of God begins with repentance and culminates in faith (i.e., repent *and* believe the good news). Since the kingdom of God is directly related to Jesus himself, entering the kingdom is directly tied to becoming a follower of Jesus.

Jesus' Disciples: The New Kingdom Community

Jesus begins his ministry by forming a community of followers or disciples. The word "disciple" means student, learner, apprentice, or follower. It's amazing to read about Jesus' first disciples leaving everything to follow him — family, profession, and property (see Mark 1:14–20 [below]; also Matt. 4:13–22):

> After John was put in prison, Jesus went into Galilee, proclaiming the good news of God. "The time has come," he said. "The kingdom of God has come near. Repent and believe the good news!"
>
> As Jesus walked beside the Sea of Galilee, he saw Simon and his brother Andrew casting a net into the lake, for they were fishermen. "Come, follow me," Jesus said, "and I will send you out to fish for people." At once they left their nets and followed him.
>
> When he had gone a little farther, he saw James son of Zebedee and his brother John in a boat, preparing their nets. Without delay he called them, and they left their father Zebedee in the boat with the hired men and followed him.

This passage leaves the impression that these guys are meeting Jesus for the first time, but John 1:35–51 suggests that there may have been previous encounters. Many of Jesus' first disciples were originally disciples of John the Baptizer and were already familiar with Jesus. When John was arrested and imprisoned, Jesus moved his public ministry to Galilee and began to call disciples. Michael Wilkins notes that "early disciples were drawn from existing networks of relatives (e.g., brothers: Andrew and Simon Peter; John and James), business partners (e.g., Peter and Andrew were partners in the fishing industry with James and John, Luke 5:10), neighbors and acquaintances (most of the Twelve were from Capernaum and Bethsaida)."[3]

It was common for Jewish rabbis to have disciples. Normally people who wanted to be disciples would seek out the most respected teacher they could find and ask permission to follow him (see Matt. 8:19, where a would-be disciple takes this approach with Jesus). But Jesus does things differently. He takes

---

3. Michael J. Wilkins, *Following the Master: A Biblical Theology of Discipleship* (Grand Rapids: Zondervan, 1992), 105.

the initiative by calling his own disciples. He is not simply one of a number of renowned religious experts whom students may pick from. Rather, he is uniquely authoritative and supremely deserving of our allegiance. Jesus' disciples are not called because of their advanced intellect or special abilities or powerful status or moral uprightness. They are called on the basis of God's sovereign grace.

The core of Jesus' community of disciples is the Twelve. They are chosen out of a much larger group of disciples to fulfill their unique role as apostles (commissioned representatives). In Luke 6:12–13 we read:

> One of those days Jesus went out to a mountainside to pray, and spent the night praying to God. When morning came, he called his disciples to him and chose twelve of them, whom he also designated apostles.

Jesus appoints the Twelve "that they might be with him and that he might send them out to preach and to have authority to drive out demons" (Mark 3:14–15). He "gave them authority to drive out impure spirits and to heal every disease and sickness" (Matt. 10:1). In other words, the Twelve are commissioned to extend Jesus' kingdom ministry of teaching and working miracles. With one exception (Judas Iscariot), these are the "founding fathers" of the church (see Eph. 2:20; 3:5; Rev. 21:14). The apostles preserve what Jesus himself taught, and their teachings have become the basis for our New Testament (Acts 2:42). The Twelve are listed in the following chart:[4]

Jesus' Twelve Disciples		
Mark 3:13–19	**Matthew 10:1–4**	**Luke 6:12–16**
Simon (Peter)	Simon (Peter)	Simon (Peter)
	his brother Andrew	his brother Andrew
James son of Zebedee	James son of Zebedee	James
John (Sons of Thunder)	his brother John	John
Andrew[1]		
Philip	Philip	Philip
Bartholomew	Bartholomew	Bartholomew
Matthew	Thomas	Matthew
Thomas	Matthew the tax collector[2]	Thomas
James son of Alphaeus	James son of Alphaeus	James son of Alphaeus
Thaddaeus	Thaddaeus	

Continued on next page

---

4. This chart is reproduced in Preben Vang and Terry Carter's *Telling God's Story: The Biblical Narrative from Beginning to End* (Nashville: Broadman & Holman, 2006), 196. The chart was originally produced by J. Scott Duvall and first made public in his unpublished New Testament Survey notes used at Ouachita Baptist University.

Mark 3:13–19	Matthew 10:1–4	Luke 6:12–16
Simon the Cananaean	Simon the Cananaean	Simon the Zealot[3]
		Judas son of James[4]
Judas Iscariot	Judas Iscariot	Judas Iscariot

[1] Mark prefers to keep the three most prominent disciples together in his list (i.e., Peter, James, and John) while Matthew and Luke prefer to keep the brothers Peter and Andrew together in their lists.

[2] We might expect Matthew to mention his profession of "tax collector."

[3] *Cananaean* is the Aramaic word for *Zealot*. Luke translates the Aramaic into Greek.

[4] It seems that Thaddaeus (Mark and Matthew) and Judas son of James (Luke) are the same person. Five of the names in the list are qualified by additional names—e.g., James son of Zebedee. The name *Judas Iscariot* suggests that there was another Judas—Judas son of James. Perhaps Mark and Matthew referred to the other Judas as Thaddaeus because of the stigma associated with Judas. Why Luke did not do so is hard to tell.

Why does Jesus choose twelve apostles and not seven or fifteen or thirty? It's because of the connection to Israel's role in the Great Story. When Jews heard the number "twelve," they would automatically think of the twelve tribes of Israel. The Jews of Jesus' day looked forward to a time when God would restore Israel (by restoring the twelve tribes) and establish his kingdom on earth. By choosing twelve apostles, Jesus is sending a strong message that he is forming the new Israel through his community of followers (see Matt. 19:28; Luke 22:30). The purpose of forming a new community is related to God's original purpose for his people. God chose and blessed Israel in order that she might be a light to the other nations (Gen. 12:1–3; Isa. 42:6–7; 49:6). Now Jesus is restoring the people of God in order that they may get back on track to carry out his purposes for the nations (think about Jesus' command to "make disciples of all nations" in Matt. 28:19).

Have you ever stopped to think about the type of people Jesus chose as his first followers? There are four fishermen (Peter, Andrew, James, and John), two "sons of thunder" or hot-tempered guys (James and John), a despised tax collector (Matthew or Levi), a super patriot (Simon the Zealot), and one who would become a traitor (Judas Iscariot). Probably not the type of people you would choose as the charter members of your new community.

It's important to note that besides the Twelve, Jesus also has other disciples. Luke mentions a group of female disciples who travel with Jesus and support him (8:1–3) as well as the seventy-two disciples sent out on a preaching and healing mission (10:1–24). In addition, crowds or multitudes follow Jesus around physically, but they are not true disciples. They are curious and benefit from Jesus' ministry (Matt. 15:29–31), but they lack the true commitment of disciples (John 6). Jesus is constantly calling the crowds to become disciples (Matt. 8:18–21; 9:35–38; 28:18).

Jesus' Miracles: Glimpses of the Final Kingdom

Once when Jesus is accused of using demonic power to perform miracles, he firmly denies that his power comes from Satan and counters, "But if it is by the Spirit of God that I drive out demons, then the kingdom of God has come upon you" (Matt. 12:28). Jesus' mighty works are empowered by the Spirit of God and are closely connected to his teaching about the kingdom of God. These miracles demonstrate that Jesus is indeed the Messiah and God's mighty power is at work through him.

The Gospels record about thirty-five miracles of Jesus, which fall into four different types: healings, exorcisms, raising the dead, and nature miracles. Certainly Jesus' healing miracles are closely connected to the kingdom of God breaking into this world. When John the Baptist is in prison, he sends disciples to ask Jesus whether he truly is the "one who is to come" (Messiah; Matt. 11:3). Jesus responds by saying, "Go back and report to John what you hear and see: The blind receive sight, the lame walk, those who have leprosy are cleansed, the deaf hear, the dead are raised, and the good news is proclaimed to the poor" (11:4–5). In other words, the healing miracles are evidence that the kingdom has arrived. Don't miss it!

On three occasions, Jesus raises people from the dead. Here Jesus resuscitates or revives the people to normal mortal life; these people eventually die again. Resurrection occurs at the end of this age when Christians receive new bodies (see 1 Cor. 15). The message is the same as with the healing miracles, only more dramatic—the kingdom of God is a kingdom of life! What Satan and sin introduced into the Great Story—death—will be defeated and completely removed when the King reigns over all.

Jesus also casts out demons. In these exorcisms the kingdom of God is launching an all-out, frontal assault on the kingdom of Satan. In an exorcism, Jesus attacks Satan and takes back a precious life that has been held captive and tortured by the enemy. These liberated captives begin to be human once again. Jesus overpowers and crushes the kingdom of Satan through his exorcism miracles.

The last category of miracles is that of nature miracles. Interestingly, the nature miracles often carry a lot of symbolic significance. For example, the feeding of the multitudes teaches that God supplies what we need for life (i.e., Jesus as the bread of life). Turning water into wine symbolizes how the "new wine" of the kingdom is replacing the "water" of legalistic Judaism. The cursing of the fig tree shows what God will do with Israel if they fail to respond to Jesus and the kingdom he inaugurates. The nature miracles also show that God is renewing the whole created order.

> ### A Glimpse of a Better World
>
> "The miracles he did perform, breaking as they did the chains of sickness and death, give me a glimpse of what the world was meant to be and instill hope that one day God will right its wrongs. To put it mildly, God is no more satisfied with this earth than we are; Jesus' miracles offer a hint of what God intends to do about it."[5]
>
> – PHILIP YANCEY

---

5. Yancey, *The Jesus I Never Knew*, 182.

Jesus' Healing Miracles

Peter's mother-in-law	Mark 1:29–31; Matt. 8:14–17; Luke 4:38–39
Man with leprosy	Mark 1:40–45; Matt. 8:1–4; Luke 5:12–15
Paralyzed man	Mark 2:1–12; Matt. 9:1–8; Luke 5:17–26
Man with withered hand	Mark 3:1–6; Matt. 12:9–14; Luke 6:6–11
Bleeding woman	Mark 5:25–29; Matt. 9:20–22; Luke 8:43–48
Deaf mute	Mark 7:31–37
Blind man	Mark 8:22–26
Blind Bartimaeus	Mark 10:46–52; Matt. 20:29–34; Luke 19:35–43
Centurion's servant	Matt. 8:5–13; Luke 7:1–10
Two blind men	Matt. 9:27–31
Woman crippled for eighteen years	Luke 13:10–17
Man with dropsy	Luke 14:1–6
Ten men with leprosy	Luke 17:11–19
Royal official's son at Cana	John 4:46–54
Paralytic at Bethesda	John 5:1–18
Man born blind	John 9:1–41
High priest's servant	Luke 22:49–51; John 18:10–11

Jesus' Resuscitation Miracles

Raising Jairus's daughter	Mark 5:22–24, 35–43; Matt. 9:18–26; Luke 8:41–42, 49–56
Raising widow's son at Nain	Luke 7:11–16
Raising Lazarus	John 11:1–45

Jesus' Exorcism Miracles

Possessed man in synagogue	Mark 1:23–27; Luke 4:33–36
Gadarene demoniac(s)	Mark 5:1–20; Matt. 8:28–34; Luke 8:26–39
Daughter of Canaanite woman	Mark 7:24–30; Matt. 15:21–28
Demon-possessed boy	Mark 9:14–29; Matt. 17:14–20; Luke 9:37–43
Blind, mute possessed man	Matt. 12:22; Luke 11:14
Mute possessed man	Matt. 9:32–34

Jesus' Nature Miracles

Calming the storm	Mark 4:35–41; Matt. 8:22–25; Luke 8:22–25
Feeding of 5,000	Mark 6:35–44; Matt. 14:15–21; Luke 9:12–17; John 6:5–15
Walking on water	Mark 6:45–52; Matt. 14:22–33; John 6:16–21
Feeding of 4,000	Mark 8:1–9; Matt. 15:32–39
Fig tree withering	Mark 11:12–14, 20–25; Matt. 21:17–22
Coin in fish's mouth	Matt. 17:24–27
First catch of fish	Luke 5:1–11
Turning water into wine	John 2:1–11
Second catch of fish	John 21:1–14

Less Talk and More Power

"[In the early church] people did not merely hear the gospel; they saw it in action, and were moved to respond. The Western Church has grown too dependent on words, and not nearly dependent enough on the power of the Holy Spirit. . . . Instead of being a community demonstrating the Lord's power, we have become one which talks incessantly. We need to remember that the 'kingdom of God is not talk, but power' [1 Cor. 4:20]. Where churches have regained dependence on God's Spirit, where they have believed that God is active among his people today, where they have prayerfully asked him to give them not only qualities of character but spiritual power, then those same gifts which we see in the New Testament have appeared today. By far the fastest growing Christian communion in the world is the Pentecostal. They have some weaknesses, to be sure, but they expect to see God at work among them. They expect to see healing. . . . And they find when they come against spiritual forces which hold men and women in bondage, these are cast out by God's Spirit and the result is a new liberation . . . It has long been fashionable for us to dismiss these gifts as unnecessary or unattainable today. We would be unwise to do so. They are part of God's equipping of his church for Evangelism."[6]

– MICHAEL GREEN

Jesus' miracles provide glimpses of how life will go when God reigns over all. The nature miracles point to a renewed creation in the new heaven and new earth (Rom. 8:18–25). The healing, exorcism, and resuscitation miracles point to God's personal presence among his people apart from the deadly consequences of sin and torment of Satan. Revelation 21:3–4 sums it up well:

> And I heard a loud voice from the throne saying, "Look! God's dwelling place is now among the people, and he will dwell with them. They will be his people, and God himself will be with them and be their God. He will wipe every tear from their eyes. There will be no more death or mourning or crying or pain, for the old order of things has passed away."

What Jesus begins through his Spirit-empowered mighty works will one day be completed.

Jesus' Teachings: Living in God's Kingdom

To equip and train his disciples about what it means to live as kingdom citizens, Jesus invests a lot of time over the course of his ministry teaching them. Much of what Jesus teaches his followers is captured in the Sermon on the Mount. Both Matthew (chs. 5–7) and Luke (6:17–49) record this sermon,

---

6. Michael Green, *Evangelism and the Early Church*, rev. ed. (Grand Rapids: Eerdmans, 2004), 26–27.

although Matthew's version is much longer. It's likely that Jesus repeated his kingdom teaching many times; we are blessed to have one of his typical sermons.

We see from the introduction to the Sermon on the Mount in Matthew 5:1–2 that Jesus' primary audience is his followers. Consequently, the Sermon on the Mount is not spelling out requirements for those who want to enter the kingdom so much as teaching those who are already following Jesus what it means to live as a community of genuine disciples. God's people are supposed to be different from the world (Matt. 6:8).

Craig Blomberg helpfully notes that the Sermon is organized into units of three or multiples of three.[7] It opens with nine "Beatitudes" (from the Latin word for "blessing") plus the salt and light sayings in 5:3–16. These are declarations of blessing on the disciples and remind us that God graciously blesses us before he makes demands on us. The word "blessed" (*makarios*) speaks of much more than superficial happiness. It refers to being in a place where God is pleased with you and pours out his favor on you. Some blessings are realized in the present, while many are reserved for the future age (see "Making Connections" below).

Jesus explains kingdom righteousness in 5:17–20, a section considered by many to be the thesis paragraph of the entire sermon. Here we see how Jesus' teachings connect to earlier parts of the Great Story. What Jesus teaches is not opposed to the Old Testament as some might expect. Jesus clearly states, "Do not think that I have come to abolish the Law or the Prophets; I have not come to abolish them but to fulfill them" (5:17). Those who want to enter the kingdom must embrace Jesus' righteousness, a heart righteousness that fulfills God's holy standards and far surpasses the hypocritical piety put forth by some of the religious leaders of Jesus' day (5:20).

Jesus' intention to fulfill the Old Testament Law is clearly spelled out in 5:21–48, where he applies kingdom righteousness in six scenarios dealing with murder, adultery, divorce, vows, retaliation, and loving one's enemies. Here Jesus stresses the true purpose and intention of the Old Testament as it is fulfilled by his life, ministry, and teachings. Jesus is the culmination and completion of the first part of the Great Story.

Living as a citizen of the kingdom of God involves authentic expressions of piety, especially prayer (6:1–18), as well as new priorities related to wealth (see 6:19–34). There are three sections in 7:1–12 on how to treat other people, culminating in what has been dubbed the "Golden Rule": "So in everything, do to others what you would have them do to you, for this sums up the Law and the Prophets" (7:12).

> ### Like a Moth to the Flame
>
> "The more I read these three chapters—Matthew 5, 6, and 7—the more I am both drawn to them and shamed by them. Their brilliant light draws me like a moth to a spotlight; but the light is so bright that it sears and burns. No room is left for forms of piety which are nothing more than veneer and sham."[8]
>
> – D. A. CARSON

---

7. Craig L. Blomberg, *Jesus and the Gospels: An Introduction and Survey*, 2nd ed. (Nashville: Broadman & Holman, 2009), 287.

8. D. A. Carson, *Jesus' Sermon on the Mount and His Confrontation with the World: An Exposition of Matthew 5–10* (Grand Rapids: Baker, 2004), 11.

Jesus concludes the Sermon on the Mount with several illustrations that make the same point: in the end we will be either for Jesus or against him (7:13–27). The narrow gate leads to life while the wide gate leads to destruction. The wise will listen to and obey Jesus' teachings, while the foolish will pay him no mind. While the primary audience is Jesus' own disciples, the secondary audience is the crowds, and they are amazed by Jesus' authoritative teaching (7:28–29).

Jesus teaches about life in the kingdom of God in many other ways, especially through his parables.[9] Approximately one-third of Jesus' teachings can be found in parables. Even people who are unfamiliar with the Bible have usually heard of the parable of the prodigal son or the parable of the good Samaritan. A *parable* (the term meaning "to throw alongside") is a short story with two levels of meaning, where certain details in the story represent something else. In the parable of the prodigal son, for example, the father represents God, the older brother represents the self-righteous, and the younger brother represents the unrighteous (see Luke 15:1).

Jesus' parables typically make more than one point but should not be understood in a wildly allegorical fashion. A good rule of thumb is that there is one main point for each main character or set of characters.[10] All the other details are there to enhance the story. The parable of the prodigal son in Luke 15:11–32 makes the following main points:

> ### Jesus' Uniquely Golden Rule
>
> "It is often pointed out that many other Jewish teachers, along with a few from other religions, taught much the same thing, but most of them phrased it negatively—in essence, 'Don't treat others the way you wouldn't want to be treated.' Jesus is the only person to state the principle in this emphatically positive form. Taking the initiative in doing good is always more challenging than simply avoiding evil."[11]
>
> – CRAIG BLOMBERG

- Younger brother: sinners may confess their sins and turn to God in repentance.
- Older brother: those who claim to be God's people should not be resentful when God extends his grace to the undeserving; rather, they should rejoice.
- Forgiving father: God offers forgiveness to undeserving people.

Jesus uses these simple but profound stories to teach about the nature of the kingdom of God. Often he begins a story with the words, "The kingdom of heaven/God is like …" (e.g., Matt. 13:44, 45, 47; Mark 4:26; Luke 13:18). It's no exaggeration to say that the kingdom of God is the central theme of Jesus' parables. Through the parables we learn a lot about who God is, what it means to live as a member of his kingdom community, and what happens if you choose to reject the King.

---

9. For a survey of the many ways that Jesus communicated his message, see Robert H. Stein, *The Method and Message of Jesus' Teaching* (Louisville: Westminster John Knox, 1994).

10. For this interpretive guideline, see the landmark work on Jesus' parables by Craig L. Blomberg, *Interpreting the Parables* (Downers Grove, IL: InterVarsity Press, 1990).

11. Blomberg, *Jesus and the Gospels*, 295.

Because it is difficult to know whether to count proverbs, riddles, metaphors, and short sayings as parables, the lists of parables found in study Bibles and other reference books vary. Here is a list of the main parables arranged according to the number of points they make.[12]

One-point parables

- Mustard seed and leaven (Matt. 13:31–33; Mark 4:30–32; Luke 13:18–21)
- Hidden treasure and pearl of great price (Matt. 13:44–46)
- Tower builder and warring king (Luke 14:28–33)

Two-point parables

- Secretly growing seed (Mark 4:26–29)
- Wise and foolish builders (Matt. 7:24–27; Luke 6:47–49)
- Householder and thief (Matt. 24:42–44; Luke 12:35–40)
- Friend at midnight (Luke 11:5–8)
- Rich fool (Luke 12:16–21)
- Barren fig tree (Luke 13:6–9)
- Lowest seat at the feast (Luke 14:7–11)
- Unprofitable servant (Luke 17:7–10)
- Unjust judge (Luke 18:1–8)

Three-point parables

- Children in the marketplace (Matt. 11:16–19; Luke 7:31–35)
- Sower and seed (Matt. 13:1–9, 18–23; Mark 4:1–9, 13–20; Luke 8:5–8, 11–15)
- Wheat and tares (Matt. 13:24–30, 36–43)
- Dragnet (Matt. 13:47–50)
- Unforgiving servant (Matt. 18:23–35)
- Laborers in the vineyard (Matt. 20:1–16)
- Two sons (Matt. 21:28–32)
- Wicked tenants (Matt. 21:33–46; Mark 12:1–12; Luke 20:9–18)
- Wedding feast (Matt. 22:1–14)
- Faithful and unfaithful servants (Matt. 24:45–51; Luke 12:42–48)
- Ten maidens (Matt. 25:1–13)
- Talents (Matt. 25:14–30; Luke 19:12–27)
- Sheep and goats (Matt. 25:31–46)
- Two debtors (Luke 7:41–43)
- Good Samaritan (Luke 10:25–37)
- Great banquet (Luke 14:15–24)
- Lost sheep and lost coin (Luke 15:4–10)

---

12. See ibid. for this listing.

- Lost (prodigal) son (Luke 15:11–32)
- Unjust steward (Luke 16:1–13)
- Rich man and Lazarus (Luke 16:19–31)
- Pharisee and tax collector (Luke 18:9–14)

Making Connections

Let's review where we are in the Great Story:

Creation and Crisis
Covenant
Calling Out
Commandments
Conquest and Canaanization
Creation of the Kingdom
Communion and Common Sense
Crumbling of the Kingdom
Captivity and Coming Home
Interlude: Time between the Testaments
➤ **Christ:**
  Jesus Enters Our World
  Jesus' Message
  Jesus' Journey to Jerusalem
  Jesus Dies on the Cross
  Jesus Is Raised from the Dead
Church
Consummation

The Jews of Jesus' day eagerly longed for the Messiah or "Anointed One" to rid the land of the Roman oppressors and establish God's righteous kingdom on earth. God had promised that he would set up a never-ending kingdom, and surely the Messiah would be a military conqueror much like King David (see 2 Sam. 7:6–18; Isa. 9:7; Dan. 2:44; Luke 1:33). Now Jesus comes on the scene proclaiming the arrival of the kingdom of God. He heals the sick, feeds the hungry, drives out demons, raises the dead, and offers spiritual freedom, but he makes no effort to overthrow Rome. Jesus' first disciples expect him to establish the kingdom convincingly during their lifetimes. You can imagine how devastated they are when Jesus is crucified. To be sure, Jesus doesn't fulfill everyone's (or even anyone's) messianic expectations.

But Jesus has started a revolution from within. Starting small and growing slowly, this kingdom movement fails to impress at first. In time, however, Jesus' kingdom revolution picks up steam. The new community of the Spirit, the church, built on the solid rock of Jesus' life, death, and resurrection, will eventually turn the world upside down. The disciples slowly begin to see

God's greater plan. The kingdom of God includes both a present reality and a future reality, with an overlap of the two ages for a lengthy period of time. As a result, Christians modify the Jewish understanding of God's kingdom in the following way:

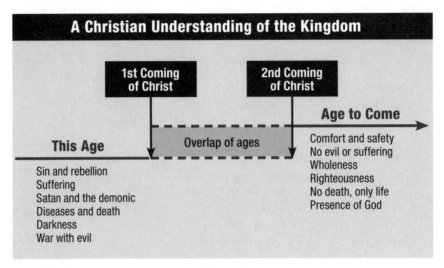

At Jesus' first coming, the kingdom of God broke into this world, a world filled with sin, rebellion, Satan, darkness, and evil. This world encounters a touch of peace, righteousness, and life from God. As people come under God's reign by following Jesus, they begin to experience "age-to-come" (or eternal) life right now (Col. 1:13). They come alive and taste heaven while still living on earth. Although God has begun his kingdom project, he has not completely finished it. The kingdom of God has *already* arrived, but it has *not fully* and completely arrived—this is what is often referred to as the "already/not yet" motif. The grand project has been launched, but it has not been finished. The kingdom has been inaugurated but not yet consummated. The kingdom of God also entails a future hope (e.g., Matt. 7:21–23; 13:36–43; 25:34; Mark 14:25; Luke 13:29–30). One day Jesus will come again to liberate creation completely from the tyranny of sin and Satan. God's enemies (far greater than the Roman Empire) will be destroyed, and he will live forever with his people in the new heaven and new earth. This reminds us of Genesis 1–2 and clarifies what God had in mind all along.

While Jesus didn't meet the immediate messianic expectations of his contemporaries, he did fulfill the ultimate expectations for God's Messiah. The Great Story finds its true and ultimate fulfillment in Jesus. Through his mighty works or miracles, Jesus begins taking back what Satan has wrongfully seized, he begins restoring creation, and he begins offering life beyond the grave—all in fulfillment of what God has promised. The poor receive good news, the prisoners are set free, the blind recover their sight, the lame walk, the lepers are healed, the deaf hear, and the dead are raised (Matt. 11:5; Luke 4:18–19; cf. Isa. 29:18–19; 35:5–6; 58:6; 61:1–2). These miracles are foretastes of the full and final kingdom yet to come. Jesus' resurrection not only vindicates his claims to be Messiah, it also guarantees our future resurrection and life in the new heaven and new earth (see 1 Cor. 15). We know from Jesus' miracles that the Great Story is a story of hope!

Through his words or teachings, Jesus explains the nature of God's kingdom and what it means to live under God's reign. Jesus did not come to set aside or ignore the first part of the Great Story. Rather, he fulfills the Story by showing its true purpose ("you have heard it said ... but I say to you"). As Moses goes up on the mountain to receive God's original Law, now Jesus goes up on a mountain to proclaim the fulfillment of that Law. Over and over again in the Sermon on the Mount, Jesus shows what God had in mind all along. God doesn't just care about outward moral behavior (e.g., no murder or adultery); he cares most about the transformation of a person's heart (e.g., no hatred or lust). Jesus' righteousness goes far beyond mere religious righteousness by becoming an inside-out, heart righteousness. With the coming of the Holy Spirit later at Pentecost (Acts 2), God's law will be written on or implanted within our hearts (Jer. 31:31–34; Jas. 1:21, 25). Jesus begins this process.

> ### Two Kinds of People
>
> "There are only two kinds of people in the end—those who say to God, 'Thy will be done,' and those to whom God says ... 'Thy will be done.'"[13]
>
> – C. S. LEWIS

Through his parables, Jesus explains even more about the true nature of the kingdom. Like a tiny mustard seed growing into a huge plant or a small amount of yeast permeating a large amount of dough, the kingdom will start small and appear unimportant but will eventually grow into a large and influential movement (Matt. 13:31–33). Jesus proclaims the message of the kingdom to all kinds of people, knowing that some will accept but many will reject (see the parable of the soils in Matt. 13:1–9, 18–23).

In fact, Jesus' parables both reveal truth to committed followers and conceal truth from those whose hearts are calloused and hardened (Matt. 13:10–17; Isa. 6:9–10). Surprisingly, Jesus makes it clear that the righteous and the wicked will coexist for the time being. Only at the final judgment at the end of the age will God separate the two, rewarding the righteous and punishing the wicked based on how they have responded to Jesus (see Matt. 13:24–30, 47–50; 25:31–46). What is clear is that the kingdom is of such value that any price is worth paying to receive it (Matt. 13:44–46).

Living the Story

We can live this aspect of the Great Story in several significant ways. First, we see that entering the kingdom of God is now connected to following Jesus as

---

13. C. S. Lewis, *The Great Divorce* (New York: HarperCollins, 2001; orig. 1946), 75.

Can We Be Christians without Being Disciples?

"The word 'disciple' occurs 269 times in the New Testament. 'Christian' is found three times and was first introduced to refer precisely to disciples of Jesus.... The New Testament is a book about disciples, by disciples, and for disciples of Jesus Christ.... The disciple of Jesus is not the deluxe or heavy-duty model of the Christian—especially padded, textured, streamlined, and empowered for the fast lane on the straight and narrow way. He or she stands on the pages of the New Testament as the first level of basic transportation in the Kingdom of God.... There is absolutely nothing in what Jesus himself or his early followers taught that suggests that you can *decide* just to enjoy forgiveness at Jesus' expense and have nothing more to do with him."[14]

– DALLAS WILLARD

a disciple. Being a member of the kingdom is not a matter of ethnicity or nationality or wealth or religious expertise or even sincerity. Rather, it is a matter of one's relationship to Jesus. Some today believe that you can be a Christian without being a disciple or follower of Jesus.

Jesus was clear that you cannot be a Christian without being a disciple. Being a disciple means to believe in and to follow Christ. If you could actually become a Christian without becoming a disciple, who would ever want to become a disciple? Why would you want the responsibilities if you already have all the privileges? But the idea that discipleship is optional is completely foreign to the New Testament. Out of the crowds Jesus calls people to follow him. He calls people to become his disciples. Those who become followers are later called *Christians* (only three times—Acts 11:26; 26:28; 1 Pet. 4:16). Some disciples are more mature than others, of course, but there is no such thing as a Christian who is not a disciple.

To become a disciple, Jesus says, requires the following (see Luke 9:23):

- *Deny self*: reject or deny anything that prevents commitment; say no to self-centeredness; refuse to allow yourself to be the center of your universe
- *Take up cross daily*: daily, ongoing, lifelong devotion to God's plan, even if that includes suffering
- *Follow me*: model your life after the person of Jesus Christ

We become disciples of Jesus when we give up on ourselves as the source of life and turn to Jesus. He then begins the lifelong process of growing us. *Discipleship* is the lifelong process of learning how to be like Jesus in every aspect of life. Jesus works from the inside out, changing our core allegiances and ambitions. He uses life experiences and spiritual disciplines to shape our desires and decisions and relationships. The goal is to be like Jesus himself (Matt. 10:24–25; Rom. 8:29; 2 Cor. 3:18; Gal. 4:19). We are not following a program or an institution but a person. As Jesus himself said, "The student is not above the teacher, but everyone who is fully trained will be like their teacher" (Luke 6:40). That is his goal—and should be ours.

The second way we can live this part of the Story is to remember that we live in the overlap between the ages. Although it is God's world, right now it is

---

14. Dallas Willard, *The Great Omission: Reclaiming Jesus' Essential Teaching on Discipleship* (New York: HarperOne, 2006), 3, 13.

occupied by enemy forces. As Jesus' followers, we are living in enemy-occupied territory between God's initial victory (Jesus' first coming) and his total defeat of evil (Jesus' second coming).

Because we live in the overlap between this age and the age to come, we will experience victories as well as struggles until Jesus returns:

- We experience God's forgiveness, but we still sin and will never be perfect in this life.
- We have victory over death, but we will one day die physically.
- We still get sick, and not all Christians will experience healing.
- We live in the Spirit, but Satan will continue to attack and may do damage.
- God lives within us, but we do not yet live in God's presence.

Because of the "already/not fully" nature of the kingdom of God, we need to adjust our expectations. Rather than being naively optimistic or desperately pessimistic, we need to be hopefully realistic about life here and now in God's kingdom.

A third way to live the Story relates to how we receive Jesus' teachings found in the Sermon on the Mount. As you read the Sermon, you will probably feel a lot of tension between God's high demands on your life and your own sinfulness. The tension is inescapable. We can't ignore God's demands for his people, but we can't always live up to them either. What are we to do? As you read the Sermon, remember three things.

> ### The Shape of Self-Denial
>
> "Every day we must open ourselves up to God's initiatives and control. Self-denial takes shape in many ways. For some, it may mean leaving job and family as the disciples have done. For the proud, it means renouncing the desire for status and honor. For the greedy, it means renouncing an appetite for wealth. The complacent will have to renounce the love of ease. The fainthearted will have to abandon the craving for security. The violent will have to repudiate the desire for revenge. On it goes."[15]
>
> – DAVID GARLAND

1. The Sermon is attainable only by those who have experienced the new birth in Christ. We enter into a relationship with God by grace through faith, and by the power of the Holy Spirit, that relationship grows into a fruitful life.
2. God takes time to accomplish his work in our lives. He will continue to work until Christ returns (see Phil. 1:6). We will always be growing and maturing in this life, but we will not be morally perfect and sinless until Christ returns. So verses like Matthew 5:48 ("Be perfect, therefore, as your heavenly Father is perfect") must be read alongside verses such as Matthew 6:12 ("Forgive us our debts").
3. We must remember that the Sermon is addressed to a community of disciples, not merely to individual disciples (e.g., knowing this helps us interpret Matthew 5:33). This doesn't let us off the hook, but it does

---

15. David E. Garland, *Mark*, The NIV Application Commentary (Grand Rapids: Zondervan, 1996), 333.

mean that we are to live like kingdom citizens with the help of our community.

Finally, we can live the Story by taking a fresh look at Jesus' miracles. We should never demand that God work a miracle for us to believe in him. Faith sometimes stands out as the reason that Jesus works a miracle, although not always; but Jesus' many miracles did not always produce faith in those who witnessed them (e.g., even the raising of Lazarus in John 11 produces mixed results). To demand miracles from God is to fall victim to one of the temptations Jesus faced in the wilderness—testing God rather than trusting him. But many of us are struggling with an opposite problem. Having been unduly influenced by a naturalistic worldview, we struggle to open ourselves to God's special activity in our lives and our churches. Have we withdrawn from the mystery of the miraculous into the comfortable confines of the materialistic and rationalistic?

Jesus should be our focus, not miracles, but the Spirit of Jesus continues to work miracles today and we should be open to them. Above all, Jesus' miracles should encourage us. They stand as God's concrete and tangible promises ("God's signature," some have said) that one day he will make things right. Jürgen Moltmann observes, "Jesus' healings are not supernatural miracles in a natural world. They are the only 'natural' things in a world that is unnatural, demonized, and wounded."[16] In other words, Jesus' miracles are visible reminders of the way things ought to be and will be one day when the kingdom of God has come in all its fullness.

> **Memory Verse**
>
> *Then he said to them all: "Whoever wants to be my disciple must deny themselves and take up their cross daily and follow me."*
> *(Luke 9:23)*

Wrapping Up

Jesus begins his public ministry by proclaiming the arrival of the kingdom of God (Mark 1:14–15). He calls people to repent and believe the good news. To enter the kingdom, people must become disciples or followers of Jesus. The kingdom revolution takes shape as Jesus forms a new community, teaches with authority, and works miracles. Over the first year or so, Jesus' kingdom revolution grows in popularity. As people are taught, fed, healed, delivered, and some even raised from the dead, they are faced with a choice: accept or reject Jesus as God's Messiah. That choice continues to this day.

---

16. Jürgen Moltmann, *The Way of Jesus Christ* (Minneapolis: Augsburg Fortress, 1995), 99.

Digging Deeper

Books

Blomberg, Craig L. *Interpreting the Parables*. Downers Grove, IL: InterVarsity Press, 1990.

Keener, Craig S. *Miracles: The Credibility of the New Testament Accounts*. 2 vols. Grand Rapids: Baker, 2011.

Snodgrass, Klyne. *Stories with Intent: A Comprehensive Guide to the Parables of Jesus*. Grand Rapids: Eerdmans, 2008.

Stein, Robert H. *The Method and Message of Jesus' Teaching*. Louisville: Westminster John Knox, 1994.

Stott, John R. W. *The Message of the Sermon on the Mount (Matthew 5–7)*. Downers Grove, IL: InterVarsity Press, 1978.

Wilkins, Michael J. *Following the Master: A Biblical Theology of Discipleship*. Grand Rapids: Zondervan, 1992.

ASSIGNMENTS

1. Study Jesus' Nazareth sermon in Luke 4:14–30. You might need to read a good commentary or two on that section of Luke's gospel (e.g., Darrell Bock in the Baker Exegetical series or Robert Stein in the New American Commentary series). Write a two-page explanation of why the people went from "praising him" to trying to kill him. What did Jesus say that was so offensive and radical?

2. Normally Jewish rabbis asked their disciples to center their lives in Torah, God's instructions found primarily in the first five books of the Old Testament. Jesus is different; he asks his disciples to center their lives in him. Study Matthew 11:28–30 and write a two-page paper explaining what he means in that passage. You might want to consult a good Bible commentary, such as the volumes by Craig Blomberg (New American Commentary) or Michael Wilkins (NIV Application Commentary).

3. In Matthew 5:17–20, the thesis paragraph of the Sermon on the Mount, Jesus says that he didn't come to abolish the Law and the Prophets but to fulfill them. Study Matthew 5:21–48 and complete the following chart for each of the six sections:

Matthew	Old Prohibition	Jesus' Fulfillment
5:21–26		
5:27–30		

Continued on next page

Matthew	Old Prohibition	Jesus' Fulfillment
5:31–32		
5:33–37		
5:38–42		
5:43–48		

4. Read through all the healing miracles mentioned above on p. 152 and ask a single question about each one: What role, if any, did faith play in the healing? Make a list of all your answers. Then write a concluding paragraph or two explaining the role of faith in the healing miracles of Jesus. Is it always present? Is it present in most or only some cases? When faith is present, whose faith is exercised?

CHRIST:
Jesus' Journey to Jerusalem

Chapter 13

Enter Here

I once attended a large church in a metropolitan area where a guy named Mike worked with homeless people. Over the years I observed Mike as he did the tiresome, thankless work of a true servant—providing food and shelter and sharing the good news of Jesus. He invested his life in serving people with few possessions and little hope. I once went to help out with a Sunday morning worship service and was blown away by how much those people loved Mike. They were captivated by his compassion. They were drawn to him as I imagined the "tax collectors and sinners" were drawn to Jesus.

As the Story of the Bible continues, we notice that Jesus has become extremely popular with the crowds. A unique part of his ministry is offering salvation to outcasts and sinners. He has truly developed a reputation as a "friend of sinners." But that popularity will soon start to fade to rejection as the conflict with the religious leaders escalates. Again, his ministry includes a year of obscurity when he starts his ministry, a year of popularity as he calls disciples, teaches, and works miracles, and a culminating final period of rejection.

This is a difficult chapter in the Story since God's plans and human expectations don't always coincide. Jesus' love for outcasts and sinners brings staunch opposition from the religious leaders. While he continues to teach and heal and feed the crowds, they are often more interested in a meal than in following him as Lord (see John 6:15, 26). Even his closest followers don't always get that Jesus came to be a Suffering-Servant Messiah. After reaffirming his destiny of dying on a cross for the sins of the world, Jesus begins the long journey to Jerusalem, where he will do just that.

Be Prepared

Read or listen to Mark 8–10; Luke 9–19; John 5–12.

The Story Continues

Jesus, a Friend of Sinners

More and more Jesus finds himself coming into conflict with the Jewish religious leaders. Along the way, he develops a reputation as a "friend of sinners" (Matt. 11:18–19; Luke 7:33–35). In that culture, the term "sinner" could refer to a person who opposes God's will (like the Samaritan woman we meet in John 4, who has been married five times and is now living with a man who is not her husband). But "sinner" could also describe a person who simply fails to measure up to the purity rules created by the religious leaders. These leaders invented a kind of religious game where they determined the winners and the losers; as a result, many people were deemed losers or outcasts, such as people with certain diseases or bodily deformities or dishonorable occupations or shameful pasts. These people had been permanently excluded from the religious and social life of Israel. They were spiritually and emotionally homeless.

Jesus breaks many of the traditional rules of piety in order to extend mercy to these outcasts. In one of his parables, the master instructs his servants to invite "the poor, the crippled, the blind and the lame" to the great banquet, symbolizing that the kingdom will be full of such believing outcasts (see Luke 14:15–24; cf. Matt. 22:1–14). To put it plainly, Jesus loves people more than empty ritual. Although he never compromises or makes excuses for their sinful behavior, Jesus purposefully extends compassion to outcasts. He touches lepers, dines with tax collectors, heals people on the Sabbath, relates to prostitutes, and habitually welcomes "sinners." They are drawn to him and feel comfortable around him. In Jesus, they see a glimmer of hope for a better life.

Often Jesus violates commonly accepted purity rules by eating with sinners. In that culture, sitting down for a meal with someone (referred to as "table fellowship") was significant because it implied that you accepted the person you were eating with. There are at least five occasions in the Gospels where Jesus enjoys table fellowship with outcasts — with Matthew the tax collector's friends (Matt. 9:9–13); with Simon the leper (Matt. 26:6–13); at a meal when he is anointed by a sinful woman (Luke 7:36–50); at a meal where he heals a sick man (Luke 14:1–6); with Zacchaeus, a chief tax collector (Luke 19:1–10).

There are many other places in Scripture where we see Jesus befriending sinners. In Luke 15:1–2 we read, "Now the tax collectors and sinners were all gathering around to hear Jesus. But the Pharisees and the teachers of the law muttered, 'This man welcomes sinners and eats with them.'" Jesus then tells three parables about finding what has been lost — a lost sheep, a lost coin, and a lost son (prodigal son). At the end of each parable there is a statement about how joyful God becomes when one lost person is found (see Luke 15:7, 10, 32).

By reaching out to sinners and other outcasts, Jesus is shouting something about the way the kingdom works. God graciously opens the doors of the kingdom to those who recognize their own sinfulness and their need for God. As Jesus himself says, "It is not the healthy who need a doctor, but the sick.

Associating with the Wrong Kind of People?

"If anything is plain in Jesus' life, it's that he welcomed the wrong kind of people. To start a movement he ought to have looked for good people with influence—professionals and theologians and community leaders, among others. Instead, Jesus consistently ate with sinners and tax collectors. Prostitutes wept over him and cleaned his feet with their hair. One of his Twelve he picked directly from the tax collecting booth, where only traitors and quislings could be found.

"When the Pharisees criticized him for these associations, Jesus made no apology. On the contrary, he implied that the Pharisees were in trouble because they thought themselves too good for such company.

"This was Jesus' persistent criticism of his beloved Israel. They had developed a pessimistically separatist outlook on the world. They had become a family that only socialized with family because the neighborhood had become too dangerous. They had become like Christians who attend Christian schools not because they value a Christian education, but because they fear the contamination of non-Christians.

"Jesus was an optimist, not in the sense that he thought the world a good and pleasant place, but in that he knew God's influence would work outward, anywhere. It was yeast, spreading through the dough. It was the mustard seed, growing mysteriously from a tiny seed into a great bush. So Jesus refused to exclude. Rather he pulled people in.... He believed and practiced that 'the one who is in you is greater than the one who is in the world' " (1 John 4:4).[1]

— TIM STAFFORD

But go and learn what this means: 'I desire mercy, not sacrifice.' For I have not come to call the righteous, but sinners" (Matt. 9:12–13).

Jesus Encounters Stiff Opposition

Unless we read the Story carefully, we might get the impression that Jesus always pleases everyone, never gets upset, and never hurts anyone's feelings. But the Story suggests that Jesus was much more than a first-century "Mr. Nice Guy." Throughout the Gospels Jesus stays embroiled in controversy. Yet we can easily neglect or ignore this significant aspect of his ministry.

The Story tells us that Jesus faces opposition from four main groups. First, as you might expect, he is opposed by Satan and the demonic. This conflict appears most clearly in the temptation accounts (Mark 1:12–13; Matt. 4:1–11; Luke 4:1–13), but it surfaces repeatedly throughout his ministry. Occasionally the demons will even publicly acknowledge Jesus as the "Holy One of God" or "Son of God" and beg for mercy (Mark 1:24; 5:7).

Second, somewhat surprisingly, Jesus also faces rejection from his own family. On one occasion as Jesus returns home after selecting his twelve apostles, his own family thinks he is "out of his mind" (Mark 3:21). This hometown rejection

---

1. Tim Stafford, *Surprised by Jesus* (Downers Grove, IL: InterVarsity Press, 2006), 90–92.

must have been difficult to take (Matt. 13:53–58; Mark 6:1–6). In the end, many of his family members put their faith in him as Lord and Messiah, but in the meantime, Jesus redefines "family" in spiritual terms as anyone who "does the will of my Father" (see Matt. 12:46–50; Mark 3:31–35; Luke 8:19–21).

Third, Jesus' own disciples resist his rescue plan. Three times in Mark's gospel Jesus predicts his own suffering and death (Mark 8:31–32a; 9:31; 10:32–34). His followers are expecting the Messiah to overthrow pagan governments, conquer enemies, and establish God's kingdom on earth. As a result, they insist Jesus is wrong when he predicts his coming death (Mark 8:32–33). Jesus patiently teaches his followers to take the long view and see his death as God's way of defeating evil and establishing the kingdom (Mark 8:33–38). Of course, the most famous case of opposition from a disciple is Jesus' betrayal by Judas Iscariot, which results in Jesus' arrest, trials, torture, and death.

Fourth, Jesus faces his strongest opposition from the Jewish religious leaders. In Mark's gospel, almost every chapter contains examples of such conflict:

- 2:1–12: for claiming to forgive sins (considered blasphemy)
- 2:13–17: for eating with sinners and tax collectors (table fellowship)
- 2:23–28: for allowing his disciples to pick heads of grain on the Sabbath
- 3:1–6: for healing a man on the Sabbath
- 3:22: over their belief that he drives out demons by Satan's power
- 7:1–23: for allowing his disciples to eat without ceremonial washings
- 8:11–13: testing Jesus by asking for a sign
- 10:2–12: testing Jesus by asking about the legality of divorce
- 11:11–19: for cleansing the temple
- 11:27–33: for claiming to have authority from God
- 12:1–12: for speaking the parable of the tenants against them
- 12:13–17: testing Jesus by asking about paying taxes to Caesar
- 12:18–27: testing Jesus by asking about the resurrection
- 12:38–40: for warning against the Jewish religious leaders
- 14:1–2: looking for a sly way to arrest and kill Jesus

In John's gospel the theme of opposition and conflict builds in chapters 5–12, eventually resulting in Jesus' crucifixion:

- 5:1–18: for healing a man on the Sabbath and calling God his own Father
- 5:19–47: follow-up conflict related to this healing
- 6:41–59: for claiming to be the bread of life from heaven
- 7:1–52: the Jewish leaders look for a way to kill Jesus
- 8:12–59: for his claims (light of the world, sent from the Father, from above, teaching the truth, Abraham's superior)
- 9:1–41: for healing the man born blind on the Sabbath

- 10:1–21: Jesus is the good shepherd while the religious leaders are wolves
- 10:22–42: for blasphemy, claiming unity with the Father (equality with God)
- 11:1–54: for raising Lazarus from the dead (seventh sign in John's gospel)
- 12:1–50: for his authoritative words and miraculous ministry

Jesus clashes with the religious leaders because his view of the kingdom of God differs radically from theirs. In short, Jesus believes that God desires to reign over all creation, including the human heart. God wants to transform the whole person so that the entire community of God's people reflects his character. In contrast, the religious leaders' strategy is to create an extensive web of rules to protect against the surrounding pagan culture, a self-centered strategy that ultimately fails to change the human heart and fulfill God's purposes.

A Turning Point: Peter's Confession

We are familiar with turning points in life. We know about critical moments in developing relationships, in careers, in sporting events, in investments, in new church starts, in movies, and so on. Turning points are real, and they are undeniably important. Many would say that the turning point of Jesus' ministry is Peter's confession of Jesus as the Christ (Messiah) and Jesus' follow-up teaching on the kind of Messiah he came to be and what it means to follow him (Mark 8:27–37).

In this pivotal moment, we see a clash of expectations. Peter and the rest of the disciples expect Jesus to be "the Christ" in a way that will benefit and empower them. They are ready to march to Jerusalem and set up the kingdom. Perhaps without even realizing it, they expect Jesus to do whatever they want. But Jesus isn't about to be domesticated. When it comes to expectations, they must be met or changed or there will be conflict. Let's see what happens in this episode.

> ### A Fighting Messiah
>
> "Jesus would not be taking up arms against the Romans; instead his own arms would in due course be stretched out on a Roman cross."[2]
>
> – PETER WALKER

During the final year of his ministry (likely AD 29), Jesus takes his disciples to the northern part of Israel, to the villages of Caesarea Philippi. (Perhaps Jesus thought it best to withdraw in order to prepare himself and his disciples for the return trip to the Holy City, where he would suffer and die for the sins of the world.) On the way, he asks them what the crowds are saying about him (Mark 8:27). They report that the people believe him to be a prophet, like John the Baptist or Elijah (Mark 8:28). Then Jesus drops the million-dollar question: "But what about you? Who do you say I am?" (The word "you" is plural, meaning that Jesus directs the question to the entire group.) Peter quickly answers for the group, "You are the Messiah" (Mark 8:29). Always careful not to entrust himself to human expectations, Jesus promptly warns them not to

---

2. Peter Walker, *In the Steps of Jesus* (Grand Rapids: Zondervan, 2007), 94.

Few Who Love the Cross

"Jesus has always many who love His heavenly kingdom, but few who bear His cross. He has many who desire consolation, but few who care for trial. He finds many to share His table, but few to take part in His fasting. All desire to be happy with Him; few wish to suffer anything for Him. Many follow Him to the breaking of bread, but few to the drinking of the chalice of His passion. Many revere His miracles; few approach the shame of the Cross. Many love Him as long as they encounter no hardship; many praise and bless Him as long as they receive some comfort from Him. But if Jesus hides Himself and leaves them for a while, they fall either into complaints or into deep dejection. Those, on the contrary, who love Him for His own sake and not for any comfort of their own, bless Him in all trial and anguish of heart as well as in the bliss of consolation. Even if He should never give them consolation, yet they would continue to praise Him and wish always to give Him thanks. What power there is in pure love for Jesus—love that is free from all self-interest and self-love!"[3]

— THOMAS À KEMPIS

tell anyone just yet (Mark 8:30). Later, the early church will confess "Jesus is the Christ," but timing is important for doing things God's way.

Jesus then plainly tells his followers that as God's Messiah or Deliverer, he "must suffer many things and be rejected by the elders, the chief priests and the teachers of the law, and that he must be killed and after three days rise again" (Mark 8:31). While Peter gives the right answer, he and the others fail to grasp exactly how Jesus will bring about God's reign. As a result, Peter pulls Jesus aside and begins to rebuke him (8:32). Peter no doubt envisions a dramatic victory in a climactic battle, followed by a glorious earthly kingdom where he will serve as a member of Jesus' inner circle. He simply cannot conceive of a "crucified Christ."

This is a crucial moment for Jesus and a matter of life and death for the whole world. Peter is telling Jesus to avoid the cross, the very thing Satan tempted him to do earlier in his ministry. Will Jesus give in to the temptation and go along with his disciples' expectations, or will he stay the course in obedience to the Father? We don't have to wait long for an answer. Peter's idea of Messiah is too small, too human, and too selfish. By opposing God's plan to save the world through the death and resurrection of the Messiah, Peter has lined up with Satan. So Jesus quickly turns and looks at the entire group before rebuking Peter: "'Get behind me, Satan!' he said. 'You do not have in mind the concerns of God, but merely human concerns'" (Mark 8:33).

Jesus then turns his attention to what it means to follow this kind of Messiah (Mark 8:34–37). He calls the entire crowd together to explain his demands for disciples. Everyone is invited to follow Jesus, but not everyone is willing to accept Jesus' terms.

---

3. Thomas à Kempis, *Imitation of Christ* 2.11.

Encouragement from Heaven: The Transfiguration

Peter's confession of Jesus as the "Christ" is a major turning point in Jesus' ministry and the disciples' faith journey. That episode concludes with Jesus speaking these words: "Truly I tell you, some who are standing here will not taste death before they see that the kingdom of God has come with power" (Mark 9:1). Then, and this is rare in the Gospels, a time reference is given that clearly connects Peter's confession to Jesus' transfiguration — "after six days" (Matt. 17:1; Mark 9:2). The transfiguration will definitely provide the disciples with a much-needed preview of kingdom glory.

Jesus takes Peter, James, and John — his inner circle — up on a high mountain. Since Caesarea Philippi is located at the base of Mount Hermon, a snow-covered peak that reaches over 9,000 feet in elevation, this is probably the place. These core leaders were also with him when he raised Jairus's daughter from the dead (Mark 5:37) and will later accompany him to the garden of Gethsemane the night before his death (Mark 14:33). Perhaps even more than the others, Peter needs to see and hear what is about to happen on this high mountain.

We are told that Jesus was "transfigured before them" so that his "face shone like the sun, and his clothes became as white as the light" (Matt. 17:2). The word translated "transfigured" (*metamorphoō*) means to be physically and visibly transformed. Rather than imagining a light shining brightly on Jesus, the idea here is that brilliant, glorious light radiates out from within Jesus. This is a temporary glorification of Jesus. Here we glimpse his divine glory, the glory he had before the creation of the world (Phil. 2:5–7) and the glory he will display again at his second coming (Dan. 7:13–14; Matt. 24:30). In this way, the transfiguration foreshadows the return of Jesus in the last days.

Motivated by fear (Mark 9:6), Peter devises a plan to build three shelters, one each for Jesus, Moses, and Elijah, thereby lowering Jesus to the level of these famous servants (Matt. 17:4). God interrupts Peter's ramblings to speak again about Jesus' identity and mission. God reminds the disciples that his plan centers on Jesus and they need to listen to him, even when he talks about suffering and dying (Matt. 17:5–9):

> While he was still speaking, a bright cloud covered them, and a voice from the cloud said, "This is my Son, whom I love; with him I am well pleased. Listen to him!"
>
> When the disciples heard this, they fell facedown to the ground, terrified. But Jesus came and touched them. "Get up," he said. "Don't be afraid." When they looked up, they saw no one except Jesus.
>
> As they were coming down the mountain, Jesus instructed them, "Don't tell anyone what you have seen, until the Son of Man has been raised from the dead."

If we read Peter's confession and Jesus' transfiguration together (as we should), what do we see? Jesus is the Christ, the King! Peter got that part right. But when Jesus announces that he will be the crucified Christ, the Suffering Servant—an idea that doesn't match Peter's expectations—Peter rebukes him. In response Jesus rebukes Peter for failing to accept God's ways and plans. Then a short time later Jesus is transfigured before them. They see a preview of the glory of the Son of God. On the mountain, out of the cloud, God himself speaks and tells Peter and the other disciples to change their expectations and listen to Jesus!

Jesus' Journey to Jerusalem

Jesus has made it clear that his mission is to suffer and die in order to set people free from their sins and offer them a relationship with God. Three times in Mark's gospel Jesus predicts his passion or suffering: 8:31–32; 9:31–32; 10:32–34. Each time the disciples respond with pride and ignorance. Peter rebukes Jesus (8:33), they argue about which one is the greatest disciple (9:33–34), and they maneuver for the most important positions in the kingdom (10:35–41). After each of the three responses, Jesus teaches them what it means to follow him. Followers of Jesus have their own cross to bear (8:34–38), they are last rather than first (9:35–37), and they are servants rather than masters (10:41–44). This leads Jesus to proclaim in Mark 10:45 (the theme verse of that gospel) that "even the Son of Man did not come to be served, but to serve, and to give his life as a ransom for many." Jesus is a Suffering-Servant King. In Jerusalem he will suffer and die, and to Jerusalem he must go.

Jesus' "journey to Jerusalem" lies at the heart of Luke's gospel. The journey begins in Luke 9:51 and runs through 19:44. That journey doesn't take a straight path to the Holy City. For example, in 10:38–42 he is in Bethany (just a short distance from Jerusalem), while later on he passes between Samaria and Galilee in the northern part of the country (see 17:11). We shouldn't imagine a strict timetable or schedule either. We call it a "journey" in a general sense to describe the phase of Jesus' ministry leading up to the final week. Although he travels in a roundabout way, Jesus' ultimate goal is Jerusalem, where he will fulfill God's plan to be a Suffering-Servant King. It is a journey of divine destiny.

Later in the book of Acts, the Christian movement will be described simply as "the Way" (Acts 9:2; 19:9, 23; 24:14, 22). It's almost as if Jesus' final journey to the Holy City becomes a pattern for the spiritual journey mapped out for his disciples. On the way, Jesus talks about loving God, about our mission to this world, about commitment in the face of opposition, about generosity, about prayer and forgiveness, about serving each other, about looking for Christ's

Mine Eyes Have Seen the Glory

"For we did not follow cleverly devised stories when we told you about the coming of our Lord Jesus Christ in power, but we were eyewitnesses of his majesty. He received honor and glory from God the Father when the voice came to him from the Majestic Glory, saying, 'This is my Son, whom I love; with him I am well pleased.' We ourselves heard this voice that came from heaven when we were with him on the sacred mountain."

– 2 PETER 1:16 – 18

return, about suffering, and much more. He teaches his followers many things about "the Way" on his way to give his life as a ransom for many.

Making Connections

Let's review where we are in the Great Story:

Creation and Crisis
Covenant
Calling Out
Commandments
Conquest and Canaanization
Creation of the Kingdom
Communion and Common Sense
Crumbling of the Kingdom
Captivity and Coming Home
Interlude: Time between the Testaments
➤ **Christ:**
    Jesus Enters Our World
    Jesus' Message
    Jesus' Journey to Jerusalem
    Jesus Dies on the Cross
    Jesus Is Raised from the Dead
Church
Consummation

God has always had a heart of compassion for outcasts. Perhaps you'll remember from the first part of the Story characters such as Ruth the Moabite or Rahab the harlot, who protected the spies, or the widow in Sidon who ministered to Elijah, or Namaan the Syrian, who was cleansed by Elisha. There are even four women mentioned in the genealogy of Jesus, something highly unusual in Jewish ancestries (Matt. 1:1–17). God desires to show mercy to the weak and helpless, and he even uses them to carry out his plans. Jesus continues that tradition.

Jesus' reference to the poor, crippled, blind, and lame in the parable of the great banquet mentioned earlier echoes Isaiah 35:5–6, which portrays the ultimate return from exile for the people of God:

Then will the eyes of the blind be opened
    and the ears of the deaf unstopped.
Then will the lame leap like a deer,
    and the mute tongue shout for joy.
Water will gush forth in the wilderness
    and streams in the desert.

In addition, some see Jesus' invitation to those who live out on the "roads and country lanes" in that same parable (Luke 14:23) as a reference to the inclusion of Gentiles among the people of God. This is not the first time that we have heard about the inclusion of non-Jews in God's Great Story. Take, for example, Isaiah 25:6–8:

> On this mountain the LORD Almighty will prepare
>   a feast of rich food for all peoples,
> a banquet of aged wine—
>   the best of meats and the finest of wines.
> On this mountain he will destroy
>   the shroud that enfolds all peoples,
> the sheet that covers all nations;
>   he will swallow up death forever.
> The Sovereign LORD will wipe away the tears
>   from all faces;
> he will remove his people's disgrace
>   from all the earth.

By sharing meals with "sinners," Jesus is announcing that he is continuing what God had in mind from the beginning, the welcoming of repentant people into his family no matter what their ethnicity or gender or income level or scandalous past. Even in the days of the Mosaic covenant, God desired "mercy, not sacrifice, and acknowledgment of God rather than burnt offerings" (Hos. 6:6; Matt. 9:13; cf. 1 Sam. 15:22). Jesus' practice regarding table fellowship also points forward to the great messianic banquet at the end of the age (Matt. 8:10–11; Luke 13:28–30).

Jesus' clash with religious leaders stems largely from their contrasting views about who belongs in God's kingdom. Unlike the religious leaders of his day, who seem to favor a quarantine approach to righteousness, Jesus does not fear being corrupted by sinners. He knows that God's grace and power can transform a person from guilt and shame to forgiveness and freedom, no matter how shady their past. As Jesus himself said, "It is not the healthy who need a doctor, but the sick" (Matt. 9:12). To the religious leaders, a "sick" person is one who fails to measure up to certain standards of piety, but Jesus describes them as blind to their own sinful condition and full of hypocrisy. As the Great Physician, Jesus didn't come into this world to avoid sinful people but to be near them in order to bring healing.

As Jesus journeys to Jerusalem, a definite turning point is Peter's confession and Jesus' transfiguration a week later. The unusual appearance of Moses and Elijah at the transfiguration suggests to some that Jesus is the fulfillment of the Law (Moses) and the Prophets (Elijah). Others associate Moses and Elijah with the beginning of the messianic age so that their presence confirms the arrival of the kingdom of God with Jesus (Mal. 4:4–6). Interestingly, both

Moses and Elijah had visions of God on a mountain—on Mount Sinai and Mount Horeb respectively (Ex. 24:15; 1 Kings 19:8–16).

The physical location of a mountain (often used in Matthew to signal key spiritual events—Matt. 4:8; 5:1; 14:23; 15:29; 17:1; 21:1; 24:3; 26:30; 28:16) and the presence of a cloud (often connected to God's glorious presence—Ex. 19:16–19) highlight the significance of the moment. Only two times in the Synoptic Gospels do we hear God speaking directly, and both times he says almost the same thing:

- Matthew 3:17 (Jesus' baptism): "This is my Son, whom I love; with him I am well pleased."
- Matthew 17:5 (Jesus' transfiguration): "This is my Son, whom I love; with him I am well pleased. Listen to him!"

As we noted earlier, "This is my Son" is from Psalm 2:7, a royal psalm first applied to King David and read at the coronation of the kings of Israel. Jesus is the King. The phrase "with him I am well pleased" is likely from Isaiah 42:1, the first of four servant songs. Jesus is also a suffering servant. Then at the transfiguration the heavenly voice adds one short phrase from Deuteronomy 18:15, "Listen to him!" Here the Father is speaking primarily to Peter, James, and John (and the rest of the disciples). They are well intentioned and, yes, Jesus is the Messiah, but they are wrong in trying to deter him from going to Jerusalem to die on the cross. Jesus is right, they are wrong, and they should "listen to him." Jesus is not only the victorious Lion; he is also the sacrificial Lamb (Rev. 5:5–6). He will suffer, die, and be raised from the dead. The disciples need to listen to him as he unveils and lives out God's plan and to adjust their expectations accordingly.

Jesus' Journey to Jerusalem		
Luke 9:51–53	**Mile Markers**	**Luke 19:41–44**
⁵¹As the time approached for him to be taken up to heaven, Jesus resolutely set out for *Jerusalem*. ⁵²And he sent messengers on ahead, who went into a Samaritan village to get things ready for him; ⁵³but the people there did not welcome him, because he was heading for *Jerusalem*.	13:22 13:33–34 17:11 18:31–33 19:11 19:28	⁴¹As he approached *Jerusalem* and saw the city, he wept over it ⁴²and said, "If you, even you, had only known on this day what would bring you peace—but now it is hidden from your eyes. ⁴³The days will come upon you when your enemies will build an embankment against you and encircle you and hem you in on every side. ⁴⁴They will dash you to the ground, you and the children within your walls. They will not leave one stone on another, because you did not recognize the time of God's coming to you."

Jesus journeys to Jerusalem because, as he puts it, "surely no prophet can die outside of Jerusalem!" (Luke 13:33). The Holy City had a reputation for killing its prophets. The prophet Uriah was killed by King Jehoiakim in Jerusalem (Jer. 26:20–23). Zechariah also died in Jerusalem (2 Chron. 24:20–22; Luke 11:51). They tried to kill the prophet Jeremiah in the city (Jer. 38:4–6), and later traditions claim that Isaiah was murdered in Jerusalem.[4] The historian Josephus reports that King Manasseh "barbarously slew all the righteous men that were among the Hebrews; nor would he spare the prophets, for he every day slew some of them, till Jerusalem was overflown with blood."[5] In the early days of the church, Stephen is stoned to death in Jerusalem (Acts 6:8–8:1). Shortly before he dies, he speaks prophetically to the religious leaders of the city:

> "You stiff-necked people! Your hearts and ears are still uncircumcised. You are just like your ancestors: You always resist the Holy Spirit! Was there ever a prophet your ancestors did not persecute? They even killed those who predicted the coming of the Righteous One. And now you have betrayed and murdered him." (Acts 7:51–52)

As the Prophet, Jesus journeys to Jerusalem to accomplish his sacrificial mission. Jerusalem for first-century Jews was like Washington, D.C., to Americans, London to the English, and Rome to the Italians. It was the center of their nation and the temple was the center of the city, the very place where they believed the presence of God resided. Jesus goes to Jerusalem to make Israel choose: Will they accept him as their king on his terms of sacrificial love, or reject him as king and attempt to fight the Romans with military and political weapons? We know the outcome. Israel rejects Jesus as king and it spells the end of their nation. In AD 70, the Romans destroy Jerusalem and its temple, reducing the place to a pile of rubble. God's original plan was to bless Israel so that Israel would bless all nations, but that plan is dead (Gen. 12:1–3). The nation had chosen unwisely by rejecting their king.

But God is beyond brilliant in his sovereign plan. By obediently and lovingly traveling to the cross, Jesus absorbs their sinfulness and sets them free for a relationship with God. The verdict of condemnation and execution is reversed by God when he raises Jesus from the dead. And some Jews take Jesus up on his offer of forgiveness and life. These followers of Jesus the Messiah constitute the true Israel, and as we will see in the book of Acts, they will journey away from Jerusalem on a mission to take the gospel to all nations.

---

4. G. K. Beale and D. A. Carson, *Commentary on the New Testament Use of the Old Testament* (Grand Rapids: Baker, 2007), 336.

5. Josephus, *Antiquities* 10.3.8 (William Whiston, *The Works of Josephus: Complete and Unabridged* [Peabody: Hendrickson, 1996]).

Living the Story

We can live this portion of the Great Story in the following ways. First, Jesus reminds us to make people a priority over certain religious rules and practices. We are shaped by our religious traditions, and in our passion to demonstrate piety, we often lose sight of the original purpose of it all.

For example, God created the Sabbath to provide human beings an opportunity to recover. The divinely designed rhythm of creation is engagement followed by recovery. We work hard most of the time and we rest some of the time. The Jewish leaders developed rules and traditions to guard the Sabbath, a worthy goal it appears. But when Jesus heals people on the Sabbath, the religious leaders strongly object. In one particular instance after healing a man on the Sabbath, Jesus asks, "Which is lawful on the Sabbath: to do good or to do evil, to save life or to kill?" (Mark 3:4; cf. John 9). Jesus reminds us that compassion and mercy are often better guides to God's will than purity rituals demanded by religious experts.

This also relates to how we connect with "outcasts" and "sinners." On this issue, Jesus clearly favors the transformation approach over the quarantine approach. Although the danger of worldliness is real (1 John 2:15–17), Jesus shows that it is possible to befriend sinners without embracing or endorsing their sinful ways—not easy, but possible. Many Christians grow up in such an insulated environment that they fail to acknowledge that unbelievers are first and foremost human beings created in God's image and loved by God. By eating with "sinners," Jesus wasn't endorsing their rebellious ways, but he was willing to be misunderstood in order to extend God's grace and forgiveness.

Jesus doesn't classify people and then reject some up front, and neither should we. It's easy to want to reach out to people who are attractive, well mannered, financially secure—the so-called "good people." But Jesus teaches us not to classify people as "redeemable" and "irredeemable" before getting to know them. All of us are spiritually sick and we can do nothing to fix our own lives. All of us stand in desperate need of God's grace and mercy.

A third application is also related. We see in this passage that the way Jesus extends hope is by publicly interacting with tax collectors and sinners. In the story from Matthew 9, Jesus doesn't go to Matthew's house merely to have fun with a bunch of crazy people. Some have taken Jesus' example as permission to engage in a solo ministry in a strip club or to hang out in bars to party it up with "sinners." We need to read the text carefully and apply it wisely. Jesus

---

Do We Only Love a Certain Kind of Person?

"When we choose to be a servant, we give up the right to be in charge. There is a great freedom in this.... When we choose to be a servant, we surrender the right to decide who and when we will serve. We become available and vulnerable."[6]

– RICHARD J. FOSTER

---

6. Richard J. Foster, *Celebration of Discipline*, 25th anniversary ed. (San Francisco: HarperSanFrancisco, 2003), 132.

Humility in Action

"We have forgotten how to flex two mental muscles at the same time: the muscle of moral conviction and the muscle of compassion to all regardless of their morality. Secular society no less than religion often operates on a narrow-minded logic: you can only love those whose lives you approve of. You can only be friends with people who agree with you. The logic can take you in two directions. The religious version reduces the number of people it loves—to match the few lifestyles it approves. The secular version increases the number of lifestyles it approves to the point of accepting virtually everything. . . .

"In both cases the logic is the same: you can only love those whose lives you approve of. But there are weaknesses in both incarnations of the logic. The weakness of the religious version is its inability to show compassion beyond the borders of its moral convictions. The weakness of the secular version is a loss of nerve about what's right and wrong in the first place.

"But there is a third way, based on a different logic. It's where we learn to respect and care even for those with whom we profoundly disagree. We maintain our convictions but choose never to allow them to become justification for thinking ourselves better than those with contrary convictions. We move beyond mere tolerance to true humility, the key to harmony at the social level."[7]

– JOHN DICKSON

gathers with Matthew and his friends primarily to celebrate Matthew's conversion. Matthew wants his friends to meet Jesus and to be forgiven by him, just as he had been. Notice also that Jesus "and his disciples" gather at Matthew's house (Matt. 9:10). In other words, Jesus was part of a "ministry team," so to speak. Jesus interacted with these "tax collectors and sinners" publicly but not in a setting so dark and evil that his message could not be heard at all.

Nevertheless, most of us struggle with the opposite tendency. We avoid any kind of interaction with outcasts and sinners. Jesus calls us to share his compassion for people, to empathize deeply with them, and get close enough to them to offer the healing grace of God. Instead of fearing sinners or running from them, we need to be willing to eat with them, to listen to them, and to relate to them as real human beings. Rather than simply bringing people to church, we need to bring Jesus to people. Sure there will be awkward, uncomfortable moments, but our Great Physician Lord calls us to break out of the religious quarantine and enter the sick ward of this world. He is already at work there, waiting for us to assist him.

An important way we can live this part of the Story relates to what the disciples learned from their confession-transfiguration experience. They rightly confess Jesus as the Christ, but they have a hard time dealing with his plan to be a crucified Christ. They had always expected the Messiah to walk a different, more glorious, road. On the mountain, the Father simply tells the disciples

---

7. John Dickson, *Humilitas* (Grand Rapids: Zondervan, 2011), 169–70.

to "listen" to Jesus (Matt. 17:5; Mark 9:7; Luke 9:35). Listening to Jesus lies at the heart of what it means to follow Jesus. His way is different from the world's way. Our task is not to redefine Jesus (found in Peter's words in Matt. 16:22: "This shall never happen to you") or to build another religious system (again, Peter's plan to build three shelters), but to listen to Jesus. In our hurried, noisy, distracted society, however, listening is easier said than done. Listening stretches our faith. It calls us to resist the quick fix, to move past our fears, and to let God alter our expectations about how he should do things. We must listen to what Jesus has revealed to us in order to please God.

Wrapping Up

Jesus has become popular with the crowds. They are captivated by his authoritative teaching, encouraged by his compassion, and helped by his miracles. Jesus even offers salvation to outcasts and sinners, an unconventional move that puts him in direct conflict with the religious leaders. As his popularity begins to diminish, Jesus takes his disciples away to talk about who he is and what he came to do. Led by the apostle Peter, the disciples understand that Jesus is the Christ (or Messiah), but they fail to understand that he came to deliver people by dying on a cross and being raised from the dead rather than forming an army and fighting the Romans. At Jesus' transfiguration, the Father clarifies Jesus' mission for the disciples and directs them to "listen to him," advice that all Jesus-followers should take seriously.

Memory Verse

"For the Son of Man came to seek and to save the lost." (Luke 19:10)

Digging Deeper

Books

Blomberg, Craig A. *Contagious Holiness: Jesus' Meals with Sinners*. NSBT. Downers Grove, IL: InterVarsity Press, 2005.

Bock, Darrell L. *Luke 9:51–24:53*. Baker Exegetical Commentary. Grand Rapids: Baker, 1996.

Yancey, Philip. *The Jesus I Never Knew*. Grand Rapids: Zondervan, 1995.

ASSIGNMENTS

1. A crucial turning point from popularity to rejection occurs in John 6 with the feeding of the five thousand and the bread-of-life teaching that follows. As you read through this whole episode, pretend that you are in the crowd on both of those days. Write a two-page personal reflection on what Jesus says and does and how it affects you emotionally as you wrestle with following him as Messiah.

2. Look up each of the following passages that speak about Jesus' having table fellowship with outcasts and sinners: Matthew 9:9 – 13; 26:6 – 13; Luke 7:36 – 50; 14:1 – 6; 19:1 – 10. As you think about all the episodes, answer the following questions: (a) Why does it upset the religious leaders so much that Jesus associates with these people? (b) How is Jesus changing the rules of their religious game? (c) Who are the outcasts in your world? (d) What can we learn from Jesus about befriending sinners without embracing or endorsing their sinful ways?

3. Read about Jesus' harsh rebuke of the religious leaders in Matthew 23. Develop a master chart or find some other way of summarizing the following: (a) What does Jesus accuse them of doing wrong or failing to do right? (b) What relational damage results from their hypocrisy? (c) What does Jesus advise them to do instead?

4. Study Mark 8:34 – 37. Explain the meaning of the three demands Jesus makes on those who want to follow him (see the last part of Mark 8:34). What do these phrases really mean? Also, explain the reason Jesus gives in 8:35 – 37 why people should accept those demands and become his disciples. How does following Jesus fulfill people's expectations in a paradoxical manner?

5. In Jesus' journey to Jerusalem (Luke 9:51 – 19:44), it's possible that the theme of "listen to him" plays a prominent role. Read Luke 9:51 – 19:44 carefully and find every place where the "listen to him" theme appears. You are not looking for the words "listen to him" so much as the idea of accepting Jesus' way of doing things, of following Jesus as Messiah. Then write a concluding paragraph in which you explain whether or not you think this is the overarching theme of this central section of Luke's gospel.

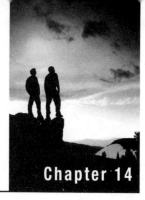

CHRIST:
Jesus Dies on the Cross

Chapter 14

Enter Here

A spider lives somewhere on the outside of Zach's Chevy truck. I'm honored to have Zach as a son-in-law, and he recently showed me a beautiful new spiderweb on the tailgate of his truck. Zach said that every morning the mystery spider produces a brand-new, masterful web just in time for him to wipe it away before work. While this may seem like an odd analogy, you could compare the Story to a spiderweb (although not one that is wiped away). Spiderwebs are beautiful, intricate works of art, displaying a myriad of connections all pointing to a unifying center. The point of the comparison is the center, both of the web and of the Story.

Think of this chapter and the next (on the cross and resurrection of Jesus Christ) as the center of the Story. The Gospels devote a large amount of space to the final week of Jesus' earthly life. Almost half of the gospel of John, for instance, focuses on what happened during Jesus' last week. Although we can do little more than survey this part of the Story because of its depth and intensity, even a simple overview makes a deep impact on us and leaves us much to think about. It's no exaggeration to say that what happened during these last few days in Jerusalem over 2,000 years ago is the climactic center of the Story. Although the Story doesn't end there, the cross and resurrection of Jesus stand as the center of human history.

Be Prepared

Read or listen to Matthew 19–27; Luke 20–23; John 11–19.

The Story Continues

The Raising of Lazarus

In the spring of AD 30 (or perhaps AD 33), near the time of the Jewish Passover, Jesus finally arrives in Jerusalem. He comes first to Bethany, a small village just under two miles away, to check on his friend Lazarus, who has taken ill. By the time Jesus arrives, Lazarus has died and his two grief-stricken sisters, Martha and Mary, turn to Jesus for help. We learn from listening in on the fascinating conversations between Jesus and the sisters recorded in John 11 that Jesus is Lord over both life and death. Angry at death and what it has done to his friends, Jesus raises Lazarus from the dead.

This miracle, the seventh "sign" in John's gospel, is the most dramatic and confrontational in the Gospels. Lazarus's resuscitation previews Jesus' own resurrection. The sheer power of the miracle persuades many of those who witness it to put their faith in Jesus (John 11:45). Ironically, however, the raising of Lazarus also causes the religious leaders to plot Jesus' death (John 11:46–57; 12:9–10). They are more convinced than ever that they must get rid of this troublemaker. By giving life, Jesus has sped up his own death.

The Triumphal Entry into Jerusalem

On the Saturday evening in Bethany just prior to Passion Week, a banquet celebration is held in Jesus' honor by his friends, including Lazarus and his sisters, Martha and Mary (John 12:2). In a humble act of worship, Mary anoints Jesus' feet with a bottle of expensive perfume and dries them with her hair. Although the thief Judas objects to the financial waste, Jesus honors her act of worship as a fitting preparation for his coming burial (12:7).

On Sunday morning Jesus enters Jerusalem, and his "triumphal entry" marks the beginning of Holy Week or Passion Week. Jesus descends the Mount of Olives into the city. This "mountain" held special significance because many believed that the Messiah would appear here in the last days (Zech. 14:4–5). Bethany was located to the east of the Mount of Olives (toward the desert). It only takes about twenty minutes to walk from the top of the Mount of Olives down into the center of Jerusalem. The population of Jerusalem swelled

The Seven "Signs" of John's Gospel

John uses the word "sign" (*sēmeion* in Greek) in the first half of his gospel to speak about events that inspire belief in Jesus (John 20:30–31). These mighty works of Jesus point beyond the miracles to Jesus' identity and mission. The seven signs are as follows:

1. Changing water into wine (2:1–11)
2. Healing the official's son (4:43–54)
3. Healing the lame man at Bethesda pool (5:1–15)
4. Feeding the five thousand (6:1–14)
5. Walking on water (6:16–21)
6. Healing the man born blind (9:1–12)
7. Raising Lazarus from the dead (11:1–44)

dramatically during Passover, and many want to see the man who has raised Lazarus from the dead (John 12:9–11). Messianic expectations are running sky high.

Jesus rides into Jerusalem not on a warhorse but on a humble donkey, fulfilling Zechariah's prophecy of a coming messianic king who would liberate the people:

> Rejoice greatly, Daughter Zion!
>   Shout, Daughter Jerusalem!
> See, your king comes to you,
>   righteous and victorious,
> lowly and riding on a donkey,
>   on a colt, the foal of a donkey. (Zech. 9:9; cf. Matt. 21:1–5)

Whereas earlier Jesus told his disciples not to reveal his identity as the Christ, now Jesus openly announces himself to the world. Jesus is the long-awaited Messiah! He is the King of the Jews. By entering on a donkey rather than a stallion, Jesus comes in humility to secure salvation. How ironic that Jesus' "triumphal entry" assumes a victory that will only come through his death on the cross. God's path to victory leads through sacrifice.

The large crowd no doubt includes a number of different groups — the Twelve, other followers of Jesus from the Jerusalem area such as Lazarus and his sisters, disciples from other places who are in the city for Passover, many curious onlookers who are not disciples of Jesus, and at least some Jewish religious leaders who are keeping tabs on Jesus (see Luke 19:39–40; John 12:19). Many of these people put their cloaks in the road ahead of the King as he descends the Mount of Olives into the city. Others lay palm branches in Jesus' path (John 12:13). This is why our church tradition refers to this Sunday as Palm Sunday. By this time, the palm branch had become a symbol of Jewish national pride and victory (see 1 Macc. 13:49–51; 2 Macc. 10:1–8).

The crowd keeps shouting, "Hosanna to the Son of David! Blessed is he who comes in the name of the Lord! Hosanna in the highest heaven!" (Matt. 21:9). The word "Hosanna" originally meant "God save us" (2 Sam. 14:4; 2 Kings 6:26), but by Jesus' day has become more of a general expression of praise to God. To refer to Jesus as the "Son of David" and the one "who comes in the name of the LORD" (Ps. 118:26) strongly suggests that many are acknowledging Jesus as the coming Messiah or Deliverer.

Their "prayer" will indeed be answered, but not in the manner they expect.

The King of Kings Rides a Donkey

"Donkeys are lowly ... slow, stubborn, the perennial work-animals of the poor ... we have Jesus as he wants to be seen: as Emmanuel, as the true God-with-us in a truly human way, at our level: God on a donkey."[1]

– FREDERICK BRUNER

---

1. Frederick Dale Bruner, *The Churchbook: Matthew 13–28* (Dallas: Word, 1990), 730.

The kingdom will be established not through military conquest but through suffering. They will be offered salvation from Satan and sin, enemies much greater than the Romans. But crowds can be fickle. Just a few days later when Jesus fails to deliver the kind of liberation they expect, the crowd will shout, "Crucify him" (Matt. 27:22).

Jesus knows that his entrance into the city will not only provide salvation, but will also bring judgment. Much that happens during Passion Week centers on judgment. He will judge the temple, the Jewish religious leaders, the nationalistic ambitions of the crowds, the impure expectations and motives of his disciples, and the sins of the people. No wonder Luke observes that when "Jesus approached Jerusalem and saw the city, he wept over it" (Luke 19:41–44).

The Fig Tree and the Temple

After his triumphal entry into Jerusalem, Jesus goes to the temple and surveys the scene. What he sees surely fills him with both sadness and righteous anger. It is already late in the day, so he returns to Bethany (Mark 11:11). On the following day Jesus reenters the city and pronounces judgment on the temple, a courageous act that (from a human perspective) costs him his life. This action puts him in deep trouble with the Jewish authorities (11:18). Confronting religious and political corruption continues to be a dangerous endeavor.

The temple stands at the center of Jerusalem and at the heart of the nation of Israel. The original temple was built by King Solomon in the tenth century BC. That first temple was demolished by the Babylonians around 587 BC. The second temple was built in its place beginning about 538 BC by those who had returned from captivity in Babylon. In 20 BC Herod the Great started a massive remodeling project on this second temple, which lasted almost fifty years (John 2:20). This is the temple of Jesus' day, and it serves as the economic, political, and religious center of Israel. In our fragmented society, it is hard for us to imagine a single place holding all the money, power, and holiness of the nation, but such is the case with the temple.

In the gospel of Mark, the cleansing of the temple and the cursing of the fig tree are "sandwiched" together. Mark often ties together the reporting of two events so that his readers will know that the two events are making a similar point (see also 3:20–35; 5:21–43; 6:7–31; 14:1–11; 14:53–72). In Mark 11, the story about the condemnation of the temple is placed inside the story of the cursing of the fig tree so that we will understand that it is more of a condemnation than a cleansing of the temple. Jesus is judging both the fig tree (a symbol of the nation of Israel) and the temple for lacking spiritual fruit.

When you first read Mark 11:12–14, you might wonder why Jesus would get mad at a poor fig tree for failing to bear figs when it wasn't the season for figs. But Mark's statement, "it was not the season for figs" in 11:13, serves as a clue to look below the surface for the symbolic meaning. Obviously, Jesus knows it isn't the season for figs. The tree serves as an object lesson for understanding what Jesus is about to do to the temple. As the tree falsely advertises through its leaves that it has fruit to offer, so the temple also leaves the false impression that it is the place where people can truly meet God. The time has come to judge the fruitless temple and to replace it with the true way to God—Jesus himself.

Like the prophets of old who often used dramatic actions to make a point, Jesus' actions announce God's rejection of the temple by temporarily disrupting its operation. In Mark 11:15–16 we see Jesus condemning the commercialism, the sacrificial system, and the worship rituals of the temple. Although the money changers probably pick up their coins and tables and resume business in a short time, Jesus has made his point through symbolic action. Rather than mediating God's presence, the temple stands under God's judgment.

As the disciples return to the city the next morning with Jesus, Peter notices that the fig tree has withered from the roots—a miraculously quick withering in a single day (see Mark 11:20–26). Jesus has condemned the temple and it will soon be destroyed, but he is putting something new in its place. Jesus himself, the incarnate Son of God, is greater than the temple and is replacing it. In Jesus Christ we find the very presence of God. The new way will be based on persevering faith in God (11:23), believing prayer to God (11:24), and ongoing forgiveness of others as we trust God to forgive us (11:25).

The Olivet Discourse

While Jesus is walking out of the temple courts (probably on the Tuesday of Passion Week), his disciples comment on the magnificence of the building itself (Matt. 24:1). Jesus abruptly announces that the whole thing will soon be torn down (24:2). This shocking pronouncement that the temple will be destroyed triggers a couple of important questions from the disciples: "Tell us, when will this happen, and what will be the sign of your coming and of the end of the age?" (24:3). Jesus' lengthy answer recorded in Matthew 24–25 and Mark 13 is called the "Olivet Discourse" since Jesus is on the Mount of Olives when he answers their questions (Matt. 24:3). Others have labeled this teaching the Eschatological or Apocalyptic Discourse since much of what Jesus says seems to apply to the end of the age.

The disciples' two questions refer to two different events: (1) the destruction of Jerusalem and its temple by the Romans in AD 70, and (2) Jesus' second coming at the end of the age. Jesus' answer, in the form of the Olivet Discourse, also speaks of these two events. He appears to use the destruction of the temple in the near future as a pattern for the judgments that will occur in the distant future when he returns. Jesus intentionally connects these two significant events and uses the first event (destruction of the temple in AD 70) as a preview of the second event (his second coming). The near future is intertwined with the far future.

Walking with Jesus through Passion Week*

Modern Calendar Days	Events of Passion Week
Friday	• Arrival in Bethany (John 12:1)
Saturday	• Evening celebration; Mary anoints Jesus (John 12:2–8; cf. Matt. 26:6–13)
Sunday	• Triumphal entry into Jerusalem (Matt. 21:1–11; Mark 11:1–10; John 12:12–18) • Jesus surveys the temple area (Mark 11:11) • Return to Bethany (Matt. 21:17; Mark 11:11)
Monday	• Cursing the fig tree on the way to Jerusalem (Matt. 21:18–22; cf. Mark 11:12–14) • Condemning the temple (Matt. 21:12–13; Mark 11:15–17) • Miracles and challenges in the temple (Matt. 21:14–16; Mark 11:18) • Return to Bethany (Mark 11:19)
Tuesday	• Reaction to cursing the fig tree on the way back to Jerusalem (Matt. 21:20–22; Mark 11:20–21) • Debates with religious leaders in Jerusalem and teaching in the temple (Matt. 21:23–23:39; Mark 11:27–12:44) • Olivet (Eschatological) Discourse on the Mount of Olives on the return to Bethany (Matt. 24:1–25:46; Mark 13:1–37)
Wednesday	• "Silent Wednesday"—Jesus and his disciples remain in Bethany for a last time of fellowship • Judas returns alone to Jerusalem to make arrangements for the betrayal (Matt. 26:14–16; Mark 14:10–11)
Thursday	• Preparations for Passover (Matt. 26:17–19; Mark 14:12–16) After sundown: • Passover meal and Last Supper (Matt. 26:20–35; Mark 14:17–26) • Upper room discourses (John 13–17) • Prayers in the garden of Gethsemane (Matt. 26:36–46; Mark 14:32–42)

Friday	Sometime perhaps after midnight:
	• Betrayal and arrest (Matt. 26:47–56; Mark 14:43–52)
	• Jewish trial—Jesus appears in three phases in front of:
	   —Annas (John 18:13–24)
	   —Caiaphas and partial Sanhedrin (Matt. 26:57–75; Mark 14:53–65)
	   —Sanhedrin fully assembled (*perhaps after sunrise*) (Matt. 27:1–2; Mark 15:1)
	• Roman trial—Jesus appears in three phases before:
	   —Pilate (Matt. 27:2–14; Mark 15:2–5)
	   —Herod Antipas (Luke 23:6–12)
	   —Pilate (Matt. 27:15–26; Mark 15:6–15)
	• Crucifixion (*approx. 9:00 a.m. to 3:00 p.m.*) (Matt. 27:27–66; Mark 15:16–39)
	• Burial (*before dark*) (Matt. 27:57–61; Mark 15:42–47)

Saturday	Jesus' body in the tomb
Sunday and beyond	• Jesus' resurrection • Resurrection witnesses (Matt. 28:1–8; Mark 16:1–8; Luke 24:1–12) • Resurrection appearances (Matt. 28:9–20; Luke 24:13–53; John 20–21)

* Adapted (with slight modifications) from Michael J. Wilkins, *Matthew*, The NIV Application Commentary (Grand Rapids: Zondervan, 2004), 709–10.

This is much like looking at a mountain range from a distance. When you look at the mountains from a great distance, they all appear as a single range far away. But as you get closer, you can tell that some peaks are in fact much closer than others. In the same way, some of what Jesus says in this discourse will be fulfilled in the first century (near future) and some at the end of the age (far future). Jesus' teaching in Matthew 24–25 is outlined below.

24:4–35	**Jesus answers the disciples' two questions — the destruction of Jerusalem and the return of the Son of Man**
24:4–14	Birth pains — events that occur in every age
24:15–20	Sharp pain of the destruction of Jerusalem
24:21–28	The interim period of great distress or tribulation
24:29–31	The coming of the Son of Man
24:32–35	Conclusion — the nearness of Christ's return
24:36–25:46	**The need to be prepared for Christ's return**
24:36	Only the Father knows the time of Christ's return
24:37–41	Illustrations of the unexpectedness of Christ's return
24:42	Therefore, stay alert!
24:43–25:30	Four parables on watchfulness
25:31–46	Final judgment and reward

Jesus begins his teaching by describing events (birth pains) that will occur throughout history but do not necessarily signal the very end (24:4–14). One especially "sharp pain" will be the destruction of Jerusalem in AD 70 (24:15–20). Then Jesus speaks about the interim period of great distress — the entire period between Jesus' first coming and his second coming or perhaps an especially intense period of time just prior to Christ's return. The return of Christ is described in 24:29–31, followed by a reminder that his return is always near (24:32–35). In the rest of chapter 24 and all of chapter 25, Jesus tells his disciples they should always be prepared for his unexpected return.

Even though the Olivet Discourse can be confusing, when we summarize Jesus' specific instructions and commands, the main message comes clearly into focus:

1. Disciples should not be deceived by false reports or false messiahs even though they may perform signs and wonders and deceive the crowds. When the real Jesus returns, everyone will know it (Matt. 24:27)!
2. Disciples should not be alarmed by chaotic world events such as wars, famines, and earthquakes. These things are going to happen throughout history and do not necessarily signal the end of time.
3. Disciples should expect opposition and persecution, perhaps even martyrdom because of their allegiance to Jesus.

4. Disciples can know that Jesus' return is a certain and sure thing.

5. The time of his return is uncertain. Although he is coming back, no one knows the time of his return. As a result, Jesus' return is always "near" or imminent, meaning that it could happen at any time. Speculation about the time of his return is useless and counterproductive.

6. Disciples should be alert and ready for Jesus' return. This is the central command of the Olivet Discourse. More than anything, Jesus wants us to be alert and prepared.

7. Disciples should be alert and be prepared by doing what God has called them to do — preaching the gospel to all nations (24:14), doing the jobs we have been assigned (24:46), and using our gifts and abilities to serve the Lord (25:14 – 30).

The Last Supper and the Lord's Supper

It's Thursday of Passion Week and only a few hours remain until Jesus goes to the cross.

Jesus' final meal with his disciples is a Passover meal — the meal that the Jews ate to remember how God delivered them from slavery in Egypt (Luke 22:15). Jesus gives Peter and John the task of making the arrangements. They go into the city, meet a man carrying a jar of water, follow him to the room, and prepare the Passover meal (Mark 14:12 – 17). When evening comes, Jesus gathers with his disciples in the upper room.

Jesus and his disciples would have sat around several low tables or couches that formed the shape of a U rather than the long, straight table portrayed in later artwork.[2] Everyone reclined on their left side, with their feet pointing outward and using their right hand to eat. Most likely the host (in this case Jesus) would be seated near the base of the tables with the honored guests on either side. Ironically, Judas probably occupies the place of an honored guest, next to Jesus.

After everyone has arrived and the meal is ready, Jesus does something unexpected and shocking. He gets up, takes off his outer clothing, and wraps a towel around his waist. Then he pours water into a basin and begins washing the disciples' feet and drying them with his towel (John 13:3 – 5).

Such a degrading, dirty task was considered too demeaning for Jewish servants and was reserved for non-Jewish slaves — those on the bottom of the social scale. Jesus' act of humility teaches his disciples an unforgettable lesson on the value of service in God's kingdom:

> When he had finished washing their feet, he put on his clothes and returned to his place. "Do you understand what I have done for you?" he asked them. "You call me 'Teacher' and 'Lord,' and rightly so, for that is what I am. Now that I, your Lord and Teacher, have washed your feet,

---

2. Darrell L. Bock, *Jesus According to Scripture* (Grand Rapids: Baker, 2002), 357 – 58.

The Slave Is Not Greater Than His Master

To serve *as Jesus served* requires humility. It requires sacrifice. It means taking up the "lesser role" for the benefit of someone else. Many stories illustrate this point, but one always comes to my mind. Dr. Robertson McQuilkin was for many years the president of Columbia Bible College and Seminary in Columbia, South Carolina. In about 1980 Dr. McQuilkin began to see signs of memory loss in his wife, Muriel. For the next decade he watched as his wife's career of conference speaking, radio shows, and television began to erode and disappear. In the mid-1980s she was diagnosed with Alzheimer's, and her deterioration continued to advance rapidly.

This situation naturally posed a crisis for Dr. McQuilkin. As president of a thriving college and graduate school, how could he meet the needs of both his wife and his job? Many Christian friends encouraged him to give Muriel over to professional care (i.e., a nursing home), but he could not bear the thought. As her condition worsened, he made a decision that was "a matter of integrity" (his words). He resigned from Columbia to care for his wife full time. "It was a choice between two loves," he writes. Columbia wisely and compassionately supported his decision and began seeking his replacement.

The striking thing about McQuilkin's personal story is its theological underpinnings. For some, he was choosing a task at remarkable social and professional cost. He was throwing away his career. Not so. His decision was grounded in God's love for him, experienced also through Muriel's unselfish forty-two-year love for him. This made his service a joy. Dr. McQuilkin writes:

It is more than keeping promises and being fair. As I watch her brave descent into oblivion, Muriel is the joy of my life. Daily I discern new manifestations of the kind of person she is, the wife I always loved. I also see fresh manifestations of God's love—the God I long to love more fully.[3]

– GARY BURGE

you also should wash one another's feet. I have set you an example that you should do as I have done for you. Very truly I tell you, no servant is greater than his master, nor is a messenger greater than the one who sent him. Now that you know these things, you will be blessed if you do them." (John 13:12–17)

Jesus does in fact hold a superior rank and position over his disciples ("Lord" is a word commonly used for God in the Greek Old Testament). But he explains that in God's kingdom, those with power and position should become servants. Jesus is setting an example or a pattern for his disciples. If the Master is willing to humble himself and serve in ways that ignore the customs of a culture, we should do the same. If God the Son stoops to perform a slave's task for us, how much more should we serve one another?

---

3. Gary M. Burge, *John*, NIV Application Commentary (Grand Rapids: Zondervan, 2000), 382–83.

As they are eating, Jesus shocks his disciples with the announcement that one of the Twelve will soon betray him. The horrible irony of Judas sharing table fellowship with Jesus while simultaneously preparing to betray him becomes clear. Psalm 41:9 foreshadows Jesus' betrayal: "Even my close friend, someone I trusted, one who shared my bread, has turned against me" (cf. John 13:18). In contrast to Mary's earlier act of worship where she anoints Jesus' body for burial with expensive perfume, Judas opens his heart to Satan (Luke 22:3; John 13:2, 27). He promises the religious leaders information about how to arrest Jesus secretly without any interference from the crowds, and this act of betrayal earns himself thirty pieces of silver—about four months' wages for a common worker (Matt. 26:15). John's gospel tells us that Judas leaves the gathering at this point (John 13:30).

The Passover meal in the Jewish tradition celebrated God's mighty deliverance of his people from slavery in Egypt. The act of deliverance was the exodus event, and the symbol celebrating that act was the Passover meal (see Ex. 12). There were six elements in the traditional Passover meal:[4]

- Passover lamb: reminder of protection by blood of lamb
- Unleavened bread: reminder that departure was so quick that they had no time to bake
- Bowl of salt water: reminder of sorrow and tears of captivity
- Bitter herbs: reminder of bitterness of slavery
- Fruit purée: reminder of the clay used to make bricks during their slavery
- Four cups of red wine mixed with water: reminder of promises of God in Exodus 6:6–7

As part of the Passover celebration, the host would normally retell the story of the exodus. As the host, Jesus now reinterprets the familiar Old Testament story in light of the coming cross and resurrection. Jesus makes four statements that capture the deeper meaning of the Last Supper and transform it into the Lord's Supper:

- "This is my body": refers to Jesus' giving his life (symbolized by the unleavened bread) as a sacrifice so that others might live. His body will be broken on the cross so that people may experience deliverance from sin.
- "This is my blood, the blood of the covenant, which is poured out for many": Jesus now portrays himself as the true Lamb of God. The cup of wine represents Jesus' blood, which is poured out for many for the forgiveness of sins (Matt. 26:28). Jesus' sacrificial death brings about the new covenant.
- "I will no longer drink of the fruit of the vine until that day when I drink it new in the kingdom of God": looks forward to Jesus' return, when God's people will share in the messianic banquet (Matt. 26:29; Mark

14:25; Luke 22:16, 18). One day the kingdom of God will arrive in fullness and glory and God will throw a huge party for his children.
- "Do this in remembrance of me" (Luke 22:19; 1 Cor. 11.23–26): a call for believers to remember Jesus' sacrificial death on the cross and anticipate his future return.

We are told that after they have sung a hymn, perhaps from Psalms 113–118, they go to the garden of Gethsemane on the Mount of Olives.

The Farewell Discourse

Before leaving the upper room Jesus talks candidly with his disciples (minus Judas) about what is about to happen. Jesus prepares his disciples for his departure. They listen like never before as Jesus speaks passionately from his heart (see John 13–17). They share a few unhurried hours together before the forces of darkness descend. Above all, his selflessness shines through. He calms their troubled hearts. He promises his Holy Spirit and peace, along with the new privilege of prayer in his name. He warns about the world's opposition, but he assures them that he is the way to the Father and urges them to abide in him and to love one another. Finally, he prays for them. Jesus has comforted his disciples; he is now ready for the cross, and the betrayer is about to arrive.

Gethsemane and Arrest

Jesus and his disciples leave the upper room and make their way to the Mount of Olives, to an olive orchard called Gethsemane or "oil press" (Mark 14:26). Jesus asks Peter, James, and John, the inner circle, to accompany him deeper into the garden for prayer. To his closest friends, Jesus confesses the enormous weight he feels pressing down on him: "My soul is overwhelmed with sorrow to the point of death" (Mark 14:34). In this place where olives are regularly crushed for their oil, Jesus is now feeling crushed by the burden of his imminent death for the sins of all humanity.

Jesus then moves a bit farther into the garden by himself to pray. He prays first that, if possible, this hour of suffering might pass him by (Mark 14:35–36a). In raw honesty, Jesus pours out his deepest thoughts and feelings to the Father. But he doesn't stop with honesty; he moves on to total submission: "*Abba*, Father, everything is possible for you. Take this cup from me. Yet not what I will, but what you will" (Mark 14:36). Three times he returns to Peter, James, and John only to find them sleeping. Finally, Jesus announces that his hour of betrayal and suffering has begun (Mark 14:41).

At this point Judas arrives with an armed crowd authorized by the religious leaders. They have been plotting to arrest Jesus for some time, but they have always feared a reaction from the common people (Mark 14:1–2). How does Judas fit into their plans? What exactly does Judas betray? He offers the leaders information. Leaving the upper room early (John 13:27–30), Judas goes to the authorities and tells them how to arrest Jesus privately without causing a scene. He then identifies the specific location of Jesus and the disciples at a time when a quiet arrest can be made away from the crowds. The disciples are familiar with Judas, and no one will suspect him of escorting trouble into the camp. Judas not only guides the arresting party to the location; he also identifies Jesus with a sign—a kiss of greeting, the normal way for a disciple to greet and show respect for his teacher.

As they arrest Jesus, Simon Peter draws his sword and cuts off the right ear of Malchus, the high priest's slave (John 18:10). Jesus tells Peter to put away his sword and then heals the slave's ear (Luke 22:51). If Jesus wanted to use military power to conquer evil, he could ask the Father to send twelve legions of warrior angels (Matt. 26:53), but he has already settled the matter in prayer. He will drink the cup of suffering and do things the Father's way (John 18:11). When Jesus is arrested and tied up, everyone forsakes him (Mark 14:50).

Trials, Crucifixion, and Burial

Soon after his arrest, the Jewish leaders begin to interrogate Jesus. The Jewish "trial" begins with an initial examination by Annas, the former high priest (AD 6–15) and father-in-law of the current high priest, Caiaphas (see John 18:13–24). They "rough up" Jesus in order to gain incriminating evidence. Later that night there is a second hearing before Caiaphas (AD 18–36) and a partial Sanhedrin (Matt. 26:57–68; Mark 14:53–65).

When Jesus doesn't defend himself against many false witnesses, the high priest asks a crucial question: "Tell us if you are the Messiah, the Son of God" (Matt. 26:63; Mark 14:61); Jesus answers, "I am"; then he adds: "And you will see the Son of Man sitting at the right hand of the Mighty One and coming on the clouds of heaven" (Mark 14:62). By quoting Psalm 110:1 and Daniel 7:13, Jesus is claiming "to be able to go directly into God's presence and work at his side, a claim that he is really their judge."[5]

When Jesus claims to have authority equal to God, the high priest tears his clothes and charges Jesus with blasphemy (Matt. 26:65–66; Mark 14:63–64). The religious leaders conclude that he deserves to die because he is a blasphemous false prophet who is leading the nation astray. And Jesus' admission that he is the Messiah (a political figure) allows the religious leaders to take him to Pilate for a Roman death sentence. Finally, the full Sanhedrin assembles after dawn to make the nighttime decision legitimate (Matt. 27:1–2; Mark 15:1; Luke 22:66–23:1). The Sanhedrin wants Jesus dead, but only the Romans can carry out a death sentence (John 18:31). So they tie him up and take him to Pilate. At this point in the Story, Matthew tells us that Judas commits suicide (Matt. 27:3–10; cf. also Acts 1:18–19).

The Roman trial consists of three phases. First, before Pilate the Jewish lead-

---

5. Bock, *Jesus According to Scripture*, 374.

ers accuse Jesus of leading the nation astray, forbidding the payment of taxes to Caesar, and claiming to be a king (Luke 23:2). Pilate finds the charges lacking, so he sends him to Herod Antipas for a second opinion (Luke 23:6–12).

Second, Jesus is interrogated by Antipas, a son of Herod the Great, who ruled Galilee and Perea from 4 BC to AD 39. Antipas is more interested in seeing Jesus perform a miracle than in providing justice. Jesus is mocked and shamed before being sent back to Pilate with another "not guilty" verdict.

Third, Jesus stands before Pilate a second time (Matt. 27:15–31; Mark 15:6–20; Luke 23:13–25; John 18:39–19:16). Pilate wants to scourge Jesus for causing trouble and set him free. He tries to release Jesus using the custom of turning back one prisoner to the people during feast time, but the attempt fails when the crowd demands Barabbas instead. And above all, Pilate wants to satisfy the crowds. Throughout the whole Story, in subtle but powerful ways Jesus offers himself as a sacrifice for guilty sinners.

Guided by their religious leaders, the people feel as if they are doing God's will by opposing a false messiah. Ironically, the religious leaders are so intent on putting Jesus to death that they claim ultimate loyalty to Caesar. They say to Pilate, "If you let this man go, you are no friend of Caesar. Anyone who claims to be a king opposes Caesar.... We have no king but Caesar" (John 19:12, 15). Pilate has Jesus scourged—a cruel and painful form of whipping— before turning him over to the soldiers to be crucified. The Roman soldiers then dress Jesus in a kingly robe and adorn him with a crown of thorns before mocking and beating him. Next, they lead him away to Golgotha ("the place of the skull" in Aramaic) to crucify him. The more common term today is Calvary, which comes from the Latin word for "skull."

> **One Son for Another**
>
> "The substitution of an innocent Jesus for a guilty Barabbas is a metaphor for the entire experience of the cross. Although none of the Gospels make anything of it, the name Barabbas means "son of the father" in Aramaic. Those who know the language and are sensitive to religious symbolism understand that one son had been exchanged for another. One condemned to die had been set free so that an innocent could die in his place."[6]
>
> – DARRELL BOCK

Crucifixion was considered a painful, humiliating way to die, so horrible that Rome would not permit its own citizens to be executed in this way. Victims normally lost a great deal of blood through the scourging process. On the cross a person usually died a slow, agonizing death from asphyxiation as they became too weak to lift their body to catch another breath. Crucifixion was reserved for lower-class criminals, slaves, and foreigners.

The writers of the Gospels describe Jesus' death in a straightforward manner. He is nailed to the cross. They offer him drugged wine, which he refuses. The soldiers gamble for his clothes, leaving the "King of the Jews" (as the inscription nailed above his head reads) to die in shameful nakedness. Jesus is crucified between two criminals, who respond to him in different ways (see Luke 23:39–43). Those who pass by the death scene mock Jesus for claiming

---

6. Ibid., 382.

The Seven Last Sayings of Jesus from the Cross

1. "Father, forgive them, for they do not know what they are doing." (Luke 23:34)
2. "Truly I tell you, today you will be with me in paradise." (Luke 23:43)
3. "Woman, here is your son!" … "Here is your mother!" (John 19:26–27)
4. "My God, my God, why have you forsaken me?" (Matt. 27:46)
5. "I am thirsty!" (John 19:28)
6. "It is finished!" (John 19:30)
7. "Father, into your hands I commit my spirit!" (Luke 23:46)

to be able to rebuild the temple in three days, for not coming down from the cross although he says he is the Son of God, and for not saving himself although he claims to be the King of Israel (Matt. 27:38–43). Jesus' last sayings from the cross speak volumes about who he is, what he has come to do, and how he faces death.

At the sixth hour (noon), darkness covers the land until the ninth hour (3:00 p.m.), at which time Jesus cries, "It is finished," and surrenders his spirit to the Father. Jesus' death is accompanied by miraculous signs (Matt. 27:51–53), along with the tearing of the massive temple curtain from top to bottom (Mark 15:38). The Synoptic Gospels all close the crucifixion scene with the ironic confession of the Roman soldier (ironic because Jesus is dying by Roman crucifixion): "Surely this man was the Son of God!" (Mark 15:39).

All four gospels report the presence of eyewitnesses at the crucifixion, and they specifically mention the women from Galilee (Matt. 27:55–56; Mark 15:40–41; Luke 23:49; John 19:25–27). The burial of Jesus is also reported in all four gospels (Matt. 27:57–61; Mark 15:42–47; Luke 23:50–56; John 19:31–42). This burial is significant because it lets the readers know that Jesus has really died. The claims of the early Christians that Jesus rose from the dead prove empty if he never really died. The burial affirms a real death.

In addition, Matthew describes how the Jewish leaders get permission from Pilate to seal the tomb and post a group of soldiers so that Jesus' disciples will not be able to steal his body and claim that he rose from the dead as he predicted (Matt. 27:62–66). There will soon be an empty tomb, but the presence of Roman soldiers guarantees that it won't be the result of human theft.

Making Connections

Let's review where we are in the Great Story:

Creation and Crisis
Covenant
Calling Out

Much as the center of a spiderweb has many connections to the rest of the web, so the center of the Story connects in many ways to other parts of the Story. We will highlight only a few. When Jesus enters Jerusalem to the praise of the crowds, he is claiming to be a king in the line of King David (Matt. 21:9; Mark 11:10; cf. Ps. 118). He is being praised as the one through whom God will deliver his people Israel. But Jesus is no typical deliverer or Messiah, as he shows by his entry into the city on a donkey rather than a warhorse. He will take the road of humility in setting his people free. God's ways are seldom our ways.

When Jesus dramatically acts against the temple, he alludes to two Old Testament passages to explain why the temple stands condemned. In Mark 11:17, Jesus says the religious leaders have turned a "house of prayer for all nations" (Isa. 56:7) into a "den of robbers" (Jer. 7:11). God's plan all along was to use his people Israel to bless other peoples. The context of Isaiah 56:1–8 says that God promises to accept and bless those who want to follow the Lord but think they have been excluded (e.g., the "foreigner" and the "eunuch").

In Jesus' day, Gentiles couldn't even go into the temple proper. Jesus says the walls must come down—one way or the other. The context from which the phrase "den of robbers" is derived (i.e., Jer. 7:1–15) helps us see that "den of robbers" is not merely describing the selfish business practices of the temple. The "den" is not actually where the robbers do their robbing but where they hide out after they have committed their crimes elsewhere.

Although the temple is huge and powerful, Jesus is replacing the temple, and people must decide between the two. Later, after Jesus ascends to the Father, God's people (both Jew and Gentile) will experience God's presence through the Holy Spirit. God cannot be confined to a building! Rather, God will dwell among his people. The temple of God will become the people of

God. As the apostle Paul told the Corinthian church, "we are the temple of the living God" (2 Cor. 6:16; cf. 1 Cor. 3:16; Eph. 2:21–22).

One of the most powerful connections relates to Jesus' words during the Passover meal. As he retells the exodus story, he transforms it in light of what is about to happen to him. God's most famous rescue now changes from the exodus event (leading people out of slavery in Egypt) to the cross and resurrection (leading people out of sin and death). The symbol celebrating that act, once the Passover, now becomes the Lord's Supper.

- Slavery in Egypt → slavery to sin
- God's deliverance through the Passover lamb → God's deliverance through Jesus, the Lamb of God (1 Cor. 5:7)
- The exodus or deliverance from Egypt → the forgiveness of sins
- The covenant at Mount Sinai → the new covenant through Jesus' blood
- The Passover → the Lord's Supper

When Jesus uses the phrase "blood of the covenant," he connects back to Exodus 24:8, where we read about Moses pouring out blood on the altar and then sprinkling blood on the people to seal the covenant between God and the people. This strange practice signified that the blood of the sacrifice would cover over the sins of the people. Jesus makes clear that his own blood, the blood of the Lamb of God, now covers over sins. Jesus' sacrifice on the cross makes "forgiveness of sins" possible.

When Jesus mentions covenant, he is alluding to the new covenant spoken of in Jeremiah 31. The new covenant will surpass the old covenant (31:32). God will put his Law in our minds and write it on our hearts (31:33). Most significantly, this new covenant will bring forgiveness of sins (31:34) and a personal relationship with God (31:33–34). The new covenant is now sealed by Jesus' death.

When Jesus dies on the cross, the curtain in the temple is ripped in two from top to bottom (Mark 15:38; cf. 1:10, where the heavens are "split apart" at Jesus' baptism). The writer of Hebrews describes in detail how the once-for-all sacrifice of Jesus has put an end to the sacrificial system and opens a new way into the presence of God, where people may find forgiveness (see Heb. 9–10). Now even Gentiles (non-Jews), once forbidden to enter the temple, may enter God's very presence through Jesus,

---

A Den of Thieves

"Jesus indirectly attacks them for allowing the temple to degenerate into a safe hiding place where people think that they find forgiveness and fellowship with God no matter how they act on the outside.... The leaders of the people think that they can rob widows' houses (Mark 12:40) and then perform the prescribed sacrifices according to the prescribed patterns at the prescribed times in the prescribed purity in the prescribed sacred space and then be safe and secure from all alarms. They are wrong. The sacrifice of animals will not enable them to evade the doom that God purposes for those guilty of lying, stealing, violence, and adultery (see 7:21–23). The sanctuary, supposedly sanctified by God, has become a sanctuary for bandits who think that they are protected from God's judgment."[7]

— DAVID GARLAND

---

7. David Garland, *Mark*, NIV Application Commentary (Grand Rapids: Zondervan, 1996), 439.

the true high priest (Heb. 4:14–5:10). In addition, we now have the amazing privilege of prayer or constant access into God's presence.

We are told in Deuteronomy 21:23 that anyone who is hung on a tree (or a cross) is under God's curse. Therefore, God's Messiah, the one sent to deliver people, could not possibly die under the curse of God on a cross. That would be total foolishness (see 1 Cor. 1:20–31). For this reason, a "crucified Christ" was deeply offensive to the Jews. But the apostle Paul writes these words to the churches in Galatia (Gal. 3:13–14):

> Christ redeemed us from the curse of the law by becoming a curse for us, for it is written: "Cursed is everyone who is hung on a pole." He redeemed us in order that the blessing given to Abraham might come to the Gentiles through Christ Jesus, so that by faith we might receive the promise of the Spirit.

We now see that Jesus' death is significant, not just because he suffered greatly (so did the two criminals, we can assume), but because he suffered as the sinless Son of God for guilty sinners. God loves all human beings and desires a relationship with them, but he is holy and must punish sin. How can God simultaneously express his holiness in judgment and his love in pardon? Answer: by providing a sinless substitute for the sinner so that the substitute receives the judgment and the sinner receives the pardon.

This very thing happened at the cross, where God substituted himself for the sinner. The "self-substitution" of God means that his love has provided what his holiness required! As John Stott says, "He was unwilling to act in love at the expense of his holiness or in holiness at the expense of his love. So we may say that he satisfied his holy love by himself dying the death and so bearing the judgment which sinners deserved."[8]

Living the Story

At every turn in this section of the Story, you will discover another way to live it. Here are a few suggestions. First, Jesus' Olivet Discourse reminds us that we don't always know how biblical prophecy will be fulfilled. Jesus uses the near view–far view technique commonly used by the Old Testament prophets. That is, they speak about the fulfillment of two significant events (e.g., the destruction of Jerusalem by the Babylonians and the day of the Lord) as if these events were closely related in time when they actually occur years apart. Jesus does the same thing when speaking of the destruction of the temple and his return.

God doesn't always (or even normally) share his timetable with us (see Acts 1:6–8). In the interim period as we wait, we can easily lose sight of what is most important. Many people become overly fascinated with end-time events

---

8. John R. W. Stott, *The Cross of Christ* (Downers Grove, IL: InterVarsity Press, 1986), 152.

and spend much of their time speculating on things they cannot possibly know. But the central command of the discourse is to stay alert and be prepared by doing what God has told us to do. So if you really want to be prepared for Christ's return, obey God in what you already know and understand. We are not all gifted in the same way, nor are we expected to be productive at the same level of competence, but we are expected to be faithful with what we have been given. That is how we stay alert and prepared for Jesus' return.

Another way to live the Story is to imitate Jesus when it comes to prayer. In the garden of Gethsemane with the weight of the world on his shoulders, Jesus is first completely open and honest with the Father. Plainly and simply, he tells the Father that he doesn't want to suffer. He doesn't pray a fake prayer or smooth over the real issue with religious language. He is honest with God, and we should be too. God is big enough to hear the deepest and most honest cries of our heart.

> ## Being Honest with God
>
> "We must lay before Him what is in us, not what ought to be in us."[9]
>
> – C. S. LEWIS

Second, Jesus submits his desires to the Father's greater plan. Jesus doesn't want to suffer on the cross, but he is willing to do so. Real faith trusts God and submits to his will above all else. Being honest with God is the best place to begin the conversation, but you may find yourself moving beyond honesty to submission. Often the right thing to do is the most difficult thing.

Our last suggestion for living the Story relates to Jesus' humble love for his followers. From the triumphal entry to his death on the cross, Jesus loves his disciples selflessly. At a time when he has the right to be preoccupied with his own circumstances, Jesus continually puts the needs of his disciples ahead of his own. He washes their feet. He comforts them regarding the future. He promises them the Holy Spirit. He prays for them. Over and over, he prepares them for what is about to happen. Then he goes to the cross to die for them.

Even while on the cross, he thinks about their needs. At the darkest point in his life, Jesus' selfless love for others does not grow cold and die. The cross becomes the supreme demonstration of God's love for us (Rom. 5:8). God's love for you includes forgiveness. No matter what kind of sin is weighing you down, if you confess those sins and turn to God, his forgiveness is available because of Christ's sacrifice (Heb. 10:21; 1 John 1:9). As you experience the freedom of receiving God's love, you will have the opportunity to love others selflessly as Jesus did. In his letter to the church in Philippi, the apostle Paul spells it out nicely for us:

> In your relationships with one another, have the same mindset as Christ Jesus:
>
> Who, being in very nature God,

---

9. C. S. Lewis, *Letters to Malcolm: Chiefly on Prayer* (Orlando: Harcourt, 1992; orig., 1963), 22.

did not consider equality with God something to be used to his
>   own advantage;
> rather, he made himself nothing
>   by taking the very nature of a servant,
>   being made in human likeness.
> And being found in appearance as a man,
>   he humbled himself
>   by becoming obedient to death—even death on a cross! (Phil.
>   2:5–8)

May Jesus empower you to love the people he has led into your life with a selfless love, knowing that you can trust him to give you strength to bear the burdens you face.

Wrapping Up

In this chapter we've talked about Jesus' final week in Jerusalem. The raising of Lazarus from the dead, an extremely provocative miracle, motivated the religious leaders to seek Jesus' death with greater urgency. But messianic expectations were running high, and Jesus' entry into Jerusalem served as the formal announcement of his messiahship. Yet Jesus enters the city in humility as one who will conquer evil by offering himself as a sacrifice. By his symbolic actions, he forces people to choose between himself and the temple as the mediator of God's presence.

His final words to his disciples are packed with meaning. They learn the deep meaning of Jesus' coming death as he transforms the Passover celebration into the Lord's Supper. Now the cross of Jesus Christ stands as the greatest saving act in God's Great Story. The way Jesus endures his hour of trial by selflessly serving his followers stands as a model of perfect love as we seek to live this part of the Story.

Memory Verse

"For even the Son of Man did not come to be served, but to serve, and to give his life as a ransom for many." (Mark 10:45)

Digging Deeper

Books

Hengel, Martin. *Crucifixion in the Ancient World and the Folly of the Message of the Cross.* Philadelphia: Fortress, 1977.

Stein, Robert H. *Jesus the Messiah.* Downers Grove, IL: InterVarsity Press, 1996.

Stott, John R. W. *The Cross of Christ.* 20th anniversary ed. Downers Grove, IL: InterVarsity Press, 2006.

ASSIGNMENTS

1. The final week of Jesus is filled with controversies with the religious leaders. After condemning the temple, the religious leaders challenge Jesus' authority (Matt. 21:23–27). He refuses to respond directly but instead tells three parables: the parable of the two sons (21:28–32), the parable of the wicked tenants (21:33–44), and the parable of the great banquet (22:1–14). The leaders know Jesus has spoken these stories against them (21:45–46). Write a short paragraph explaining each parable; then write a concluding paragraph explaining how Jesus uses these stories to criticize the religious leaders.

2. Beginning with the triumphal entry into Jerusalem, you will notice that Jesus often uses symbolic actions to communicate during this final week (e.g., riding into town on a donkey, overturning a few tables in the temple, washing the disciples' feet). First, identify all the symbolic acts of Jesus during his final week. Then write a paragraph explaining why you think Jesus communicated in this way at this time. Finally, write a short paragraph explaining how symbolic acts have been used to strengthen your faith.

3. Throughout the Jewish trial, Simon Peter proceeds to deny Jesus three times. Read the following passages about Peter's denials and write a two-page reflection on the whole experience from Peter's viewpoint: Matthew 26:69–70, 71–72, 73–75.

4. Jesus' seven last words from the cross tell us much about what he thought was most important. Study each of these seven statements (see the chart on the seven "words" earlier in this chapter), and write a short paragraph for each one, explaining what it means and why it is important.

CHRIST:
Jesus Is Raised from the Dead

Chapter 15

Enter Here

The disciples have been following Jesus for several years now, looking forward to the day when his promises will come true. But now he is dead. They had been challenged by his authoritative teaching, captivated by his wondrous miracles, and drawn to his love and compassion. They felt surely this was the Anointed One, the Messiah, sent from God to deliver Israel from her enemies and establish God's kingdom on earth. But a Roman crucifixion has dashed their hopes—the Romans knew how to kill a person with maximum pain and suffering. Jesus' body was now lying in the new tomb of Joseph of Arimathea. He had been buried hurriedly just before the Sabbath began on Friday at 6:00 p.m. All that is left is for the women to anoint his body with spices for permanent burial. Jesus is really dead.

Most of us have experienced the death of someone close to us—a family member or close friend perhaps. We have experienced the shocking numbness, the overwhelming grief, the pain of loss. We can picture the funeral service, and we remember our attempt to return to "normal life." Can you imagine what it might have been like two days after the funeral to answer the doorbell and find _____ (you supply the name) standing there, very much alive? If you can imagine for a few seconds what it would mean for _____ to rise from the dead and appear to you again, you can begin to feel how those early Christians felt. At first, they simply cannot believe that Jesus has truly risen from the dead. They are initially afraid, skeptical, doubtful, and leery. Their first reaction is a mixture of paralyzing fear and unspeakable joy, much like you might feel if you saw _____ standing at your front door.

Be Prepared

Read or listen to Matthew 28; Mark 16; Luke 24; John 20–21; 1 Corinthians 15.

The Story Continues

The Resurrection and Appearances

The first visitors to Jesus' tomb early on a Sunday morning are a few women who have come to complete the partial embalming process that occurred on Friday. They had rushed his burial on the day of preparation for the Sabbath, and this meant postponing the full burial ritual. These few women dutifully return to the tomb to finish the job. They are in for quite a surprise. We read in Luke 24:1–6:

> On the first day of the week, very early in the morning, the women took the spices they had prepared and went to the tomb. They found the stone rolled away from the tomb, but when they entered, they did not find the body of the Lord Jesus. While they were wondering about this, suddenly two men in clothes that gleamed like lightning stood beside them. In their fright the women bowed down with their faces to the ground, but the men said to them, "Why do you look for the living among the dead? He is not here; he has risen! Remember how he told you, while he was still with you in Galilee."

Over the next forty days Jesus appears to a diverse group of witnesses in a variety of places. Although each gospel writer emphasizes different aspects of the resurrection accounts, they share a basic story line (see "A Harmony of the Post-Resurrection Appearances of Jesus").

The resurrection of Jesus Christ stands at the center of the Christian faith. As the apostle Paul told the Corinthian Christians, "If there is no resurrection of the dead, then not even Christ has been raised. And if Christ has not been raised, our preaching is useless and so is your faith" (1 Cor. 15:13–14). The entire Christian faith is founded on the bodily resurrection of Jesus Christ. Yet throughout history, and especially in modern times, some have denied that the resurrection ever happened. They have proposed several rationalistic alternatives to the bodily resurrection of Jesus.

1. *Coma*: Jesus didn't really die, but only appeared to die. According to this explanation, Jesus fainted or even lapsed into a coma. He was placed in the tomb alive but unconscious. He later regained consciousness, escaped from the tomb, appeared to his disciples, and eventually died from his injuries suffered earlier on the cross.

2. *Theft*: Jesus' tomb was indeed empty, not because he actually rose from the dead but because someone stole his body from the tomb (see Matt. 28:11–15).

3. *Wrong tomb*: The women who first discovered the empty tomb got confused. They did find an empty tomb, but it was the wrong tomb. They reported this discovery to the disciples, who also went to the wrong tomb. The disciples then began preaching that Jesus had risen from the dead.

A Harmony of the Post-Resurrection Appearances of Jesus[1]

1. A group of women come to the tomb near dawn, with Mary Magdalene possibly arriving first (Matt. 28:1; Mark 16:1–3; Luke 24:1; John 20:1).

2. Mary and the other women are met by two young men who in reality are angels, one of whom acts as the spokesman and announces Jesus' resurrection (Matt. 28:2–7; Mark 16:4–7; Luke 24:2–7).

3. The women leave the garden with a mixture of fear and joy, at first unwilling to say anything but then resolving to report to the Twelve (Matt. 28:8; Mark 16:8). Mary Magdalene may have dashed on ahead, telling Peter and John in advance of the arrival of the other women (John 20:2).

4. Jesus meets the remaining women en route and confirms their commission to tell the disciples, along with his promise to meet them in Galilee. The women obey (Matt. 28:9–10; Luke 24:8–11).

5. Peter and John meanwhile returned to the tomb, having heard Mary's report, and discover it to be empty (John 20:3–10; Luke 24:12).

6. Mary also returns to the tomb after Peter and John have left. She sees the angels and then Jesus, although at first she supposes him to be a gardener (John 20:11–18).

7. Later that afternoon, Jesus appears to Cleopas and his unnamed companion on the road to Emmaus and, in a separate incident, to Peter (Luke 24:13–35).

8. That same Sunday evening, Jesus appears to the ten (the Twelve minus Judas and Thomas) behind locked doors in Jerusalem (Luke 24:36–43; John 20:19–23).

9. A week later he appears to the eleven disciples in the same setting, with Thomas present (John 20:24–29).

10. Further appearances take place over a forty-day period, including in Galilee, with over five hundred seeing him altogether (Acts 1:3; John 21; 1 Cor. 15:5–7).

11. A climactic commissioning in Galilee instructs the disciples to spread the news throughout the world (Matt. 28:16–20).

12. Perhaps only shortly thereafter, Jesus gives his parting instructions to await the coming Holy Spirit and ascends into heaven (Luke 24:44–53; Acts 1:4–11).

4. *Legends created by the church*: Jesus' disciples began having dreams or visions about Jesus being alive. Their dramatic emotional and spiritual experience led the church to invent stories (legends) about Jesus being raised from the dead in order to support their faith. As a result, the resurrection stories in the Bible are seen as later inventions by the church. This view says the New Testament records of Jesus' resurrection are historically unreliable and can't be trusted.

The central question is: "Did Jesus really rise from the dead?" This is a question of history, not of science. The scientist tests a theory by performing various experiments in the lab. This is not possible for historians; they must test their explanations or reconstructions by seeing how well they account for

---

1. See Craig Blomberg, *Jesus and the Gospels*, 354–55.

the evidence. The historian looks for the explanation that exceeds rival explanations. We all want our faith to rest on explanations that are true. There are indeed persuasive reasons for believing that the bodily resurrection of Jesus really happened.

1. *Jesus really died.* Jesus' death is indicated by the brutal beating, the six hours on the cross, the spear thrust through his side that caused the loss of fluid and blood, the partial embalming, the wrapping in grave clothes, and the sealing in the tomb. It takes a great deal more faith to believe that Jesus did not die than to believe that he did. The Romans knew how to kill.

2. *Jesus was buried.*
   - Joseph of Arimathea and Nicodemus. The early Christians felt strongly that the Jewish leaders were responsible for putting Jesus to death (Acts 2:23–24; 3:15; 4:10; 5:30; 10:39–41). Joseph was a prominent member of the Jewish Sanhedrin (Mark 15:43; cf. "the whole Sanhedrin" in Mark 14:55) and a secret disciple of Jesus (John 19:38). Nicodemus, a Pharisee and (like Joseph) a member of the Sanhedrin (3:1), came to Jesus at night (3:2), perhaps for fear of being seen with Jesus during the day. The early Christians simply would not have invented a story with members of the Jewish Sanhedrin doing something good for Jesus unless it really happened that way. Besides, Mark 14:50 indicates that Jesus' closest followers all ran away at his arrest; would anyone who has the freedom to make up a story make their own top leaders look bad?
   - There is no other burial tradition. "If the burial of Jesus in the tomb by Joseph of Arimathea is legendary, then it is strange that conflicting traditions nowhere appear, even in Jewish polemic. That no remnant of the true story or even a conflicting false one should remain is hard to explain unless the gospel account is substantially the true account."[2]
   - Jesus was buried late on the Day of Preparation. "According to Jewish regulations, the body had to be buried on Friday evening before nightfall (John 19:42) and would not have been allowed to remain on the cross overnight—this would have defiled the land."[3]
   - The burial was observed by women. The women are said to witness the crucifixion, burial, and empty tomb of Jesus (Mark 15:40–41, 47; 16:1–6). Because women in Jewish society were not qualified to serve as legal witnesses, it is hard to imagine why the gospel writers would have recorded the women (instead of the male disciples) playing this significant role, unless it actually happened that way.

2. William Lane Craig, "Did Jesus Rise from the Dead?" in *Jesus under Fire*, ed. Michael J. Wilkins and J. P. Moreland (Grand Rapids: Zondervan, 1995), 149.

3. Ibid., 148.

3. *The tomb was empty.* One objection is that Jesus' body was stolen. There are persuasive reasons, however, why the disciples would not have stolen the body. Although Jews typically believed in a general resurrection of the righteous at the end of the age, the disciples never expected Jesus to rise from the dead only a short time after his death in spite of what he himself had predicted. They even initially doubted the first reports of Jesus' resurrection (Luke 24:11). Although they may have been willing to die for what they believed to be true, it's highly doubtful that they were willing to suffer torture and death for what they knew to be false (i.e., a lie).

Some have claimed that the Jews (rather than the disciples) stole the body of Jesus. But the earliest Jewish explanation presupposes an empty tomb. In Matthew 28:13–15 the Jewish leaders do not deny the tomb was empty. Rather, they take it for granted that the tomb was empty and devise a plan to say that the Christians stole the body. Also, Christians were preaching the resurrection of Christ. If the Jews wanted to stop the preaching that was turning their world upside down, all they had to do was produce the corpse of Jesus. William Lane Craig writes, "The simple fact that the Christian fellowship, founded on the belief in Jesus' resurrection, came into existence and flourished in the very city where he was executed and buried is powerful evidence for the historicity of the empty tomb."[4]

4. *Other evidence for the resurrection.*
   - The gospel accounts are matter of fact and appear immediately, in contrast to the apocryphal accounts that begin appearing in the second century. The presence of living eyewitnesses would hinder any tendency to invent a legend (see 1 Cor. 15:6). The Gospels are records of eyewitness testimony rather than a later invention by the church.[5]
   - Regarding spiritual visions, there is great variety in the post-resurrection appearances: different people, places, times, numbers (see 1 Cor. 15:5–8). As Mark Strauss says, "Religious visions are generally personal and subjective, not communal. It is unlikely that so many different people would have had the same vision."[6]
   - The record of the discovery of the empty tomb by women is unlikely unless it is true. Again, Craig writes, "Why would the Christian church humiliate its leaders by having them hiding in cowardice in

---

4. Ibid., 152.

5. See the tour de force of Richard Bauckham, *Jesus and the Eyewitnesses: The Gospels as Eyewitness Testimony* (Grand Rapids: Eerdmans, 2008).

6. Mark L. Strauss, *Four Portraits, One Jesus: An Introduction to Jesus and the Gospels.* (Grand Rapids: Zondervan, 2007), 520.

Jerusalem, while the women boldly carry out their last devotions to Jesus' body, unless this were in fact true?"[7]

- The rapid and long-term spread of Christianity—a faith based on the resurrection of Jesus Christ that was first preached in Jerusalem—is hard to explain unless the resurrection was a reality.
- The disciples are transformed from frightened, discouraged men (Mark 14:50, 66–72; John 20:19) into bold witnesses. Also, Paul's conversion from persecutor to preacher assumes a resurrection.
- The Jewish setting of early Christianity supports the resurrection. Craig Blomberg concludes:

> Had Christianity been born in Greece and later migrated to Israel, one might find more credible the story of a spiritual rebirth later being reclothed in the language of a bodily resurrection. But most Jews had always believed in a very literal reenfleshment of skeletons (cf. e.g., Ezek. 37), while it was the Hellenistic world that accepted only the immortality of the soul. So for a religion born in Judaism and later transplanted into the Greco-Roman world, the hypothesis of development from spirit to body turns out to run backwards.[8]

- The disciples began observing the first day of the week (Sunday) as the day of worship rather than the Sabbath (Saturday). Something dramatic and powerful must have happened to cause these Jewish disciples to make the switch after thousands of years of Sabbath observance.
- Neither the Jews nor the Romans ever produced evidence to the contrary.

The earliest Christians, who were far closer to the scene than we are, believed in the bodily resurrection of Jesus and announced his resurrection as historical event. This same faith has been around ever since. If God raised Jesus from the dead, his claims are true, and he has achieved a salvation that is now available to all.

The Great Commission

After the resurrection, Jesus appears to many people over a period of forty days. On one occasion he appears to some women in Jerusalem and instructs them to tell his eleven disciples (minus Judas) to meet him up north in Galilee:

> The angel said to the women, "Do not be afraid, for I know that you are looking for Jesus, who was crucified. He is not here; he has risen, just as he said. Come and see the place where he lay. Then go quickly and tell his dis-

---

7. Craig, "Did Jesus Rise from the Dead?" 151.
8. Blomberg, *Jesus and the Gospels*, 353.

ciples: 'He has risen from the dead and is going ahead of you into Galilee. There you will see him.' Now I have told you."

So the women hurried away from the tomb, afraid yet filled with joy, and ran to tell his disciples. Suddenly Jesus met them. "Greetings," he said. They came to him, clasped his feet and worshiped him. Then Jesus said to them, "Do not be afraid. Go and tell my brothers to go to Galilee; there they will see me." (Matt. 28:5 – 10)

A short time later Jesus meets the eleven disciples in Galilee on a mountain (a significant place throughout the Story). When they see him, some worship him while others aren't sure how to react (the term "doubted" in 28:17 probably indicates hesitation rather than unbelief). Jesus then gives his disciples marching orders for a worldwide mission. Actually, because Jesus joins us in the mission, it's commonly called the "Great Commission."[10]

> **A Resurrection-Shaped Dent**
>
> "The evidence for the resurrection of Jesus is good in the sense that we have the kind of historical evidence you would expect to be left behind if a man did in fact rise again, and more evidence pointing in that direction than you would expect if he did not. Put another way, there is a resurrection-shaped 'dent' in the historical record. This is why the topic is still taken seriously, even by those who do not personally believe that a resurrection is possible."[9]
>
> – JOHN DICKSON

Then Jesus came to them and said, "All authority in heaven and on earth has been given to me. Therefore go and make disciples of all nations, baptizing them in the name of the Father and of the Son and of the Holy Spirit, and teaching them to obey everything I have commanded you. And surely I am with you always, to the very end of the age." (Matt. 28:18 – 20)

The layout or organization of this Great Commission is important. Look at each item below and the role it plays in Jesus' charge to the first disciples and to us.

- *The command giver.* All authority has been given to Jesus by the Father, as the "all" words indicate — "*all* authority ... *all* nations ... obey *everything* ... with you *always*." Because of this supreme authority, Jesus has the right to tell his people what to do. And he sends his followers out to the nations not on a military-political conquest but to share the good news. Yet again, Jesus demonstrates that he came to be a different kind of Messiah.
- *The commission.*
  "Go": This is a supporting command that is essential for carrying out the main command. We cannot make disciples of "all nations" unless we reach out to all nations, whether across the sea or across the street.
  "Make disciples": This is the central command of the commission. A disciple is a committed follower of a teacher or a leader. To "make

---

9. John Dickson, *Life of Jesus* (Grand Rapids: Zondervan, 2010), 157.

10. Christopher Wright argues that the missionary activity of the church relies not just on the Great Commission but on the larger understanding of these Jewish Christians of their participation in the Great Story. See *Mission of God's People*, 35 – 36.

disciples" of Jesus involves (1) inviting people to enter a relationship with Jesus and (2) helping them grow in that relationship. In other words, followers of Christ are to help others become followers of Christ. We are to make disciples of all "nations" or all peoples, excluding no one. The two actions that follow explain how we are to carry out this command.

"Baptizing": This is the onetime, public initiation into the Christian community. Baptism represents the birth phase of the new life in Christ. Baptism is "in the name [singular] of the Father and of the Son and of the Holy Spirit" (one God in three persons).

"Teaching": This speaks of the lifelong process of growing as a Christian. Evangelism alone does not fulfill the Great Commission! In Jesus' culture, only privileged men had access to the leading rabbis. Jesus, however, invites *all* people to follow him and learn from him. Teaching lies at the heart of the growth process, but this kind of teaching is much more than a theoretical discussion. Jesus does not say "teaching them to know," but rather "teaching them to obey." Discipleship is education that results in life-changing obedience (Matt. 12:49–50).

- *The promise of the presence.* Along with the responsibility comes the privilege. Jesus promises to be present with us as we carry out the commission. The fulfillment of this promise begins at Pentecost (Acts 2) when the Holy Spirit comes to live within believers (cf. John 14:16, where Jesus promises to send "another advocate" or counselor, i.e., another of the same kind).

The Ascension

After appearing a number of times to his disciples, Jesus ascends into heaven. Luke describes Jesus' ascension both at the end of his gospel and at the beginning of Acts:

> When he had led them out to the vicinity of Bethany, he lifted up his hands and blessed them. While he was blessing them, he left them and was taken up into heaven. Then they worshiped him and returned to Jerusalem with great joy. And they stayed continually at the temple, praising God. (Luke 24:50–53)

> In my former book, Theophilus, I wrote about all that Jesus began to do and to teach until the day he was taken up to heaven, after giving instructions through the Holy Spirit to the apostles he had chosen. After his suffering, he presented himself to them and gave many convincing proofs that he was alive. He appeared to them over a period of forty days and spoke about the kingdom of God....

> After he said this, he was taken up before their very eyes, and a cloud hid

Great Commission — Outward, Inward, and Upward

"*Outward looking.* The Great Commission obviously looks outward because of its impelling missionary thrust to make disciples of all nations. The world out there is lost and dying without a Savior. Jesus' final Great Commission makes sure that we do not become ingrown, complacent, or callous. We must look outward and bring the good news of the gospel of the kingdom of heaven to people of all nations.

"*Inward looking.* The Great Commission also looks inward because it speaks to the ongoing transformation of those who have become disciples of Jesus. . . . But this cannot be accomplished alone. More mature disciples must teach other disciples how to obey all that Jesus commanded. The community of disciples looks within itself to provide concrete examples, compassionate encouragement, and structured and informal teaching of Jesus' life and words.

"*Upward looking.* The Great Commission also looks upward because disciples are to have only the risen and ascended Jesus as Master, Teacher, and Lord. No other master can ever supplant Jesus, and we must never consider ourselves to be master of any other disciples. . . . What makes this possible is that Jesus promises to be with us always, to the very end of the age."[11]

— MICHAEL WILKINS

him from their sight. They were looking intently up into the sky as he was going, when suddenly two men dressed in white stood beside them. "Men of Galilee," they said, "why do you stand here looking into the sky? This same Jesus, who has been taken from you into heaven, will come back in the same way you have seen him go into heaven." (Acts 1:1–3, 9–11)

Honestly, most Christians don't pay much attention to the ascension of Jesus. He returns to heaven and that's that. And Luke doesn't overdramatize the event himself. But the New Testament writers do focus on the importance of the event in ways that we sometimes miss. From the passages below, notice how the ascension concludes Jesus' earthly ministry and at the same time expands his heavenly ministry in a number of ways:

- Jesus has now been exalted to "the right hand of God" (symbol of ultimate power) as Lord and Christ where he reigns in glory (Ps. 110:1; Acts 2:32–36; 5:30–31; Eph. 1:20–21; Phil. 2:8–11; 1 Tim. 3:16; Heb. 1:3; 2:9; 10:12; 12:2; 1 Peter 3:22; Rev. 1:12–18; 3:21).
- Jesus has poured out his Spirit to live within and empower his people (John 14:12; 16:5, 7, 28; Acts 2:32–33).
- Jesus also gave gifts to the church to equip us for ministry (Eph. 4:7–12).

---

11. Michael Wilkins, *Matthew*, 963–64.

- As our faithful high priest, Jesus now intercedes for us (Rom. 8:34; Heb. 4:14; 6:19–20; 7:25; 8:1; 9:24).
- Jesus is preparing a place for us (John 14:2).

The hope of the early Christians was not just "Christ has died" and "Christ is risen," but also "Christ will come again" (see Acts 1:11). The ascension reminds us that Christ will indeed come again.

Making Connections

Let's review where we are in the Great Story:

Creation and Crisis
Covenant
Calling Out
Commandments
Conquest and Canaanization
Creation of the Kingdom
Communion and Common Sense
Crumbling of the Kingdom
Captivity and Coming Home
Interlude: Time between the Testaments
➤ **Christ:**
　　Jesus Enters Our World
　　Jesus' Message
　　Jesus' Journey to Jerusalem
　　Jesus Dies on the Cross
　　Jesus Is Raised from the Dead
Church
Consummation

As the foundation of the Christian faith, the resurrection stands as significant in a number of ways. First, the resurrection tells us something important about Jesus. The apostle Paul sums it up well at the beginning of his letter to the Christians in Rome:

> Paul, a servant of Christ Jesus, called to be an apostle and set apart for the gospel of God—the gospel he promised beforehand through his prophets in the Holy Scriptures regarding his Son, who as to his earthly life was a descendant of David, and who through the Spirit of holiness was appointed the Son of God in power by his resurrection from the dead: Jesus Christ our Lord. (Rom. 1:1–4)

Through the resurrection, you might say that heaven announces to earth that Jesus is the Son of God. At the cross, Jesus was judged by the religious and political leaders to be a messianic pretender, but at the resurrection God vindicates Jesus as Messiah and Lord! Drawing on Psalm 16 and especially Psalm 110, the apostle Peter concludes his Pentecost sermon in Acts 2 with these words: "Therefore let all Israel be assured of this: God has made this Jesus, whom you crucified, both Lord and Messiah" (Acts 2:36). The human verdict has been turned upside down. The earliest Christian confession, "Jesus is Lord!" rests firmly on the historical reality of the bodily resurrection of Jesus Christ.

The resurrection also relates to the larger Story of Scripture. The problem of sin and death that first intruded on God's good creation in Genesis 3 has been dealt a fatal blow at the resurrection of Jesus. By Jesus' dying on the cross to atone for our sins and by his being raised from the dead, the curse of sin has been broken, the archenemies of God have been decisively defeated, and eternal life begins now for those in Christ. God has kept his covenant promises by conquering evil. Now we know that the Story will end well. God is faithful!

Jesus' resurrection also connects to the final part of the Story and, more specifically, to what will happen to his followers. The early Christians came to describe Jesus as the "firstborn" from among the dead (Col. 1:18; Rev. 1:5) and Jesus' resurrection as the "firstfruits" of a greater harvest to follow (Acts 26:23; 1 Cor. 15:20, 23). At the return of Christ, followers of Jesus will be raised from the dead and receive resurrection bodies fit for life in a new heaven and new earth (1 Cor. 15:20–26, 50–55; 1 Thess. 4:13–18). What happened to Jesus will also happen to us as his bodily resurrection becomes the promise and guarantee of our future resurrection.

Jesus' Great Commission connects to God's earlier promise to Abraham in Genesis 12:3 that through him all peoples on earth will be blessed. Jesus had called twelve disciples as a symbol of reforming faithful Israel as a means of fulfilling God's original promise. Now, after the cross and resurrection, Jesus commissions his disciples to "bring the message of light to his own people and to the Gentiles" (Acts 26:23). This is Jesus' purpose for coming to earth—to launch the kingdom of God, a multicultural kingdom. At the end of the Story we are told that God's people will come from "every nation, tribe, people, and language" (Rev. 5:9; 7:9).

Living the Story

As with the last chapter on the cross of Christ, there are also scores of ways we can live this section of the Story. The resurrection of Jesus means that our faith is more than wishful thinking. The disciples came to believe in Jesus as Messiah and Lord as a result of the resurrection, not the other way around. It's reassuring to remember that you are not just making up this stuff, that you are not just believing in an idea with no connection to reality. Our faith is based on an event that actually happened in history.

The resurrection of Jesus also means that our future involves more than just going to heaven when we die. A popular Christian belief in America is that when we die, our souls are released from our bodies and spend eternity in heaven in an invisible, disembodied state—perhaps drifting through clouds listening to harp music forever. But the Story is crystal clear that Jesus' resurrection guarantees our future resurrection. We too will be raised from the dead and given new, resurrection bodies (Rom. 8:18–25; 1 Cor. 15:35–58; 1 Thess. 4:13–18). We will live in a new heaven *and* a new earth (Rev. 21:1–5; 2 Peter 2:13)!

God's plan involves more than just preparing a place for invisible souls. He will raise us from the dead and give us new bodies. The great Christian hope is not being raptured out of trouble or remembering our loved ones or going to heaven when we die; it is a bodily resurrection from the dead and life in God's new creation! A day will come when death is fully and finally defeated, a day when death will die forever. As a result, we can do exactly what Paul tells the Corinthian Christians to do at the end of his resurrection chapter: "Therefore, my dear brothers and sisters, stand firm. Let nothing move you. Always give yourselves fully to the work of the Lord, because you know that your labor in the Lord is not in vain" (1 Cor. 15:58).

The Great Commission brings us back down to earth and reminds us that there is much to be done before Christ returns. Jesus clearly spells out our mission of making disciples of all nations. Our mission is not just evangelism or community ministry or doing church. Our mission is to follow Jesus ourselves, to invite others to follow Jesus, and to help one another obey Jesus' teachings.

The ascension of Jesus reminds us that the resurrected Jesus now reigns in heaven and will one day return. When he ascended, Jesus didn't just evaporate or dissolve; he physically went up to heaven in the sight of the disciples, meaning that we now have a representative in heaven with a resurrection body, and we await his return (Acts 1:11). N. T. Wright makes the point that we need to "grasp firmly that the church is *not* Jesus and Jesus is *not* the church ... the truth of the ascension, that the one who is indeed present with us by the Spirit, is also the Lord who is strangely absent, strangely other, strangely different from us."[13]

The Story is not complete until Jesus' rule includes the new heaven and new earth. Until that day, we continue to "wait for the blessed hope—the appearing of the glory of our great God and Savior, Jesus Christ" (Titus 2:13).

Life after Life after Death

"Resurrection isn't a fancy way of saying 'going to heaven when you die.' It is not about 'life after death' as such. Rather, it's a way of talking about being bodily alive again *after* a period of being bodily dead. Resurrection is ... about 'life *after* "life after death."' After you die, you go to be 'with Christ' ('life after death'), but your body remains dead.... What is promised *after* that interim period is a new bodily life within God's new world ('life *after* "life after death"')."[12]

– N. T. WRIGHT

---

12. N. T. Wright, *Simply Christian: Why Christianity Makes Sense* (New York: HarperOne, 2006), 114–15, 218–19.

13. N. T. Wright, *Surprised by Hope: Rethinking Heaven, the Resurrection, and the Mission of the Church* (New York: HarperOne, 2008), 113.

We continue to pray the Lord's Prayer: "Our Father in heaven, hallowed be your name, your kingdom come, your will be done, on earth as it is in heaven" (Matt. 6:9–10). We continue to pray the ancient Aramaic prayer— *maranatha*—"Come, Lord Jesus" (Rev. 22:20; cf. 1 Cor. 16:22).

Wrapping Up

After the cross, the disciples' hopes in Jesus as Messiah are completely crushed. In their despair, they certainly aren't expecting the shock of the resurrection. But Jesus' resurrection demonstrates that he is indeed Lord and Messiah! God is faithful to keep his promise to rescue his creation from the grip of sin and death. All things will be made new. In the meantime, Jesus gives his followers clear instructions about their mission in this world—"Go and make disciples of all nations" (Matt. 28:19). Jesus' ascension concludes his earthly ministry but expands his heavenly ministry and serves as a reminder that he will return again. The next part of the Story relates to how the followers of Jesus, the church, should live as they wait for the final consummation of God's kingdom.

Memory Verse

The angel said to the women, "Do not be afraid, for I know that you are looking for Jesus, who was crucified. He is not here; he has risen, just as he said." (Matt. 28:5–6)

Digging Deeper

Books

Bauckham, Richard. *Jesus and the Eyewitnesses: The Gospels as Eyewitness Testimony*. Grand Rapids: Eerdmans, 2008.

Craig, William Lane. "Did Jesus Rise from the Dead?" In *Jesus under Fire*. Edited by Michael J. Wilkins and J. P. Moreland. Grand Rapids: Zondervan, 1995.

Wright, N. T. *The Resurrection of the Son of God*. Philadelphia: Fortress, 2003.

———. *Surprised by Hope: Rethinking Heaven, the Resurrection, and the Mission of the Church*. New York: HarperOne, 2008.

ASSIGNMENTS

1. One of the most powerful discussions on the resurrection occurs in 1 Corinthians 15. Study this chapter with the help of a good Bible commentary. Then make an extended outline of the chapter so that you can follow Paul's line of thought throughout the chapter. Write a concluding paragraph about the significance of the resurrection of Jesus Christ for believers.

2. Return to John 11 and the account of Jesus' raising Lazarus from the dead. Read that story again from the viewpoint of someone (perhaps even Martha) who now lives on this side of the resurrection of Jesus. Write a two-page explanation of Jesus' words and actions in light of his coming resurrection. For example, think about Martha's statement that everyone will rise again at the resurrection on the last day in 11:24 as the typical Jewish view of the last days, along with Jesus' response to her in 11:25.

3. Simon Peter's journey through the last days of Jesus is a spiritual rollercoaster ride. For example, he boasts that he will never deny Christ before denying him three times. He then decides to return to his old profession of fishing before seeing the risen Christ on the beach. By reading all four gospels, compile a record of what happens to Peter from the triumphal entry through the ascension of Jesus. Then write a concluding paragraph or two about how these events and experiences must have forever changed Simon Peter.

4. Imagine that we really will be raised from the dead and be given new bodies perfectly prepared for life in a whole new world. Put aside the idea of living forever as a disembodied soul and think in fresh ways about eternal life in a physical world, a brand-new world with mountains and rivers and beaches and cities. In this new world, there will be no temptation or sin or sickness or war or pain or hunger or violence or death or evil of any kind. In this perfectly beautiful new creation, you will find family and friends who love Jesus. You will have true community with people from various cultures because you will all have the main thing in common: a relationship with God through Jesus Christ. And you also will have a brand-new body. Write a two-page personal reflection of how you would like to spend the first ten years of your new life in the new heaven and new earth.

CHURCH:
The Coming of the Spirit

Chapter 16

Enter Here

Growing up, I was a big fan of the TV series *Batman*. On many afternoons after school I would watch Bruce Wayne transform into the Caped Crusader and rescue Gotham City from villains such as the Joker, the Riddler, the Penguin, Catwoman, and Mr. Freeze. Most episodes began with the villain committing a crime. Police Commissioner Gordan and Chief O'Hara would then decide that Batman was the only one who could help, and they would call him on the Batphone. Alfred the butler normally answered the Batphone at Wayne Manor and would interrupt the leisurely business of Bruce and Dick, who would then race to the Batpoles behind the bookcase and drop into the Batcave. Now transformed into Batman and Robin, the dynamic duo would race out of the Batcave in the Batmobile to fight crime and save their beloved city.

Some episodes were cliffhangers. At the end of such episodes, Batman and Robin found themselves in deep trouble, usually on the verge of death with no apparent way of escape. Just as the crime fighters were about to breathe their last, the words "To Be Continued" would flash on the screen and conclude the episode. I was not a happy camper when I saw those words because I knew it meant that I had to wait another week to see how good would triumph over evil.

In some ways, the book of Acts is like the concluding episode of a cliffhanger. Of course, Batman doesn't compare to Jesus as a superhero, but Acts does serve as the follow-up episode to the Gospels chapter in the Story. In fact, originally, the gospel of Luke and the book of Acts were two volumes of a single work. While we have four versions of the life and ministry of Jesus in Matthew, Mark, Luke, and John, we only have one account of the life of the early church—Acts. This unique book describes the first Christian generation from Jesus' resurrection (about AD 30) to the end of Paul's ministry (mid AD 60s). Acts gives us a glimpse into how God's Story continues after Jesus' ascension into heaven.

Be Prepared

Read or listen to Luke 1:1–4; 24:36–53; Acts 1–2; Jeremiah 31.

The Story Continues

In the gospel of Luke, we see the beginning of God's plan to offer salvation to the world through Jesus Christ. In the second volume, the book of Acts, we see how God continues to work out his redemptive purposes through his people now empowered by his Spirit. What Jesus started, the Spirit now continues through the church. This ongoing work of Jesus is implied in the first verse of Acts: "In my former book, Theophilus, I wrote about all that Jesus *began to do and to teach* …" (1:1, italics added). The kingdom of God has been introduced, but it has not yet fully come. Between the first coming of Jesus and his second coming, there is a worldwide mission. Jesus' work will continue through his people; that is the focus of the book of Acts.

Preparation for Pentecost (Acts 1)

In the chart on page 217, you can see how the end of Luke's gospel links to the beginning of Acts as a seamless transition from one part of the Story to another. What Jesus began to do in the gospel, he now continues to do in Acts. Because of Jesus' death and resurrection, the good news of forgiveness may

Luke and Theophilus

Luke was a well-educated Gentile, a physician, and a missionary coworker of the apostle Paul (Col. 4:14; Philem. 24). You might never guess it, but Luke wrote more words in the New Testament than any other author, including Paul. He was probably not an eyewitness of Jesus, but he did careful research in preparation for writing his two volumes (Luke 1:1–4). He was also skilled with language since Luke-Acts displays excellent literary Greek. Most likely, Luke accompanied Paul on some of his missionary journeys (note the use of the pronoun "we" in certain sections of Acts: 16:10–17; 20:5–21:8; 27:1–28:16; cf. 2 Tim. 4:11).

Both Luke and Acts are addressed to "most excellent Theophilus" (Luke 1:3; Acts 1:1). His title indicates that he is a person of rank and wealth and quite possibly the one who paid for Luke-Acts to be copied for wider distribution. What Luke says in Luke 1:1–4 makes it likely that Theophilus is a recent convert to faith in Christ (i.e., the events "fulfilled among us" in 1:1 and a reference to previous instruction in 1:4). Luke probably wants to instruct and encourage Theophilus in his new faith. Most scholars believe that Luke-Acts was also intended for a wider audience, perhaps Gentile Christians throughout the Roman Empire.

End of Luke → Beginning of Acts

Luke 24:46–53	Acts 1:1–11
He told them, "This is what is written: The Messiah will suffer and rise from the dead on the third day, and repentance for the forgiveness of sins will be preached in his name to all nations, beginning at Jerusalem. You are witnesses of these things. I am going to send you what my Father has promised; but stay in the city until you have been clothed with power from on high." When he had led them out to the vicinity of Bethany, he lifted up his hands and blessed them. While he was blessing them, he left them and was taken up into heaven. Then they worshiped him and returned to Jerusalem with great joy. And they stayed continually at the temple, praising God.	In my former book, Theophilus, I wrote about all that Jesus began to do and to teach until the day he was taken up to heaven, after giving instructions through the Holy Spirit to the apostles he had chosen. After his suffering, he presented himself to them and gave many convincing proofs that he was alive. He appeared to them over a period of forty days and spoke about the kingdom of God. On one occasion, while he was eating with them, he gave them this command: "Do not leave Jerusalem, but wait for the gift my Father promised, which you have heard me speak about. For John baptized with water, but in a few days you will be baptized with the Holy Spirit." Then they gathered around him and asked him, "Lord, are you at this time going to restore the kingdom to Israel?" He said to them: "It is not for you to know the times or dates the Father has set by his own authority. But you will receive power when the Holy Spirit comes on you; and you will be my witnesses in Jerusalem, and in all Judea and Samaria, and to the ends of the earth." After he said this, he was taken up before their very eyes, and a cloud hid him from their sight. They were looking intently up into the sky as he was going, when suddenly two men dressed in white stood beside them. "Men of Galilee," they said, "why do you stand here looking into the sky? This same Jesus, who has been taken from you into heaven, will come back in the same way you have seen him go into heaven."

now be preached to all nations, beginning in Jerusalem. In the gospel of Luke, Jesus travels to Jerusalem for his divine appointment with the cross. In Acts, the church will journey away from Jerusalem to be witnesses to all the world of what Jesus has accomplished. The disciples must wait in Jerusalem, however, until they are "clothed with power from on high"—the promised Holy Spirit.

The disciples are waiting—forty days from the resurrection of Jesus to his ascension and ten more days until Pentecost. During that waiting period, four important events take place: (1) they receive instructions about the coming of the Spirit and their role as witnesses (Acts 1:6–8); (2) they see Jesus ascend into heaven (1:9–11); (3) they meet together consistently to pray (1:12–14); and (4) they replace Judas with Matthias as the twelfth apostle (1:15–26). Throughout Acts, these realities remain important—power supplied by the

Spirit, Jesus' commission to witness, the exalted Lord who guides the mission, the importance of prayer, and the central role of the apostles.

Notice that in both Luke and Acts, Jesus specifically says that the good news will be preached to all nations (Luke 24:47; Acts 1:8). The scope of God's rescue plan stands in contrast to what the disciples have in mind when they ask in Acts 1:6: "Lord, are you at this time going to restore the kingdom to Israel?" They are expecting a national kingdom ("Israel") while Jesus speaks of a universal kingdom (including all nations), as promised to Abraham. They are expecting the kingdom to arrive at any moment, perhaps in conjunction with the coming of the Spirit, while Jesus implies that the kingdom will arrive fully and completely only at his return. He warns them not to speculate about "times or dates" and turns their attention to the job assigned to them in the interim (Acts 1:8). They continue to wait on the promised gift from the Father, the Holy Spirit.

Exalted to God's Right Hand

"Then Jesus is taken up into heaven (Acts 1:9), or 'exalted to the right hand of God,' as Peter says later (Acts 2:33; 5:31). This is coronation day! The Messiah now shares the throne of God over all creation and all peoples. It is important to understand the significance of that *place* described as 'the right hand of God.' Though many Jews believe that the Messiah will share the throne of God, they expect God's throne to be in Jerusalem, from which the Messiah will rule a worldwide Jewish empire. However, the throne of the Messiah as Peter describes is not in Jerusalem at all: it stands entirely above the world, in heaven at the right hand of God. This is the place of *highest* authority and honor. God's kingdom has no boundaries of any kind. Jesus does not merely sit on the throne of our hearts and reign there: that is much too narrow a concept of his authority. Jesus reigns over all of human life, all history, and all nations."[1]

– CRAIG BARTHOLOMEW
AND MICHAEL GOHEEN

Pentecost: The Coming of the Holy Spirit (2:1–47)

After all their waiting and praying, the gift of the Holy Spirit finally arrives in a mighty way (2:1–13). The Jewish festival of *Pentecost* (from a Greek word meaning "fiftieth") was also called the Feast of Weeks. Fifty days after Passover, the Jews celebrated Pentecost as their annual grain harvest. During this time they thanked God for his faithful provision throughout the year and celebrated their deliverance from slavery in Egypt as God's covenant people (Deut. 16:9–12; Lev. 23:15–22; Num. 28:26–31). Later, Pentecost came to celebrate the giving of the Law to Moses on Mount Sinai. It was a pilgrimage festival, so during this time the population of Jerusalem would grow dramatically with visitors from around the world. The 120 believers are together in one place when the miracle of Pentecost occurs:

> Suddenly a sound like the blowing of a violent wind came from heaven and filled the whole house where they were sitting. They saw what seemed to be tongues of fire that separated and came to rest on each of them. All of them were filled with the Holy Spirit and began to speak in other tongues as the Spirit enabled them. (Acts 2:2–4)

---

1. Craig G. Bartholomew and Michael W. Goheen, *The Drama of Scripture: Finding Our Place in the Biblical Story* (Grand Rapids: Baker, 2004), 172.

Wind and fire are often connected with the powerful presence of God in the Bible. In Ezekiel's vision of the dry bones, the life-giving breath of God comes as a wind to make the dead bones live again (Ezek. 37). During the exodus event, God appears to Moses as a burning bush, and later the Lord descends in fire to appear to Moses on Mount Sinai (Ex. 19). The coming of the Spirit is the coming of the very presence of God. Like wind and fire, it comes with great power.

Throughout the Greco-Roman Empire, Greek was the official language, much like English is today in much of the world. But most people were multilingual and could also speak in a local language. Jews from around the Mediterranean world have gathered in Jerusalem for Pentecost. A large group of these Jews from other nations hears the loud sound and gathers near the house where the believers are praying to see what is going on. They soon realize that they are hearing these 120 Galilean Christians speak of the "wonders of God," but surprisingly, they are hearing these praises in their own local language from back home (Acts 2:5–12).

"Tongues" in this context refers to known languages (Acts 2:6, 8, 11). This seems different from the gift of tongues described in 1 Corinthians since here the Jews from the surrounding nations can understand the message in their own language. (The gift of tongues Paul later describes seems to have been used for private times of prayer and praise.) Most who observe what is happening to these believers are amazed and curious, while others mock and ridicule them (Acts 2:12–13).

> ### God Expects Us to Use His Power
>
> "Imagine visiting a town at night that appears to have no lights, no television—not even alarm clocks. And then imagine learning that the town's power supply is virtually infinite, but that no one in the town had thought to turn any of their electrical appliances on. Wouldn't that town seem like a silly place to you? Yet the Church is all too often like that town. God has given us the power of His Spirit to fulfill His mission in the world, yet few Christians have even begun to depend on His power."[2]
>
> – CRAIG KEENER

For Christians, Pentecost became much more than an annual Jewish festival. Pentecost represents a new chapter in God's Story when God the Spirit comes to live permanently within individual followers of Jesus Christ.

Peter Explains the Importance of Pentecost (Acts 2:14–41)

Simon Peter now stands up and explains what has just happened. These believers aren't drunk, he insists, because "it is only nine in the morning" (Acts 2:14–15). Rather, the Holy Spirit has just been poured out on God's people, as predicted by the prophet Joel (Acts 2:16–21; see Joel 2:28–32). The coming of the Spirit marks the beginning of the "last days," the time period stretching from the first coming of Christ and the outpouring of the Spirit to the return of Christ. Joel had said that God would pour out his Spirit on all

---

2. Craig S. Keener, *Three Crucial Questions about the Holy Spirit* (Grand Rapids: Baker, 1996), 17.

A Learning Community

"Anti-intellectualism and the fullness of the Spirit are mutually incompatible, because the Holy Spirit is the Spirit of truth. Nor did those early disciples imagine that, because they had received the Spirit, he was the only teacher they needed and they could dispense with human teachers. On the contrary, they sat at the apostles' feet, hungry to receive instruction, and they persevered in it.... The two references to the apostles, in verse 42 (their teaching) and in verse 43 (their miracles), can hardly be an accident. Since the teaching of the apostles has come down to us in its definitive form in the New Testament, contemporary devotion to the apostles' teaching will mean submission to the authority of the New Testament. A Spirit-filled church is a New Testament church, in the sense that it studies and submits to New Testament instruction. The Spirit of God leads the people of God to submit to the Word of God."[3]

— JOHN STOTT

people (family members as well as servants, men and women, young and old). These people would prophesy or declare the wonders of God. In essence, every believer would become a prophet or one who declares the wonders of God. This is what just happened to the 120 believers.

Peter now uses more Scripture to show how the Spirit continues what Jesus began. During his life, Jesus performed mighty miracles that demonstrated the coming of God's kingdom (Acts 2:22). People were set free from disease and demonic oppression, and even death. But Jesus died a violent death at the hands of the religious leaders (2:23). God, however, raised Jesus from the dead and exalted him to the highest place (2:24–35; cf. Ps. 16:8–11; 110:1). In other words, "God has made this Jesus, whom you crucified, both Lord and Messiah," and this has resulted in the pouring out of the Holy Spirit (Acts 2:33, 36).

The listeners are "cut to the heart" with conviction and ask what they should do (Acts 2:37). Peter calls them to repentance and public confession of faith through baptism, at which point they will receive the gift of the promised Holy Spirit (2:38–39). Amazingly, about three thousand people become followers of Jesus (2:40–41).

A New Community of the Spirit (Acts 2:42–47)

Now Luke describes the new community formed by the Spirit, a community through whom he will work to finish the Story. This new Spirit community or church is characterized by certain practices and qualities. First, they are committed to the Word of God: "They devoted themselves to the apostles' teaching," a teaching authenticated by "wonders and signs" (Acts 2:42–43).

As eyewitnesses of Jesus, the apostles pass on teachings that focus on the

---

3. John R. W. Stott, *The Message of Acts* (Downers Grove: InterVarsity, 1994), 82.

life, ministry, death, and resurrection of Jesus. These teachings become the foundation of truth for the new community.

Second, the new community is a loving and generous community. They devote themselves to "fellowship," and they are eager to give up their possessions to help those in need (Acts 2:42, 44–45). The concept of "fellowship" (*koinōnia*) involves generosity in sharing, giving, or participating. People matter greatly in the new community.

Third, the new community is a worshiping community. They devote themselves to "the breaking of bread and to prayer" (2:42), and they break "bread in their homes" and eat together "with glad and sincere hearts, praising God" (2:46–47a). The breaking of bread probably refers to the early Christian practice of observing the Lord's Supper as part of an ordinary fellowship meal. The reference to "prayer" is literally "the prayers" and suggests times of praying together rather than just times of private prayer. They worship with "glad and sincere hearts," meaning that their gatherings are characterized by joy and authenticity.

Fourth, as a result of their commitment to God's Word, their devotion to loving and sharing with one another, and their passionate worship of God, the Lord adds to their number. The new community is an open and growing community that enjoys the "favor of all the people" (2:47). No doubt they have opportunities as they meet together in the temple courts to explain why they have put their faith and hope in Jesus as Messiah (2:46). And the Lord honors that witness as those who are being saved are added to the new community (2:47).

Community and Solitude

"*Let him who cannot be alone beware of community.* He will only do harm to himself and to the community. Alone you stood before God when he called you; alone you had to answer that call; alone you had to struggle and pray; and alone you will die and give an account to God. You cannot escape from yourself; for God singled you out. . . .

"But the reverse is also true: *Let him who is not in community beware of being alone.* Into the community you were called, the call was not meant for you alone; in the community of the called you bear your cross, you struggle, you pray. You are not alone, even in death, and on the Last Day you will be only one member of the great congregation of Jesus Christ.

"We recognize, then, that only as we are within the fellowship can we be alone, and only he that is alone can live in the fellowship."[4]

– DIETRICH BONHOEFFER

4. Dietrich Bonhoeffer, *Life Together* (New York: Harper & Row, 1954), 77.

Making Connections

Let's review where we are in the Great Story:

Creation and Crisis
Covenant
Calling Out
Commandments
Conquest and Canaanization
Creation of the Kingdom
Communion and Common Sense
Crumbling of the Kingdom
Captivity and Coming Home
Interlude: Time between the Testaments
Christ
➤ **Church:**
    The Coming of the Spirit
    In Jerusalem, Judea, and Samaria
    The Mission to the Gentiles
    The Gospel Spreads from Jerusalem to Rome
Consummation

As Peter explains the meaning of Pentecost, everything rests on what happened to Jesus. As one Jew to another, Peter in effect says to the crowd, "You thought you got rid of this troublemaker from Nazareth by killing him on a cross, but God had other ideas. God has raised him from the dead, and Jesus' resurrection demonstrates that he is both Israel's Messiah and the sovereign Lord of the universe" (see Acts 2:23–24, 31–32, 36). When Jesus was exalted to God's right hand, the Spirit was poured out on God's people just as he promised. This has fulfilled the Old Testament prophecies that God would make a new covenant with his people by writing his law on their hearts and living them, as Jeremiah 31:31–34 predicts:

> "The days are coming," declares the LORD,
>   "when I will make a new covenant
> with the people of Israel
>   and with the people of Judah.
> It will not be like the covenant
>   I made with their ancestors
> when I took them by the hand
>   to lead them out of Egypt,
> because they broke my covenant,
>   though I was a husband to them,"
>   declares the LORD.

"This is the covenant I will make with the people of Israel
    after that time," declares the LORD.
"I will put my law in their minds
    and write it on their hearts.
I will be their God,
    and they will be my people.
No longer will they teach their neighbor,
    or say to one another, 'Know the LORD,'
because they will all know me,
    from the least of them to the greatest,"
                               declares the LORD.
"For I will forgive their wickedness
    and will remember their sins no more."

God originally formed the nation of Israel to bless all the peoples of the world (Gen. 12:1–3), but Israel failed to carry out its calling and actually opposed God's Messiah. Yet God remains faithful to keep his promise to restore his people and to use them to accomplish his mission of restoring all of creation. Jesus begins to restore the people of God by calling twelve apostles, symbolizing the restoration of the twelve tribes of Israel. Scripture had predicted that the Spirit would be poured out at an important time in the restoration process (Ezek. 36:24–28; 37:14; 39:29; Joel 2:28–29). Now the Spirit has been poured out on the "true Israel" in order to bring the message to all nations, thus fulfilling God's original purpose (Rom. 9:6; Gal. 6:16; Eph. 3:6). God is working through this new Spirit community to fulfill his promise to Abraham so that everyone may have the opportunity to enter into a relationship with God.

God's larger purpose relates to his desire to be present among his people in a personal way. The phrase in Jer. 31:33—"I will be their God, and they will be my people"—connects to a much bigger promise found throughout the Story, a promise that brings hope like nothing else. This promise often appears with three parts (see Lev. 26:12; Ezek. 37:27; 2 Cor. 6:16):

- I will be your God;
- You will be my people;
- I will live among you.

This is God's biggest promise—bigger than "getting saved" or "going to heaven" or "doing ministry." From the beginning God has been working to create a community so that they could enjoy perfect fellowship with him in a restored creation.

On the night before he went to the cross, Jesus had promised that the Holy Spirit (the "helper" or "advocate" in John 14:16, 26; 15:26; 16:7) would make his presence known to the disciples.

God Has Always Wanted to Live with His People

- Garden of Eden with Adam and Eve (Gen. 3:8)
- Special appearances to people like Abraham, Isaac, Jacob, Moses, and the Prophets
- The tabernacle (Ex. 25:8)
- The temple (1 Kings 8; 2 Chron. 6:18; Ezek. 10:18)
- The Word (Jesus) became flesh, Immanuel, God with us (John 1:1, 14)
- The new community of the Spirit, the church (John 14:16; 1 Cor. 3:16)
- God will live with his people face-to-face in the new heaven and new earth (Rev. 21:3)

As a continuation of what Jesus began to do, the coming of the Spirit at Pentecost is a major leap forward in God's master plan. The new community has been formed. God's Holy Spirit will live within believers and use them to bring the good news of the kingdom to all peoples. God is making a new covenant with his people and fulfilling his promise to live among them.

Living the Story

Living the Story at this point becomes relevant since we stand with the early Christians on this side of the cross, resurrection, and Pentecost. The first way we can live this aspect of the Story is to know that we were created to be with God, not just corporately but also individually. The "tongues of fire" come to rest on each of the believers at Pentecost (Acts 2:3). All of them are filled with the Spirit (2:4). The Spirit of God now dwells within individual believers who are formed into a community of the Spirit. We were created to be connected to God in a deeply relational way. A pencil was made to write or draw. A hammer was made to hit or remove nails. Glasses were made to improve vision, and so on. Human beings were made to relate to God and to God's creation, including other people. Our deepest needs are relational. Pentecost made the long-term vision of God living among his people more of a reality than ever before. You don't have to wait until heaven to experience God's presence. Life with God starts now, thanks to the presence of the Holy Spirit.

What's more, we not only have the Spirit; we also have each other. We are part of a new community in which the barriers that have separated human beings since sin entered the Story begin to come down. At Pentecost, God

What Is Life without Hope?

"Living without hope is no longer living. Hell is hopelessness and it is not for nothing that at the entrance to Dante's hell there stand the words: 'Abandon hope, all you who enter here.'"[5]

— JÜRGEN MOLTMANN

---

5. Jürgen Moltmann, *Theology of Hope* (Minneapolis: Fortress, 1993), 32.

is praised in different languages. Men and women prophesy or proclaim the wonders of God; young and old alike experience communion with the Lord. God delights in making people one without making them all the same. Different doesn't mean better; it just means different.

It's good to remember that God doesn't destroy the unique cultures of the world in order to create a one-Christian world culture. He joins us together in Christ and forms us into one community in Christ, but we live out those relationships in a variety of cultural expressions. What's important is making sure that you are part of a local community. Are you connected to a local church where you can grow in your understanding of God's Word, live in community where giving and sharing are commonplace, and worship the Lord with a joyful heart? Living the Story is much harder, if not impossible, without a connection to a local community of the Spirit.

Just as Jesus needed to walk in the strength of the Holy Spirit during his public ministry, so we too need to depend on the Spirit. As the Spirit does his transforming work within us, we will talk about the Lord and, as a result, outsiders will be attracted to God and to our community. Notice how often speech is emphasized throughout the Pentecost episode (e.g., tongues of fire, other languages, the fulfillment of prophecy, Peter's sermon). Human beings talk about what they love. If we love a sport or a hobby, we will talk about it. If we love our family, we will talk about them. So too, if we love the Lord, we will talk about him.

At Pentecost, believers receive a new power for talking about God. It's encouraging to remember that Peter, the guy who once vehemently denied even knowing Jesus, is the same person who later preaches the powerful Pentecost sermon. Only the Spirit can change a person from a fearful failure into a bold and engaging witness for Jesus. The Spirit continues to change people like that.

Wrapping Up

The book of Acts is unique as the one story in the Bible about the life of the early church. Acts takes up where the Gospels (especially the gospel of Luke) leave off. What Jesus began to do during his earthly ministry, he now continues to do through the Holy Spirit and the church.

After watching Jesus ascend into heaven, the disciples wait in anticipation of the coming of the promised Holy Spirit. One day while they are praying together, the Holy Spirit descends on the group of 120 believers at Pentecost. From that point forward, the Spirit of God now lives among the people of God, both corporately and individually, empowering them to work with God in his mission of rescuing people and restoring his creation.

Memory Verse

They devoted themselves to the apostles' teaching and to fellowship, to the breaking of bread and to prayer. (Acts 2:42)

Digging Deeper

Books

Fernando, Ajith. *Acts*. The NIV Application Commentary. Grand Rapids: Zondervan, 1998.

Peterson, David G. *The Acts of the Apostles*. Pillar New Testament Commentary. Grand Rapids: Eerdmans, 2009.

Polhill, John B. *Acts*. New American Commentary. Nashville: Broadman, 1992.

ASSIGNMENTS

1. Acts emphasizes the importance of fellowship, and fellowship involves sharing and giving. Read Acts 1:1–6:7 carefully, looking specifically for references to generous giving or sharing among the believers. For example, in Acts 2:45 we read that they sold property and possessions and gave to "anyone who had need," but in verse 46 we learn that they "broke bread in *their* homes," meaning that many still owned homes. Make a list of all the references to giving and sharing (or failing to do so) and write a concluding paragraph or two explaining the importance of fellowship in the early church.

2. In Acts 2:42–47 we read about the new community of the Spirit. Read that section again, paying special attention to the characteristics of this new community. Then write a two-page essay on how churches today could pursue those same qualities. What would such a church look like in terms of organization? What would it do or not do? What kind of priorities would it have? How would it incorporate the elements of Acts 2:42–47 into its life and ministries, and so on?

3. Read the entire book of Acts, looking for every place that the Spirit comes on a person or group of people (e.g., Acts 4:8, 31; 7:55; 8:15–17; 9:17–19). Make a list of all those occurrences and ask one important question of all the instances: What happens when people are filled with the Spirit? Write a concluding paragraph or two summarizing your findings and explaining their significance.

CHURCH:
In Jerusalem, Judea, and Samaria

Chapter 17

Enter Here

In August of 2004, I got in on the early stages of planting a church. A small group of people had recruited a colleague of mine to help in leadership the previous year, and my wife and I were deeply excited when they asked us to join them. We live in a college town, and it wasn't long before we were having more and more students attend our worship gatherings. The church's philosophy was simple—gather to worship on Sunday mornings, meet in home groups on Sunday night to share life (and food) together in a time centered around the Story, and the rest of the week seek to be the church in the community.

It's been eight years and Fellowship Church of Arkadelphia is still going strong, but a lot has happened in those eight years. We have seen God do some amazing things within our community and beyond. While we haven't faced persecution, we have worked our way through some opposition to our form of church government (elder-led congregationalism). We've faced the struggles of organizing in a way that maintains biblical priorities and meets practical needs. We've wrestled with the scarcity of older adult leaders, and money always seems to be an issue. On top of all that, we desire to be a multicultural congregation in the southern United States, and that brings another set of obstacles. But through it all, the Spirit has cultivated an attitude of unity and generosity among us that is contagious. Most exciting of all, I would say, the Spirit has encouraged us to become a "sending church," that is, a church that values sending people out on mission more than investing ever-greater resources into growing a bigger organization here.

My experience at Fellowship Church has given me a taste of what the early days of the church must have been like. Not perfect by any stretch (just read Acts 5 again), but alive and dynamic as the Spirit worked among the people to accomplish his mission. Let's pick up the adventure just after Pentecost.

Be Prepared

Read or listen to Acts 3–12; Hebrews 8–12; James 1–3; 1 Peter 1–2; Jude.

The Story Continues

Many consider Acts 1:8 to be an outline of Acts in a single verse: "But you will receive power when the Holy Spirit comes on you; and you will be my witnesses in Jerusalem, and in all Judea and Samaria, and to the ends of the earth." The Spirit empowers the early church to be witnesses first in the city of Jerusalem, where Jesus was crucified and raised from the dead. Then, just as Jesus journeyed to Jerusalem to die for the sins of the world, so now the church takes the good news of God's forgiveness away from that city to the rest of the world. In this chapter you will see how this early Christian witness occurred within Jerusalem itself before moving outward in ever-expanding waves to the surrounding regions of Judea and Samaria. In the following chapters, you will see this message move all the way to Rome itself and beyond, clearly showing God's heart for the nations. In the three chapters dealing with Acts 3–28, we will also introduce you to many of the letters of the New Testament so that you can see for yourself the inner workings and heartbeat of the early church.

In Jerusalem: The Spirit Works through the Apostles (Acts 3:1–4:31)

As Jewish Christians, the believers retain their custom of going to the temple for prayer. One day as Peter and John are entering the complex through the Beautiful Gate (Acts 3:1–4), they meet a crippled beggar desperate for help.

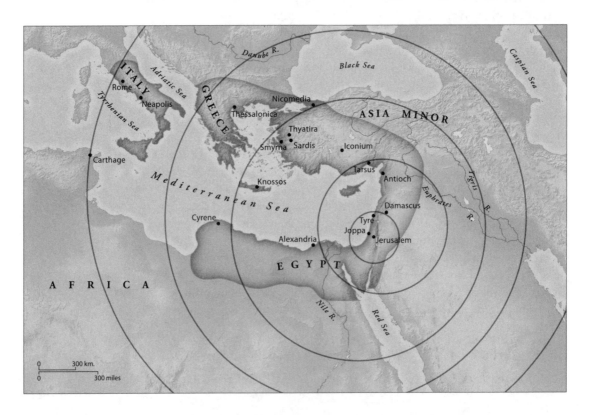

Although they cannot offer him money, they do offer him physical healing in the name of Jesus (Acts 3:5 – 7). The healed man then celebrates by jumping for joy as he praises God in the temple courts, and the people watch in amazement (3:8 – 10). This guy had been begging a very long time.

As in the Gospels, miracles are often signs that point to a greater message. Peter now preaches a second sermon in which he uses Scripture to connect the beggar's healing to Jesus as the crucified and resurrected Messiah, the one Abraham, Moses, and the Prophets had spoken about (Acts 3:11 – 26). Peter challenges the people to repent and turn to God in order to experience life.

Because many people are trusting in Jesus because of the man's healing, the Jewish Sanhedrin arrests Peter and John for questioning (Acts 4:1 – 22). They are disturbed that the apostles are proclaiming the resurrection from the dead and that the people are starting to believe their message. Peter, the same guy who once denied Jesus, now boldly proclaims not only that Jesus is responsible for this man's healing but also that he provides the only way of salvation. When warned by the Sanhedrin to speak no more in Jesus' name, Peter and John take their stand: "Which is right in God's eyes: to listen to you, or to him? You be the judges! As for us, we cannot help speaking about what we have seen and heard" (Acts 4:19 – 20). After being released, the apostles report everything to the other believers, who praise God and ask for courage to be faithful as God continues to work (Acts 4:23 – 31).

> ### Embodied Spirituality
>
> "The gospel may remain a mystery to the surrounding culture unless the church lives out the gospel in the form of its life together. It is the pattern of the believing community's relationships that embodies the story of Jesus in concrete terms that outsiders can comprehend. Only when the gospel is linked to such concrete illustrations can outsiders say, 'I see what you mean.' "[1]
>
> **– BRAD KALLENBERG**

In Jerusalem: The Spirit Works in the Community (Acts 4:32 – 5:11)

Once again, the Spirit inspires generosity and sharing within the community so that "there were no needy persons among them" (Acts 4:34). One especially encouraging person is Barnabas, who sells a field and gives the money to the apostles to distribute to those in need (Acts 4:36 – 37). In contrast to his integrity and generosity, we read about the greed, hypocrisy, and deception of Ananias and Sapphira, who sell property and pretend to give all the proceeds to the church but secretly keep some for themselves (5:1 – 11). For lying to the Spirit and deceiving the community, both serious threats to the young church, the couple is harshly punished with physical death.

In Jerusalem: More Power and More Persecution (Acts 5:12 – 42)

The Christians go on meeting together in Solomon's Colonnade, and the Lord keeps adding to their number. As they speak the message about Jesus and as the apostles perform signs and wonders, it becomes apparent that Jesus is

---

1. Brad Kallenberg, *Live to Tell: Evangelism to the Postmodern Age* (Grand Rapids: Brazos, 2002), 50.

still doing through his Spirit and his apostles what he began to do during his earthly ministry (Acts 5:12–16).

But as the miracles continue and more people put their faith in Jesus, the pressure from the religious authorities mounts. Motivated by jealousy, they arrest the apostles once again and put them in jail (Acts 5:17–18). This time the Lord rescues them during the night and commands them to return to the temple courts and to resume speaking about new life in Christ, which they do (5:19–21). Once discovered, they are rearrested and interrogated by the high priest before the Sanhedrin. When asked why they have not stopped speaking about Jesus, Peter and the other apostles reply:

> We must obey God rather than human beings! The God of our ancestors raised Jesus from the dead—whom you killed by hanging him on a cross. God exalted him to his own right hand as Prince and Savior that he might bring Israel to repentance and forgive their sins. We are witnesses of these things, and so is the Holy Spirit, whom God has given to those who obey him. (Acts 5:29–32)

The religious leaders are furious and are ready to kill the apostles, when a Pharisee named Gamaliel intervenes. He persuades the Sanhedrin to punish and release the apostles in hopes that the movement will die out. If the movement is from God, however, the Jewish leaders don't want to be fighting against God (Acts 5:33–39). They have the apostles brutally beaten and then release them with the warning not to speak anymore about Jesus. The apostles leave the Sanhedrin, rejoicing that they have been considered worthy of suffering for Jesus' sake. We are then told that "day after day, in the temple courts and from house to house, they never stopped teaching and proclaiming the good news that Jesus is the Messiah" (5:42).

In Jerusalem: The Church Organizes to Maintain Priorities and Meet Needs (Acts 6:1–7)

In addition to dealing with hypocrisy within the community (i.e., Ananias and Sapphira) and persecution from the Sanhedrin, the young church also faces the logistical challenge of caring for more and more people. Some of the widows of the Greek-speaking Jewish Christians are being overlooked in the daily distribution of food (Acts 6:1–2). The apostles act quickly to remedy this injustice. They propose that seven wise, Spirit-filled men be appointed to oversee this important ministry, while the apostles themselves will continue to focus on prayer and the ministry of God's Word (6:3–4). (Two of the seven, Stephen and Philip, will play significant roles in the next few chapters of Acts.) The solution works well and unity is preserved. Luke summarizes the story up to this point with one of his progress reports, indicating that the number of disciples in Jerusalem is increasing rapidly and, surprisingly, a large number of Jewish priests are becoming followers of Jesus (6:7).

Progress Reports in Acts

Luke pauses in telling the story of the early church to indicate the progress of the gospel and the growth of the Christian community. There are five such reports and one final summary at the very end of the book:

- *Acts 6:7*: "So the word of God spread. The number of disciples in Jerusalem increased rapidly, and a large number of priests became obedient to the faith."
- *Acts 9:31*: "Then the church throughout Judea, Galilee and Samaria enjoyed a time of peace and was strengthened. Living in the fear of the Lord and encouraged by the Holy Spirit, it increased in numbers."
- *Acts 12:24*: "But the word of God continued to spread and flourish."
- *Acts 16:5*: "So the churches were strengthened in the faith and grew daily in numbers."
- *Acts 19:20*: "In this way the word of the Lord spread widely and grew in power."
- *Acts 28:30–31*: "For two whole years Paul stayed there in his own rented house and welcomed all who came to see him. He proclaimed the kingdom of God and taught about the Lord Jesus Christ—with all boldness and without hindrance!"

In Jerusalem: The Ministry and Martyrdom of Stephen (Acts 6:8–8:4)

One of the seven chosen in Acts 6, Stephen is described as a "man full of God's grace and power," who "performed great wonders and signs among the people" (Acts 6:8). Along with playing a role in making sure the widows receive food, Stephen also does a magnificent job of defending Jesus and the gospel in public debate (6:9–10). His opponents falsely accuse him of speaking blasphemous words against Moses and against God (6:11). He is arrested and brought before the Sanhedrin, where he is accused of speaking against the temple and the law (6:12–15).

Stephen makes his defense in a lengthy speech in Acts 7. He retells much of the Story from Abraham to David, emphasizing that true worship of God can't be restricted to one place such as the temple in Jerusalem, and that the Jews always have rejected God's messengers, including Jesus the Messiah. He concludes by saying:

> You stiff-necked people! Your hearts and ears are still uncircumcised. You are just like your ancestors: You always resist the Holy Spirit! Was there ever a prophet your ancestors did not persecute? They even killed those who predicted the coming of the Righteous One. And now you have betrayed and murdered him—you who have received the law that was given through angels but have not obeyed it. (Acts 7:51–53)

This drives the religious leaders mad with rage, and they drag him out of the city and stone him to death as the young man named Saul (later known as Paul) cheers them on (Acts 7:57–8:1). Stephen imitates Jesus in the way he dies, with trust in the Father and forgiveness for his enemies (7:59–60).

From the time of Stephen's martyrdom, a great persecution breaks out against the church in Jerusalem, forcing many people except the apostles to scatter throughout Judea and Samaria (Acts 8:1). Luke also tells us that Saul begins to persecute the church intensely (8:3).

In Judea and Samaria: Philip the Evangelist (Acts 8:5–40)

Ironically, the persecution actually results in the scattering of the church and in further missionary work. Another one of the seven, Philip, travels to Samaria, where he proclaims Christ, casts out demons, heals the sick, and encourages the people (Acts 8:4–8). Many people believe in Jesus as a result of Philip's evangelistic ministry, including a famous Samaritan named Simon, who had amazed people with his magical arts (8:9–13). The power available from the Holy Spirit through the disciples is far superior to the wonder-working power of ancient magic.

When the apostles in Jerusalem hear that many in Samaria have received the gospel, they send Peter and John to verify the events (Acts 8:14–25). The apostles play an important role in the giving of the Spirit to the Samaritans because of the bitter division between Jews and Samaritans. The human confirmation of the work of the Spirit across ethnic lines helps establish unity within the multicultural church. Peter and John eventually return to Jerusalem, preaching the gospel in many Samaritan villages.

Meanwhile, God sends Philip to a desert road that connects Jerusalem

James: Authentic Faith Acts!

This letter is probably written by James, the half brother of Jesus and leader of the Jerusalem church (Acts 1:14; 12:17; 15:12–21; 21:18; Gal. 1:18–19). He becomes a follower of Jesus after the resurrection (1 Cor. 15:7). James is believed to have died as a martyr around AD 62.

The letter is addressed to "the twelve tribes scattered among the nations" (Jas. 1:1), likely a reference to Jewish Christians living outside of Palestine. These believers may have been part of the Jerusalem church that had to leave the city when persecution hit hard (Acts 8:1; 11:19). Perhaps they had been converted at Pentecost and then returned to their original homes scattered outside of Palestine. Many scholars believe that James may have been the earliest New Testament letter written, dating as early as AD 45–50.

James sees a few problems in these scattered congregations and reminds these believers (and us) of the importance of living out the faith in practical ways. James insists that true faith works! He offers practical advice for everyday godly living, such as how we face trials, how we use money, how we talk about others, and, generally speaking, how we live. There are many parallels with Jesus' Sermon on the Mount, and James often reflects the Old Testament book of Proverbs with a heavy emphasis on instructions and commands. James would say that godly wisdom is proved not only by its theological content but also by its actions. We should trust God in trials, use our possessions to promote justice and meet needs, and use our words both to praise God and to edify our brothers and sisters in Christ.

with Gaza for a divine encounter (Acts 8:26–40). Philip meets an Ethiopian finance minister returning from a long journey to Jerusalem where he has worshiped—likely as a God-fearer or convert to Judaism. The man is a eunuch, which means that he has been castrated. As such, he has no doubt experienced social and religious rejection, since the law excluded eunuchs from public worship and considered them ritually impure (see Lev. 21:20; 22:24; Deut. 23:1). The man is sitting in his chariot reading from Isaiah, perhaps because that section of Isaiah gives hope to eunuchs (see Isa. 56:3–8). But he has trouble understanding what the larger passage means. Philip takes the opportunity to explain that Isaiah 53 is fulfilled in Jesus, the Lamb of God. This leads the man to faith in Christ, and he is baptized before continuing on his journey with newfound joy. Philip is then taken away by the Spirit and travels through various towns preaching the gospel.

In Judea and Samaria: The Conversion of Paul (Acts 9:1–31)

The conversion of the man from Ethiopia marks the beginning of a mission to Gentiles, non-Jews living all over the world. That mission takes shape even more with the calling of Saul (whose Roman name is Paul), the man specifically set apart by God to be the apostle to the Gentiles. (We read of his conversion/call three times in Acts: 9:1–30; 22:3–21; 26:2–23.)

Earlier, Paul looked on with approval when Stephen was stoned to death (Acts 8:1). Now, under the authority of the Jewish Sanhedrin, Paul zealously tracks down Christians in order to persecute them (Acts 9:1–2). On his way to Damascus, however, he is thrown to the ground, blinded by a heavenly light, and confronted by a heavenly voice:

> "Saul, Saul, why do you persecute me?"
> "Who are you, Lord?" Saul asked.
> "I am Jesus, whom you are persecuting," he replied. (Acts 9:4–5)

By persecuting Jesus' disciples, Paul has actually been persecuting Jesus. For several days Paul is blind and helpless, perhaps fearing that he will be in that condition for good as punishment for his evil deeds.

The Lord then commands Ananias, a disciple living in Damascus, to meet with Paul and pray for his physical and spiritual healing. Ananias is told that Paul "is my chosen instrument to proclaim my name to the Gentiles and their kings and to the people of Israel" (Acts 9:15). Thus begins the amazing transformation of one of the leading enemies of the church into a leading witness for Christ.

Paul doesn't waste any time preaching Jesus as the Son of God and Messiah in the synagogues of Damascus, stupefying those who know him only as a persecutor of the Way (Acts 9:19–22). Even though the local Jews hatch a plan to kill Paul, his friends secretly smuggle him out of the city. He returns to Jerusalem and tries to meet with the disciples there, but they are deathly afraid of him. Barnabas, whose name means "son of encouragement," vouches for Paul so that the believers in Jerusalem cautiously receive him. Paul then speaks out boldly for Christ in Jerusalem until the Jews there try to kill him also and he has to leave. At this point Luke inserts his second progress report: "Then the church throughout Judea, Galilee and Samaria enjoyed a time of peace and was strengthened. Living in the fear of the Lord and encouraged by the Holy Spirit, it increased in numbers" (Acts 9:31).

In Judea and Samaria: The Ministry of Peter beyond Jerusalem (Acts 9:32–11:18)

God uses the apostle Peter to minister in dramatic ways outside the city of Jerusalem, and this becomes the doorway, if you will, for the gospel to reach the ends of the earth. As Peter travels through the coastal towns of Judea, God uses him to perform miracles. He heals a paralytic named Aeneas in Lydda (Acts 9:32–35) and raises from the dead a disciple named Tabitha ("Dorcas" in Greek) in the town of Joppa (Acts 9:36–43). As a result, many people begin to follow the Lord.

Just up the coast in Caesarea Maritima, a Roman centurion named Cornelius has a vision from God telling him that God has answered his prayers and he should send for Peter in Joppa (Acts 10:1–8). Meanwhile, Peter has a corresponding vision in which he is told three times to kill and eat unclean animals that have been lowered from heaven on a sheet (10:9–16). The point is that Peter is not to "call anything impure that God has made clean" (10:15). The animals, he will soon discover, represent Gentiles, whom God himself is accepting into his family. The Holy Spirit then tells Peter to go with men coming from Caesarea (10:17–23).

Peter arrives and enters the house of Cornelius the Gentile, an unlawful act for devout Jews, and the two men share their respective visions from the Lord (Acts 10:24–33). Peter begins to speak to all who have gathered about what God has done through Jesus Christ and how God is now accepting people from every nation who fear him (10:34–43). While Peter is still speaking, the gift of the Holy Spirit is poured out on all the Gentiles in the room, an

Paul's Personal Testimony

If someone else thinks they have reasons to put confidence in the flesh, I have more: circumcised on the eighth day, of the people of Israel, of the tribe of Benjamin, a Hebrew of Hebrews; in regard to the law, a Pharisee; as for zeal, persecuting the church; as for righteousness based on the law, faultless.

But whatever were gains to me I now consider loss for the sake of Christ. What is more, I consider everything a loss because of the surpassing worth of knowing Christ Jesus my Lord, for whose sake I have lost all things. (Phil. 3:4–8)

1 Peter: "Stand Firm in God's Grace"
2 Peter: "Stand Firm in God's Truth"
Jude: "Contend for the Faith"

The early church regularly faced persecution from outsiders and false teaching from within. First Peter was written to help Christians endure persecution, while 2 Peter and Jude provide wisdom for responding to false teaching.

Both 1 and 2 Peter claim to have been written by Peter, the fisherman who became an apostle of Jesus Christ (1 Peter 1:1; 2 Peter 1:1). Peter confessed Jesus as the Messiah at Caesarea Philippi but subsequently failed to grasp the significance of his own words. Peter is famous for denying Jesus three times on the night before the cross. After the resurrection, however, Jesus restored Peter and used him in a mighty way in the early church. Peter not only witnessed Christ's sufferings, but he also suffered himself. He writes with the help of "Silas" (or Silvanus) from Rome (5:12–13). The author of Jude describes himself as a "servant of Jesus Christ and a brother of James" (Jude 1). Christian tradition identifies Jude as the half brother of Jesus and the brother of James, who wrote the letter of James (Matt. 13:55; Mark 6:3).

Peter is probably writing from Rome (1 Peter 5:13) to believers scattered throughout the provinces of Asia Minor who are facing persecution for their faith (1 Peter 1:1; 2:19–21; 3:14, 17; 4:1, 12–16; 5:9–10). If the letter he mentions in 2 Peter 3:1 is 1 Peter, the audience for both letters is probably the same. Early Christian tradition says that Peter was martyred when the Roman emperor Nero began persecuting Christians in the mid 60s. Consequently, 1 Peter may have been written around AD 63–64 and 2 Peter shortly before his death about AD 68 (2 Peter 1:14–15). Second Peter and Jude look a lot alike and one may have borrowed from the other. Most scholars assume that Jude was written prior to (but close to the same time as) 2 Peter.

Peter praises God for providing salvation through the death and resurrection of Jesus Christ. He exhorts believers to grab hold of this living hope by standing firm in God's grace (1 Peter 5:12). God's grace will strengthen them to know their true identity, live holy lives, and stay faithful even in the midst of suffering. After all, as God's people they are God's holy temple and should live godly lives before unbelievers in hopes of encouraging a positive response to the Lord.

In 2 Peter and Jude the problem is internal as false teachers seem to be rejecting the power of the Scriptures, promoting godlessness, and denying the return of Christ or future judgment. When faced with false teaching, believers need to grow in the knowledge of the Lord (2 Peter 3:18). The best antidote to falsehood is to be rooted and grounded in God's truth. In a similar manner, Jude urges believers to "contend for the faith that was once for all entrusted to God's holy people" (Jude 3).

event that astonishes the Jews traveling with Peter since the assumption up to this point was that only Jewish believers will share in the blessings of God (10:44–48).

Peter travels back to Jerusalem to answer criticism from Jewish Christians about entering a Gentile's house (Acts 11:1–3). Peter explains what has just happened and concludes: "So if God gave them the same gift he gave us who believed in the Lord Jesus Christ, who was I to think that I could stand in God's way?" (11:17). The Jewish Christians grant their approval and praise God that he has given the Gentiles the opportunity to repent and find life in Jesus. Cornelius's conversion represents a major step forward in the Christian mission. From this point on, the focus of Acts is on the mission to the nations.

Transition: The Gospel Spreads in Spite of Obstacles (Acts 11:19 – 12:25)

Most who fled Jerusalem after the persecution connected with Stephen's martyrdom share the gospel with Jews, but some talk also with Gentiles about the Lord. This results in the planting of a church in Antioch (Acts 11:19 – 21). Antioch was the third-largest city in the Roman Empire next to

Hebrews: "God's Final Word Is Jesus"

No one really knows who wrote the book of Hebrews. Paul always identifies himself as the author in his letters, whereas this author does not. The person who wrote this letter had an extensive knowledge of the Old Testament and tremendous skill in developing persuasive arguments. Apollos appears to be a likely candidate, but we can't be certain that he is the author (see Acts 18:24 – 28). The book is probably written around the time of Nero's persecution of the church (mid 60s AD) to a Christian house church composed of believers with a Jewish background. They likely live near Rome and have been Christians for a while (Heb. 5:11 – 6:3; 13:24).

The letter is specifically called a "word of exhortation" or a sermon (Heb. 13:22; cf. Acts 13:15). These believers are growing weary of facing constant pressure, and some are tempted to give up on the Christian faith and return to the Jewish synagogue in order to avoid more persecution (Heb. 10:25; 32 – 34; 12:4). As an ancient religion, Judaism was exempt from persecution by the Roman government and provided a "safe" alternative to Christianity.

The author of Hebrews sees the situation as critical and writes to persuade them to persevere as followers of Jesus. He focuses on a central theme: God's final word is Jesus! He shows that Jesus is the supreme revelation of God and is superior to all previous forms of revelation, including angels, Moses, and the priests and ministries of the old covenant. To convince these believers not to turn their backs on Jesus, he warns them sternly (Heb. 2:1 – 4; 3:7 – 19; 4:12 – 13; 6:4 – 8; 10:26 – 31; 12:25 – 29) and assures them repeatedly (6:9 – 12, 19 – 20; 7:25; 10:14, 32 – 39). The sermon also shifts back and forth between teaching about Christ (exposition) and commands to live out that teaching (exhortation).

Jesus is the focus of Hebrews. He existed before the creation of the world and is the sovereign Lord of the universe. As our compassionate high priest, he thoroughly understands our human weakness. As the sacrifice himself, he has provided sufficient payment for our sins. Jesus Christ is the only reliable object of trust. He will never let us down. We must stay strong in the faith, fixing our eyes on Jesus, God's ultimate revelation of himself to us.

Rome and Alexandria. When the news reaches Jerusalem, they send Barnabas to Antioch, and he confirms that this is a genuine work of God (11:22–24). Barnabas recruits Paul to help with the ministry in Antioch, and they spend a year teaching the believers. Luke tells us that "the disciples were called Christians first in Antioch" (11:26). Following Jesus' example, the first Christians were concerned not just with a person's soul but with the whole person. When the believers at Antioch hear about a severe famine, they take up a collection for the Christians in Judea and send the gift with Barnabas and Paul (11:27–30).

The early church also faces stiff political opposition. Herod Agrippa I, the grandson of Herod the Great, who had tried to kill baby Jesus, persecutes the church in Jerusalem. He has James, the brother of John and one of Jesus' twelve apostles, put to death and puts Peter in prison (Acts 12:1–4). In answer to prayer, however, the Lord miraculously rescues Peters and restores him to the fellowship (12:5–19). God's judgment falls on Agrippa I, who dies a rather bizarre death (12:19–23). In spite of numerous difficulties, the word of God continues to increase and spread (12:24).

Nothing can stop what God is doing! Barnabas and Paul return to Antioch with John Mark in preparation for the first missionary tour among the Gentiles (12:25). From this point on, the focus in Acts moves away from the church in Jerusalem to the apostle Paul and the mission to the ends of the earth.

Making Connections

Let's review where we are in the Great Story:

Creation and Crisis
Covenant
Calling Out
Commandments
Conquest and Canaanization
Creation of the Kingdom
Communion and Common Sense
Crumbling of the Kingdom
Captivity and Coming Home
Interlude: Time between the Testaments
Christ
➤ **Church:**
   The Coming of the Spirit
   In Jerusalem, Judea, and Samaria
   The Mission to the Gentiles
   The Gospel Spreads from Jerusalem to Rome
Consummation

There are many connections that could be made between this part of the Story and the whole Story, but we will make just five. First, the miracles performed by the Holy Spirit through the apostles and other early Christian leaders reflect the climactic miracle—the resurrection of Jesus Christ from the dead. When a miracle is performed in the book of Acts, those humanly responsible usually point to the risen Lord as the one who is ultimately responsible for the miracle. We will always find the death and resurrection of Jesus at the heart of the biblical Story. All miracles seem to either foreshadow (the exodus event) or reflect (such as miracles in Acts) that central miracle.

Second, God has always been interested in caring for the whole person, and this appears once again in Acts 6:1–7. In the garden of Eden, God provided for the physical needs of Adam and Eve along with their relational needs. As Israel traveled through the wilderness, God provided quail and manna to sustain them. The only miracle besides the resurrection to be recorded in all four gospels is Jesus' feeding of the five thousand. And now in Acts 6 we see that the distribution of food is an essential ministry of the church. God cares for the whole person, and so should we.

Third, we see in Stephen's long sermon how Christianity differs from Judaism. Although the two were running along the same track for much of their shared history, a definite split occurred with Jesus. If Jesus is Messiah and Lord and God's people (rather than the temple) now constitute God's dwelling place, one must accept Jesus as Lord and Messiah in order to rightly relate to God. We see even more clearly in Acts that Jesus has fulfilled the Old Testament Story.

Fourth, although human opposition such as that experienced by the early Christians does bring real pain and suffering, it does not hinder or stop God's sovereign plan to redeem his people and restore his creation. For Peter, John, and James, for example, life was not easy as a Christian leader. They suffered imprisonment, beatings, and even death for the cause of Christ. But as Luke constantly reminds us, the word of God continued to spread and have a huge impact on the world. God can even bring good out of evil events like the persecution of his people. As Paul would later write in Romans 8:28: "And we know that in all things God works for the good of those who love him, who have been called according to his purpose." Although God's people suffer temporarily, God's purposes are still accomplished!

Fifth, we see clearly in this part of the Story God's heart for the nations. From the beginning God has invited all people to become members of his family. He has always desired a multicultural people. In Acts 3–12 we see the good news of life in Jesus go to those who have been previously rejected, like a crippled beggar and a eunuch. We also see the gospel move outside of Jerusalem to the Samaritans and the Gentiles. Even a Roman soldier and a persecuting Pharisee, representing those who put Jesus to death, are welcomed into God's family.

Living the Story

If Jesus occupies the very center of the Story, then listening to Jesus remains our top priority. You remember back a bit in the Story when Peter confessed Jesus as the Christ at Caesarea Philippi? Peter then tried to tell Jesus that he didn't have to go to the cross, but Jesus sternly rebuked him. A week later on the Mount of Transfiguration, the voice from heaven tells Peter to "listen" to Jesus (Matt. 17:5). Peter has to learn the hard way, as do many of us, so he goes on to deny Jesus three times. After his resurrection, Jesus restores Peter on the shore of the Sea of Galilee. Humbled and restored, Peter is now in a place to be used by God. Interestingly, in Acts 3 when Peter preaches his second sermon, he makes a big deal of this idea of listening to God:

> Now, fellow Israelites, I know that you acted in ignorance, as did your leaders. But this is how God fulfilled what he had foretold through all the prophets, saying that his Messiah would suffer. Repent, then, and turn to God, so that your sins may be wiped out, that times of refreshing may come from the Lord, and that he may send the Messiah, who has been appointed for you—even Jesus. Heaven must receive him until the time comes for God to restore everything, as he promised long ago through his holy prophets. For Moses said, "The Lord your God will raise up for you a prophet like me from among your own people; you must listen to everything he tells you. Anyone who does not listen to him will be completely cut off from their people." (Acts 3:17–23)

We too must listen to Jesus. This could mean many things for you. It could mean allowing God to replace your ideas of God's plan for your life with God's ideas. It could mean allowing suffering to play a role in your future rather than trying to do everything possible to prevent suffering. It could mean something as basic as opening the Bible each day, reading God's Word, and spending time pouring out your heart to God in prayer. Listening to Jesus requires a reorientation of one's heart and an opening of one's heart to what God thinks is best.

Another way we can live this part of the Story is to imitate the generosity of the early church in our own communities. Without a doubt, our culture prizes material possessions. Many people find their identity and self-worth through buying, consuming, or accumulating stuff. Throughout Acts, we see a bountiful generosity that is both beautiful and attractive. In Acts 4:32–37 we read:

> All the believers were one in heart and mind. No one claimed that any of their possessions was their own, but they shared everything they had. With great power the apostles continued to testify to the resurrection of the Lord Jesus. And God's grace was so powerfully at work in them all that there were no needy persons among them. For from time to time those who owned

No Solitary Christian

"We cannot live the Christian life in isolation, like some religious Robinson Crusoe. Membership in the church is not an optional extra. The fact is, we cannot be fully Christian without belonging to the church. As we study the New Testament we find that to be a Christian is to be 'in Christ,' and that this means being a member of a new society of which Christ is the living Head—the church. The New Testament knows nothing of unattached Christians. Consider the matter in a more mundane way. What would we think of a man who said that he wanted to be a soldier but insisted that he could be a perfectly good one without joining the army? An unattached soldier is nonsense—and so is the notion of a solitary Christian."[2]

– BRUCE SHELLEY

land or houses sold them, brought the money from the sales and put it at the apostles' feet, and it was distributed to anyone who had need.

Joseph, a Levite from Cyprus, whom the apostles called Barnabas (which means "son of encouragement"), sold a field he owned and brought the money and put it at the apostles' feet.

You know the Spirit of God is at work when people are willing to let go of their things for the good of others. "There were no needy persons among them," we are told. Amazing! Do things have a grip on your life to the point where it would be really hard, too hard perhaps, to give them away to meet needs within your own community? Are you aware of the needs within your own community? Are you using the resources God has given you to help someone who is struggling just to have the basics, such as food, clothing, and a safe place to live? There is much we can learn from the generosity of the early church.

This also brings up another point. God never wants merely to use people to accomplish his mission; he always wants to do a genuine, transforming work among his people first and then use them to accomplish the mission. In other words, people are not just tools or instruments to God; they are valuable in and of themselves. As the community experiences genuine transformation, much of the mission of the community flows out of that. The Spirit works in the church first and then through the church in the world. Many people in our world will be attracted first to a local community where they see the gospel at work, and only then will they listen to the Story. Much like a healthy marriage, living in Christian community is both extremely humbling and deeply rewarding. If you are an integral part of a local community, you are doing more than you realize to spread the gospel to the world.

---

2. Bruce Shelley, *Theology for Ordinary People* (Downers Grove, IL: InterVarsity Press, 1993), 146.

Wrapping Up

In Acts 3–12 we see Jesus' Great Commission given earlier to his disciples finally take shape. After Pentecost, the Spirit continues to work through the apostles in the city of Jerusalem. People are healed, the message about Jesus gets out, and many believe. But the success of the mission is not without opposition as both religious and political powers—such as the Sanhedrin and Herod Agrippa I—try to silence the witnesses. Yet although God's people suffer, God's mission continues unhindered.

The Spirit works within the community producing the fruit of generosity, but the church must now adapt in order to teach the Word and meet new practical needs. After the martyrdom of Stephen, a strong persecution runs many believers out of the city, but God uses this to accomplish his mission. Even Paul, who formerly persecuted the church, becomes a believer. Philip goes to Samaria, Peter to Cornelius's house, and Paul and Barnabas to Antioch, the city that will serve as home base for the expanded Gentile mission that follows.

Memory Verse

"But you will receive power when the Holy Spirit comes on you; and you will be my witnesses in Jerusalem, and in all Judea and Samaria, and to the ends of the earth." (Acts 1:8)

Digging Deeper

Books

Bock, Darrell L. *Acts*. Baker Exegetical Commentary on the New Testament. Grand Rapids: Baker, 2007.

Stott, John R. W. *The Message of Acts*. The Bible Speaks Today. Downers Grove, IL: InterVarsity Press, 1990.

ASSIGNMENTS

1. The idea of "witnessing" shows up a lot in Acts. Interestingly, that word is often understood today to mean nothing more than giving a personal testimony about what God has done in your life. That's certainly important, but is that what "witness" meant in Acts? What exactly were the apostles witnessing about? Look carefully at each of the following verses in Acts: 1:22; 2:32; 3:15; 5:32; 10:39, 41; 13:31. Write a short description of what the people were witnessing about in each verse. Then write a concluding paragraph or two explaining the primary meaning of the word "witness" in Acts.

2. Write a short personal history of your relationship to the local church. Describe each church you have been a part of and something about the theology and practices of that church. Conclude with a paragraph or two

about how you plan to relate to the local church in the next five years. What kind of church do you hope to be part of, and how do you plan to contribute?

3. In Acts 3 – 12 we see an interesting encounter between three realities: God's power at work through Christian leaders, stiff opposition from religious and secular authorities, and the progress of God's mission to the nations. Create a chart or diagram that depicts the relationship between these three realities in this part of Acts.

CHURCH:
The Mission to the Gentiles

Chapter 18

Enter Here

Have you ever looked on the back of a water bottle to see the nutritional value of water? If not, here is what you will find:

Calories – 0 grams
Total Fat – 0 grams
Sodium – 0 milligrams
Total Carbs – 0 grams
Protein – 0 grams

But just try to live without water. Although I'm not a nutritionist, even I know that the "Nutrition Facts" on the back of the bottle don't tell the whole story. Sometimes what is needed for an individual to be healthy is not mentioned in the standard facts and figures. The same holds true for local churches.

Many churches in the West believe that you can do church perfectly fine without sending anyone out on mission. We organize precisely, advertise intensely, teach faithfully, care consistently, budget efficiently, and trust that we are doing everything we are supposed to do. But the Story calls us to include something not on that list, and without that something, local churches eventually wither and die. This section of Acts focuses on how the Holy Spirit uses the local church to send out missionaries to speak the gospel and establish other local churches. Acts suggests that being a sending church lies at the heart of God's Story.

Be Prepared

Read or listen to Acts 13–21; Galatians 5–6; 1 Thessalonians 4–5; 2 Thessalonians 2; 1 Corinthians 12–15; 2 Corinthians 3–5; Romans 1; 3–6; 8; 12.

The Story Continues

The two main human characters in Acts are Peter and Paul. Peter is the leading figure in the mission to the Jews in Acts 1–12, while Paul takes the lead in ministry to the Gentiles in Acts 13–28. In truth, the leading figure in all of Acts is the Holy Spirit, who works through both Peter and Paul in similar ways, as the following chart indicates.[1]

Peter	Paul
Peter's sermon at Pentecost (2:22–29)	Paul's sermon at Pisidian Antioch (13:26–41)
Healing of a lame man (3:1–10)	Healing of a lame man (14:8–11)
Shaking of a building by prayer (4:31)	Shaking of a building by praise (16:25–26)
Rebuke of Ananias and Sapphira (5:1–11)	Rebuke of Elymas (13:8–12)
Healing by the shadow of Peter (5:15–16)	Healing by the handkerchiefs of Paul (19:11–12)
Laying on of hands (8:17)	Laying on of hands (19:6)
Rebuke of Simon the sorcerer (8:18–24)	Rebuke of Jewish sorcerer (13:6–11)
Resuscitation of Tabitha (9:36–42)	Resuscitation of Eutychus (20:7–12)
Removal of chains in prison (12:5–7)	Removal of chains in prison (16:25–28)

To the Ends of the Earth: First Missionary Journey (Acts 12:26–14:28)

As the multicultural church in Antioch is worshiping, the Spirit calls them to set apart Barnabas and Paul to take the gospel to the Gentiles (Acts 13:1–3). The persecution connected with Stephen's death had forced many believers to leave Jerusalem, and they took the good news of Jesus with them. But now the Spirit-led church strategically commissions missionaries to go to the ends of the earth. Incidentally, at this point in Acts, Paul's name changes from "Saul" to "Paul," not because of his conversion, but because the Roman name Paul is more fitting for ministry among the Gentiles.

Accompanied by John Mark, Barnabas and Paul leave Antioch and sail to the island of Cyprus, where they proclaim the gospel first in the Jewish synagogue in Salamis (Acts 13:4–5). In fact, Paul's standard practice, at least early on, is to gain a hearing in the synagogues. At Paphos, the proconsul Sergius Paulus is converted (13:6–12). When the team sails to the mainland at Perga, for unknown reasons, Mark calls it quits and returns to Jerusalem (13:13).

Paul and Barnabas make the rugged journey to Pisidian Antioch, where Paul again preaches in a Jewish synagogue. In his sermon (recorded in Acts 13:14–41), Paul demonstrates how God's promises to his people recorded in

---

1. *Grasping God's Word*, 272.

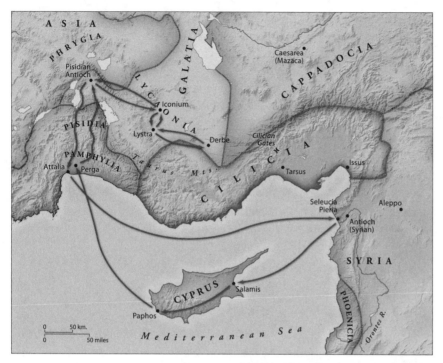

PAUL'S FIRST MISSIONARY JOURNEY

the Old Testament have been fulfilled in Jesus Christ. In other words, Paul's preaching is based on the Great Story of the Bible. He invites the listeners to accept the forgiveness available in Jesus and warns them about the consequences of rejecting God's offer. The people agree to talk more, but on the following Sabbath, Paul and Barnabas face stiff opposition from the Jewish leaders. Having fulfilled their obligation to speak the word of God first to the Jews, who apparently do not consider themselves worthy of receiving eternal life, Paul and Barnabas turn to the Gentiles (13:46–47). Many Gentiles believe the message, but opposition forces them to leave the city.

Paul and Barnabas travel to Iconium, Lystra, and Derbe, where a similar pattern emerges (Acts 14:1–20). They share the good news, the Spirit

"God-fearers"

In the book of Acts, a "God-fearer" is a Gentile or non-Jew who has formally associated with the Jewish community, perhaps out of a desire to worship the one God of Israel (see Acts 10:2, 22; 13:16, 26, 43, 50; 17:4, 17; 18:7). They seek to live in a way that honors God, either through attending the synagogue or doing good works. They aren't necessarily proselytes or converts who have completely joined the Jewish community. The first Christian missionaries often found these God-fearers willing to listen to their message about Jesus the Messiah.

confirms the message with signs and wonders, some people become followers of Jesus, and they encounter opposition from the Jewish leaders. At Lystra, an essentially pagan city, they are first thought to be gods, but later Paul is stoned and dragged outside the city to die.

On this missionary journey, they have not just been preaching the gospel; they have also been planting churches. Paul knows the value of establishing local communities, not just isolated Christians. They now retrace their steps through the same cities, where they appoint elders in these churches and

Paul's Life and Letters

Date of events	Date of letters	Events/letters
5–10		Paul's birth
30/33		Jesus' death and resurrection
32–34		Paul's conversion
35–36		Paul's first visit to Jerusalem
46–47		Barnabas and Paul take famine relief to Jerusalem
47–49		First missionary journey (Acts 13–14)
	49	? Galatians (Antioch)
49		Jerusalem Council (Acts 15)
50–52		Second missionary journey (Acts 15:36–18:21)
	51–52	1 and 2 Thessalonians (Corinth)
53–57		Third missionary journey (Acts 18:22–21:16)
	53	? Galatians (Ephesus)
	54	1 Corinthians (Ephesus)
	56	2 Corinthians (Macedonia)
	57	Romans (Corinth)
57–59		Arrest in Jerusalem (Acts 21:26–33) and two-year imprisonment at Caesarea
59		Journey to Rome (Acts 27:1–28:14)
60–62		Two-year house arrest in Rome (Acts 28:30)
60–62		Prison Letters: Philemon, Colossians, Ephesians, Philippians (Rome)
63		Release from prison and more missionary work
63–67		Pastoral Letters: 1 Timothy, Titus, 2 Timothy (at some point imprisoned again)
66–68		Martyrdom in Rome

Galatians: Free to Love!

There is little doubt that the apostle Paul wrote the letter to the Galatians, but the time of its writing is a matter of debate (Gal. 1:1; 5:2). The letter is addressed to "the churches of Galatia" (1:2; 3:1; 4:8–9), likely Gentile Christians living in the towns that Paul visited on his first missionary journey (Acts 13–14). Paul either wrote Galatians during his third missionary journey between AD 53 and AD 58 (Gal. 2 = Acts 15), or he wrote the letter from Antioch soon after returning from his first journey in about AD 48–49 (Gal. 2 = Acts 11). We favor the early date prior to the Jerusalem Council in Acts 15, making Galatians Paul's earliest letter.

Soon after Paul planted the churches on his first journey, false teachers arrived and demanded that the Gentile Christians be circumcised and fulfill other Jewish religious requirements in order to be full-fledged Christians (Gal. 4:9–10; 5:2–4; 6:12–13). These opponents were corrupting the gospel, hindering the faith journey of the Galatian Christians and turning the churches against Paul, their father in the faith. This false message was appealing to the new believers, who were tempted to think that adding works of law to their new faith in Christ would result in a more "spiritual" life. A childlike trust in Christ was being replaced by fleshly attempts to keep the law.

Paul deals with the crisis by treating the underlying theological issue—what makes a person fully Christian? He first defends his apostleship and authority (Gal. 1:1–2:14) because the integrity of the gospel is tied to the integrity of the messenger. Next, Paul clarifies the true gospel as one that rests on Christ alone (2:15–4:11). In doing so, Paul appeals to the Great Story (notice the reference to Abraham in Gal. 3). Paul then calls the Galatians to keep on following the Spirit who empowers love—the true evidence of spirituality (4:11–6:10).

Galatians reminds us that salvation is by grace through faith in Christ, not a result of works. There is nothing we can do to add to the faithfulness of Jesus Christ. Through his life, death, and resurrection, he has set us free, but we are not free to pursue our own selfish agendas. Rather, we are empowered by the Spirit to love and serve one another, and such love fulfills the Law (Gal. 5:14; 6:2).

remind the disciples that "we must go through many hardships to enter the kingdom of God" (Acts 14:22). After returning to Antioch, where they were originally commissioned, they report "all that God had done through them and how he had opened a door of faith to the Gentiles" (14:27). They stay in Antioch for a long time with the disciples.

To the Ends of the Earth: The Jerusalem Council (Acts 15:1–35)

If you remember from Acts 1:8, Jesus said his disciples would be witnesses in Jerusalem, Judea and Samaria, and then to the ends of the earth. Paul's first missionary journey into Gentile territory had been a success, but the early church now struggles with how much Gentile Christians should honor the traditions and practices of Jewish Christians. Before the Gentile mission can continue, the church needs to agree on how that mission is to be conducted. This question is addressed at the Jerusalem Council in Acts 15.

Some men from Judea came to Antioch insisting that Gentiles must be circumcised in order to be saved (Acts 15:1). Paul and Barnabas strongly disagree, and the church in Antioch appoints them to go to Jerusalem and discuss the matter with the apostles (15:2). They arrive and report all that God did among the Gentiles, including pouring out his Spirit on those who believe (15:3–4, 8). While some believing Pharisees contend that Gentiles must be circumcised and required to obey the Law of Moses (15:5), Peter, James, Paul, and Barnabas argue that Gentile Christians should not be burdened with either (15:6–21).

The council sides with the apostles and decides that Jewish Christians should not make it hard for Gentiles to turn to God (Acts 15:19). They send word back to the church in Antioch that Gentile believers do not have to submit to circumcision and obedience to the Law in order to follow Christ (15:22–35). They do ask, however, that Gentile Christians avoid things that are particularly offensive to Jewish Christians (e.g., eating food offered to idols) so that the two groups may enjoy table fellowship together (15:20, 29).

To the Ends of the Earth: Second Missionary Journey (Acts 15:36–18:22)

The second missionary journey also begins from Antioch, but the composition of the mission team changes. Paul and Barnabas disagree about the role Mark should play after his actions on the first journey, so Barnabas takes

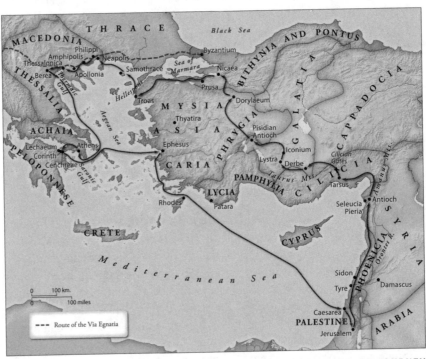

PAUL'S SECOND MISSIONARY JOURNEY

1 – 2 Thessalonians: How to Live in Light of Christ's Return

These two letters are sent by "Paul, Silas and Timothy," but most believe that Paul is the primary author (1 Thess. 2:18; 3:5; 5:27; 2 Thess. 2:5; 3:17). After only a brief stay in Thessalonica, the missionary team had to leave due to violent opposition. The young, fragile church now faces tremendous challenges alone. Paul had attempted to return to Thessalonica numerous times but without success (1 Thess. 2:18). He writes these two letters from Corinth in the early AD 50s for the purpose of encouraging and instructing this new church.

In both letters, Paul focuses on how Christians ought to live in light of Christ's second coming. He mentions Jesus' return near the end of every chapter in 1 Thessalonians, and almost 40 percent of 2 Thessalonians deals with this topic. Paul writes as a compassionate pastor who is concerned with the well-being of the community of believers. He repeatedly emphasizes the hope we have in Christ. He reminds them of how they bravely received the good news of Christ in spite of suffering. He reminds them of his faithful ministry among them to prevent any second guessing of his motives for leaving. He tells them plainly how to live as they await Christ's return.

Between the first and second letter, the external pressure grows stronger, and some seem to have misunderstood Paul's previous teaching. He writes his second letter to clear up any confusion about Christ's return and encourages them to persevere in holy living.

In our day, Christians seem to be either totally consumed with the topic of Christ's return or entirely unaware of its importance. These two letters offer balance and wisdom on this issue. We are reminded that Jesus is coming again and we should live each day with that reality in mind. No matter what we face now, we have a strong and sure hope that will not be shaken.

Mark and returns to Cyprus while Paul takes Silas and heads north. When Paul and Silas pass through Derbe and Lystra, the very place where Paul was almost killed, they meet a disciple named Timothy, who joins the team. From the place of great suffering comes one of Paul's greatest blessings.

They continue through South Galatia and Phrygia, but the Spirit prevents them from going north into Asia or Bithynia (Acts 16:6 – 7). At Troas, Paul has a vision calling him to preach the gospel in Macedonia (16:8 – 10). So Paul, Silas, and Timothy, accompanied now by Luke, travel to Philippi, where they meet Lydia, a businesswoman and a God-fearer. She and her whole household respond to the gospel and are baptized (16:11 – 15). While in Philippi, Paul casts out a spirit from a girl, and her owners blame him and Silas for their fortune-telling business faltering. The city officials strip them, beat them, and throw them in prison (16:18 – 24). As they sing praises to God in prison, God miraculously delivers them through an earthquake. In the process, the jailer and his household come to faith in Christ (16:25 – 34).

They continue on to Thessalonica, where they preach again in the Jewish synagogue with similar results: a number of converts and opposition from the Jews for claiming that Jesus is Lord (Acts 17:1 – 9). They travel on to Berea, where the response is positive; but when opposition from Thessalonica catches up with them, Paul must move on to Athens (17:10 – 15).

In Athens, Paul speaks about Christ in both the Jewish synagogue and in the marketplace. He even addresses a group of philosophers at a meeting of the city council (Acts 17:16–21). In this setting he attempts to persuade not by appealing to the biblical Story but by presenting God as Creator and the only one worthy of true worship (17:22–25). He completes his talk to the philosophers by revealing that a person may turn from pagan idolatry and find God through the resurrected Jesus (17:26–31). Paul receives a mixed response from this audience because of his emphasis on the resurrection of Jesus (17:32–34).

Paul moves on to Corinth where he spends most of his time reasoning in the synagogue and testifying that Jesus is the Messiah (Acts 18:1–6). Crispus, the synagogue ruler, comes to faith in Christ, and many Corinthians become believers (18:7–8). Paul is encouraged through a vision from the Lord and continues his teaching ministry in Corinth for a year and a half (18:9–11). Again he comes under attack from Jewish opponents, but the Roman proconsul Gallio rules in Paul's favor (18:12–18). Finally he returns to the sending church in Antioch (18:18–22).

To the Ends of the Earth: Third Missionary Journey (Acts 18:23–21:16)

Once again Paul departs from Antioch and travels through Galatia and Phrygia, strengthening the disciples before arriving in Ephesus (Acts 18:23; 19:1). Acts 19 provides a window into Paul's lengthy ministry in Ephesus.

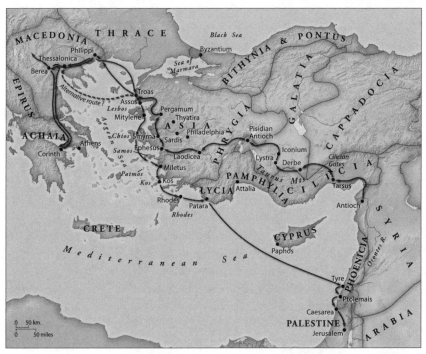

PAUL'S THIRD MISSIONARY JOURNEY

1 – 2 Corinthians: Solving Problems in the Church

In these two letters we see clearly into Paul's pastoral heart. He planted the church in Corinth on his second missionary journey (Acts 18:1 – 18). The city adopted various philosophies, religions, and lifestyles, and it was known especially for its sexual immorality (e.g., to "Corinthianize" meant to act like a prostitute). The church in Corinth challenged Paul more than any other church largely because it struggled to pull away from the influence of its pagan environment. Paul wrote both letters while on his third missionary journey: 1 Corinthians from Ephesus around AD 54 and 2 Corinthians from Macedonia about AD 56.

The church at Corinth had problems stemming from incorrect beliefs, pride and arrogance, and, perhaps most of all, spiritual immaturity. While ministering in Ephesus, Paul receives disturbing news from Chloe's household (1 Cor. 1:11) along with a letter from the church raising many issues. In response to these reports and the letter, Paul writes 1 Corinthians. He deals with divisions within the church, a case of incest and the lack of church discipline, lawsuits among believers before pagan judges, sexual immorality, marriage, eating food sacrificed to idols, the use of spiritual gifts in public worship, the resurrection from the dead, and the collection for the Jerusalem church.

After Paul writes 1 Corinthians, his relationship with the church goes from bad to worse. Paul probably makes a personal (and painful) visit to the church (2 Cor. 2:1), followed by a severe letter (2 Cor. 2:4; 7:8 – 9). Second Corinthians, then, is likely Paul's fourth letter to this difficult church. Paul's enemies within the church manage to turn some church members against him so that the congregation is divided over whether Paul is a legitimate apostle. Because of his visit some church members have repented and now support Paul, but a minority still questions his apostleship. He writes 2 Corinthians, perhaps his most emotional and personal letter, to defend his apostolic authority as a means of upholding the gospel of Jesus Christ and the Corinthians' own spiritual well-being.

These two letters relate to the nitty-gritty life of the local church. In 1 Corinthians you find practical wisdom about how things should work in the church. For Paul (and for us too hopefully), theology is practical. The biblical Story is meant to be lived out, not just studied and admired. In 2 Corinthians we see that reconciliation with fellow believers can be painful, disruptive to our plans, and emotionally taxing, but it is worth pursuing. When you read 2 Corinthians 2:12 – 13 and the jump over the digression to 7:5 – 7, you get a feel for the joy and relief that can come when reconciliation does happen.

After preaching for three months in the Jewish synagogue, he is forced to move to a public lecture hall. There he teaches for two more years "so that all the Jews and Greeks who lived in the province of Asia heard the word of the Lord" (Acts 19:10).

In addition, in this center of magic and false religion called Ephesus, the Spirit confirms the authenticity of the gospel through miraculous works (Acts 19:11–16). As a result, many Christians break completely with their pagan past (19:17–20). Paul, however, faces intense opposition from those who profit from the worship of the pagan god Artemis (19:21–20:1).

While in Ephesus, Paul responds to problems that have arisen in the church across the Aegean Sea in Corinth (see the chart on Paul's contact with the Corinthian church). He leaves Ephesus and travels through Macedonia to Corinth, where he spends three months (Acts 20:1–3a). He then travels by land back through Macedonia and begins sailing his way back to Judea. In every letter written on his third journey, Paul mentions a collection of money he has been taking up for the impoverished believers in Jerusalem

Paul's Contact with the Corinthian Church

Date	Event	Description
50–51	Visit 1	Evangelizes Corinth on second journey (Acts 18:1)
		Leaves Corinth and goes through Ephesus on his way back to Caesarea (Acts 18:18–22)
54	Letter 1	"Previous letter," now lost (1 Cor. 5:9)
		Paul returns to Ephesus (Acts 19:1) and stays for three years (Acts 20:31). In Ephesus he receives a visit from someone from Chloe's household (1 Cor. 1:11) reporting factions in the church, and he receives a letter from Corinth asking for advice and guidance (1 Cor. 7:1, 25; 8:1; 11:2; 12:1; 15:1; 16:1). Paul then writes 1 Corinthians in response (1 Cor. 16:8–9).
54	Letter 2	**1 Corinthians** (from Ephesus) on third journey
54		Paul sends Timothy to Corinth on a special mission (1 Cor. 4:17; 16:10). A powerful opponent in Corinth attacks Paul, and Timothy is unable to deal with it (2 Cor. 2:5–11). Timothy returns to report this to Paul.
55	Visit 2	"Painful visit" (2 Cor. 2:1) from Ephesus to Corinth and back
55	Letter 3	"Tearful letter" (2 Cor. 2:4; 7:8–9; 12:14; 13:1) probably written from Ephesus after the painful visit and carried by Titus
55		Paul goes to Troas, hoping to meet Titus with the report about Corinth (2 Cor. 2:12–13). Unable to find Titus, Paul travels to Macedonia.
56		In Macedonia, Paul finds Titus, who gives a good report about the church in Corinth (2 Cor. 7:5–8).
56	Letter 4	**2 Corinthians** (from Macedonia) on third journey (carried by Titus to Corinth)
57	Visit 3	Paul joins Titus in Corinth (Acts 20:2–3), spends the winter there, and writes Romans.

Romans: A Righteousness from God

With the secretarial help of Tertius, the apostle Paul writes the letter of Romans (Rom. 1:1; 16:22). Many of the first Christians in Rome were Jewish Christians, perhaps converts on the day of Pentecost. But in AD 49, Emperor Claudius expelled the Jews from Rome, and many Jewish Christians had to leave the city as well (Acts 18:1–3). As a result, the Gentile Christians had to assume leadership responsibilities in the church. When Claudius died in AD 54 and the Jewish Christians were allowed to return, the church in Rome (probably a number of small house churches) had a Gentile majority and a Jewish minority with some tension between the two groups.

Paul writes Romans after arriving in Corinth in AD 57 near the end of his third missionary journey (Acts 20:2–3). Following a period of conflict and reconciliation with the Corinthian church in his own ministry, Paul writes Romans to encourage reconciliation among the various house churches in that congregation. He encourages unity because he knows that unity as much as anything advances the mission of the church. To promote unity, he focuses on the gospel itself. The heart of Romans may be summarized in this way:

Gospel → Unity of the Church → Mission of the Church

By presenting the good news of a righteousness from God (the gospel), Paul hopes to persuade the Jewish and Gentile Christians in Rome to unite. He emphasizes the gospel or "good news" of God at the beginning (1:1, 2, 9, 15–17), in the middle (2:16; 10:15, 16; 11:28), and at the end (15:16, 19, 20; 16:25) of his letter. As the gospel brings unity, unity becomes the platform for launching the mission of the church, including Paul's own desire to take the gospel to Spain (Rom. 15:22–29). The outline of Romans reflects this purpose:

1:1–17	Introduction
1:18–3:20	Our problem: all are sinful and guilty
3:21–5:21	God's solution: righteousness
6:1–8:39	The result: our participation with Christ
9:1–11:36	An important concern: God has been faithful to keep his promises
12:1–15:13	Practical implications: relational righteousness
15:14–16:27	Conclusion

This letter is probably the clearest and most powerful presentation of the gospel in the entire Story. The gospel begins with bad news—human beings are sinful and guilty before a holy God. Just before we are driven to despair over our wretched sinfulness, we read that God has come to our rescue in Christ. He has done something for us that we could never do for ourselves. By his grace he offers us forgiveness and membership in his covenant community with the promise never to condemn us. We mysteriously participate in the life, death, and resurrection of Jesus Christ, with the result that we are no longer slaves to sin but are now free to follow Christ. The practical implications of this grace life are many, and Paul details them in the last part of the letter. The gospel of grace, however, is much bigger than God's saving a few individuals; he has been keeping his covenant promises all along. He aims to restore all of creation and to reverse the curse of sin and death. He wants to live forever with his people in a new creation free from all forms of evil. To him be the glory!

(Rom. 15:25–33; 1 Cor. 16:1–4; 2 Cor. 8:1–9:15). No doubt he hopes that a monetary gift from the Gentile churches to the Jewish Christians will not only meet basic needs but also promote unity within the body of Christ.

Paul and his traveling companions hope to reach Jerusalem by Pentecost (Acts 20:13–16). They sail past Ephesus but stop in nearby Miletus, where Paul meets with the elders of the church in Ephesus (20:17). His farewell speech to these leaders is one of the most moving accounts in all Scripture concerning the challenges and rewards of ministry (see 20:18–38). Paul then sails to Tyre and then to Caesarea before arriving in Jerusalem, likely in the spring of AD 57. He has been repeatedly warned that going to Jerusalem will bring suffering, but he presses on (21:1–14).

Paul arrives in the city to a warm welcome from his Jewish Christian friends and the church leaders there (Acts 21:17–18). He gives them the details on all that God has done among the Gentiles through his ministry (21:19). They rejoice with him but express concern about his negative reputation among the many Jews who have become followers of Christ. They have heard that Paul insists that Jewish Christians must ignore their traditions and live like Gentile Christians, a charge that is entirely untrue (21:20–21). They recommend that Paul join in the Jewish purification rites with four other men at the temple, and that's where the trouble begins—to be continued (21:22–26).

Making Connections

Let's review where we are in the Great Story:

    Creation and Crisis
    Covenant
    Calling Out
    Commandments
    Conquest and Canaanization
    Creation of the Kingdom
    Communion and Common Sense
    Crumbling of the Kingdom
    Captivity and Coming Home
    Interlude: Time between the Testaments
    Christ
➤ **Church:**
        The Coming of the Spirit
        In Jerusalem, Judea, and Samaria
        The Mission to the Gentiles
        The Gospel Spreads from Jerusalem to Rome
    Consummation

This part of Acts and the corresponding letters of Paul connect to the rest of the Story in powerful ways. First, we notice God's heart for the nations. Once again we mention Genesis 12:1–3 and God's promise to bless all nations through Abraham. How easy it would have been for the Spirit to stop the expansion of the church after Jerusalem, Samaria, and Judea. You could even argue that once the gospel reaches Antioch, a major city located outside of Judea where Gentiles are converted, that the commission to go to "the ends of the earth" has been fulfilled.

But while the church is worshiping, the Spirit of God specifically separates Barnabas and Paul for a mission much deeper into the Gentile world. We are reminded that God's redeemed people will come from "every tribe and language and people and nation" (Rev. 5:9). And God's promise in Genesis 12 comes in the context of Genesis 1–11. God is creating a people who will fulfill his original intentions for the creation and who will be his instrument to draw all peoples to himself as part of his master restoration project.

It also becomes clear, the more you read this section of the Story, that Paul and the other missionaries are focused on the gospel. Suffering the consequences of sin, humanity is unable to fulfill God's righteous requirements. As a result, we deserve to experience his condemning wrath. But in his great mercy, God sends a Savior, Jesus Christ, to rescue those who put their trust in him. This rescue or salvation is made possible by God's grace as the letters to the Galatians and Romans so masterfully proclaim.

This gospel—the focus of the missionary vision—centers on Jesus Christ, and specifically on his death, resurrection, and lordship. In fact, "Jesus is Lord" becomes the earliest Christian confession among Gentile Christians (Rom. 10:9). Among Jewish Christians, the confession of Jesus as Lord is often combined with the confession of Jesus as the Messiah (e.g., Luke 2:11; Acts 2:36). When Paul preaches his sermon in the synagogue at Pisidian Antioch (Acts 13:14–41), he traces the Old Testament Story from the choosing of Israel through the exodus, the entrance into the Promised Land, the judges, and the prophets, all the way to King David. Then he affirms that the Old Testament Story is fulfilled in Jesus as the prophesied descendant of David, the promised Savior for Israel.

Yet in spite of God's gracious provision, Israel has rejected her Messiah by crucifying him. God, however, raises Jesus from the dead, and Paul now proclaims: "I want you to know that through Jesus the forgiveness of sins is proclaimed to you. Through him [Jesus] everyone who believes is set free from every sin, a justification you were not able to obtain under the law of Moses" (Acts 13:38–39). The one who died under a curse turns out to be the risen Lord and Redeemer sent by God (Gal. 3:13–14). Since Jesus is both Messiah and Lord, the kingdom of God has arrived, and now is the day of salvation (2 Cor. 5:17; 6:2). That is the heart of Paul's message.

We also see in this section of Acts that Paul is committed to establishing healthy communities of faith and not merely to evangelizing individuals. This reminds us that God is all about community. The triune God is the perfect community and has always been keen on cultivating a people who will share in that community. Think about how much time Paul spent in Ephesus (almost three years), Corinth (a couple of years), and Antioch (several years). That's about two-thirds of his time as a missionary between the start of his first journey and his arrest in Jerusalem. Yes, travel was more difficult in that day and he needed time to earn a living, but we still see Paul's clear commitment to nurturing healthy local churches. He invests time in these communities so that they will become mature and consistent witnesses to the surrounding world. We clearly see what happens when the local community is not healthy (Corinth) and what becomes possible when a community is healthy (Romans and the mission farther west).

Finally, we are reminded that having a clear picture of how the Story ends is important for living out the Story in present circumstances. In other words, hope is (and has always been) a crucial ingredient in God's kingdom. God is a God of promises — to Abraham, to Moses, through the Prophets to his people, through Jesus, and now through his apostles. God's kingdom has arrived, but it has not yet been finalized. The consummation of the kingdom awaits Christ's return.

Paul writes to the Thessalonians repeatedly about this topic, encouraging them to remember that their hope will be fulfilled when Jesus returns (1 Thess. 1:9–10; 2:19–20; 3:12–13; 4:13–18; 5:1–11, 23–24; cf. also Rom. 8:23–24). God is not satisfied with the Story as long as Satan, sin, and death are around to harm his creation (Rev. 21:1–8). There will be a day when God will restore all things beyond anything we can imagine, a time with no more death or suffering or pain. Until then, we persevere, anticipating Christ's return. Should we die prior to his return, our hope lies in resurrection from the dead, and Christ's own resurrection is God's promise that he will raise us also (1 Cor. 15:20–26, 50–55; 1 Thess. 4:13–18).

Living the Story

One of the first ways we can live this section of the Story is to have an outward mindset when it comes to our faith. I believe it was the master teacher Howard Hendricks who once compared two types of people (or churches) using boxes and lines with arrows. On one box, the arrows (symbolizing our mindset and commitments) are all pointing toward the center, representing those who are selfish and, as a result, dying. On the other box, the arrows are all pointing outward from the center, representing those who are giving and sharing and, as a result, truly living. It reminds us of something Jesus said several times: "Whoever wants to save their life will lose it, but whoever loses their life for me and for the gospel will save it" (Mark 8:35). What is the focus of your life?

What occupies most of your time and energy and resources? To truly live, we must pour ourselves out in service to others.

The Jerusalem Council of Acts 15 illustrates a saying often attributed to Saint Augustine: "In essentials, unity; in nonessentials, liberty; in all things, charity." During that important early church meeting, the believers decided to stay united on the core issue of the gospel and to practice flexibility on peripheral issues. As we think about how that applies to us, one sure way to weaken your faith is to elevate every aspect of it (convictions, persuasions, and opinions) to the same level and attempt to hold them all with equal intensity.

For example, a person who contends equally not only for the core conviction that Jesus is divine but also for his or her personal persuasion that Christians should not should watch R-rated movies will ultimately be fighting to the death over every issue. When one of their persuasions is threatened or over-turned, their faith will become vulnerable and fragile. Our core belief system should be centered around Jesus Christ and his gospel, and we should be flex-ible on noncore issues. For a clear understanding of the gospel, look no further than Paul's letter to the Romans.

Another way to live the Story is to persevere in the midst of trials. Through-out the book of Acts and the ministry of Paul, we read of believers suffering. Here is Paul's own testimony about how difficult life has been for him as a missionary:

> Are they servants of Christ? (I am out of my mind to talk like this.) I am more. I have worked much harder, been in prison more frequently, been flogged more severely, and been exposed to death again and again. Five times I received from the Jews the forty lashes minus one. Three times I was beaten with rods, once I was pelted with stones, three times I was ship-wrecked, I spent a night and a day in the open sea, I have been constantly on the move. I have been in danger from rivers, in danger from bandits, in danger from my fellow Jews, in danger from Gentiles; in danger in the city, in danger in the country, in danger at sea; and in danger from false believers. I have labored and toiled and have often gone without sleep; I have known hunger and thirst and have often gone without food; I have been cold and naked. Besides everything else, I face daily the pressure of my concern for all the churches. (2 Cor. 11:23–28)

Most of us will never know that kind of suffering, but we will face trials of our own as we seek to follow Jesus. Hang in there! Keep the faith! Persevere! God can use even trials to change your character in deep ways, to draw other people to him, and to bring glory to his name (Jas. 1:2–4).

We also see from this part of the Story that reconciliation can be difficult, but it is well worth the effort. Paul expends much emotional energy on the Corinthian congregation. To put it mildly, they are his problem children. Even

One Big Mosaic

"Community is like a large mosaic. Each little piece seems so insignificant. One piece is bright red, another cold blue or dull green, another warm purple, another sharp yellow, another shining gold. Some look precious, others ordinary. Some look valuable, others worthless. Some look gaudy, others delicate. As individual stones, we can do little with them except compare them and judge their beauty and value. When, however, all these little stones are brought together in one big mosaic portraying the face of Christ, who would ever question the importance of any one of them? If one of them, even the least spectacular one, is missing, the face is incomplete. Together in one mosaic, each little stone is indispensable and makes a unique contribution to the glory of God. That's community, a fellowship of little people who together make God visible in the world."[2]

— HENRI NOUWEN

when God opens a door for fruitful ministry, Paul cannot walk through it because he is so distressed over his relationship with the Corinthians (2 Cor. 2:12–13). God has given us the gift of forgiveness to heal our deep hurts even when the other person refuses to change. But surely God's hope is that there will be repentance, forgiveness, and reconciliation.

Jesus said, "If you are offering your gift at the altar and there remember that your brother or sister has something against you, leave your gift there in front of the altar. First go and be reconciled to them; then come and offer your gift" (Matt. 5:23–24). When Christians fight among themselves, it brings dishonor to God and pushes unbelievers even further away from the kingdom. Jesus prayed that his followers would be united because that in itself makes a powerful statement about who Jesus is (John 17:23). Are there relationships in your life that need to be repaired?

Even when working far away from Jerusalem, Paul still remembers the poor in that city. As we said earlier, his collection of money from the Gentile churches for the poor believers in Jerusalem is one of his top priorities. Being on mission from God is not just about speaking words or setting up organizations or completing projects. It is primarily about helping people, and people need clothes to wear and food to eat. The Story is full of commands from God to take care of the poor among us. Do we even know who they are?[3]

---

2. Henri J. M. Nouwen, *The Only Necessary Thing* (New York: Crossroad, 1999), 124.

3. A good place to begin is to understand what the Story says about material possessions and how they should be used. We recommend Craig L. Blomberg's *Neither Poverty nor Riches: A Biblical Theology of Material Possessions* (Grand Rapids: Eerdmans, 1999).

Wrapping Up

In Acts 12–21 the church's mission of taking the good news of Jesus to the ends of the earth is on full throttle. From Antioch, definitely a sending church, the Spirit launches missionary tours across the Greco-Roman world using Paul and Barnabas and others. They speak first to the Jews in the synagogue before moving on to the marketplace and lecture halls to speak to the Gentiles about Jesus. Local churches are planted and nourished in places like Galatia, Ephesus, Philippi, Thessalonica, and Corinth. Paul then writes letters to these believers to encourage them or instruct them about a particular situation. Although he appoints local leaders, Paul serves as their apostolic father in the faith from a distance through his letters. This section ends with Paul's returning from his third missionary journey to Jerusalem with the collection for the poor believers there. The next phase of Paul's life will be even more difficult than he expected.

Memory Verse

There is no difference between Jew and Gentile, for all have sinned and fall short of the glory of God, and all are justified freely by his grace through the redemption that came by Christ Jesus. (Rom. 3:22b–24)

Digging Deeper

Books

Bird, Michael F. *Introducing Paul: The Man, His Mission and His Message.* Downers Grove, IL: InterVarsity Press, 2008.

Capes, David B., Rodney Reeves, and E. Randolph Richards. *Rediscovering Paul: An Introduction to His World, Letters and Theology.* Downers Grove, IL: InterVarsity Press, 2007.

Polhill, John B. *Paul and His Letters.* Nashville: Broadman & Holman, 1999.

ASSIGNMENTS

1. Read the text in Acts that describes Paul's three missionary journeys (Acts 13–21). Look carefully for any missionary principles you find. Make a list of all the ones you discover. Write a concluding paragraph or two explaining how you think Paul's missionary strategies could be used more effectively today.

2. Compare and contrast Paul's evangelistic approach in his synagogue sermon in Acts 13:16–41 with his speech before the Areopagus in 17:22–31. After you have identified what they have in common and how they differ, write a brief explanation of how Paul changed his message to match his audience in each case and why this might be important in evangelism.

3. The book of Romans presents a terrific summary of the gospel. Outline the letter of Romans in one page. Take a second page to explain how the outline of the letter summarizes the gospel.

4. In 1 Corinthians Paul deals with some complicated church issues. Read this important letter again and identify the following for each major problem that he addresses: (a) What is the specific problem? (b) What solution does he propose? (c) What does Paul's solution say about his view of God and the way things should work in God's kingdom?

CHURCH:
The Gospel Spreads from Jerusalem to Rome

Chapter 19

Enter Here

Several years ago I took up the sport of cycling. I bought an entry-level road bike and all the gear and started riding. At first I celebrated riding five, then fifteen, thirty, and eventually fifty miles. Then I got ambitious and set my sights on peddling a century. Riding a bicycle a hundred miles is a challenge. If you've trained properly, the first twenty-five to thirty miles of the race is usually easy and enjoyable. You feel as if you could maintain the pace forever. Around the fifty-mile mark, you become well aware that you're in for a long day in the saddle. When you hit mile seventy, major fatigue sets in, but the doubts never hit me until around mile eighty. From that point on, you hurt both mentally and physically until the end. Finishing a century is a test of endurance, pure and simple.

Endurance is also an important biblical virtue. In the last part of Acts we read about the later stages of Paul's ministry, and it wasn't an easy road. He spent years in prison, and things didn't always go as planned for this veteran missionary. Through it all he persevered so that God's purposes were fulfilled in his life. There may be times you want to quit. We pray that this part of the Story will encourage you to endure to the end.

Be Prepared

Read or listen to Acts 21–28; Ephesians; Philippians 2–3; Philemon; 1 Timothy 3; 2 Timothy 4.

The Story Continues

To the Ends of the Earth: Paul's Witness in Jerusalem
(Acts 21:17–23:35)

In the previous episode, Paul had arrived in Jerusalem to a warm welcome. He told all about what God had done through his ministry among the

Gentiles, and the Jewish Christians rejoiced. They express concern, however, that many Jewish believers view Paul as an enemy of their traditions since he seems to be preaching against the temple and the Law. Paul thus agrees to undergo Jewish purification rites at the temple as a way of demonstrating that although he ministers among the Gentiles, he is not anti-Jewish.

In the process of purification, some Jews from Asia (perhaps Ephesus) see him in the temple area and accuse him of stirring up trouble (Acts 21:27–29). A riot results, and the mob is about to beat Paul to death when Roman soldiers intervene to arrest him (21:30–36). As they are taking him to the army barracks, Paul gets permission to speak to his persecutors. He speaks in Aramaic, the ancient language of the Jews living in this area. He repeats the story of his former life in Judaism and his encounter with the risen Christ (21:37–22:21). The mob listens until he mentions his vision in the temple through which God sent him on mission to the Gentiles, at which point they demand his death (22:17–22). Paul's Roman citizenship prevents the soldiers from flogging him without a trial.

The next day Paul defends himself before the Jewish Sanhedrin by claiming that he is on trial for his belief in the resurrection of the dead, a doctrine accepted by Pharisees but rejected by Sadducees (Acts 22:30–23:6). This clever strategy divides the Sanhedrin, and the hearing degenerates into a violent argument between the two groups. The following night the Lord speaks to Paul: "Take courage! As you have testified about me in Jerusalem, so you must also testify in Rome" (23:11).

Since Paul's life is being threatened by the Jews, the Roman commander transfers him from Jerusalem to Caesarea under heavy military guard. Paul is kept in Herod's palace until Felix, the Roman governor of Judea at the time, can hear his case (Acts 23:12–35). It may not seem like much is happening in God's plan, but Paul is staying faithful in his witness, and his journey to Rome has in some ways already begun.

To the Ends of the Earth: Paul's Witness in Caesarea (Acts 24:1–26:32)

When Paul's Jewish opponents arrive in Caesarea, Felix hears the case. They accuse Paul, as the leader of the "Nazarene sect," of stirring up trouble among the Jews all over the empire and, most recently, of desecrating the temple (Acts 24:1–9). Paul claims that the charges against him are false but admits to worshiping the God of his Jewish ancestors as a follower of the Way (Christianity). Paul has not been causing trouble in Jerusalem. On the contrary, he came to the city with a gift from the Gentile churches. Paul does admit to his belief in the resurrection of the dead. Governor Felix puts off any decision and keeps Paul in prison with limited freedom.

Paul has the opportunity a few days later to give witness again to Felix and his wife, Drusilla, a Jewish woman and a daughter of Herod Agrippa I (Acts 24:24–26). Paul talks about Jesus Christ, about righteousness, and about the judgment to come. Then for the next two years Paul stays in prison in Caesarea (24:27). This must have been a difficult time for Paul, knowing that his mission is on hold for no apparent reason. Yet he continues to trust God.

Fast-forward two years when Festus takes over for Felix as Roman procurator. The Jewish leaders want Paul transferred back to Jerusalem to stand trial there (with plans to kill him along the way), but Festus tells the Jews to come to Caesarea where he will hear the case (Acts 25:1–5). They bring serious charges against Paul, none of which can be proven. Paul insists that he has done nothing against the Law, the temple, or even against Caesar, and when Festus considers moving the trial to Jerusalem, Paul appeals to Caesar (25:6–12).

> ### A Person Totally Committed to God
>
> "It has often been devotionally said: 'The world has yet to see what God can do with a man wholly committed to Him.' Paul was such a man, and the world has witnessed the effect."[1]
>
> – RICHARD LONGENECKER

Paul was a Roman citizen by birth, and citizenship had its privileges, one of which was the right to have your case heard before the Roman emperor. Rather than risk death by ambush or a corrupt trial in Jerusalem, Paul will take his case to Rome. The Lord's words to Ananias at the time of Paul's conversion continue to be fulfilled (9:15–16): "This man is my chosen instrument to proclaim my name to the Gentiles and their kings and to the people of Israel. I will show him how much he must suffer for my name."

Luke records yet another opportunity in Caesarea for Paul to bear witness to "kings." When King Agrippa II and his sister Bernice come to visit Festus, they want to listen to Paul (Acts 25:13–22). Paul once again tells the story of his former life in Judaism, his zeal in persecuting Christians, his Damascus road conversion, and his commission from Christ (26:1–18; cf. 9:1–19; 22:3–16). Paul has been obedient to God by speaking about Jesus and his resurrection and the need for people to repent and believe. Paul does his best to persuade Agrippa to become a believer, but he is unsuccessful. Agrippa tells Festus that Paul has done nothing to deserve death and that if he hadn't appealed to Caesar, he could have been released. But God has greater plans for Paul, and so his journey to Rome and his audience with the emperor will soon begin.

To the Ends of the Earth: Paul's Witness in Rome (Acts 27:1–28:31)

Paul travels to Rome by ship along with almost three hundred other passengers (Acts 27:1). Luke provides many details of their adventuresome voyage in Acts 27–28. They face violent storms at sea, and when all seems lost, Paul has another vision from the Lord assuring him that he must stand trial (bear witness) before Caesar and that everyone on the ship will be safe (Acts 27:21–26). They finally make land on the tiny island of Malta and all 276

---

1. Richard N. Longenecker, *The Ministry and Message of Paul* (Grand Rapids: Zondervan, 1971), 112.

Paul's Prison Letters: Philemon, Colossians, Ephesians, Philippians

These four letters are often grouped together as the Prison Letters for the simple reason that Paul was in prison when he wrote them. There is little disagreement that the apostle Paul wrote Philemon and Philippians, though some have doubted that he wrote Colossians and Ephesians because of their different language and style, theological emphases, and the author's lack of familiarity with his audience (in the case of Colossians). Nevertheless, Paul's claim to be the author, early church support, the first-person presentation of personal information, the overall purpose of the letters, and the likely use of a trusted secretary offer sufficient reasons for affirming Paul as author.

Most likely, Paul wrote these letters when he was a prisoner in Rome in the early AD 60s. Some have suggested that he wrote during his imprisonment in Caesarea, and that is a possibility, but the traditional view that he wrote from Rome remains the most persuasive. Tychicus carries Ephesians and Colossians and likely Philemon to their respective readers, suggesting that they were written from the same place (Eph. 6:21 – 22; Col. 4:7 – 9). If Philippians was written from this same Roman prison (and the place of writing for Philippians is the most debated of the four letters), it may have come near the end of his imprisonment, since more time was needed for communications between Paul and the Philippian church.

The short letter of **Philemon** tells how a Jewish Christian apostle (Paul), a wealthy Gentile slave owner (Philemon), and a runaway slave (Onesimus) are united together by their common faith in Christ. Philemon is a slave owner who has become a Christian through Paul's ministry. Onesimus is a runaway slave who comes in contact with Paul and becomes a believer. Paul writes to persuade Philemon to welcome back Onesimus as a brother in Christ, without putting him to death or punishing him — the normal treatment for runaway slaves in the Roman world. The letter reminds us that our connection to Christ also unites us to people of different social, racial, and economic situations, and we should treat them as fellow believers in spite of what the world says.

The church in **Colossae** is being threatened with a false teaching that promises a deeper, mysterious experience with God but also pushes Jesus Christ to the side and produces arrogance and division within the fellowship. This "hollow and deceptive" teaching depends on "fine-sounding arguments," private visions and special knowledge, mystical experiences, and strict religious regulations (Col. 2:4, 8, 16 – 18, 21 – 23). The basic problem is that this teaching gives Christ "a" place rather than "the" place as it blends together Jewish beliefs, folk religion, and pagan ideas such as magic and astrology, along with a few Christian elements. Paul's solution in Colossians is simple: Jesus Christ is the supreme revelation of God, and he provides the deepest possible experience of God. Christ is above all spiritual powers and is absolutely enough for the Colossian Christians. Rather than being paralyzed by superstition or living in fear of what fate might bring, we have been given spiritual fullness and abundance in Christ. He is supreme and all-sufficient and worthy of our complete devotion.

Paul didn't write **Ephesians** to deal with any crisis in particular. Rather, he wrote to house churches in Ephesus and the region about God's great plan for his people. More specifically, he focuses on our new life in Christ, the new community we now share with other believers, and our new responsibility to live as God's people. Ephesians is both majestic and intensely practical. God's grace offered in Christ rescues us from our sinful trajectory and transforms our lifestyle and our relationships. Because of all that God has done for us in

Christ, we should live a life worthy of this calling from God.

Paul writes **Philippians** to a church he planted on his second missionary journey, a church that supported him financially more than any other church. When they heard he was in prison, they sent a gift to support him (Phil. 2:25; 4:18). He now writes this letter to thank the church for being generous (1:5; 4:10–19), to update them on his circumstances (1:12–26; 4:10–19), to prepare for an upcoming visit (2:19–24), to warn them against false teachers (3:1–4, 18–19), and to exhort them to unity (2:1–11; 4:2–5). Philippians reminds us of the importance of giving generously, of rejoicing rather than worrying, of pursuing Christ's example of humility in order to maintain unity in the church, and of trusting in Christ's righteousness rather than our own.

PAUL'S JOURNEY TO ROME

people on the ship are saved. God's sovereign protection of Paul becomes evident since it would have been easy to miss such a small island. When warming himself around the fire on the beach, Paul is bitten by a poisonous snake, but it doesn't harm him so the people of Malta declare him to be a god (28:1–6). Paul and the small group of believers traveling with him are welcomed into the home of the chief official on the island, where God uses Paul to heal many who are sick (28:7–11).

In the spring, they continue their voyage and arrive on the mainland of Italy, where they find some believers and spend a week with them before arriving in Rome. Paul and his traveling companions are welcomed to Rome by other Christians, and he is allowed to live by himself with a soldier to guard him. Soon after arriving, Paul meets with Jewish leaders to explain his story. They claim that they've heard nothing negative about him and express interest in hearing more about the Christian sect since everyone is talking about it. Paul meets with them and explains what the Scriptures say about the kingdom of God and Jesus as Messiah. Some are convinced while others reject the message. Paul then declares that God has offered his salvation to the Gentiles, who will listen.

The book of Acts concludes with these words:

> For two whole years Paul stayed there in his own rented house and welcomed all who came to see him. He proclaimed the kingdom of God and taught about the Lord Jesus Christ—with all boldness and without hindrance! (Acts 28:30–31)

Paul's Pastoral Letters: 1–2 Timothy and Titus

First and Second Timothy and Titus are known as the Pastoral Letters because they are written to two pastors: Timothy, who is leading the church in Ephesus, and Titus, who is serving on the island of Crete. All three letters claim Paul as their author, but his authorship has been questioned by some scholars because of their different literary style and doctrinal emphases. In addition, the chronology of Acts doesn't seem to have a place for these letters. In spite of these objections, there are persuasive reasons for holding to Paul's authorship of the Pastorals. The different subject matter, purposes, and circumstances account for many of the peculiarities. It is also plausible that Paul used a trusted scribe, perhaps even Luke (see 2 Tim. 4:11), and gave him added freedom when composing the letters.

The book of Acts closes with Paul awaiting his audience with the emperor. Early church tradition says that Paul was eventually released from his first Roman imprisonment (AD 60–62) and that he continued his missionary ministry for a while before being rearrested, imprisoned in Rome a second time, and eventually martyred (about AD 67–68). Sometime between AD 63 and AD 67, Paul wrote to his two trusted coworkers with advice and encouragement about church ministry.

In 1 Timothy Paul writes to correct false teaching within the leadership of the Ephesian church and to teach believers how to conduct themselves as the church (see Acts 20:30; 1 Tim. 1:3–7; 6:3–5). The focus of 1 Timothy is on teaching the truth. In Titus, Paul spells out how the church should live in a pagan society, a difficult challenge for the Christians on Crete. The main theme of Titus is doing what is good (Titus 1:8, 16; 2:7, 14; 3:1–8, 14). Second Timothy is Paul's personal farewell to Timothy, his lifelong friend and partner in ministry. This letter is Paul's final good-bye to a loyal friend, urging him to stay faithful and endure hardship, always relying on God's grace.

Paul's Pastoral Letters speak to Christians today in powerful ways. They emphasize the importance of living godly lives so that our witness has integrity, of doing what is good as a demonstration of our faith, and of taking church leadership responsibilities seriously. They also stress the need to persevere and endure in spite of hardship and opposition.

Paul has finally made it to Rome, but not as he expected. He arrives as a prisoner rather than a free traveler. He has suffered greatly for the cause of Christ, but he remains a faithful witness in spite of his chains. Yet while Paul is bound, the gospel is free and goes out to all who will listen. It's fitting that the last word of the book ("without hindrance" is one word in Greek) describes the liberating influence of the gospel and fulfills Jesus' words in Acts 1:8 that the message will go to the ends of the earth.

Making Connections

Let's review where we are in the Great Story:

Creation and Crisis
Covenant
Calling Out
Commandments
Conquest and Canaanization
Creation of the Kingdom
Communion and Common Sense
Crumbling of the Kingdom
Captivity and Coming Home
Interlude: Time between the Testaments
Christ
➤ **Church:**
    The Coming of the Spirit
    In Jerusalem, Judea, and Samaria
    The Mission to the Gentiles
    The Gospel Spreads from Jerusalem to Rome
Consummation

Jesus said that the kingdom would have a small beginning but would eventually exert widespread influence. For example, in his parables of the mustard seed and yeast in Matthew 13:31–33, Jesus contrasts the kingdom's small start to its eventual large growth and influence. In this section of Acts, we see the fulfillment of Jesus' prediction as the kingdom expands across the entire Roman Empire. Consider the following statements about the influence of the Christian movement:

- Acts 24:5: "We have found this man [Paul] to be a troublemaker, stirring up riots among the Jews all over the world. He is a ringleader of the Nazarene sect."
- Acts 26:26: "The king [Agrippa] is familiar with these things, and I can speak freely to him. I am convinced that none of this has escaped his notice, because it was not done in a corner."

- Acts 28:22: "But we [the Jewish leaders in Rome] want to hear what your views are, for we know that people everywhere are talking against this sect."

From small beginnings in Palestine with Jesus and his band of believers to tens of thousands of followers all across the empire, Jesus' words have come true. The kingdom of God has expanded beyond Judea and Samaria to the ends of the earth (Acts 1:8).

As the message has been proclaimed across the empire, the resurrection of Jesus has remained at the center of the Story. The apostles witnessed to Jesus' resurrection from the first to the last of Acts. In Peter's sermon at Pentecost, he emphasized the resurrection as central (Acts 2:23–24, 31–33, 36). Much later in Acts, in Paul's speech to King Agrippa, he also concentrates his message on Jesus' resurrection (26:8, 23). Most importantly, Paul identifies this resurrection message as the hope of Israel (26:6–7). This is precisely what God promised to Paul's Jewish ancestors, that the Messiah would offer eternal life to both Jews and Gentiles. Because the Jews accusing Paul didn't see God's heart for the nations, they refused to believe.

Although Paul is the apostle to the Gentiles, he never stops sharing the good news with the Jews. In the last chapter of Acts, Paul calls together the Jewish synagogue leaders and speaks to them about the "hope of Israel"—the gospel centering on the death and resurrection of Jesus (Acts 28:20, 23). The tragedy of Jewish unbelief is their rejection of Jesus as the central figure in all of human history. In Acts 28:26–27 Paul quotes Isaiah 6:9–10, a passage quoted earlier by Jesus, to explain why the Jews are rejecting their Messiah, but Paul never gives up on them. His heart hurts because his own people generally refuse to believe in Jesus, yet he holds out hope: "Brothers and sisters, my heart's desire and prayer to God for the Israelites is that they may be saved" (Rom. 10:1; cf. 11:11–26). Jesus focused his ministry on Israel but didn't neglect Gentiles (Matt. 15:21–28), while Paul focuses on Gentiles but doesn't neglect Jews. As a result, Gentile Christians now have a huge role to play in evangelizing the Jewish people.

One last connection we want to make between this part of Acts and the rest of the Story relates to God's sovereignty. In spite of the struggles and setbacks throughout Acts, God's purposes are moving forward. God had made it clear that he chose Paul to "proclaim my name to the Gentiles and their kings and to the people of Israel" (Acts 9:15). Along the way Paul encountered plenty of trials. Paul expressed a desire in the early 50s to visit Rome (19:21), but it was ten years later that he finally arrived in the city. Even then, Paul didn't arrive in the manner he expected—as a traveling missionary. Rather, he arrived as a prisoner awaiting a trial before the most powerful person on earth, the Roman emperor.

Yet God has always brought good out of suffering. For example, he used Joseph's abandonment to save Israel, and he delivered his people from slavery in Egypt. His purposes will not be frustrated. In Acts alone, God overrules imprisonment, human travel plans, the powerful Jewish Sanhedrin, violent storms at sea, human errors in judgment, and more to accomplish his purposes.

Living the Story

God's plan is focused more on the success of the gospel than the health and wealth of the witnesses. The apostle Paul had a tough life. He was falsely accused, beaten, imprisoned for years, and he probably wondered many times how his circumstances would fit into God's calling on his life. We often deal with the same tension—what God seems to want us to do as a life calling and our current predicament don't match up. Through it all, Paul revealed a more God-centered attitude and perspective. Paul was more concerned about how he fit into God's plan than about how God was blessing his life. We see this in many places, including this passage from Philippians:

> And because of my chains, most of the brothers and sisters have become confident in the Lord and dare all the more to proclaim the gospel without fear.... I eagerly expect and hope that I will in no way be ashamed, but will have sufficient courage so that now as always Christ will be exalted in my body, whether by life or by death. (Phil. 1:14, 20)

Paul had learned not to focus on his life calling or his circumstances but on God's larger purposes and how God could use his situation to glorify Christ and edify the church. That was his prayer and his focus, and it should be ours as well.

In spite of Paul's larger vision, he was still an individual dealing with tough circumstances. God didn't forget about him. We learn from Paul's experience that when life hits rock bottom, we can always rely on God's presence with us. Yes, our sins have been forgiven (our past) and God has promised us a place in the new heaven and new earth (our future), but life can get pretty rough in the present. At several points in Acts when things appear hopeless, the Lord speaks to Paul in special ways to remind him that he is with him and that he is still working:

- Acts 23:11: "The following night the Lord stood near Paul and said, 'Take courage! As you have testified about me in Jerusalem, so you must also testify in Rome.'"
- Acts 27:23–24: "Last night an angel of the God to whom I belong and whom I serve stood beside me and said, 'Do not be afraid, Paul. You must stand trial before Caesar; and God has graciously given you the lives of all who sail with you.'"

Throughout the Story, God has reminded his people that he is always with them. To Abraham, Moses, David, the Prophets, and now the church, God promises his faithful presence to see us through even the darkest of days.

As Paul moves through the Roman legal system in this part of Acts, we also note how he uses his Roman citizenship in a wise manner. Yes, there are times when Paul doesn't play the citizenship card to prevent suffering (e.g., in Acts 16, where they were beaten and imprisoned at Philippi and he only later mentioned his citizenship). Paul doesn't run from suffering for the sake of Christ, but neither does he suffer without purpose or find a bizarre pleasure in suffering. There are times when he appeals to his citizenship to stop a beating (22:23–29) or to prevent an unfair trial (25:10–11). In other words, Paul uses his citizenship to promote justice and to prevent meaningless persecution when possible. We can pray for wisdom in knowing how to use tools like citizenship to advance God's purposes.

This section of the Story also challenges us to regard evangelism as a priority for the church. Throughout Acts we read about Christians evangelizing or bearing witness to the "kingdom of God" and the "Lord Jesus Christ" (Acts 28:31). First of all, this entails living like God's people in all of life and not just in the "sacred" sphere. We witness first with our lives and actions before we witness with our words. Next, it also involves verbally pointing people to Jesus Christ as the crucified and resurrected Lord. Paul repeatedly attempts to persuade people to repent and believe the gospel. Finally, we join with other believers in embracing God's kingdom purposes in every arena of society, whether business or politics or family or sports or education or whatever. This will keep us from fixating on the salvation of individuals to the neglect of God's larger purpose of redeeming all of creation. You can begin by asking God to open your eyes to people who need to hear the greatest Story ever and the hope it brings.

Wrapping Up

Paul returns to Jerusalem after his third missionary journey with the collection from the Gentile churches. His hopes of bringing unity between Jew and Gentile are quickly dashed as he is accused of stirring up trouble by bringing a Gentile into the temple area. Paul is arrested and imprisoned. He makes a defense before the Jewish Sanhedrin, but he is kept in prison and eventually transferred to the coastal town of Caesarea. He stays in prison in Caesarea for two years, testifying before rulers such as Felix, Festus, and Herod Agrippa II. To avoid being transferred back to Jerusalem, Paul takes advantage of his rights as a Roman citizen and appeals to Caesar. He then makes the long voyage to Rome, and Acts concludes with Paul in a Roman prison awaiting his trial before Emperor Nero.

Memory Verse

For it is by grace you have been saved, through faith — and this is not from yourselves, it is the gift of God — not by works, so that no one can boast. For we are God's handiwork, created in Christ Jesus to do good works, which God prepared in advance for us to do. (Eph. 2:8–10)

Digging Deeper

Books

Schnabel, Eckhard J. *Paul the Missionary: Realities, Strategies and Methods.* Downers Grove, IL: InterVarsity Press, 2008.

Walker, Peter. *In the Steps of Paul: An Illustrated Guide to the Apostle's Life and Journeys.* Grand Rapids: Zondervan, 2008.

ASSIGNMENTS

1. Paul spent a lot of time in Ephesus. Look up "Ephesus" in a Bible dictionary or Bible handbook and write a general, one-page description of the city during the first century. Now locate every place in Acts where it describes Paul's ministry in Ephesus. Make a list of what happens in the city in connection with Paul's ministry. Conclude with an evaluation of Paul's relationship to this church and city, including both highs and lows.

2. Read Acts 21–28 from Paul's perspective. Imagine that God had called you to be the apostle to the Gentiles, yet you are experiencing difficult circumstances. Trace Paul's situation throughout this part of Acts in half a page and then write a two-page personal journal of the spiritual struggles and victories Paul might have had as he lived through these circumstances.

3. Read 1–2 Timothy and summarize any wisdom you can find about what makes a local church a healthy church. For example, in 1 Timothy 1:3–7, Paul instructs Timothy to command the teaching elders not to teach false doctrines. One characteristic of a healthy church from this passage is that healthy churches are doctrinally sound.

CONSUMMATION:
The Happy Ending to the Great Story

Chapter 20

Enter Here

Can you imagine how frustrating it would be to cut out the ending to all the movies you watch and all the books you read? A story is really not a story without an ending. In places like the Prophets, the teachings of Jesus, and other parts of the New Testament, we have seen previews of how God's Story will end, but the ending is most thoroughly described in the book of Revelation. You see, the Bible is not just a collection of sixty-six individual books. It is also a single book with sixty-six chapters, and the final chapter is the book of Revelation.

This book is known as "the revelation of Jesus Christ" (Rev. 1:1 NRSV). This phrase could denote a "revelation *about* Jesus Christ" (the central character) or a "revelation *from* Jesus Christ" as he reveals a divine message to John. Perhaps Revelation includes some of both. In the final chapter in the Great Story, God pulls back the curtain to reveal his plans for human history, plans that center around Jesus Christ.

Revelation presents in colorful language and powerful imagery the ending to the Story, where God defeats the powers of evil, reverses the curse of sin, restores his creation, and lives among his people forever. While the details of this awesome and mysterious book are often debated, the main idea is not. God wants us to read Revelation to transform us so that we will live faithfully in this fallen world until Jesus returns. The final book of the Bible not only tells us much about how the Story will end; it also confronts us with our place in the Story.

To better understand Revelation, we need to learn about its literary and historical context and its overall purpose as well as how the book unfolds. We also need to understand how Revelation connects with (and concludes) the rest of the Story.

Be Prepared

Read or listen to Revelation.

The Story Continues

Literary Context

You don't have to read far in the book of Revelation before you realize that this is no ordinary book. We see a colorful description of "someone like a son of man" (Jesus) in 1:13–16 and his dramatic presence among seven churches in Revelation 2–3. Then the scene shifts to heavenly worship in chapters 4–5. It only gets more bizarre as we read about locusts with human faces and tails that sting like scorpions (9:7–10), a woman clothed with the sun (12:1), a beast with seven heads and ten horns (13:1), Babylon, the mother of prostitutes (17:5), and so on. Revelation is very, very strange. But why?

One reason Revelation is different from other New Testament books is that it combines three different types of literature: letter, prophecy, and apocalyptic. We are constantly confronted with different types of literature — a flirty text, a menu, a church announcement sheet, a phone bill, a political ad, and the like. We instinctively know how to read (or interpret) these different types of literature. But Revelation combines several literary types in one book.

First, Revelation is a *letter*. The book contains a typical letter greeting (1:4–5) as well as a closing benediction (22:21). The entire book should be viewed as a single letter written specifically to seven churches in Asia Minor (1:11). A quick glance at a map of Asia Minor shows that the cities are named in the order that a letter carrier might visit them, starting from Patmos (John's location at the time) and moving in a clockwise circle. Because the num-

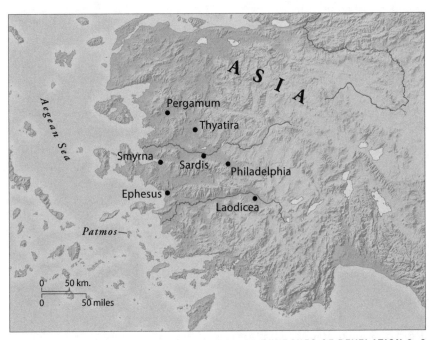

THE SEVEN CHURCHES OF REVELATION 2–3

ber seven symbolizes wholeness or completeness in Revelation, this letter to seven specific churches also functions as a letter to the universal church, which includes Christians today.

New Testament letters were meant to be read aloud to believers gathered for worship. Revelation 1:3 pronounces a blessing on the one who reads the letter aloud and on the congregation that courageously gathers to listen. Also, the book closes with a warning to anyone who tries to change the content of the book in any way (22:18–19).

What is perhaps most important about New Testament letters is that they were written to address a particular situation or problem. (The historical context of Revelation discussed shortly describes this situation.) The message of Revelation certainly extends beyond the first-century audience, but it must include the original audience. Any approach to Revelation that ignores its message to the seven churches of Asia Minor will distort the meaning of the book in a potentially harmful way.

Second, Revelation is clearly described as a *prophecy* (Rev. 1:3; 22:7, 10, 18–19; cf. 19:10; 22:9). Alongside other prophetic books in the Bible, Revelation includes both *prediction* about the future (foretelling) and *proclamation* about the present (forthtelling). Surprisingly, biblical prophecies stress the second of these two elements. Interestingly, in the very places where Revelation is described as a prophecy, the readers are commanded to *obey* the prophecy (1:3; 22:7, 18–19). That's right, we are supposed to obey or keep this prophecy. That only makes sense when we understand prophecy as first and foremost a proclamation rather than a prediction. How would you obey a prediction anyway? Revelation certainly has something to say about the future and we don't want to downplay that aspect, but Revelation speaks primarily about how God wants his people to live here and now.

Third, Revelation is an *apocalypse*. In Revelation 1:1 we are told that the book is a "revelation" (*apokalypsis* in Greek), a term that means "to unveil" or "to reveal" what has been hidden. In the Old Testament, we see examples of apocalyptic literature in books like Daniel and Zechariah as well as certain other sections of the Prophets (e.g., Ezek. 38–39). There were also Jewish apocalyptic works that arose in the time between the Old and New Testaments (e.g., *1* and *2 Enoch*, *Jubiliees*, *2* and *3 Baruch*, *4 Ezra*, and the *Apocalypse of Abraham*). Jesus' Olivet Discourse (Matt. 24–25; Mark 13) even displays an apocalyptic tone.

Apocalyptic literature includes God's promise to a well-known person (like John or Daniel) that he will intervene in the course of history to overthrow evil empires and set up his kingdom. This type of literature communicates primarily through the use of visual images. Revelation 1:1 serves notice that we should expect symbolic communication throughout the book when it says that the revelation was "made known" (*sēmainō*) to John through an angel (cf. Dan. 2:45). This term means "to make known through symbols." Revelation uses picture language to speak a powerful message. It might help to know a bit more about the specific situation faced by the original audience.

Historical Context

Most scholars date the book of Revelation near the end of the first century (around AD 95) during the reign of Emperor Domitian. It had been about sixty-five years since Jesus was crucified and resurrected, and the Christian faith had spread across much of the Roman Empire (as we have seen in the book of Acts). Jesus had promised that he would return, and the first Christians lived in expectation of the great event. But life was not always easy for Christians living under the rule of Rome.

Throughout Asia Minor, the imperial cult (i.e., the worship of the Roman emperor) was alive and well. For example, Domitian (AD 81–96) wanted his subjects to address him as *dominus et deus noster* ("our Lord and God"). The imperial cult was a force to be reckoned with precisely because it united political, social, and economic elements into a single, dominating religious force. Since the earliest and most basic Christian confession was "Jesus is Lord," when Christians refused to confess "Caesar is Lord," they were considered disloyal to the state and were subject to persecution.

The book of Revelation leaves the clear impression that some Christians are suffering for their faith and that many more should prepare to suffer in the near future. John has been banished to the island of Patmos "because of the word of God and the testimony of Jesus" (Rev. 1:9). John describes himself as a "brother and companion in the suffering and kingdom and patient endurance that are ours in Jesus" (1:9). Antipas, a believer in Pergamum, has been put to death (2:13), and Jesus himself tells the church in Smyrna that they should expect the situation to get worse (2:10):

> Do not be afraid of what you are about to suffer. I tell you, the devil will put some of you in prison to test you, and you will suffer persecution for ten days. Be faithful, even to the point of death, and I will give you life as your victor's crown.

There are also numerous references throughout the book to pagan powers shedding the blood of God's people (Rev. 6:10; 16:6; 17:6; 18:24; 19:2). There is little doubt that many of these early Christians are feeling the effects of war with the dragon (12:17), and some have paid the ultimate price (2:13; 6:9; 20:4). Revelation addresses a situation in which false religion has formed a partnership with pagan political power. As a result, those who claim to follow Christ are facing increasing pressure to conform to the imperial cult at the expense of faithfulness to Christ.

But not all Christians in Asia Minor are standing firm. When faced with the possibility of suffering, some believers have compromised their faith in order to avoid persecution. The temptation to turn away from Christ and join with the world system shows up clearly in the messages to the seven churches. The church in Ephesus has forsaken its first love (2:4). Some in Pergamum and Thyatira are following false teachers (2:14–15, 20). The church in Sardis has a reputation of being alive, but it's really dead (3:1). And then there is the lukewarm church in Laodicea, which the Lord is about to spit out of his mouth (3:16).

To summarize, the historical context of the book is one in which false religion has teamed up with pagan political power. As a result, faithful Christians are under pressure to conform to this worldly system while others are compromising with it. Revelation comforts those who are persevering in loyalty to

1 John: "True Christian Belief and Behavior"
2 John: "Walk in Love and Truth"
3 John: "Imitate What Is Good"

John wrote these three letters to Christians living in the region of Ephesus near the end of the first century, about the same time he wrote Revelation. The churches were under attack from an early form of Gnosticism that promoted a special knowledge, rather than love, as the way to relate to God, and they degraded the human body as evil. The focus on this "special knowledge" led to arrogance, while their low view of the human body led some to deny that Jesus was fully man and fully God, a truth the Bible clearly affirms. The false teachers were claiming that Jesus couldn't have had a real human body because physical matter is evil and only spirit is good.

On top of all that, those who were buying into this false teaching were leaving the fellowship (1 John 2:19), claiming they had already attained sinless perfection (1:8, 10; 3:9–10). John writes to reinforce the traditional teaching about Jesus Christ and the true Christian faith, identifying the true marks of a believer in 1 John and then applying those to specific situations in 2–3 John.

In 1 John we are given three characteristics of a true believer: obedience to God (vs. moral self-indulgence), love (vs. arrogance), and a correct belief about Jesus (vs. a belief that the body is evil). The two purpose statements in 1 John indicate that John is warning believers about the false teaching (2:26) and writing to help them know that they have eternal life (5:13).

Second John was written to a particular congregation, warning them against false teachers, encouraging them to love one another, and instructing them to be discerning when welcoming and supporting traveling teachers. At that time, when Christians traveled they relied heavily on the hospitality of other Christians for food and lodging. We learn from 2 John to be discerning when it comes to whether or not to support a Christian ministry.

Third John speaks even more directly to the importance of providing hospitality to other believers. Apparently an authoritarian leader has rejected some traveling teachers sent out by John himself. John writes to correct the problem. We learn from this letter not to let our love grow cold toward all Christian ministries just because some are deceptive.

Christ and warns those who are selling out. This double message of comfort and warning also relates to the overall purpose of the book.

Overall Purpose

Simply put, the overall purpose of Revelation is to show how God's Great Story ends in order to give hope to the persecuted and to challenge the complacent. Revelation uses images and symbols to accomplish this purpose. The book creates a kind of virtual world in which readers may live while they are hearing the book read aloud. In this symbolic world the readers see reality from God's perspective. They see that God is more powerful than evil. They see that God is sovereign and, in the end, will conquer all their enemies. The scholar Richard Bauckham illustrates how this works with Revelation 17:

> For example, in chapter 17 John's readers share his vision of a woman. At first glance, she might seem to be the goddess Roma, in all her glory, a stunning personification of the civilization of Rome, as she was worshipped in many a temple in the cities of Asia. But as John sees her, she is a Roman prostitute, a seductive whore and a scheming witch, and her wealth and splendor represent the profits of her disreputable trade. For good measure there are biblical overtones of the harlot queen Jezebel to reinforce the impression [read about Jezebel in 1 Kings 16–21]. In this way, John's readers are able to perceive something of Rome's true character — her moral corruption behind the enticing propagandist illusions of Rome which they constantly encountered in their cities.[1]

Where There's Hope, There's Life

" 'While there's life, there's hope' is an old and true saying. It is probably just as true to say, 'While there's hope, there's life.' Hope is one of the most fundamental human motivations. When we lose this sense of something better beyond our present experience, we are apt to slip into a dark pit of depression from which it is difficult to escape."[2]

– PAUL SPILSBURY

After seeing reality from a heavenly perspective, they are then able to reenter their own world and live faithfully. Loyal believers are reminded over and over in this book that Jesus is Lord, that what they believe is not crazy but totally true and reliable.

Basically, Revelation answers the question, "Who is Lord?" During times of oppression and impending persecution, the righteous suffer and the wicked seem to prosper. This begs the question, "Is God still on his throne?" Revelation says that in spite of how things appear, Caesar is not Lord and Satan is not Lord, but Jesus is Lord and he is coming soon to restore his creation and establish his eternal kingdom. The powers of evil will not have the final word. In the end, God wins! Those who are faithfully persevering are reminded of the rock-solid foundation of their hope in

---

1. Richard J. Bauckham, *The Theology of the Book of Revelation* (Cambridge: Cambridge Univ. Press), 17–18.

2. Paul Spilsbury, *The Throne, the Lamb and the Dragon: A Reader's Guide to the Book of Revelation* (Downers Grove, IL: InterVarsity Press, 2002), 129.

Christ. Those who are selling their souls to the pagan powers are shown God's future so as to shock them into repentance. Revelation is truly a transforming vision of God's sovereign rule over all reality.

Overview of Revelation

Introduction (1:1–20). Revelation 1 begins with a prologue (1:1–8) and a detailed description of the risen, glorified Christ (1:9–20). In this first chapter we are introduced to the main characters of the divine drama.

The prologue begins by indicating the source of the revelation: God → Jesus → an angel → John → the rest of God's servants. A blessing (the first of seven such beatitudes) is pronounced in 1:3 followed by a greeting in 1:4–8. The greeting comes from the triune God: from God the Father "who is, and who was, and who is to come," from "the seven spirits [the Holy Spirit] before his throne, and from Jesus Christ, who is the faithful witness, the firstborn from the dead, and the ruler of the kings of the earth." After the greeting come a doxology of praise to Jesus, a promise of his return, and an affirmation that God is sovereign over all history.

John, who has been exiled to the island of Patmos because of his faithful testimony about Jesus, receives a commission to write down what he sees and to send it to the seven churches in Asia Minor (1:9–11). John's vision focuses on Jesus Christ in all his glory and on Jesus' ongoing presence among the seven lampstands or churches. Using language from Daniel 7 and 10, Jesus is described as a powerful figure who has authority over the powers of evil because of his death and resurrection (1:12–16). John is told not to fear but to faithfully record the vision, which concerns the past, the present, and the future (1:17–20).

Messages to the seven churches (2:1–3:22). Chapters 2 and 3 contain particular messages to seven churches in Asia Minor: Ephesus, Smyrna, Pergamum, Thyatira, Sardis, Philadelphia, Laodicea. These messages follow a similar literary pattern with a description of Jesus, a commendation of the church's good works, an accusation against the church because of some sin, an exhortation followed by a warning or an encouragement, an admonition to listen to the Spirit, and a promise to those who overcome. While Jesus does commend several congregations for their faithful perseverance in the face of persecution, the more dominant picture is of churches that are spiritually weak because of their idolatry and immorality.

These compromising churches are called to repent before it is too late. Each message ends with a promise to those who overcome, a key theme in Revelation. These future rewards are for all believers who are faithful to Jesus (e.g., the right to eat of the tree of life, protection from the second death, authority over the nations, eternal security in the presence of God).

A vision of the heavenly throne room (4:1–5:14). The seven messages set the scene on earth where the church faces the dual threat of persecution and compromise. Now in Revelation 4–5 the scene shifts to heaven, where God reigns in majestic power. Here we see the centering vision for the entire book, a glimpse of the center of reality—God on his throne! All of heaven worships God for his eternal holiness and for his magnificent work as Creator. Worship is certainly the most important activity of heaven.

God is holding a scroll sealed with seven seals that seems to represent his redemptive plan. At first no one is found worthy to open the scroll, and John weeps in despair until he is told about the Lion of Judah. When he looks to see this Lion, however, he sees a Lamb looking as if it had been slain. The Lamb's wounds are from his sacrificial death on the cross. Only Jesus, the Lion-Lamb, is worthy to fulfill God's plan. He is worthy because he died and rose again to redeem a people for God from all the peoples of the world. Because of Jesus, God's purposes can now be fulfilled. While God is praised as Creator, Jesus is also worthy of ceaseless praise as Redeemer.

The opening of the seven seals (6:1–8:1). The stage has been set and the unveiling of God's ultimate victory formally begins—a victory that will involve his judgment of evil. Here we see the first of three judgment visions, each with seven elements: the seal judgments (6:1–8:1), the trumpet judgments (8:2–11:19), and the bowl judgments (15:1–16:2). Revelation 6 begins with the opening of the first four seals—the famous four horsemen of the apocalypse: conquest, war, famine, and death. The fifth seal consists of the martyrs' question, "How long, Sovereign Lord, holy and true, until you judge the inhabitants of the earth and avenge our blood?" (6:10). The sixth seal concludes with the question, "Who can withstand it?" or who can survive the wrath of the Lamb?

The answer comes in Revelation 7 with two visions of people belonging to God—the 144,000 on earth sealed with divine protection and the great multitude in heaven standing before God's throne. These two visions appear to describe the same group of people from two different perspectives—before and after their deaths. The church on earth should prepare to endure persecution while the church in heaven rejoices in victory. Those who can withstand God's judgment are those who truly belong to him. God's people will experience persecution/tribulation, but they will never experience God's wrath.

The sounding of the seven trumpets (8:2–11:19). The trumpets continue to show God's judgment on a wicked world. They are patterned after the plagues of Egypt leading up to the exodus. In spite of the ever-intensifying judgments, however, the wicked refuse to repent (9:20–21). As with the other judgments, God's people are "sealed" or protected against divine wrath (9:4).

Once again, before the seventh element in the series, there is an interlude consisting of two visions: the angel and the little scroll (10:1–11) and the two witnesses (11:1–14). As before, these two visions offer God's people encouragement and instruction as God carries out his purposes in history. The "How much longer?" question of 6:10 is now answered in 10:6: "There will be no more delay!"

God's plan is moving forward (the scroll is sweet to the taste), but it will involve the suffering of God's people (the scroll turns bitter in John's stomach). The two witnesses of Revelation 11 probably symbolize the witnessing church. Although God's people will face persecution and even martyrdom as they bear witness, they are assured of spiritual protection and a secure future in the presence of God through resurrection. The seventh trumpet returns us again to the scene of heavenly worship.

The people of God versus the powers of evil (12:1–14:20). Revelation 12–14 forms an extended interlude between the second (trumpets) and third (bowls) series of judgments. Revelation 12 explains why God's people face tribulation and hostility in this world. It all relates to the larger cosmic conflict between God and Satan. A woman (probably representing the true Israel) gives birth to a male child—Jesus the Messiah. Satan (the red dragon) tries to destroy Christ (the male child) but is decisively defeated by Christ's death and resurrection. As a defeated enemy, Satan now vents his anger on the people of God. Knowing the real reason for persecution along with the certainty of God's future victory encourages believers to persevere to the end.

Chapter 13 introduces Satan's two agents for waging war against God's people—the beast out of the sea (13:1–10) and the beast out of the earth (13:11–18), sometimes referred to as the Antichrist and the False Prophet, although Revelation never actually uses the term "Antichrist." These two beasts likely represent pagan political power and false religion. An unholy trinity now emerges: the dragon and the two beasts, whose goal it is to seduce and destroy God's people.

Revelation 14 gives the reader another glimpse of the future blessings God has in store for his people. We see again the 144,000, this time showing that they have safely arrived in heaven. This confirms our understanding of the 144,000 and the great multitude in Revelation 7 as the people of God. These are the ones who "follow the Lamb wherever he goes" (14:4). In spite of the difficulties they face in their discipleship to Jesus, one day they will stand in God's presence and sing a new song of redemption. Chapter 14 concludes with three angelic messages proclaiming the coming judgment of God, exhorting people to repent, and encouraging believers to remain faithful to Jesus.

The pouring out of the seven bowls (15:1–16:21). Chapter 15 prepares for the third series of judgments by describing seven angels with seven golden bowls filled with the wrath of God. In chapter 16 these seven bowls are poured out on the unrepentant world. These judgments are devastating, uninterrupted, universal manifestations of God's anger toward sin and evil. In response, unbelievers not only refuse to repent; they go so far as to curse God (16:9, 11, 21) and gather together to make war against him for the last time (Armageddon). But God's judgment falls on Babylon the Great (the Roman Empire in the first century) as he makes her drink the "wine of the fury of his wrath" (16:19).

The judgment and fall of Babylon (17:1–19:5). Revelation 17 and 18 depict the death of Babylon, a pagan power said to be "drunk with the blood of God's holy people, the blood of those who bore testimony to Jesus" (17:6). Babylon undoubtedly represents Rome, the leading pagan power center of the first century, as well as future centers of pagan power. From here on, Revelation contrasts two cities: the city of man (Babylon, destined for destruction) and the city of God (the heavenly Jerusalem, where God will live with his people forever). Chapter 18 provides the world's funeral lament for the deceased Babylon.

God's ultimate victory (19:6–22:5). Here we see God's ultimate victory over the forces of evil and the final reward for God's people. The scene opens and the announcement of the wedding of the Lamb (19:6–10) and the return of Christ for his bride (19:11–16). Christ comes now as a Warrior, intent on destroying the two beasts and their allies in the lake of burning sulfur (19:17–21). Satan is bound (20:1–3), during which time Jesus' faithful followers reign with him (20:4–6). Satan is then released from his temporary prison and immediately begins to deceive the nations once again but is defeated by God once and for all and now joins the two beasts in eternal torment (20:7–10).

The dead are judged by him who sits on the great white throne, and those whose names are not found in the book of life are also thrown into the lake of fire (20:11–15). At this point death itself is judged. Having judged sin and Satan and death, God ushers in the eternal state of glory. There is a general description of "a new heaven and a new earth" in 21:1–8, followed by a more detailed presentation in 21:9–22:5. God's longtime promise to live among his people is now fulfilled (21:3). There is no temple in this heavenly city because God Almighty and the Lamb are its temple (21:22). God's victory is complete, and the fellowship he first sought with Adam and Eve is restored in a new garden-city complete with a tree of life (22:1–2). The curse of sin is removed, and redeemed humanity is again able to walk with God and see his face (22:4).

Conclusion (22:6–21). Revelation closes with a final blessing on those who keep "the words of the prophecy written in this scroll" (22:7) and a warning for those who practice sexual immorality, idolatry, and the like (22:15). The book is an authentic revelation from God and should be read faithfully to the churches (22:6, 16). Jesus assures his people that his return is imminent (22:7, 12, 20). And John responds with a prayer statement that Christians of all times can make their own: "Come, Lord Jesus." In the meantime, John writes, "the grace of the Lord Jesus be with God's people. Amen" (22:21).

Making Connections

Let's review where we are in the Great Story:

Creation and Crisis
Covenant
Calling Out

Commandments
Conquest and Canaanization
Creation of the Kingdom
Communion and Common Sense
Crumbling of the Kingdom
Captivity and Coming Home
Interlude: Time between the Testaments
Christ
Church
➤ **Consummation**

To see how Revelation connects to the Story, we begin with a brief survey of the five main ways scholars have tried to interpret the book of Revelation:

1. *Preterist*: Revelation primarily deals with what was happening in the first century. John uses figurative language to communicate to first-century Christians how God plans to deliver them from the evils of the Roman Empire.
2. *Historicist*: Revelation supplies a prophetic overview of church history from the first century until the future coming of Christ.
3. *Futurist*: Revelation is concerned with what will happen at the end of history.
4. *Idealist*: Revelation is a symbolic description of the ongoing battle between God and the devil. Revelation offers timeless spiritual truths to inspire Christians of all times as they endure persecution, suffering, and injustice.
5. *Eclectic*: This approach combines the strengths of several approaches (e.g., value in the message to the original readers, some portions of the book await future fulfillment, and a relevant spiritual message for the church of every age).

Although it can be useful to know more about the major interpretive approaches and the millennial views, we believe it's even more constructive to understand how Revelation's main themes show the consummation of God's Great Story. The main themes of Revelation include God on his throne, the enemies of God, Jesus the Lion-Lamb, the people of God, God's judgment of evil, and the new heaven and new earth.

God on His Throne

Although God is never described in detail in Revelation, he constitutes the center of reality. Throughout the book, God is shown to be sovereign, worthy of worship, and a loving Father to his people. The opening salutation introduces God as the "Alpha and Omega," the one "who is, and who was, and who is to come," and "the Almighty" (1:8).

The vision of God on his throne in Revelation 4–5 adds to this picture of

Major Millennial Views

Postmillennialism ("post" meaning "after"): Christ will return after the millennium. The gospel of Christ will eventually triumph and bring about the millennial age. The progress of the gospel will usher in the spiritual reign of Christ. The millennium will be followed by the return of Christ, a general resurrection and judgment, and the eternal kingdom.

Amillennialism ("a" meaning "not"): There will not be a visible, earthly millennial reign of Christ. Revelation 20:4–6 should be interpreted as symbolizing (1) the heavenly reign of Christ with Christians who have already died and are now with the Lord, or (2) the spiritual reign of Christ during the present age in the hearts of believers on earth. Satan has been bound by the work of Christ and his gospel. At the end of history there will be the return of Christ, a general resurrection, and a last judgment.

Premillennialism ("pre" meaning "before"): Christ will return before establishing an earthly reign with his people. This may or may not be a literal thousand-year period of time, but it will be a full and complete earthly reign. Revelation 19–21 portrays a sequence of events that will occur at the end of the age. Christ will return (Rev. 19), Satan will be bound, and the saints will be resurrected to reign with Christ for a thousand years (20:1–6). Then Satan is released for a final rebellion before his ultimate defeat (20:7–10). Then come the resurrection and the final judgment (20:11–15), followed by the new heaven and new earth (Rev. 21).

There are two major types of premillennialism: (1) historic premillennialism and (2) dispensational premillennialism, and there are two major types of dispensational premillennialism: classic and progressive.

God as the creator and sovereign ruler of the universe. For all he has done, God is worthy of worship (4:11; cf. 14:7; 19:6). God is intent on judging evil, vindicating his people, and restoring his creation (e.g., 16:5–7; 19:1–2). Through it all, God consistently reveals himself as one who loves his people deeply by protecting and comforting them (7:2–3, 15, 17; 21:4). In the end, God will fulfill his longstanding promise to live among his people in perfect fellowship (21:6–7; 22:1–5).

God's Enemies

Not every creature worships God as the sovereign and loving Creator. Even God has his enemies. There are four main enemies named in Revelation. God's archenemy, the dragon or Satan, seeks to ruin the plans of God. Revelation 12 explains why Satan hates God and his people so much—he has been decisively defeated and now vents his rage against God's people.

The dragon's two primary partners are the "beast out of the sea" and the "beast out of the earth" (see Rev. 13). John's original audience would have identified the first beast (commonly known as the Antichrist) as the Roman Empire, but the reference likely extends beyond the first century to include any worldly power that competes with God for allegiance or worship. The second beast represents religious power that supports the first beast. In the first century, this would have referred to the worship of the Roman emperor. The dragon and the two beasts constitute the satanic trinity.

The fourth enemy of God includes human beings (i.e., "inhabitants of the earth") who give themselves to idolatry and immorality (17:2), worship of the beast (13:8, 12), and the persecution of believers (6:10; 11:10). In the end, all of God's enemies will face his condemning wrath.

Jesus, the Lion-Lamb

God carries out his plan to rescue humanity and restore his creation through his Son, Jesus Christ, who is described in Revelation as both a Lion and a Lamb (5:5–7). Revelation consistently emphasizes Jesus' oneness with God in that he shares in the authority, glory, and worship reserved for God (1:4–5, 14–16; 5:6, 9–14; 7:10, 17; 12:10; 21:22–23; 22:1, 3).

Through his sacrificial death and subsequent resurrection, Jesus overcomes evil and secures for God a people from every nation (1:5; 5:9). As the slaughtered yet risen Lamb, he is able to empathize with his people, who now endure tribulation as part of their identification with him (1:9; 12:17; 20:4). Jesus has also promised to return, no longer as the sacrificial Lamb, but as a Warrior-Judge (1:7; 3:11; 16:15; 19:11–21). At his return, he will completely conquer the forces of evil and usher in the eternal kingdom.

The Seven Beatitudes of Revelation	
1:3	**Blessed** is the one who reads aloud the words of this prophecy, and **blessed** are those who hear it and take to heart what is written in it, because the time is near.
14:13	Then I heard a voice from heaven say, "Write this: **Blessed** are the dead who die in the Lord from now on." "Yes," says the Spirit, "they will rest from their labor, for their deeds will follow them."
16:15	"Look, I come like a thief! **Blessed** is the one who stays awake and remains clothed, so as not to go naked and be shamefully exposed."
19:9	Then the angel said to me, "Write this: **Blessed** are those who are invited to the wedding supper of the Lamb!" And he added, "These are the true words of God."
20:6	**Blessed** and holy are those who share in the first resurrection. The second death has no power over them, but they will be priests of God and of Christ and will reign with him for a thousand years.
22:7	"Look, I am coming soon! **Blessed** is the one who keeps the words of the prophecy written in this scroll."
22:14–15	**Blessed** are those who wash their robes, that they may have the right to the tree of life and may go through the gates into the city. Outside are the dogs, those who practice magic arts, the sexually immoral, the murderers, the idolaters and everyone who loves and practices falsehood."

God's People

Revelation refers to God's people in a variety of ways: "church" (e.g., 1:4, 11; 2:1; 3:1; 22:16), "saints" (e.g., 5:8; 13:10; 14:12; 17:6), "servants" (1:1; 2:20; 6:11; 7:3; 19:2), the "144,000" (7:4; 14:1, 3), the "great multitude" (7:9; 19:1, 6), the "bride" of the Lamb (18:23; 21:2, 9; 22:17), and the "new Jerusalem" (21:2, 10), just to name a few. These are people who have been redeemed by the blood of the slain Lamb (1:5; 5:9). They come from every "tribe and language and people and nation"; that is, God is creating a multicultural people (5:9; 7:9; 10:11; 11:19; 13:7; 14:6; 17:15). Above all, they are people who "keep God's commands and hold fast their testimony about Jesus" (12:17).

As they "follow the Lamb wherever he goes" (14:4) and refuse to worship worldly powers, they experience ridicule, persecution, and even death (1:9;

The Beginning	Genesis	The End	Revelation
"In the beginning, God …"	1:1	"I am the Alpha and the Omega, the Beginning and the End."	21:6
God creates first heaven and earth, eventually cursed by sin.	1:1	God creates a new heaven and earth where sin is nowhere to be found.	21:1
Water symbolizes unordered chaos.	1:2	There is no longer any sea.	21:1
God creates light and separates it from darkness.	1:3–5	No more night or natural light; God himself is the source of light.	21:23; 22:5
God gives humans dominion over the earth.	1:26–30	God's people will reign with him forever.	20:4, 6; 22:5
"Marriage" of Adam and Eve	1:27–28; 2:7, 18–25	Marriage of Last Adam and his bride, the church	19:7; 21:2, 9
Satan introduces sin into the world.	3:1–7	Satan and sin are judged.	19:11–21; 20:7–10
The serpent deceives humanity.	3:1–7, 13–15	The ancient serpent is bound "to keep him from deceiving the nations."	20:2–3
Death enters the world.	3:3; 4:6–8; 6:3	Death is put to death.	20:14; 21:4
Sin enters the world.	3:6	Sin is banished from God's city.	21:8, 27; 22:15
Sinful people refuse to serve/obey God.	3:6–7; 4:6–8; 6:5	God's people serve him.	22:3
Community forfeited	3:8; 4:8	Genuine community experienced	21:3, 7
God abandoned by sinful people	3:8–10; 6:5	God's people (new Jerusalem, bride of Christ) made ready for God; marriage of Lamb	19:7–8; 21:2, 9–21
Sinful people ashamed in God's presence	3:8–11	God's people will "see his face."	22:4
People rebel against the true God, resulting in physical and spiritual death.	3:8–19	God's people risk death to worship the true God and thus experience life.	20:4–6

Continued on next page

2:9–10; 6:9–11; 12:10; 13:7, 15). Their challenge is to persevere or "overcome" rather than to compromise (chs. 2–3; 12:11; 15:2; 21:7). While Christians may suffer earthly defeat at the hands of Satan through persecution and even death, they actually conquer him by holding fast to their testimony of Christ crucified and resurrected. Satan's victory over them is at the same time their victory over Satan. They overcome in the same way that their Lord overcame—victory through suffering (3:21; 5:5–6).

God's Judgment of Evil

Throughout the Story, God has promised to judge evil once and for all. We see that judgment culminate in the book of Revelation. Throughout the book there are three series of seven judgments—the seals (6:1–8:1), the trumpets

The Beginning	Genesis	The End	Revelation
Sin brings pain and tears.	3:16–17; 6:5–6	God comforts his people and removes crying and pain.	21:4
Sinful people are cursed.	3:16–19	The curse is removed from redeemed humanity and they become a blessing.	22:3
Sinful people are forbidden to eat from the tree of life.	3:22–24	God's people may eat freely from the tree of life.	22:2, 14
Sinful people are sent away from life.	3:22–24	God's people have their names written in the book of life.	20:4–6, 15; 21:6, 27
Exclusion from bounty of Eden	3:23	Invitation to marriage supper of Lamb	19:9
Sinful humanity is separated from presence of holy God.	3:23–24	God's people experience God's holiness (cubed city = Most Holy Place).	21:15–21
Sinful people are sent away from garden.	3:23–24	New heaven/earth includes a garden.	22:2
Sinful people are banished from presence of God.	3:24	God lives among his people.	21:3, 7, 22; 22:4
Sinful humanity is cursed with wandering (exile).	4:10–14	God's people are given a permanent home.	21:3
Sinful humanity suffers a wandering exile in the land.	4:11–14	God gives his children an inheritance.	21:7
Creation begins to grow old and die.	5:6, 8, 14, 17, 20, 27, 31; 6:3	All things are made new.	21:5
Sin results in spiritual sickness.	6:5	God heals the nations.	22:2
Water is used to destroy wicked humanity.	6:1–7:24	God quenches thirst with water from spring of life.	21:6; 22:1
Sinful people are scattered.	11:3–9	God's people unite to sing his praises.	19:6–7
Languages of sinful humanity are confused.	11:8–9	God's people are a multicultural people.	21:24, 26; 22:2

(8:2–11:19), and the bowls (16:1–21). These judgments seem to be modeled on the plagues against Pharaoh in the book of Exodus, where God judges his enemies and vindicates his people. Revelation 14 also sends a strong message related to judgment: either fear God and give him glory (14:7), or face God's terrible judgment reserved for Babylon the Great and those who worship the beast (14:8–9).

Revelation 17–20 describes God's final judgment of evil. At the last "battle," the Lamb triumphs over the dragon and the two beasts and throws all three into the lake of fire, where they suffer eternal torment (19:20; 20:10). While unbelievers are repeatedly warned to repent, those who refuse to do so also experience God's wrathful judgment (20:14–15). Finally, Death and Hades are thrown into the lake of fire, paving the way for the restoration of creation.

The New Heaven and New Earth

What God began in Genesis 1–2, he now finishes in Revelation 21–22 (see "The Beginning" and "The End" in the chart on pages 286–87).[3] This is the happy ending to God's Great Story. Having destroyed his enemies and rescued his people, he now restores his creation. Revelation 21 announces "a new heaven and a new earth," where God will make good on his promise to live forever among his people. In this garden city known as "the new Jerusalem," there will be no evil of any kind, only God's light-giving presence, comforting love, and abundant provision (21:4–7; 22:1–2). God's promise to Abraham to bless all the nations through him (Gen. 12:1–3) is now fulfilled as redeemed people from all nations of God inhabit the new creation (22:2). The greatest blessing of all is that God will live in intimate fellowship with his people.

> No longer will there be any curse. The throne of God and of the Lamb will be in the city, and his servants will serve him. They will see his face, and his name will be on their foreheads. There will be no more night. They will not need the light of a lamp or the light of the sun, for the Lord God will give them light. And they will reign for ever and ever. (Rev. 22:3–5)

The communion that God desired with Adam and Eve is finally realized with those who have been redeemed by Jesus Christ, the Last Adam. In the restored paradise, there will be no more Satan, no more sin, and no more suffering or death. God's glory will completely banish all night and darkness. He will live among his people, and they will know him face-to-face. They will join the multitude of angels worshiping and serving God forever.

Living the Story

Revelation truly is a transforming vision. As we enter into this book by reading it or hearing it read, we begin to see reality as God sees it. We gain heavenly

---

3. J. Daniel Hays and J. Scott Duvall, *The Baker Illustrated Bible Handbook* (Grand Rapids: Baker, 2011), 30–31.

perspective. Entering into John's vision allows us to see several things clearly. First, Revelation provides hope. Biblical hope is much more than wishful thinking. Rather, it is the confident expectation that God will keep his promises. Hope anchors the future in the character of God. Revelation reminds us that God has already defeated evil at the cross and resurrection of Jesus and that he will completely destroy evil and make all things new in the future. We can trust God to keep his promises because he has always kept his promises.

Second, Revelation helps us adjust our expectations about the nature of the Christian life. Revelation never promises Christians that they will be free from struggles, persecution, and even martyrdom. While Revelation makes it crystal clear that believers will never experience the condemning wrath and judgment of God, it also makes it clear that believers should expect to suffer persecution and hardship precisely because they follow Christ. Jesus himself told his first disciples, "In this world you will have trouble [or 'tribulation']. But take heart! I have overcome the world" (John 16:33). His words apply to us as well.

Over and over in the messages to the seven churches in Revelation 2–3, Jesus challenges believers to be faithful in the face of persecution. In those messages, Jesus' promises apply to those who overcome, not to those who do everything possible to escape hardship. Rather than expecting to be exempt from suffering and persecution, we should expect to endure persecution or tribulation. Revelation calls us to change our expectations. No longer should we expect to be exempt from trials. Rather, we should prepare to face trials for the sake of Christ (Rev. 12:11; cf. 1 Peter 4).

Third, Revelation clarifies what it means to overcome. God and his people are at war with the forces of evil. Through his life, death, and resurrection, Jesus dealt a death blow to sin and Satan, but believers still live in enemy territory with its assorted trials and temptations. Negatively, to overcome includes rejecting false teaching, abstaining from immorality, resisting idolatry, and refusing to compromise. Positively, overcoming includes faith (and good works, prayer, and worship that demonstrate its authenticity) along with perseverance even in the face of suffering. Overcoming also includes participating in God's larger mission to the nations by embracing the testimony of Jesus. To summarize, overcoming involves making decisions to follow the Lamb with one's whole life until the end of one's life.

> ## Hope
>
> "Hope is one of the Theological virtues. This means that a continual looking forward to the eternal world is not … a form of escapism or wishful thinking, but one of the things a Christian is meant to do. It does not mean that we are to leave the present world as it is. If you read history you will find that the Christians who did most for the present world were just those who thought most of the next.… It is since Christians have largely ceased to think of the other world that they have become so ineffective in this. Aim at Heaven and you will get earth 'thrown in': aim at earth and you will get neither."[4]
>
> – C. S. LEWIS

---

4. C. S. Lewis, *Mere Christianity* (New York: Simon & Schuster, 1996; orig. 1943), 119.

Wrapping Up

There have been times throughout history when false religion has forged a partnership with pagan political and military might to create a power center that demands total allegiance. The rulers who personify such a system (e.g., the Roman emperor Domitian or Adolf Hitler) will often claim to be Lord. Those living under this kind of pagan power will be tempted to compromise their faith in order to avoid persecution. Revelation reminds us that Jesus is Lord and that God will be victorious over the powers of evil in the end. No matter how things appear now, God is in control, and we should not lose hope. One day the Lord will destroy evil completely, restore his creation, and live among his people forever in the new heaven and the new earth. Revelation is a God-given vision that shows us reality from a heavenly perspective so that we may live faithfully now.

Memory Verse

"They triumphed over him
by the blood of the Lamb
and by the word of their testimony;
they did not love their lives so much
as to shrink from death." (Rev. 12:11)

Digging Deeper

Books

Hays, J. Daniel, J. Scott Duvall, and C. Marvin Pate. *The Dictionary of Biblical Prophecy*. Grand Rapids: Zondervan, 2007.

Keener, Craig S. *Revelation*. The NIV Application Commentary. Grand Rapids: Zondervan, 2000.

Mounce, Robert H. *The Book of Revelation*. Rev. ed. New International Commentary on the New Testament. Grand Rapids: Eerdmans, 1997.

Osborne, Grant. *Revelation*. Baker Exegetical Commentary on the New Testament. Grand Rapids: Baker, 2001.

ASSIGNMENTS

1. Make a chart of the seven messages to the churches in Revelation 2–3. Organize the biblical text in terms of the pattern used for all the churches: the description of Jesus, the commendation for good works, Jesus' accusation of some sin, the exhortation followed by warning or encouragement, the admonition to listen, and the promise to those who overcome. Then add an eighth church to your chart—your home church or the church you are now attending—and write in the message you think Jesus would have for that church.

2. Find the sidebar labeled "The Seven Beatitudes of Revelation" in this chapter. Study each statement of blessing in an attempt to answer the following question: How do these beatitudes help us to understand what Revelation means by "overcome"?

3. Write a two- to three-page summary of the main message of Revelation to a close friend who has asked you to explain what it means in plain language.

4. Read again the section on the "Olivet Discourse" in chapter 14 (page 185). Now write a two- to three-page paper comparing the message of Jesus' discourse found in Matthew 24–25 and Mark 13 with the central message of Revelation.

CONCLUSION

"What is the real story of which my life story is a part?"[1]

— LESLIE NEWBIGIN

"The mission [of the church] has to do with the whole church taking the whole gospel to the whole world ... using the whole Bible."[2]

— CHRIS WRIGHT

The 2002 film *The Emperor's Club* tells the story of the relationship between William Hundert (Kevin Kline), a passionate classics professor, and the students he taught and mentored over the years at St. Benedict's Academy, an all-boys prep school. Near the end of the movie, Mr. Hundert is reunited with many of his students, now successful men. In a moving speech, he quotes the school's Latin motto to drive home a moral lesson: *Finis Origine Pendet*—"The end depends upon the beginning." The idea that a person's beginning plays a major role in the overall outcome of their life can also apply to the Great Story of the Bible, although the beautiful ending God desired took a long time to orchestrate.

"In the beginning God created the heavens and the earth"—a good and beautiful place, a perfect place (Gen. 1:1). The triune God wanted to share the perfect community with creatures made in his own image—human beings. That's the kind of God he is—a loving, giving, sharing God. Later in the Story, God makes the ultimate sacrifice in giving his only Son so that we might live in this perfect community.

> ## The Perfect Community
>
> "God did not create human beings because he was lonely or bored.... [God] did not create because he was needy. God created human beings because he was so in love with community that he wanted a world full of people to share it with."[3]
>
> — JOHN ORTBERG

1. Leslie Newbigin, *The Gospel in a Pluralist Society* (Grand Rapids: Eerdmans, 1989), 15.

2. C. H. J. Wright, *Mission of God's People* (Grand Rapids: Zondervan, 2010), 266.

3. John Ortberg, *Everybody's Normal Till You Get to Know Them* (Grand Rapids: Zondervan, 2003), 38.

A Review of the Great Story

This is how the Great Story begins: God and his creation living in perfect harmony. Adam and Eve, the first human beings, enjoy intimate fellowship with the Lord God. They walk with him, speak with him, and flourish in the wonder and abundance of these perfect relationships: with their God, with each other, and with God's creation. Again, it couldn't possibly get any better.

But, sadly, it could get worse. The evil serpent (Satan) deceives Adam and Eve into thinking that they are missing something. He tricks them into believing that God is keeping something from them. As a result, they say yes to the serpent's invitation to sin and rebel against their God. Sin enters God's perfect world. By this one act of rebellion, all the perfect relationships are broken. When Adam and Eve look beyond God to some other source of life and fulfillment and purpose, they discover that all the other options are inadequate, temporary, and deeply flawed compared to the Lord God, the only true source of life.

The consequences of their sin, however, are disastrous. People are banned from the perfect garden and now experience pain, suffering, and death. People begin to hate and murder each other. This kind of wicked behavior becomes "normal" in a broken world, and people try their best to live without God. It's no exaggeration to say that sin has caused broken relationships all around.

God does not abandon his creation project, however, and so he begins the long, arduous task of fixing the sin problem and restoring his creation. He begins to restore it by entering into a covenant with Abraham. The Abrahamic covenant (Gen. 12–17) is God's response to the sin problem described in Genesis 3–11. God calls this one man to leave his own country and begin a faith journey. Abraham responds by trusting God, and God counts his response as righteousness (15:6). God and Abraham are in right relationship, and God plans for this righting of wrongs to spread far and wide. God promises to bless Abraham and make him into a great nation and through him to bless all the peoples of the earth (12:1–3). God creates out of Abraham a single people, Israel, which he plans to use to bless the other peoples of the earth.

God sets up the Abrahamic covenant by binding himself in a covenant ceremony (see Gen. 15). Much of the Great Story revolves around how God acts in human history to bring about the fulfillment of these promises to Abraham, promises that will lead to the restoration of all of creation. Abraham's response of faith allows him to participate in the covenant established by God. We see something similar in the new covenant established by Jesus.

The Story continues with Abraham's descendants: Isaac, Jacob, and Jacob's twelve sons. These twelve sons are the origin of the twelve tribes of Israel. God reminds Abraham's descendants of his original promise to Abraham, and he cares for them through a series of difficult circumstances, the central one being their slavery in Egypt (e.g., Gen. 26:24; 28:3–4, 14; 45:7; cf. 50:20).

Four hundred years after God makes his covenant with Abraham, God's people find themselves enslaved. Yet this captivity becomes the occasion for God's mighty deliverance. To fulfill his promise to Abraham, God delivers his people from slavery in Egypt. This "exodus" or deliverance from slavery is God's most powerful act of redemption in the Old Testament and points forward to God's ultimate act of deliverance from sin and evil through his Son Jesus Christ.

After rescuing his people from slavery, he calls them into a special relationship with himself, spelled out in the Mosaic covenant. God's deliverance always precedes our response of worship and holiness:

> "You yourselves have seen what I did to Egypt, and how I carried you on eagles' wings and brought you to myself. Now if you obey me fully and keep my covenant, then out of all nations you will be my treasured possession. Although the whole earth is mine, you will be for me a kingdom of priests and a holy nation." These are the words you are to speak to the Israelites. (Ex. 19:4–6)

The Mosaic covenant seems to depend on the people's response of obedience to keep the covenant in place. The key question at this point is whether the people will keep God's commands. In the Mosaic covenant, God reveals his character as a holy God and shows the people how he expects them to live in relationship with him as his holy people. God's expectations relate to all of life, not just their "religious" life, and the most famous explanation of these expectations can be found in the Ten Commandments (see Ex. 20 and Deut. 5). If they obey him, they will be blessed, but if they disobey him, they will be cursed.

The people obey for a time as God leads them into the Promised Land, but their loyalty doesn't last. Eventually they disobey and rebel against God and experience the devastating consequences. All along, God's prophets warn the people by reminding them of God's expectations. But the people continue to rebel against God, mainly by committing acts of idolatry, immorality, social injustice, and religious ritualism. Because they fail to heed the Prophets' warnings, they face God's judgment. Their enemies defeat them and take them into captivity once again. But in spite of the people's disobedience, there is another, more hopeful, aspect to the Prophets' message: God promises a future restoration that extends beyond his judgment.

The Abrahamic covenant is still in place. God will still fulfill his promises to Abraham. At this point, the main way he keeps his promises to Abraham is through the Davidic covenant. God promises King David that he will raise up a ruler like David to shepherd his people (2 Sam. 7:9–29). This ruler will be the Messiah and his kingdom will never end. Jesus Christ is the Messiah and the Davidic King who came to establish this everlasting kingdom. God's promise to Abraham to bless all nations through him will be fulfilled through Jesus, the Davidic King.

The Gospels make sure we don't miss this important connection between Abraham, David, and Jesus. Matthew opens his gospel with these words: "This is the genealogy of Jesus the Messiah the son of David, the son of Abraham" (Matt. 1:1). Zechariah (father of John the Baptizer) also hits this note in his song of praise in Luke 1:68–73:

> "Praise be to the Lord, the God of Israel,
> because he has come to his people and redeemed them.
> He has raised up a horn of salvation for us
> in the house of his servant David
> (as he said through his holy prophets of long ago),
> salvation from our enemies
> and from the hand of all who hate us—
> to show mercy to our ancestors
> and to remember his holy covenant,
> the oath he swore to our father Abraham."

Jesus is the Davidic Messiah who fulfills the covenant promises made to Abraham.

People who rebelled against God under the Mosaic covenant broke that covenant and experienced God's judgment. But God's faithfulness alone established the Abrahamic and Davidic covenants. Ultimately, an individual can only break these covenants by rejecting Jesus, the Messiah. By accepting Jesus, people enter into the new covenant and experience God's gracious provision of salvation. They become citizens in the kingdom of God, Jesus' favorite topic in his teaching. By rejecting Jesus, however, people refuse God's provision of salvation and are left to face his condemning judgment.

The apostle Paul reminds the Galatians (and us) that the Abrahamic covenant came before the Mosaic covenant by more than four hundred years. Is there any value at all in the Mosaic covenant? Why was it added? The Mosaic covenant clarifies God's character and expectations for his people and shows how those expectations extend to all of life. Here we see clearly God's standard for life under his rule. Jesus upheld these covenant standards and even took them a step further by making them a matter of the heart as well as outward behavior (see Jesus' Sermon on the Mount in Matt. 5–7). But although the Mosaic covenant shows us God's standards, it fails to provide a way to meet those standards. It points out God's expectations, but it doesn't provide a permanent way to live up to them. The temporary provisions it does make point forward to the ultimate provision of salvation in the Messiah. They are the copies of which the work of Jesus Christ is the original.

Now we can understand Paul's explanation to the Galatian Christians about how all this fits together (Gal. 3:19–22):

> Why, then, was the law given at all? It was added because of transgressions until the Seed to whom the promise referred had come. The law was given

through angels and entrusted to a mediator. A mediator, however, implies more than one party; but God is one.

Is the law, therefore, opposed to the promises of God? Absolutely not! For if a law had been given that could impart life, then righteousness would certainly have come by the law. But Scripture has locked up everything under the control of sin, so that what was promised, being given through faith in Jesus Christ, might be given to those who believe.

The Law (Mosaic covenant) was given not only to show us God's character and standards but also to show us how we fail to live up to those standards (i.e., "because of transgressions" in Gal. 3:19). The Mosaic covenant, however, could not "impart life" since it could not make unrighteous people righteous. But coming before and stretching beyond the Mosaic covenant is God's covenant promise to Abraham that becomes a reality through Jesus, the Davidic King and Messiah.

We are told clearly in the New Testament that the Mosaic law is no longer binding as a means of salvation. We are also told that we should continue to be concerned about God's standards as Jesus has fulfilled them. Jesus is our perfect model for understanding both God's character and God's standards. We are also told that when we follow the Holy Spirit, who empowers us to love one another, we will fulfill God's standards (Rom. 13:10; Gal. 5:14, 18; 6:2). So although the Mosaic covenant has been broken and Christians are no longer bound to live under that covenant, we still fulfill God's good law as we follow Jesus and walk by his Spirit.

In summary, God initiates his covenant with Abraham to solve the sin problem of Genesis 3–11. The covenant with Abraham is ultimately fulfilled in Jesus, the Davidic Messiah. Jesus establishes the new covenant, the fourth and final major covenant in the Bible. The prophet Jeremiah predicted the establishment of this new covenant (Jer. 31:31–34), a covenant established by Jesus' death and resurrection (see Mark 14:22–25; 1 Cor. 11:23–26). Through his teaching, mighty works, sacrificial death, and resurrection, Jesus did what Israel failed to do. God's covenant promises are fulfilled in Jesus, the obedient Son.

The power and beauty of what Jesus has done can also be described this way: in Jesus, God himself provides the righteousness that he requires of his people. Through Jesus the Messiah, God will create a people from all the peoples on the earth. God's desire all along has been to live among his people.

The major covenants of the Bible provide the primary means God uses to fulfill his ultimate goal of restoring his creation and living among his people, a multicultural people. When the people were delivered from slavery in Egypt, God gave them instructions for setting up a temporary dwelling place for his presence—the tabernacle. Later, during the time of King Solomon, the people build a magnificent temple for God. Sadly, because of the people's sin, the glorious presence of God left the temple in Jerusalem (see Ezek. 10). Eventually

Temples of the Bible		
Proto-temple	God's presence in the garden of Eden	Mankind banished from the Garden due to sin
Temple #1	Built by King Solomon in tenth century BC	Destroyed by the Babylonians in 587 BC
Temple #2	Zerubbabel's temple built after the return from exile around 536 BC	Later expanded by Herod the Great
(Temple #3)	Herod the Great greatly expands Zerubbabel's temple (19/20 BC–AD 64). This is the temple during the time of Jesus.	Destroyed by the Roman army in AD 70
Temple of the Spirit	The church is referred to as the temple of God's Spirit (e.g., 1 Cor. 3:16–17; 6:19; 2 Cor. 6:16; Eph. 2:21–22; Heb. 3:6; 1 Peter 2:4–5).	God's people experience God's personal presence now through the Holy Spirit.
The new Jerusalem	There is no physical temple in the new heaven and new earth "because the Lord God Almighty and the Lamb are its temple" (Rev. 21:22).	God lives among his people for eternity in the eternal garden-city.

this temple was destroyed and later rebuilt during the time of Ezra. The Old Testament closes with the hope that God's glorious presence will one day live again among his people.

When Jesus the Messiah walks through the gates of the temple in Jerusalem, the glorious presence of God has finally returned. God's presence is no longer restricted to a tabernacle or a temple. God's presence is made known in a person: Jesus the Christ. Jesus replaces the temple as the primary place where people experience God's presence. Near the end of his ministry Jesus promises to send the Holy Spirit to live among his people after he ascends to the Father. With the coming of the Holy Spirit at Pentecost (Acts 2), the people of God become the temple of God's Spirit. God now lives among his people.

Throughout Acts, we also see God's heart for his people to be a multicultural people. As Jews, Samaritans, and finally Gentiles become followers of Jesus, we see the beginning of the fulfillment of God's promise to Abraham to bless *all the peoples* of the earth through him. The beginning of the Story shapes the end of the Story.

God's promises to Abraham have been partially fulfilled with the coming of the Holy Spirit, but they await a final, complete fulfillment. God still wants to provide a perfect place to live among his people in an even more permanent and personal way. Place is important! One day God will destroy evil and wickedness and provide this perfect place—a new heaven and new earth. The book of Revelation describes this perfect garden-city, the new Jerusalem, where God will live among his people in unhindered intimacy:

> Then I saw "a new heaven and a new earth," for the first heaven and the first earth had passed away, and there was no longer any sea. I saw the Holy City, the new Jerusalem, coming down out of heaven from God, prepared as a bride beautifully dressed for her husband. And I heard a loud voice from the throne saying, "Look! God's dwelling place is now among the people, and he will dwell with them. They will be his people, and God himself will be with them and be their God. 'He will wipe every tear from their eyes. There will be no more death' or mourning or crying or pain, for the old order of things has passed away."
>
> He who was seated on the throne said, "I am making everything new!" Then he said, "Write this down, for these words are trustworthy and true."
>
> He said to me: "It is done. I am the Alpha and the Omega, the Beginning and the End. To the thirsty I will give water without cost from the spring of the water of life. Those who are victorious will inherit all this, and I will be their God and they will be my children." (Rev. 21:1–7)

The long restoration project is finally complete. People from every tribe and language and people and nation who follow Jesus the Messiah are welcomed into this perfectly restored creation. There is no need for a temple in the new heaven and new earth because the entire place will be a temple as God lives among his people forever (Rev. 21:22). What sin and Satan once ruined, God has now restored. God has kept his promises.

The Great Story has been a long story. We wonder what it would have been like if Adam and Eve had obeyed God instead of sinning. We'll never know. But we do know that God has brilliantly and masterfully and compassionately provided a way to right these wrongs and restore his creation. In the new heaven and new earth, all our relationships will be made whole and new—with the Lord God, with other people, and with creation itself. Until then, as the author of Hebrews puts it: we "run with perseverance the race marked out for us, fixing our eyes on Jesus, the pioneer and perfecter of faith" (Heb. 12:1–2).

So What? Discovering Our Place in the Great Story

Stories shape our lives like nothing else. If you were asked to describe the three most important moments of your life, you would probably tell a story. Your story would likely involve important relationships (characters), a significant series of events (plot), an unforgettable place (setting), a problem or challenge (conflict), and a purposeful ending (resolution). Can we even imagine life without stories? What's more, foundational or grand stories claim to explain the whole world, and for this reason they are truly life-changing. Whether or not we realize it, everyone lives by some great story or grand narrative. The only question is which one.

Although the Bible is a collection of sixty-six diverse books, it also tells an overarching Story, the Great Story. We (and millions of others) believe that the Great Story of the Bible provides the best grand story when compared to competing grand stories (e.g., the Enlightenment story, the Muslim story, the Postmodern "story"). Christopher Wright explains:

> We live out of the story or stories we believe to be true, the story or stories that "tell it like it is," we think. So what does it mean to live out *this* story? Here is *The Story*, the grand universal narrative that stretches from creation to new creation, and accounts for everything in between. This is The Story that tells us where we have come from, how we got to be here, who we are, why the world is in the mess it is, how it can be (and has been) changed, and where we are ultimately going. And the whole story is predicated on the reality of this God and the mission of this God. He is the originator of the story, the teller of the story, the prime actor in the story, the planner and guide of the story's plot, the meaning of the story and its ultimate completion. He is its beginning, end, and center. It is the story of the mission of God, of this God, and no other.[4]

There are several reasons we believe the Great Story of the Bible is the best grand story.[5] Unlike other grand stories, the Great Story doesn't force itself on you. You won't find coercion in either the hero Jesus or the climax of the Story (the cross and resurrection). Jesus is a suffering Messiah who pours out his life for others. Also, in the Great Story, God plans and works for a truly diverse people to live in his presence. This Story doesn't try to pack everyone into the same mold or favor just one class of people. Rather, the Great Story celebrates God-given diversity (i.e., "every tribe and language and people and nation" of Revelation). In addition, by living according to the Great Story of the Bible, we find the best answers to the foundational questions of life:

1. Where are we? What kind of world do we live in? The Great Story says we are in a world created and sustained by God. There is more to this world than science or technology or progress or our own imaginations.
2. Who are we? What does it mean to be a human being? The Bible says that we are human beings created in God's image for the purpose of

---

4. C. H. J. Wright, *The Mission of God* (Downer's Grove, IL: InterVarsity, 2006), 533. In his masterful work, Wright contends that the mission of God is the best interpretive lens through which to see the whole Bible clearly.

5. See Michael W. Goheen's public lecture: "The Urgency of Reading the Bible as One Story in the 21st Century" (given at Regent College, Vancouver, B.C., November 2, 2006).

being in loving relationship with God and other human beings. We are not just autonomous selves in control of our own destiny or multiple selves dependent on our environment.

3. What's wrong? What is the essential problem with us and the world? Scripture says that the problem is sin. We have chosen to rebel against our Creator, and sin has damaged our relationships. We can't just blame outside circumstances.

4. What's the solution? What can fix the problem? The Bible says that God has come to our rescue in Jesus Christ, whose life, death, and resurrection provide a way to God. We do need saving, and we can't save ourselves, but Jesus can save us.

5. Where are we in the Story? Where do we belong and how does the Story affect our lives right now? We are citizens of the kingdom of God living between the decisive victory of the cross and resurrection and the final consummation. We are called to join God in his mission.

When a person decides to follow Jesus Christ, they are basically saying, "I want to become part of God's Story. I want his Story to become my story." At conversion, we merge into the Great Story or, if you prefer, God begins to weave our lives into his magnificent Story tapestry. Embracing the Great Story as your personal story not only answers the most important questions of life, but also calls you to join God in his mission. This is another way in which we discover our place in God's Story. Participating in God's mission in this world brings us ultimate meaning and purpose in life because it centers our life in God himself and his purposes rather than in ourselves.

God's mission can be portrayed as a web or cluster of five central spiritual realities:

The Mission of God

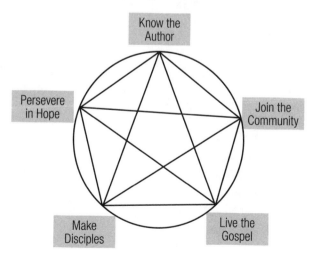

Know the Author

John 17:3: *"Now this is eternal life: that they know you, the only true God, and Jesus Christ, whom you have sent."*

The initial way we participate in God's mission is by knowing and relating to the Author of the Story, God himself. We do so by following Jesus Christ as Lord and Messiah. Repeatedly the Bible calls us to put our faith in Jesus (e.g., John 3:16; Rom. 10:9 – 10; Eph. 2:8 – 9).

Join the Community

Acts 2:42: *"They devoted themselves to the apostles' teaching and to fellowship, to the breaking of bread and to prayer."*

We can't carry out God's mission by ourselves. We must be part of the community of faith, the church — the community that follows Jesus and lives by the Great Story. In this life together, what was lost when sin entered the Story begins to be redeemed and restored. The church plays a central role in carrying out God's mission.

Live the Gospel

Romans 8:14: *"For those who are led by the Spirit of God are the children of God."*

The mission of God affects us first of all. In the Old Testament, "living the gospel" might be summarized by Micah 6:8b: "To act justly and to love mercy and to walk humbly with your God." Jesus calls us to live as kingdom citizens (see Matt. 5 – 7). The apostle Paul might say that living the gospel is the same as being led by the Spirit (e.g., Gal. 5:18). Here we live the Story ourselves before we turn outward to tell the Story to others.

Make Disciples

Matthew 28:19 – 20: *"Therefore go and make disciples of all nations, baptizing them in the name of the Father and of the Son and of the Holy Spirit, and teaching them to obey everything I have commanded you. And surely I am with you always, to the very end of the age."*

Beyond joining the community and living the gospel, the church is also called to bear witness to the gospel. Jesus told his disciples that he was sending them out into the world just as the Father had sent him into the world (John 20:21). He empowered them with his Spirit to bear witness to him throughout the world (Acts 1:8). Making disciples entails much more than passing out evangelistic tracts or going on a mission trip. We envision a holistic approach to bearing witness to the gospel that affects all of life, including entertainment, sports, business, politics, art, education, and so on. This is what Goheen and Bartholomew refer to as a comprehensive vision of cultural engagement.[6] We don't just need Christians being called into "full-time Christian ministry"; we need Christians who will live the Story faithfully in all areas of life.

---

6. Goheen and Bartholomew, *Living at the Crossroads*, 1 – 10.

Persevere in Hope

Rev. 12:11: *"They triumphed over him by the blood of the Lamb and by the word of their testimony; they did not love their lives so much as to shrink from death."*

The people of God live in hope that God will one day fulfill his promises to redeem his creation completely. Part of our mission involves enduring and persevering. The book of Revelation says enduring faithfully is how we "overcome" or "triumph" (e.g., Rev. 21:7). Living the Story and fulfilling God's mission will not be easy in a broken world replete with spiritual enemies and obstacles. But we persevere in hope that God will finish the work of restoration that he began.

Decision Time

The Great Story calls for our full participation. A person will never truly experience the Great Story if they remain content with adding bits and pieces of it to their life, especially if they are really living according to a different grand story. The Story of the Bible is much too powerful to be reduced to "spiritual sprinkles." It demands a 100 percent commitment. When you merge onto the superhighway of God's Great Story, you accelerate and never look back. Is such a commitment worth it?

Consider the following statements:[7]

- Rather than asking, "Where does God fit into my life?" we should be asking, "Where does my life fit into God's Great Story?"
- Rather than focusing on God's purpose for my individual life, we should be asking, "How my life can fit into God's mission for this world?"
- Instead of talking so much about applying the Bible to our lives, we should be asking how we can "apply our lives to the Bible."
- Instead of wondering "what kind of mission God has for *me*," we should be asking "what kind of me God wants for *his* mission."

Discovering our place in God's Story involves much more than paying tribute to how much space we are giving God while we keep ourselves firmly planted at the center of our reality. The adventure of discovering our place begins when we allow God to take his rightful place as the one, true Center of all reality, ours included. This is what Jesus meant when he challenged people to deny themselves, to take up their cross, and to follow him. Conversion involves a change of place. Notice also that Jesus made promises for those who denied themselves the center and allowed him to occupy that place — they would save their own life in the process (Mark 8:34–35). Isn't this what everyone is searching for? What could possibly be more important than life itself?

"In the beginning God created the heavens and the earth." This is how the Great Story begins. We were created to experience God's perfect community,

---

7. Adapted from Wright, *Mission of God*, 533–34.

but something went terribly wrong. Satan and sin invaded God's good world and introduced brokenness and death. Because of his great love, God did not abandon his creation. Rather, Jesus, God's one and only Son, entered this world to redeem it. Through the life, death, and resurrection of Jesus, God began to reverse the curse of sin and restore his creation. Now, as the Spirit-empowered church, we join God in fulfilling his mission—the ultimate redemption and restoration of his creation. We long for the day when God will make all things new, when there will be no more death or crying or pain, and when God will live among his people in a perfectly beautiful place (Rev. 21:1–4; 22:3–5). We long for that day and pray the prayer: "Come, Lord Jesus" (22:20). Yes, this Story is worth our full attention and total devotion. It is, after all, God's Great Story.

ASSIGNMENTS

1. In the Introduction to this book (p. 20), you completed the following assignment:

   The biblical story and the story of Western civilization are often incompatible. Write out short answers to the five basic questions mentioned in this chapter, first from the point of view of the Western story and then from the point of view of the biblical Story. Your answers need to be thoughtful but not necessarily lengthy. Then write a concluding paragraph showing where the two stories overlap and where they are radically different.

   Now we ask you to do the same assignment again (without looking at your previous answers) to see how much you have learned in the process.

2. We mention in this chapter that God's mission may be portrayed as a cluster of five spiritual realities. Write a two-page paper in which you discuss all five of these realities and the role you think each plays in God's mission. In addition, write a concluding paragraph explaining what, if anything, you think should be added to this list of five realities.

3. The Great Story is a foundational story calling for total commitment. Write a two-page paper explaining your connection to the Great Story at this point in your life. Do you accept the Great Story 100 percent? Are you dabbling with the Great Story, or do you reject it as your foundational story? Please explain the reasons for your relationship to the Story. This should be a personal reflection.

SCRIPTURE INDEX

AUTHOR INDEX

A Curriculum for Life

HERMENEUTICS
COLLEGE / UNIVERSITY

THIRD EDITION

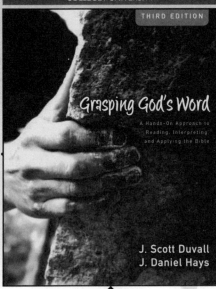

Grasping God's Word
A Hands-On Approach to
Reading, Interpreting,
and Applying the Bible

J. Scott Duvall
J. Daniel Hays

Living God's Word
ISBN: 9780310292104

J. Scott Duvall and J. Daniel Hays invite lay and college-level Bible students to see how their faith journey relates to the big picture of the Bible. *Living God's Word* presents a broad narrative framework that encompasses every book of the Bible and demonstrates how students make this story their own.

BIBLE SURVEY

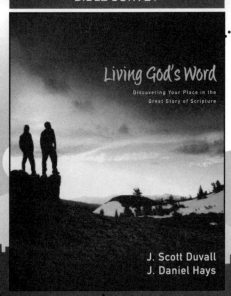

Living God's Word

Discovering Your Place in the
Great Story of Scripture

J. Scott Duvall
J. Daniel Hays

Grasping God's Word
ISBN: 9780310492573

Grasping God's Word Workbook
ISBN: 9780310492597

Grasping God's Word Laminated Sheet
ISBN: 9780310275145

Understanding the Bible correctly and rightly relating its meaning to life require using the right approach and tools to dig deeper into Scripture. This popular text is an indispensable guide to reading, interpreting, and applying the Bible that teaches college students how to read the Word of God carefully and in context.

UNIVERSITY

From the Classroom to the Church

Journey into God's Word
ISBN: 9780310275138

Journey into God's Word helps Bible readers acquire the skills necessary in order to successfully read, interpret, and apply the Bible to life. An ideal resource for teaching hermeneutics in churches, especially for leaders who have previously used *Grasping God's Word*.

PREACHING

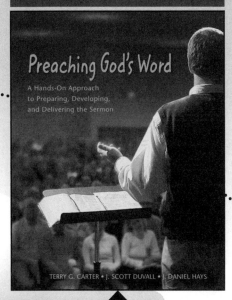

Preaching God's Word
A Hands-On Approach to Preparing, Developing, and Delivering the Sermon

TERRY G. CARTER • J. SCOTT DUVALL • J. DANIEL HAYS

HERMENEUTICS
CHURCH

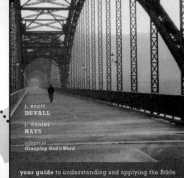

j. scott **DUVALL**
j. daniel **HAYS**
authors of *Grasping God's Word*

your guide to understanding and applying the Bible

JOURNEY INTO GOD'S WORD

Preaching God's Word
ISBN: 9780310248873

This user-friendly practical textbook helps preachers and homiletics students develop and deliver biblically based expository sermons relevant for the twenty-first century.

We want to hear from you. Please send your comments about this book to us in care of zreview@zondervan.com. Thank you.

ZONDERVAN.com/
AUTHORTRACKER
follow your favorite authors